MW00630454

LIFE AT
400 Beacon Street

Working in Mary Baker Eddy's Household

By Heather Vogel Frederick

Heather Vogel Frederick

Longyear Museum Press
Chestnut Hill, Massachusetts, U.S.A.

This book was designed by Sarah Nichols. It was printed on Endurance Silk 80# Text and 120# Cover by Puritan Capital in Hollis, N.H., and bound by Superior Bindery in Braintree, Mass. Puritan Capital is an environmentally friendly printer, which uses vegetable-based inks printed on FSC-certified paper.

The text face is Adobe Caslon Pro. For her Caslon revival, designer Carol Twombly studied specimen pages printed by William Caslon between 1734 and 1770. The headline face is Clarendon Text Bold. Clarendon Text is a contemporary remake by Patrick Griffin of the truly classic slab serif typeface with a distinctively clear and legible visibility.

© 2019 Longyear Museum
All rights reserved
ISBN: 978-0-578-40482-0

Longyear Museum Press
1125 Boylston Street
Chestnut Hill, MA, U.S.A. 02467-1811
617-278-9000
www.longyear.org

Printed in the United States of America

Front cover: Ella Rathvon, Irving Tomlinson, William Rathvon, and Ella Hoag set off down the front drive at 400 Beacon Street, circa 1910.
Longyear Museum collection

Back cover, clockwise from top: Hand-colored image of 400 Beacon Street, circa 1910; Calvin Frye seated at his desk; Mary Baker Eddy on a carriage ride in the summer of 1909 — Frank Bowman is at the reins, and Calvin Frye is beside him.
Longyear Museum collection

LIFE AT
400 Beacon Street

Working in Mary Baker Eddy's Household

By Heather Vogel Frederick

Mary Baker Eddy's home at 400 Beacon Street in Chestnut Hill, Massachusetts.

Contents

Foreword

Twelve years ago this month, thanks to the overwhelming generosity of our members and friends, Longyear was able to purchase Mary Baker Eddy's final residence at 400 Beacon Street in Chestnut Hill, Massachusetts. Over the past dozen years, as we've cared for the property and shared it with thousands of visitors, we have gained a deep affection for the home and for all that it represents. This book is an outgrowth of that affection.

Life at 400 Beacon Street: Working in Mary Baker Eddy's Household examines a family of workers brought together for a common purpose: To support the Cause of Christian Science by serving its Leader. The significant work Mrs. Eddy was doing during the three years she lived here (1908-1910) shines through the pages of the book, as does the tender, motherly care she expressed toward her staff. As each chapter unfolds, the reader is able to catch a glimpse of what it meant for the members of the household to live and work in their Leader's home, the qualities that were required, the lessons they were learning under her direction, and the blessings that flowed from faithful service. We are delighted to be adding this book to the shelf of Longyear Museum Press publications.

The author, Heather Vogel Frederick, heads up Longyear's Research and Publications department. Like all Longyear projects, the book was a team effort, with many staff contributing to the final product. But it was Heather who saw the potential of sharing the stories this house has to tell in print, and it was Heather who spent many long months putting pen to paper — or rather, fingers to keyboard! We're grateful for her inspired scholarship and for shepherding the project from start to finish.

As the book goes to press, the Longyear Trustees and staff are deep into planning for the final phase of restoration at 400 Beacon Street. Just as "the windows of heaven" (Malachi 3:10) opened in 2006 when we purchased the house, so, too, they have opened in recent years to enable us to preserve this home for the next century. We feel privileged to be doing this work and look forward to welcoming visitors to a fully-restored home in a few years.

And thanks to several recent gifts from The First Church of Christ, Scientist, in Boston—gifts of original furniture, artwork, and decorative items—when 400 Beacon Street is ready to open its doors once again, visitors will be able to see the furnishings that graced the home when Mrs. Eddy and her household family lived and worked here together. Photographs of a number of these original pieces are used as illustrations in the book.

In April 1910, while living at Chestnut Hill, Mrs. Eddy wrote:

"When will mankind awake to know their present ownership of all good, and praise and love the spot where God dwells most conspicuously in His reflection of love and leadership?" (*The First Church of Christ, Scientist, and Miscellany*, 356)

Through the pages of this book, and the restoration of 400 Beacon Street, Longyear is striving to do its part to help ensure that Mrs. Eddy's efforts for mankind—her "love and leadership"—will be more widely recognized and valued.

Sandra J. Houston, President
Chestnut Hill, Massachusetts
December 2018

Preface

I still remember the first time I visited 400 Beacon Street. I was a student in the Christian Science Sunday School in a nearby town, and one weekend our teacher took the class on a "field trip" to visit several of Mary Baker Eddy's former homes, driving us first to Lynn and Swampscott, Massachusetts, and then to Chestnut Hill. My first impression of 400 Beacon Street was that it was big. Very big! All that house for just one person?

Fast forward to the fall of 2015. As a newly-minted member of the Longyear Museum staff, I found myself standing in the kitchen of 400 Beacon Street with a preservation architect and a team of colleagues. We were poring over flooring samples, looking for a close match to a thrilling discovery — a scrap of the original linoleum found beneath a cupboard in the pantry. The first phase of restoration at the house was in full swing, and the kitchen was in the process of being transformed back to its original appearance in 1908, when Mrs. Eddy and her household moved in. As I looked around the room, I thought, "I wonder what it would have been like to work here?"

That simple question sparked a series of articles for Longyear's website, which in turn mushroomed into something much larger, as we realized that we had enough material for a book. The research we were doing for the restoration put us in a unique position to dive deeply into this question and learn more about what occurred during Mary Baker Eddy's Chestnut Hill years. This book provides an avenue for sharing some of what we have learned.

This house has so many stories to tell! First and foremost, there is Mrs. Eddy's own story and the story of all that she accomplished while living here, including founding *The Christian Science Monitor,* making final revisions to her published writings, settling the succession question, and cementing in place the structure that would carry her Church forward in the years to come. In addition, there are also the stories of the men and women who left home and hearth (sometimes at no little cost to themselves) to offer Mrs. Eddy the practical support that she needed to carry out her work. Grateful for lives transformed by Christian Science, these individuals were eager to serve in whatever way they could. Mrs. Eddy's household staff were for the most part ordinary people in extraordinary circumstances, in many cases plucked from obscurity and from all walks of life and invited to come live and work in one of the most mentally active, high-profile households in the world: The home of the Discoverer, Founder, and Leader of Christian Science.

And this is key to what had been lost on middle-school me: 400 Beacon Street was not just Mrs. Eddy's home, it was also the executive headquarters of the Christian Science movement. As such, perhaps more than any of her other homes, this house represents Mary Baker Eddy's role as Leader. By the time she moved to Chestnut Hill, she was a national figure—arguably the most famous woman in the United States—her viewpoint sought and valued, her every move tracked by the press to satisfy a curious public. Approaching ninety but far from retirement, she continued to be actively engaged in the work of her Church, and this gracious home reflects her stature as a respected religious leader and Christian reformer at the summit of her career.

Fortunately for future historians, Mary Baker Eddy's household recognized the fact that they were witnessing history in the making and took the time to record their experiences. Some kept diaries; others wrote home to family and friends; most would later write reminiscences. This wealth of material, combined with other primary sources, such as newspaper accounts of the day, some of which are only now coming to light, is pure gold for researchers—and, we hope, for readers.

A word about the structure of the book. It is not a biography of Mary Baker Eddy or of those who worked in her home. Rather, using the house as a backdrop, it allows Mrs. Eddy and those who served her to speak for themselves about this significant period in her life. Organized thematically rather than chronologically, each of the dozen chapters details a different aspect of life in Mrs. Eddy's household, from the nature of the work that went on upstairs in her study to the daily routine of her staff. Readers will witness Mrs. Eddy mentoring her household; glimpse what went on behind the scenes in the kitchen, the secretarial offices, the sewing room, and so on; get to know Mrs. Eddy as a grandmother; learn about the music that she and her household enjoyed; travel with staff members on a memorable outing; find out how holidays were celebrated, and much more. Over the course of the book, nearly two dozen individuals are profiled. We trace their early years, explore the circumstances that led them to Christian Science, and explain their specific roles in the household and the contributions they made to the movement afterwards. Some of these men and women, like Adam Dickey and Laura Sargent and Calvin Frye, may be familiar; others, like Frances Thatcher and Frank Bowman and Anna Machacek, may not be. All of them have inspiring insights to share about Mrs. Eddy and about the work that went on under her roof.

And she has inspiring insights to share about them, including a message she wrote at Chestnut Hill in 1910. It reads in part:

"The Christian Scientists at Mrs. Eddy's home are the happiest group on earth. Their faces shine with the reflection of light and love; their footsteps are not weary; their thoughts are upward; their way is onward, and their light shines. The world is better for this happy group of Christian Scientists; Mrs. Eddy is happier because of them; God is glorified in His reflection of peace, love, joy." (*The First Church of Christ, Scientist, and Miscellany*, 355)

Telling these stories about "the Christian Scientists at Mrs. Eddy's home" affords us the opportunity to share never-before-seen images and artifacts from the Museum's collection, along with photographs and items that have been generously shared with us by private collectors and by The Mary Baker Eddy Library. We also went further afield for visual material to sources as diverse as local historical societies, Harvard University, and the Smithsonian Institution.

One key component to the book's design was inspired by the house itself. In keeping with the style of the day, most of the rooms and hallways were (and still are) wallpapered. The patterns are largely floral, reflecting Mrs. Eddy's love of flowers, and we chose four to feature in the book. Motifs were developed from each pattern, which in turn inspired the color schemes and decorative elements.

Many people — myself included — grew up calling the house simply "Chestnut Hill." One question I'm occasionally asked is, "Why does Longyear call it 400 Beacon Street?" It's true that in Mrs. Eddy's day, the street number for the house was 384. However, in 1933 this designation was changed by the City of Newton to 400, and so it has remained for nearly a century. As this is the number on the marker by the front gate, and as this is the number visitors look for in finding the house, 400 is what we at Longyear use. That being said, we also refer to it as "Chestnut Hill." Both are valid, and the house is referenced both ways in this book.

Another question I've been asked in recent months is if I have a favorite from the large cast of household members who inhabit these pages. The answer is, "How could I possibly choose?" Each one has taught me a great deal, from dining room worker Elizabeth Kelly getting up at 4:00 a.m. every morning in order to have time to read the Christian Science Bible Lesson before work, to secretary Adam Dickey stoutly declaring his willingness to shovel snow if that's what Mrs. Eddy needed him to do, to sweet Anna Machacek, the Czech émigré housekeeper, whose hunger for all that Christian Science had to offer impelled her, as a young domestic servant, to spend part of her meager earnings on lamp oil. Why? So that she could study the Bible and *Science and Health with Key to the Scriptures,* by Mary Baker Eddy, late into the night. There's so much that these men and women have to teach readers. I have come to know this house and its former occupants very well by now, and it's been tremendously enriching, on both a professional and a personal level, to have spent so much time in their company.

I hope that readers will find their company enriching, too, and come away from the book with a heightened respect for their contributions to the Christian Science movement and with an even deeper appreciation for all that Mrs. Eddy accomplished during the crowning years of her mission to mankind.

And now, welcome! Please come in—the door is open, and 400 Beacon Street awaits.

Heather Vogel Frederick
Chestnut Hill, Massachusetts
December 2018

Chapter 1
A New Home for Mary Baker Eddy

 hortly before 2:00 p.m. on January 26, 1908, a line of horse-drawn carriages pulled up to the railroad depot in Concord, New Hampshire. It was a quiet Sunday afternoon, and as the occupants alighted and made their way to the private train that had been chartered for them, they attracted little attention. Once aboard, the travelers awaited the final—and most important—member of their party.

The member in question had taken a longer route to the station, her carriage wending its way through the city as it usually did on her daily drive. But this time, instead of returning home, the carriage made a detour to the depot, where the woman inside stepped out.

Of medium height and slender, she was dressed in gray velvet, her traveling outfit completed by a fur cape, white kid gloves, and, perched atop her snowy white hair, a gray hat with purple and white ostrich plumes.[1]

Vintage postcard of the railroad depot in Concord, New Hampshire, circa 1907.

As she walked swiftly toward the waiting train, there was a stir throughout the station.

"The news spread like wildfire," recalled one who was among those already aboard. "People scurried. Reporters tried to board the train, but were gently brushed off."[2]

Who was this unassuming woman who ignited such sudden interest? Where was she going? And who were the people traveling with her?

"I have much work to do"

Her name was Mary Baker Eddy, and she was the most famous woman in Concord—and, arguably, the United States. Mayor Charles Corning would speak of her to the press later that same day as the city's "most distinguished citizen."[3] Just three weeks earlier, Clara Barton, founder of the American Red Cross, had told a reporter that "Mrs. Eddy should have the respect, admiration and love of the whole nation, for she is its greatest woman."[4] And the previous year, *Human Life* magazine had dubbed her "the most famous, interesting and powerful woman in America, if not in the world, today."[5]

As Discoverer, Founder, and Leader of Christian Science, Mary Baker Eddy had devoted the last forty years to the welfare of mankind. Raised in a deeply Christian household, she was a life-long student of the Bible, which had been her comfort and mainstay during early years marked by ill health, struggle, and loss. The trajectory of her life changed dramatically shortly after the end of the Civil War, with a remarkable healing through prayer alone of the aftereffects of a severe fall. From that point on, all her time and effort were dedicated to understanding and sharing the spiritual law behind her recovery and teaching others to heal as Christ Jesus did.

To that end, she had written 16 books (she would publish one more in 1910), including her cornerstone work and most important doctrinal statement, *Science and Health with Key to the Scriptures,* the textbook of Christian Science. During two fruitful decades working in and around Boston, she had established a church, chartered a college to teach this Science, started a publishing company, and launched a monthly magazine, among other endeavors. A poet, writer, teacher, preacher, and healer, she was also a noted philanthropist, and as a national figure her opinion was highly regarded and widely sought. As her fame had grown, however, rather than bask in the limelight, Mrs. Eddy had left the bustle of Boston behind and come to Concord seeking peace and quiet in which to continue her work. Nearly two more equally productive decades followed. Now, at 86, she still had no plans for retirement. Her sights were set firmly on the future.

"I have much work to do," she had told a journalist the previous summer. "I trust in God, and He will give me strength to accomplish those things which have been marked out for me to do."[6]

Those accomplishments would include founding a daily newspaper that set a new ethical standard in an era rife with yellow journalism, making final revisions to her writings, surmounting serious challenges to her leadership, and securing the organizational structure she had put in place to shepherd her Church forward into the future.

Carrying out this work, however, meant uprooting from her native state of New Hampshire and leaving behind a home that she loved dearly. Mary Baker Eddy had lived in Concord since 1889, and at Pleasant View, her tranquil residence on the outskirts of town, since 1892. It could not have been an easy choice for her to make, but like everything else in her life, the decision came about as the result of prayer.

"I trust in God, and He will give me strength to accomplish those things which have been marked out for me to do."
— Mary Baker Eddy

"She made her moves as God directed her," noted one who was traveling with her that day.[7]

After she boarded her private car, the press clamored for answers: Where was Mrs. Eddy going? How long would she be away? Was she leaving Concord for good?[8]

"My lips are sealed," replied Reverend Irving Tomlinson, a former minister who was serving as First Reader of the Christian Science church in Concord and who would accompany Mrs. Eddy on her journey.[9] The others in the party were equally tight-lipped.

For now, all questions would have to wait. The train was ready to depart.

Top right: Front gate at Pleasant View. Pictured (left to right) are Pamelia Leonard, Lida Fitzpatrick, and Joseph Mann. | LONGYEAR MUSEUM COLLECTION
Right: Pleasant View in full bloom. | LONGYEAR MUSEUM COLLECTION

A "perfect beehive of reconstruction industry"

Meanwhile, some 70 miles to the south in Chestnut Hill, Massachusetts, everything was in readiness for Mrs. Eddy's arrival. The move had been in the works for months but was kept under tight wraps at her request.

"The whole affair, including the preparation of the house, was in keeping with Mrs. Eddy's usual way of doing things," Church spokesman Alfred Farlow later explained to the press. "She weighs matters deliberately and carefully, then acts quickly."[10]

Sometime during the summer of 1907, Mrs. Eddy had begun thinking about relocating back to Boston, and that September she directed Archibald McLellan, one of the trustees of her estate and chairman of the Christian Science Board of Directors, to begin looking for a suitable property.[11]

"Mrs. Eddy had pictures sent her of different residences that were for sale in Brookline," Rev. Tomlinson would recall. Eventually, an estate in Chestnut Hill near a picturesque reservoir was decided upon.[12]

Purchased without fanfare in October 1907 through an intermediary for Mary Baker Eddy, 400 Beacon Street was originally built in 1880 as a home for a prosperous Boston wool merchant and his family.[13] The residence was imposing, situated on the crest of a rise within eight and a half leafy acres and vastly different in style from the New Hampshire farmhouse that Mrs. Eddy would be leaving behind.[14] Instead of a simple wood-framed structure cloaked in clapboard, the Chestnut Hill mansion was constructed of Roxbury pudding-stone trimmed with brick.

Like Pleasant View, it offered a lovely view — of the surrounding countryside and the distant Blue Hills, rather than New Hampshire's Merrimack Valley. Unlike Pleasant View, it offered privacy. Mrs. Eddy's home in Concord fronted

Top: 400 Beacon Street entrance hall as it originally looked. | Private collection
Bottom: The interior layout was redesigned to echo Pleasant View, including moving the staircase in the entrance hall. | Longyear Museum collection

Above: Front entrance of 400 Beacon Street during renovation prior to Mrs. Eddy's arrival. | Longyear Museum collection
Overleaf: Mrs. Eddy's Chestnut Hill home, circa 1910.
Photograph by John Salchow, courtesy Library of Congress

almost directly onto the avenue that ran before it, but the new house was set well back from busy Beacon Street, reached by a long semi-circular drive, book-ended with handsome iron gates.

The Boston real estate agency working with Robert Walker, a Christian Scientist who acted on Mrs. Eddy's behalf in the transaction, would describe the Chestnut Hill residence as "of that substantial English architecture and construction that is, and always will be, in good taste."[15] That may have been the case, but as it stood, it wasn't large enough to house Mrs. Eddy and her staff. Chicago-based architect Solon Spencer Beman, who had recently served as an architect for the Extension of The Mother Church in Boston, was hired to expand it.

The new wing he designed essentially doubled the home in size, and at Mrs. Eddy's direction he was also tasked with remodeling the layout of the original structure to resemble more closely the floor plan of Pleasant View.[16] In the mansion's front hall, the main staircase was relocated to echo the placement of the one back in Concord. A grand fireplace and imposing archway were replaced by the simple, clean lines of a New England farmhouse. Upstairs in Mrs. Eddy's study, a bay window, similar to the one she enjoyed at Pleasant View, was added near to where her desk would be placed.

Additions included a room above the newly-built porte-cochère. From this vantage point, Mrs. Eddy could sit and watch the passing flow of traffic, just as she was accustomed to doing in a similar room in Concord. Throughout the house, the original, rather baronial interior was lightened in an effort to make it more familiar and homey. Elaborate paneling was removed and the walls cheerily papered, much of the woodwork was brightened with paint, and the dark hardwood floors were carpeted. The house was modernized to expand the lighting and heating systems, and it would be further brought up to date with the installation of an intercom system and an elevator. (A second private elevator for Mrs. Eddy's use was added several months after her arrival.) The back porch, or piazza, was also overhauled, its rustic wood framing replaced with brick, concrete, and steel.

All of this work required a massive effort on the part of contractors and builders, who were rumored to have been instructed to "hurry the work through at a record pace, without regard to expense."[17]

The transformation did not go unnoticed by the local press.

"Big gangs of mechanics have been working steadily night and day for the past two months in the effort to complete the job so that the building may be turned over to the owner," the *Boston Herald* reported. The front-page story ran under a headline describing the worksite as "a perfect beehive of reconstruction industry" and described some 300 men working on the mansion by day "and as many more" by gas torches at night.[18]

Speculation as to the home's new owner was fueled by reports of two large concrete-and-steel vaults built into the walls and institutional-quality fireproofing of the structure.[19] The focus of the conjecture narrowed as word filtered out that the architect had also worked on the Extension of The Mother Church, that Archibald McLellan had been spotted on the Chestnut Hill premises, and that Robert Walker, a Christian Scientist who had acted before on behalf of Mrs. Eddy and her Church in realty transactions, was involved in the purchase. Could this be the site of the new "Eddy college," an educational institute for Christian Scientists that was said to be in the works?[20]

Reporters scrambled to connect the dots, but no one would or could confirm the rumors.[21]

"It's all nonsense," scoffed head contractor Arthur English. "Mr. Walker is paying for the building and will reside there when everything is completed."[22]

Asking the laborers themselves also proved fruitless.

"All the workmen on the mansion have been as silent as oysters," the *Washington Post* reported, although one "oyster" opened up enough to tell the *Boston Herald,* "Neither I nor anybody else, so far as I have been able to learn, knows what use is to be made of this estate when our work is completed."[23]

That use would very shortly become apparent.

The "Eddy Special"

Back in Concord, reporters raced for the telephones to alert their colleagues in Boston to the breaking news. Promptly at 2:00 p.m., "the Eddy Special," as the chartered train would be christened by the press, pulled out of the depot, bearing "one of the most notable railroad parties which recent years has known."[24] A pilot engine had been sent ahead to ensure the tracks were clear, while a second followed behind as a rear guard, precautions that one newspaper would note were not even taken for presidential visits.[25]

"Down through the Merrimack Valley the train flew, passing through Manchester and Nashua without stopping," wrote the *Boston Post*.[26] Snow was in the forecast, but as the train steamed south, the weather remained calm.[27] Mrs. Eddy was comfortably ensconced in the drawing room of a private car belonging to the president of the Boston & Maine Railroad.[28] A coach car and a "combination" car (one that accommodated baggage as well as passengers) followed.[29]

Right: Mary Baker Eddy's move made headlines nationwide, including these from the Los Angeles Herald *and* Boston Post, *January 27, 1908.*

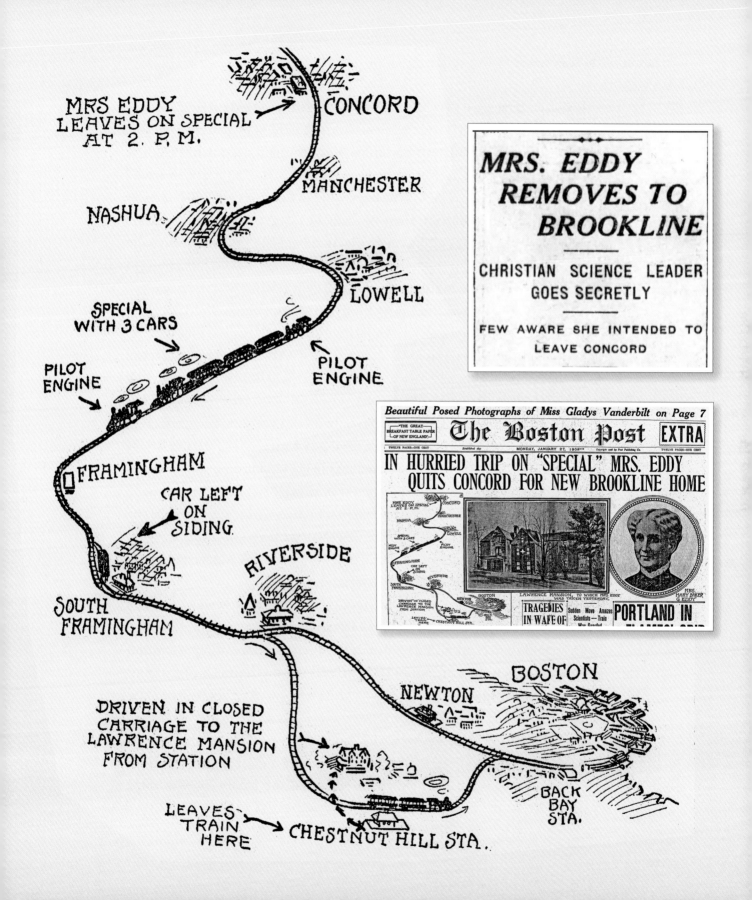

MRS EDDY LEAVES ON SPECIAL AT 2. P. M.

CONCORD

MANCHESTER

NASHUA

LOWELL

SPECIAL WITH 3 CARS

PILOT ENGINE

PILOT ENGINE

FRAMINGHAM

CAR LEFT ON SIDING.

RIVERSIDE

SOUTH FRAMINGHAM

DRIVEN IN CLOSED CARRIAGE TO THE LAWRENCE MANSION FROM STATION

NEWTON

BOSTON

BACK BAY STA.

LEAVES TRAIN HERE

CHESTNUT HILL STA.

MRS. EDDY REMOVES TO BROOKLINE

CHRISTIAN SCIENCE LEADER GOES SECRETLY

FEW AWARE SHE INTENDED TO LEAVE CONCORD

Beautiful Posed Photographs of Miss Gladys Vanderbilt on Page 7

"THE GREAT BREAKFAST TABLE PAPER OF NEW ENGLAND"

The Boston Post

EXTRA

TWELVE PAGES-ONE CENT   Established 1831   MONDAY, JANUARY 27, 1908   Copyright 1908 by Post Publishing Co.   TWELVE PAGES-ONE CENT

IN HURRIED TRIP ON "SPECIAL" MRS. EDDY QUITS CONCORD FOR NEW BROOKLINE HOME

LAWRENCE MANSION, TO WHICH MRS. EDDY WAS TAKEN YESTERDAY.

MRS. MARY BAKER G. EDDY

TRAGEDIES IN WAKE OF

Sudden Move Amazes Scientists --- Train Was Boarded

PORTLAND IN FLAMES

It was the first time that Mary Baker Eddy had been on a train in almost ten years.[30] Traveling with her was a full complement of staff, from longtime compatriots Calvin Frye and Laura Sargent, who had been with her since 1882 and 1890 respectively, to such newcomers as Adelaide Still, a young Englishwoman who had joined the household in the spring of 1907 and was serving as her personal maid. There were about a dozen other staff members aboard that afternoon as well, along with Archibald McLellan; a porter who worked for the president of the railroad; the ticket agent who had arranged the charter; and Alpheus Baker Morrill, a distant relative of Mrs. Eddy.[31]

"The fact was, he was the only relative at hand," household member Minnie Scott would later explain, noting that Mrs. Eddy's cousin Henry Baker, with whom she was close, was in Washington, DC, at the time. Having someone from the family accompany Mrs. Eddy was important, it was felt, as her staff "could not have it said we lured her away."[32]

The trip was largely uneventful. The only hiccup was the discovery of an overheated axle bearing in one of the coach cars, which was deemed potentially dangerous and necessitated the disabled car being shifted to a side track. Its occupants were packed into the private car in which Mrs. Eddy was traveling, with some of the men standing for the roughly 15 miles that remained of the trip.

When they finally pulled into the Chestnut Hill station shortly before 5:00 p.m., seven horse-drawn carriages were waiting in the winter twilight to convey the travelers to Mrs. Eddy's new home.

"We arrived just as the sun had set," recalled Elizabeth Kelly, another of the household in the party. "The house was ablaze with light. . . ."[33]

Despite the precautions taken to foil the press, a horde of reporters and photographers were waiting by the entrance to the house to document Mrs. Eddy's arrival.

"Can you get me out of this, John?" Mrs. Eddy asked her trusted handyman and groundskeeper, John Salchow, who had accompanied her on the train.[34]

Scooping her up in his arms, the "tall, powerfully built man, with deep-set eyes, a sandy mustache and high cheek bones," as the *Boston Post* described

400 Beacon Street at twilight.

> ## "We arrived just as the sun had set.
>
> ## The house was ablaze with light. . . ."
>
> ## — Elizabeth Kelly

him, shouldered his way through the crowd and carried Mrs. Eddy through the front door and directly upstairs, where he gently deposited her in a chair in her new study.[35]

"Well, we beat them that time, didn't we?" Mrs. Eddy said to him, laughing in delight.[36]

"I am thinking of moving"

"John, dear, I am thinking of moving to Brookline," Mary Baker Eddy confided to John Salchow in June 1907. She went on to ask if he would be willing to move with her, adding, "because if you will not go with me, I will not go at all."[37]

Mr. Salchow quickly assured her of his complete willingness to accompany her, and seven months later, when Mrs. Eddy boarded the train that would take her from New Hampshire back to Massachusetts, John was among the household members who moved with her.[38]

The reasons for Mary Baker Eddy's move back to Boston have long been debated. Was it because she felt that the New Hampshire court system had failed to protect her from the Next Friends suit in 1907 — the trumped-up legal action financed by the *New York World* newspaper and brought against her by relatives in an effort to wrest control of her finances and affairs? Did she feel that laws in Massachusetts might better shield her, were there to be further attempts to revive this lawsuit in the future? Or did she simply want to be closer to her Church and its activities?

The answer is likely all of the above, and more.

Mrs. Eddy told Thomas Hatten, a member of the Committee on Business who was tasked with helping find staff for her household, that "her object in making the move was to be nearer the Mother Church and the Christian Science Publishing House in doing the work that she had to do, that no one else could do."[39]

"This move was not prompted by any sudden decision. . . . Her purpose is to be more convenient to the Mother Church of the denomination, near its headquarters."

— Alfred Farlow

On a practical level, she and her staff had outgrown Pleasant View. Messengers and visiting Church officials, who frequently took the train to Concord to see Mrs. Eddy, had to sleep on cots set up in the parlor or the hallway if they needed to stay overnight. Additionally, the house was very close to the street, affording little privacy for its famous occupant, and it also needed repairs, which, as one staff member noted, "would have hindered her work. . . ."[40] Plus, there was a dearth of facilities.[41]

Whatever the overriding reason, Church spokesman Alfred Farlow had this to say to the press about the move: "This move was not prompted by any sudden decision. It is known to some of Mrs. Eddy's friends that she has for some years been considering the advisability of returning to this city. Her purpose is to be more convenient to the Mother Church of the denomination, near its headquarters."[42]

"A great barn of a place"

Much careful thought and preparation had gone into ensuring that Mrs. Eddy's new surroundings would look and feel familiar, enabling her routine and work to continue uninterrupted. The furnishings in her suite of rooms back in Concord had been duplicated,[43] her china and table linens and knick-knacks spirited to Boston over the previous weeks in trunks sent along with visiting Church officials.[44] But as Mrs. Eddy explored her new home, her initial enthusiasm waned.

"Altogether, the rooms did not seem cozy and homelike, and were a great disappointment to her," Adelaide Still would recall, adding that Mrs. Eddy described her enormous study as "a great barn of a place."[45] She had consented to having her own rooms a little larger than at Pleasant View, but her study and bedroom were nearly twice the size of what she was accustomed to. On top of that, the wallpaper, though handsome, was too dark, and the windowsills near her desk were too high, blocking her view when seated.

Something would have to be done.

During the weeks that followed, Mrs. Eddy directed a complete overhaul of her rooms as plans were drawn up to cut her study and bedroom down to a more modest size, add a private elevator that could whisk her directly to a side door on the ground floor for her daily carriage ride, swap out the dark wallpaper for a lighter floral pattern, and enlarge the bank of windows so that she could look out when seated at her desk. As construction got underway, Mrs. Eddy moved upstairs to the third floor and temporarily took over seamstress Nellie Eveleth's quarters. She would later say that Miss Eveleth had the best rooms in the house, thanks to the beautiful view. The snug bedroom in particular pleased her. She pronounced it "the most homelike room she had seen since she left Concord."[46]

By mid-March, Mrs. Eddy was settled back downstairs in her newly remodeled suite. Now that things were finally beginning to feel like home, she was ready to tackle the work that lay ahead.

Clockwise from top: Rear view of 400 Beacon Street as it looks today; interior first floor hall and stairway; front entrance. Inset: Aerial view of the estate.

Living and working as a family

With the move to Chestnut Hill, the household would expand to accommodate the additional staff needed to assist Mrs. Eddy in accomplishing "those things that had been marked out" for her to do. These individuals came with hearts brimming with gratitude for lives that had been healed and regenerated through Christian Science. Each one had enthusiastically embraced the new religion and was only too happy to have the opportunity to serve in whatever way he or she could.

Mary Baker Eddy's household reflected the changing landscape of a still-young America. Some were U.S. citizens; others were first- and second-generation immigrants, whose roots stretched to Canada, Scotland, England, Ireland, Germany, Norway, and Bohemia (now the Czech Republic). These latter were pilgrims of a different sort, whose initial paths may have echoed the typical American immigrant experience but who had also sought and found a higher sense of freedom — that of liberation from sickness, sorrow, and other limitations.

In the end, these strangers who came together under Mrs. Eddy's roof were held together by a common goal: The desire to support and care for their Leader. And she in turn supported and cared for them. She considered them family, and they lived as a family. As with all families, particularly large ones — the 400 Beacon Street staff numbered from 17 to 25 at various times — there was inevitably some chafing. Despite occasional conflict and tensions, by and large the arrangement worked.[47]

The value of making it work was clear. The demands placed on them would be many, including long hours with little time for leisure. But the rewards of living "at the fountainhead," as Mrs. Eddy termed it, could be tremendous, including being mentored on a near-daily basis by the one who had given Christian Science to the world.[48] As Mrs. Eddy noted a few years prior to her move, "loyal Christian Scientists, called to the home of the Discoverer and Founder of Christian Science, can acquire in one year the Science that otherwise might cost them a half century."[49]

Household staff (and Archibald McLellan) at 400 Beacon Street, circa 1908. Left to right: Alice Peck, Mr. McLellan, Elizabeth Kelly, Irving Tomlinson (seated), Nellie Eveleth, Katharine Retterer, Adam Dickey, Jonathan Irving, Frances Thatcher, Adelaide Still, Margaret Macdonald, Minnie Scott, Adolph Stevenson. | LONGYEAR MUSEUM COLLECTION

Those who rose to the occasion—who had the character and humility to tackle even the most menial tasks, recognizing that there was in fact no menial work in a household committed to approaching every task from a metaphysical basis—would eventually return home battle-tested, strengthened, and well equipped to be of further use to the Christian Science movement. Many would go on to serve as Christian Science practitioners. Some would become Christian Science teachers. One would become a Christian Science nurse; another, an editor of the Christian Science periodicals. They would serve as lecturers, as Normal class teachers, and as members of the Christian Science Board of Directors, as well as in other key roles both at The Mother Church and in the movement's wider ranks.

For each of these dedicated men and women, the years they spent in Mary Baker Eddy's household would change their lives forever.

Chapter 2
Help Wanted

ary Baker Eddy stood firmly at the helm of what by this point in time was rapidly becoming a worldwide religious movement. As the Discoverer, Founder, and Leader of Christian Science, she needed practical, professional, and prayerful support on the home front, since her residence doubled as the executive headquarters of the thriving movement.

"The demands on Mrs. Eddy were so many that at times several secretaries were required to care for the correspondence," noted Calvin Hill, who helped Mrs. Eddy with staffing. "Resident secretaries and other workers necessitated a large household staff. The work of cook, waitress, housemaid, laundress, seamstress, and personal maid had to be done by sincere, unselfish Christian Scientists."[1]

With the move to Chestnut Hill, additional staff would be needed, and someone had to locate these men and women. For several years, that responsibility had been shouldered by Calvin alone.

"It was difficult work, and I must confess that I was not always wholly successful in my missions," he would admit. "Helpers for [Mrs. Eddy's] household were hard to find, and especially those who were both physically and mentally qualified for such positions of trust."[2]

To be successful, individuals needed a rare combination of spiritual mindedness, humility, and practicality, among other strengths.

Finding qualified staff was one thing — keeping them was another.

> *"Resident secretaries and other workers necessitated a large household staff. The work of cook, waitress, housemaid, laundress, seamstress, and personal maid had to be done by sincere, unselfish Christian Scientists."*
>
> *— Calvin Hill*

"Some who began their work with inspiration found it difficult to retain their joy and spiritual vision, especially if their assigned work seemed to be menial," Calvin explained. "Others could not continue because of strong home ties or for other personal reasons."[3]

As Adam Dickey, who served as a secretary at 400 Beacon Street, pointed out, "Many people seemed to be inspired with a belief that there could be no pleasanter occupation in the world than to work for Mrs. Eddy. They failed to

Top: Hand-tinted photograph of Pleasant View. | Longyear Museum collection

Right: Calvin Hill at Pleasant View, circa 1907. For several years, he was largely responsible for finding staff for Mrs. Eddy's household. | Longyear Museum collection

Above: 400 Beacon Street today.

realize that what Mrs. Eddy wanted and actually required of those about her was the mental support which she found necessary to receive from students in order that she might be uninterrupted in her work for her Cause and for mankind."[4]

"I went with God"

Being uninterrupted in her work was of paramount importance to Mrs. Eddy. As she told a reporter just a few months before her move to Chestnut Hill, after she placed her estate in the hands of trustees, "I had come to a place where I could not carry on my work of Christian Science and attend to my business affairs." By taking this practical step, she explained, "I was not only relieved of the burden of caring for my business, but I was also relieved of what I call the inconsistency of bearing the burden, for one cannot serve two masters, and I chose the spiritual. I went with God. I have shut out society; I haven't time for it. I have things of more value to my life and to mankind to attend to."[5]

For much the same reason that Mrs. Eddy needed competent individuals to manage her business interests, she needed competent staff to oversee her household interests. And the more stable that staff remained, the better. Calvin Hill was sensitive to the strain that continual comings and goings in the household placed on her.

"I dread to change help," she confided to him at one point. "[I]t is such a care and toil to fit them for the situation...."[6]

Mrs. Eddy was keenly aware of the challenges involved in finding suitable help, and Mr. Hill would eventually have official reinforcements. In February 1906, Mrs. Eddy sent the Christian Science Board of Directors a draft of a new *Church Manual* By-law establishing a Committee on Business, whose responsibilities included providing metaphysical support at her direction and locating workers for her home.

The first appointees were Calvin Hill, James Neal, and Thomas Hatten. The trio began their work together in March of that year and were soon joined by Daisette McKenzie. Later, others would serve on the Committee as well.[7]

Caring for the "aged reformer"

"After a hard and successful career reformers usually are handsomely provided for," Mary Baker Eddy writes in her *Message to The Mother Church for 1901.* "Has the thought come to Christian Scientists, Have we housed, fed, clothed, or visited a reformer for that purpose? Have we looked after or even known of his sore necessities? . . . [M]ortals in the advancing stages of their careers need the watchful and tender care of those who want to help them. The aged reformer should not be left to the mercy of those who are not glad to sacrifice for him even as he has sacrificed for others all the best of his earthly years."[8]

Mrs. Eddy could very well have been speaking of her own experience. If anyone had earned the right to "watchful and tender care," she had. By this point in her life, she had labored for the Cause of Christian Science for nearly forty years, and, as her personal maid, Adelaide Still, would later point out, "had passed through

Early members of the Committee on Business. From top: Calvin Hill, James Neal, Thomas Hatten, Daisette McKenzie. | Longyear Museum collection

Illustration from the June 24, 1901, Boston Globe *depicts scenes from the previous day's Communion services at The Mother Church.*

many battle-scarred years, which seemed to take their toll of her physical strength so that she required more tenderness and care than in the earlier years."[9]

Mrs. Eddy's message was read aloud to the nearly 8,000 men and women who attended the four packed Communion services on June 23, 1901.[10] It touched the hearts of many that day, including Minnie Scott and her husband, Clarence. The young couple had taken up the study of Christian Science just a few years earlier. Their Leader's words would come back to them when Minnie was eventually called to serve in Mrs. Eddy's household. Remembering the reminder to help care for the "aged reformer," Minnie didn't hesitate.[11]

> *"The individual who loves most, does most, and sacrifices most for the reformer, is the individual who soonest will walk in his footsteps."*
> *— Mary Baker Eddy*

And there would be others like her, faithful men and women whose gratitude for Christian Science ran deep and who were consequently willing to leave home and hearth to aid Mrs. Eddy in her important work for her Church and the wider world. Mary Baker Eddy could have been speaking of them when, in that same 1901 address, she writes, "All honor and success to those who honor their father and mother. The individual who loves most, does most, and sacrifices most for the reformer, is the individual who soonest will walk in his footsteps."[12]

Her words would prove prophetic.

What would you do for Christian Science?

Initially, Calvin Hill was instructed by Mrs. Eddy to scout for helpers among her own students. "She said that if such were physically fit, they were the ones to serve in her home, because she knew what God had planted in their thought through her teaching, and at the proper time she could awaken that and make use of it."[13] As time went on, however, the search necessitated a wider pool of candidates. The Committee took to the road, following leads on prospective employees and sending initial assessments back to Mrs. Eddy. The most promising individuals were brought to Boston for further interviews, often with the Christian Science Board of Directors. Finally, in most cases, those who passed muster were sent on for an interview with Mrs. Eddy herself.

"She appeared to be a woman of medium height, quite elderly in appearance, not what you would call robust but rather of slight stature," noted Adam Dickey. Describing Mrs. Eddy's "wonderfully intelligent face," he adds that she "was quick and active in her mental perception and recognition of what was going on about her; she had a wonderful capacity for reading character and understanding the thought of those with whom she came in contact...."[14]

Ultimately, Mrs. Eddy had the final say as to who was hired.

At her request, the Committee's work was kept confidential. Sometimes, even the practitioners and teachers with whom individual Committee members spoke, hoping to gain clues about likely prospects, didn't have an inkling of the real purpose behind such conversations. At other times, only the prospects themselves were kept in the dark.

"[I]t might be thought unnecessary to cloak one's movements with so much secrecy," Calvin explained. "But Mrs. Eddy understood better than most of us, the necessity for keeping our activities to ourselves no matter how seemingly unimportant they might be."[15]

She was specific in her requirements for household help.

"Get one who loves to work for the Cause and is willing to take up the cross for it as I have done," Mrs. Eddy told the Committee.[16]

She provided a long list of questions to ask, directing them to inquire about a prospect's former religion and subsequent Christian Science teaching, their family ties, financial dependence, and physical well-being — this was demanding work, both mentally and physically. Her household was no place for lingering ailments or for the possibility of relapse, as Mrs. Eddy knew that the "carnal mind," as Saint Paul termed it in his letter to the Romans, would press on these points.[17] She wanted to know if a candidate was accustomed to "hard and constant activity," to being up early and late, and if he or she could handle the "close confinement" that came along with both living and working at her home.[18] Specific qualities of thought were essential — qualities that included humility, love, orderliness, promptness, alertness, accuracy, amiability, truthfulness, fidelity, and consecration — but Mrs. Eddy also counseled the Committee to report back on each prospect's age, appearance, and disposition.

"Get one who loves to work for the Cause and is willing to take up the cross for it as I have done."
— Mary Baker Eddy

Their assessments are refreshingly candid. Frances Thatcher, for instance, who would go on to join the housekeeping staff at Chestnut Hill, was described as 39 years of age, "small in stature, wiry, dark hair and eyes; pleasing in manner, accurate, competent."[19] Fifty-year-old Katharine Retterer, who would also work at 400 Beacon Street as a housekeeper, was raised on a farm, the Committee reported, and overall struck them as one who "loves to work," who was a "good whole-souled woman," ever "cheerful and capable."[20] Ella Rathvon, who would join the household as a metaphysical worker, was 45, of medium

Some members of Mrs. Eddy's household outside the service entrance at 400 Beacon Street.
Left to right: Frances Thatcher (seated), Nellie Eveleth, Adam Dickey,
Minnie Scott, Katharine Retterer (seated), Elizabeth Kelly, Adelaide Still.
Longyear Museum collection

height, rosy and plump, and portrayed as possessing a "sunny" disposition and "fearless" nature.[21]

There were more questions, too. Could the individual keep a confidence? Stand rebuke? Mrs. Eddy wanted to know about their success in the healing practice, and she also instructed the Committee to ask how a prospect felt about his or her obligation to their Leader—specifically: "What would you do for Christian Science?"[22]

Katharine Retterer told the Committee that she was "willing to do anything" for Mrs. Eddy. Ella Rathvon said that she was "holding herself in readiness to respond to a call," while her husband, William Rathvon, declared, "I am ready to come whenever you may want me."[23]

Formidable favors

One of the most important requirements that Mrs. Eddy directed the Committee to investigate was a prospect's ability to handle successfully what she termed "animal magnetism"—the carnal mind's resistance to all that is good.

Mrs. Eddy was keenly aware of the adverse winds of thought that buffeted her home. She knew that it required a certain stoutness of heart to live and work in a household that at times came under withering attack. Once, after interviewing a candidate, she commented, "[I] like her appearance but no one can tell till tried what another will be under fire."[24]

"Whenever personal ambition and the desire to be near our Leader for selfish reasons ruled one of those chosen, their stay was brief."

— Calvin Hill

And not everyone who joined her household was able to hold up under fire.

"Whenever personal ambition and the desire to be near our Leader for selfish reasons ruled one of those chosen, their stay was brief," noted Calvin Hill.[25]

Some washed out within days or weeks; others, even sooner. Groundskeeper and handyman John Salchow famously told of his strategy when sent to the train station to meet prospective workers.

"I would always try to engage the person in conversation," he recalled, "and from the character of his remarks, I could judge pretty well as to whether he could help Mrs. Eddy or not. If I sensed any personal pride or self-exaltation, I always left the horse hitched when we arrived . . . for I knew it would not be

*Above: Historic photo of Adam Dickey's room at 400 Beacon Street shows a framed portrait
of Mary Baker Eddy above the mantel mirror.* | LONGYEAR MUSEUM COLLECTION
Right: Today, that same portrait, by artist Anne D. Hearne, is part of Longyear's collection.

long before that person would be starting back to the station—and there were quite a few who went back."[26]

In a frank letter to his sister Bertha and other family members back home in Kansas, John also confided: "People sometimes say to me, you work for Mrs. Eddy. I say yes. O! how lovely it must be. What a good time you must have, and so on until I get tired, and I think if they could have a real try at it, for five minutes, how much would be left of them, for in spite of all the blessings, those that come here (many of them) will squirm as if you were throwing hot water on their backs."[27]

Ella Hoag, a student of Mrs. Eddy's who would serve on several different occasions of varying length at 400 Beacon Street as a metaphysical worker and who called that service a "very great privilege,"[28] also quietly acknowledged its challenges. Years later, when "a gushing Christian Scientist said to her … 'How *wonderful* it must have been to live in our Leader's home!' Mrs. Hoag replied laconically with a quotation from Mrs. Eddy's sermon *Christian Healing*: 'Heaven's favors are formidable.'"[29]

The "dearest spot on earth"

While 400 Beacon Street was unquestionably the executive headquarters of the Christian Science movement, it was also first and foremost a home.

"Home is the dearest spot on earth," Mrs. Eddy writes in *Science and Health with Key to the Scriptures*—words made all the more poignant coming from one who had not had a settled sense of home, practically speaking, for nearly two decades during an earlier period in her life.[30]

Home had always been important to Mrs. Eddy. She declared to a student at one point, "Meekness and love and home are my elements."[31] And to another she said, "The strongest tie I have ever felt, next to my love of God, has been my love for home."[32]

Mrs. Eddy had always taken a keen interest in domestic details—the decoration, the arrangement of artwork and furniture, the planning of meals. Here at Chestnut Hill, she was as solicitous of her household's comfort as she was of her own. One of the first things she did after her arrival at the new house was to visit each of her household workers' rooms in order to ensure that they were comfortable, and she later arranged for easy chairs for everyone.[33]

"I want you all to feel this is your home, and if you do not and I can do anything to make it so, you must tell me and I will do it," she told William Rathvon, who joined the secretarial staff in November 1908.[34]

Mrs. Eddy ensured that each staff member had a comfortable chair, like this one in Adam Dickey's room.

LONGYEAR MUSEUM COLLECTION

Such thoughtfulness was typical of Mary Baker Eddy and often remarked on by those who lived and worked side by side with her.

"While Mrs. Eddy was very generous in her donations to public interests . . . I think it was the smaller examples of loving interest to those within her immediate circle that counted most with me," observed Minnie Weygandt, who cooked for Mrs. Eddy at Pleasant View and occasionally filled in at Chestnut Hill. "It is easy enough to be large-handed in public, but what really tells the story about one is his attitude toward others in private life. I always felt she had a genuine affection for everyone."[35]

Mrs. Eddy considered her staff to be family, and she spoke of them that way. Irving Tomlinson, another of her secretaries, told of an instance when everyone was called to her study at 400 Beacon Street. At first, only the metaphysical workers and secretaries came. When Mrs. Eddy inquired where the rest of the household was, then "Mrs. Wilcox, Katharine Retterer,

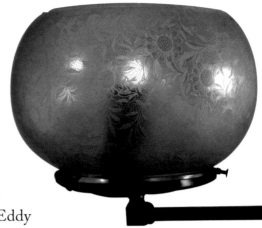

Restored light fixture at 400 Beacon Street.

Mrs. Kelly, Mrs. Minnie Scott, Miss Margaret Macdonald, Miss Eveleth came. While they were coming she said, 'I love every one of my family.'"[36]

"I want you all to feel this is your home...."
— Mary Baker Eddy

As a family of workers, Mrs. Eddy's staff was brought together for a common purpose: To support the Cause of Christian Science by serving its Leader. Their quiet labors were largely behind the scenes and would largely go unsung. But not unnoticed — especially by Mrs. Eddy. Together, they would help to make her new house a home.

Overleaf: Heading up the drive in winter.

37

Chapter 3

Serving Their Commander-in-Chief

ary Baker Eddy and her staff were still settling in at 400 Beacon Street when a newcomer arrived by sleigh one wintry February morning. He joined the household at the breakfast table, then was shown upstairs to the room he would occupy for most of the next three years.

"I found it equipped as an office, as well as a bedroom," he would later recall. "There were house telephones connecting with every room in the house except those occupied by Mrs. Eddy. The room was large, light, airy, and well furnished."[1]

After a face-to-face interview with the Leader he had come to serve ("my heart gave a few extra flutters, for this was to me the supreme moment in my Christian Science career"), Adam H. Dickey rolled up his sleeves and got to work.[2]

The big, bluff Midwesterner would go on to become Mrs. Eddy's private secretary and one of her most trusted lieutenants, but he got off to a rocky

Adam Dickey's room at 400 Beacon Street. | Longyear Museum collection

start. While it's unclear exactly what prompted it, a mere two weeks after his arrival, Mrs. Eddy called him in and told him "lovingly and kindly" that he "was not suited to the work here and that it might take years to train [him] properly."[3]

Adam informed his colleagues that he would be departing, telegraphed his wife, packed his trunk, and went to bed.

By 9:00 a.m. the following morning, however, Mrs. Eddy had changed her mind. She called him back into her study and told him he was to stay, then sent a letter brimming with gratitude to Lillian Dickey for her willingness to part with her husband. She ended it, "May the divine Love reward you for your kindness to me, and fill your consciousness with peace and power divine."[4]

Mr. Dickey took this turn of events to heart, thanking Mrs. Eddy for her vote of confidence and telling her that he "was beginning to learn what it meant to *strive*."

"Yes," she replied. "[T]hat's just the point. You must strive. I have to do it [and] so must you. This human 'I' is the very element of error and must be overcome in all points."

That night, Adam was given the prayerful watch from 3:00 to 5:00 a.m.—"and you better believe I kept it," he noted in his diary.[5]

Old and new

While the number and makeup of the secretarial staff fluctuated occasionally, there were four men who maintained a steady presence at 400 Beacon Street during the Chestnut Hill years: Calvin Frye, Irving Tomlinson, Adam Dickey, and William Rathvon.[6]

The latter two were members of what has been described as the "new guard"—unfamiliar faces to Mrs. Eddy who were among a new generation of practitioners and teachers not taught by her.[7] Both were vigorous men who hailed from points west—Adam Dickey from Kansas City; William Rathvon from Colorado—both had been successful businessmen, and both would bring fresh outlooks and approaches to Chestnut Hill.

Calvin Frye and Irving Tomlinson, on the other hand, were members of the old guard, although the younger Tomlinson had a foot in both camps. Calvin's New England roots ran as deep as Mrs. Eddy's; Irving was a transplant but had lived in the area for decades and was thus familiar and comfortable with Yankee ways.[8] Additionally, both men had been instructed personally by Mrs. Eddy, and both had gained experience in her household at Pleasant View.

In fact, Calvin Frye's association with Mrs. Eddy stretched all the way back to Lynn, Massachusetts, and the infancy of her Church. After his mother's healing of mental illness, Calvin became interested in Christian Science and

received instruction from Mrs. Eddy while she was living there at 8 Broad Street.[9] He'd been part of her household since 1882 — responding immediately when Mrs. Eddy sent for him to assist her after the passing of her husband, Asa Gilbert Eddy, and remaining with her for the next 28 years.

"In the early days," Irving Tomlinson wrote, "Calvin Frye faithfully undertook whatever duties and tasks required his attention: he kept her books, superintended the household buying, took her dictation, typing or writing in longhand a vast number of her letters and most of her articles."[10]

By 1908, however, while many of his duties remained the same — Calvin continued to keep the books and supervise the household buying at 400 Beacon Street, among other things — circumstances had changed.

"At the opening of the century," Irving noted, "Mrs. Eddy's household at Pleasant View was small, consisting only of a secretary or two, a companion, a cook, a housekeeper, and additional outside workers; but as the Cause grew and her work became more exacting, others were called to meet various needs of the household."[11]

For Calvin Frye, the expansion of Mrs. Eddy's inner circle to include those "others" — a necessary by-product of the need for additional help — must have been difficult. Biographer Robert Peel doesn't mince words: "It was a bitter pill for Calvin Frye to find himself superseded in many respects by Dickey."[12]

Mrs. Eddy was sensitive to her long-time aide's feelings,

From top: Adam Dickey, Calvin Frye, William Rathvon, and Irving Tomlinson. | LONGYEAR MUSEUM COLLECTION

and in March 1908 she sent Adam a short note: "Mr. Frye needs <u>encourage-ment</u> . . . the dear man has shared my deprivations many years hoping they would cease and so give him release as well as myself. Encourage him to find all happiness in <u>divine</u> <u>Love</u>, life spiritual here and now. . . ."[13]

> *"Encourage him to find all happiness in*
>
> <u>*divine*</u> <u>*Love*</u> *, life spiritual here and now. . . ."*
>
> *— Mary Baker Eddy*

As Mary Baker Eddy's longest-serving worker, Calvin was trusted for his unfailing honesty and obedience and for his willingness to do whatever was needed, including donning livery and riding alongside the coachman on Mrs. Eddy's daily carriage outings. His protectiveness of her prompted a response from fellow secretary William Rathvon that points up the tension between the old and new guard: "We have two aims in our work here: first, to protect our Leader; and second, to protect the Cause. [Frye] has shown his are: first, to protect our Leader; and second, to protect our Leader."[14]

For Calvin, protecting Mrs. Eddy *was* protecting the Cause — through long decades of experience at her side, and as an eyewitness to the struggles she had endured, he had come to see the absolute inseparability of the two.[15]

And if he was protective of Mrs. Eddy, Mrs. Eddy was also protective of him. In May 1908, for example, she wrote a corrective note to the editor of the *New York Herald,* which had mistakenly identified Calvin as her coachman.[16] Arguably a trivial point — but perhaps not to Calvin, who was no doubt cheered at his Leader's prompt defense of his dignity.

Calvin Frye

The quality of faithfulness

"God had been graciously preparing me during many years for the reception of this final revelation of the absolute divine Principle of scientific mental healing," writes Mary Baker Eddy in *Science and Health*.[17] In like manner, Calvin Frye was prepared for his life work, although he couldn't have known it at the time.

Just a year younger than Mrs. Eddy's son, George Washington Glover II,

Calvin A. Frye | LONGYEAR MUSEUM COLLECTION

Calvin Augustine Frye was born in the summer of 1845 into a venerable New England family. His great-grandfather fought in the Revolutionary War, and his hometown of Frye Village, Massachusetts, was named for his great-great-great-grandfather, Samuel Frye, a prosperous miller of grain and lumber.[18] Calvin's father, Enoch, was educated at prestigious Phillips Andover Academy and later at Harvard University (Ralph Waldo Emerson was a classmate), but his teaching career was cut short when a crippling illness left him lame and a semi-invalid. He managed to eke out a living running a grocery store, later moving the family to the neighboring mill town of Lawrence.

"It was not possible for [Enoch Frye] to educate his sons as he had been educated," wrote journalist Sibyl Wilbur, and consequently Calvin received only a village school education, although he would remain a life-long learner.[19]

Like Mrs. Eddy, Calvin grew up in the Congregational church. Like Mrs. Eddy, he would serve as a Sunday School teacher, among other posts. He, too, was no stranger to tragedy, experiencing a string of early losses. Of his four siblings, one brother died in infancy, and another perished in the Civil War, as did his brother-in-law.[20] His mother struggled with mental illness and was periodically institutionalized.

To help support the family, Calvin apprenticed as a machinist and afterward went to work in the Pacific Mills along the banks of the Merrimack River in Lawrence, Massachusetts.

"To be a first-class machinist,"

Engraving of Pacific Mills, circa 1860. Calvin Frye worked here as a machinist when a young man.
Courtesy Kheel Center, Cornell University

observed William Lyman Johnson, who knew Calvin and whose father labored shoulder to shoulder with him during the early days of the Christian Science movement, "means primarily accuracy, and great accuracy, for he has to work in the radius of a thousandth of an inch." Noting also the patience required, he continued, "the work of a fine machinist becomes an art, and demands thought, intelligence, energy and accuracy. Hardly a better training could have been given to Mr. Frye, combined with natural qualities that were inherently within him, and which were afterwards developed to a very remarkable degree, for his work with Mrs. Eddy."[21]

Calvin would prove a capable employee at the textile mill, rising to become an overseer.[22] The future must have looked promising when he met and married Ada Brush, a young Canadian weaver of Irish descent. He was 26; his bride just 22. Sadly, however, Ada died of consumption barely a year after their marriage. Calvin moved back in with his parents and widowed sister, Lydia.[23]

Onto this cheerless and desolate scene came Christian Science, with a burst of light that would transform Calvin's life. Introduced to the new religion through the healing of a relative, Calvin and his sister sought treatment for their mother. Within a short time, she was well.[24]

Calvin and Lydia immediately took up the study of Christian Science, and in the fall of 1881, Calvin went to Lynn to receive instruction from Mrs. Eddy.[25] During the class, he boarded with the Eddys at their home at 8 Broad Street, which gave them the opportunity to size him up.

After the class finished, Calvin returned to Lawrence and went into the public healing practice. At some point in the following months, Asa Gilbert Eddy paid a visit to Calvin's pastor to make inquiries about his character, sensing in Calvin a suitable and trustworthy man to assist his wife.[26]

"If Mr. Frye is not a Christian there is not one on earth," the minister told him.[27]

And so it was that in August 1882, just two months after her husband's passing and at the end of a period of quiet mourning in Vermont, Mrs. Eddy sent for Calvin Frye. He dropped everything to meet her train home to Boston. He was 37 years old, and for the next 28 years, he would hardly leave her side.[28]

Mrs. Eddy's "useful man"

Toward the end of Calvin's life, a visiting acquaintance remembers him speaking "feelingly of Mrs. Eddy's need in the early days of her work, of someone on whom she could depend."[29]

Calvin Frye was that someone. Plain speaking and plain dealing, he was trustworthy, obedient, earnest, and honest as the day is long. Above all, "the quality of faithfulness was preeminently his," wrote Sibyl Wilbur.[30]

"Only a great love and devotion to our Leader, and to the Cause, could have held him through so many years of struggle and self-sacrifice," recalled Adelaide Still, who worked closely with Calvin at Pleasant View and 400 Beacon Street. "No one else was so continually on duty: he was subject to call day or night, and I never heard of his having a vacation."[31]

Calvin Frye, circa 1882, around the time he went to work for Mrs. Eddy. | LONGYEAR MUSEUM COLLECTION

During the busy decade of the 1880s, with the Massachusetts Metaphysical College in full swing and the fledgling Christian Science church rapidly taking root in Boston, Calvin was Mrs. Eddy's man-of-all-work, willing to serve in whatever way would best support her mission.[32] He kept the books, paid the bills, tended the furnace, learned typing and shorthand in order to take dictation and help answer correspondence, organized classes, oversaw the household, and more. He was also fully engaged publicly with the growing movement, serving as President of the Christian Scientist Association after Mrs. Eddy's resignation in 1888, and even filling the pulpit at Hawthorne Hall on occasion.

"He preached fluently, with good poise, with subjects applicable to the time, and with a spiritual comprehension of the text," commented one who heard him.[33]

There were no lengths to which Calvin would not go to protect his Leader. After a startled horse nearly upended her carriage one day while out for a drive, he donned livery and sat beside the coachman, keeping a watchful eye on her daily outings. And when she visited The Mother Church for the first time and stayed overnight in the Mother's Room, "Mr. Frye slept across the doorway outside her room, so that no one could reach her without stepping over his body."[34]

He was, in short, "her useful man," as he told the *Denver Republican* in a 1912 interview.

It was a role that Calvin was happy to fill. As he explained to the Colorado newspaper, "My own mother was an invalid for so long that I did not know a mother's care until I went to Mrs. Eddy. Mrs. Eddy was not only my spiritual guide but my second mother."[35]

Described as "an active, careful agent for Mrs. Eddy's personal affairs,"[36] Calvin Frye's account books bear this out. The machinist who mastered his painstaking trade is evident in the meticulous records he kept. So scrupulously honest was he, in fact, that when the household books were audited during the Next Friends lawsuit in 1907, it was found that Calvin was actually *owed* money![37]

"Whenever there was an entanglement, I used to take money from my own pocket to straighten it out," he explained.[38]

A physically unprepossessing man with deep brown eyes and a calm demeanor, Calvin had a quick wit, which Mrs. Eddy and those in her household appreciated.[39] Others, too, remarked on his good nature.

"Delightful of manners, easy, and graceful, Mr. Frye has a bright smiling eye," reported the *New York Herald*,[40] and Concord newspaper editor Michael Meehan observed that Calvin "keeps his own business and the business of Mrs. Eddy entirely to himself," that he was "kind but firm, seeks no favors, strives not at conciliation, never becomes entangled in the affairs of others, speaks plainly of things concerning which there must be no doubt, moves softly but with dignity, and grasps the hand of a friend heartily."[41]

Calvin had an artistic bent and could play the piano and sing (he had a "surprisingly good tenor" voice, according to John Salchow). He also enjoyed amateur photography and learned to print and develop his own film.[42] And there was one particular snack for which he had a weakness — "Frye is a regular squirrel for nuts," Mrs. Eddy once told cook Minnie Weygandt, who kept a plentiful supply on hand for him.[43]

The boy whom circumstances had deprived of a higher education continued a lifelong course of self-improvement by reading widely.[44] A look at Mr. Frye's book collection reveals a broad range of interests, from natural history, poetry, and literature — including Chaucer, Dickens, and Sir Walter Scott — to astronomy, investing, Bible study, and musical theory, among other topics. His thirst for self-improvement is also evident in books on subjects like public speaking, grammar, and etiquette.[45]

"A quiet corner and a good book are all he requires, he has told the writer good-humoredly, after his daily duties are performed," noted Sibyl Wilbur.[46]

Calvin attended three classes taught by Mrs. Eddy, receiving the designation C.S.D.[47] He was also present at her final class in 1898. Humble to the core, he was content to play a supporting role, and when at one point in 1910 Mrs. Eddy offered him a spot on the Christian Science Board of Directors, he declined, telling her, "No, Mother, I have been in the limelight long enough. Let someone else take the position."[48]

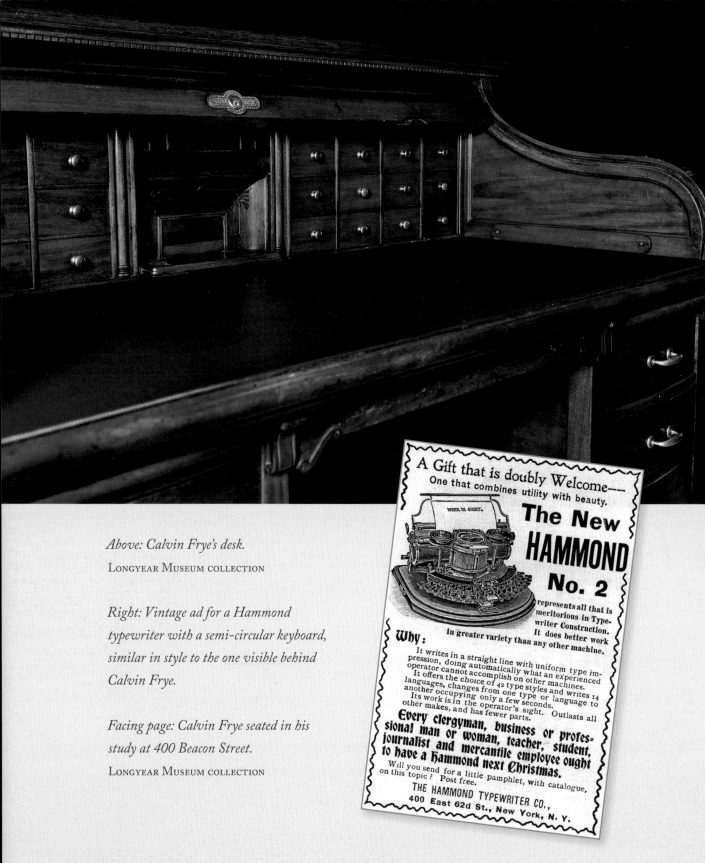

Above: Calvin Frye's desk.

Longyear Museum collection

Right: Vintage ad for a Hammond typewriter with a semi-circular keyboard, similar in style to the one visible behind Calvin Frye.

Facing page: Calvin Frye seated in his study at 400 Beacon Street.

Longyear Museum collection

A Gift that is doubly Welcome---
One that combines utility with beauty.

WORK IN SIGHT.

The New
HAMMOND
No. 2

represents all that is meritorious in Typewriter Construction. It does better work in greater variety than any other machine.

Why:

It writes in a straight line with uniform type impression, doing automatically what an experienced operator cannot accomplish on other machines.
It offers the choice of 42 type styles and writes 14 languages, changes from one type or language to another occupying only a few seconds. Outlasts all other makes, and has fewer parts.
Its work is in the operator's sight.

Every clergyman, business or professional man or woman, teacher, student, journalist and mercantile employee ought to have a Hammond next Christmas.

Will you send for a little pamphlet, with catalogue, on this topic? Post free.

THE HAMMOND TYPEWRITER CO.,
400 East 62d St., New York, N. Y.

"Pulling and hauling"

The move to 400 Beacon Street and subsequent addition of staff brought subtle and not-so-subtle cross-currents into Calvin Frye's life. Conflicts with the "new guard," who didn't always fully appreciate the long history that he and Mrs. Eddy shared, must have been unsettling.

"[I]t can be imagined what a lot of 'pulling and hauling' went on out there at Chestnut Hill, much of which Mrs. Eddy felt or sensed, and all of which hurt her," observed Calvin Hill.[49]

The divide between the old and new guard is even evident in the diaries that each of the secretaries kept. William Rathvon, Irving Tomlinson, and Adam Dickey all seem to have had one eye on posterity.

"These are history making days," Rathvon would write in a 1909 letter, and that sense of being an eyewitness to larger-than-life events carries over into his diary and chatty reminiscences.[50] Tomlinson's *Twelve Years with Mary Baker Eddy* is drawn from his diary and reminiscences, which run into the hundreds of pages, and Dickey would also mine his diaries for a memoir. Calvin's entries, on the other hand, are largely as dry and matter-of-fact as might be expected from such a circumspect Yankee.

Despite her deep fondness for Calvin, Mrs. Eddy could find him exasperating at times, once calling him "the prince of blunderers."[51] On another occasion, she said to her household, "When Mr. Frye is himself, he can accomplish the work of fifty men in mental practice, but he is liable the very next day to be off again."[52] One of his colleagues at 400 Beacon Street recalled Calvin's "gusts of temper"—although he hastened to add that they were short-lived, "and always followed by a deep repentance and return to his normal joking self."[53]

Still, there was arguably no one in the household to whom Mrs. Eddy was closer. In January 1908, she would write, "Calvin dear, Because I love you most of persons on earth I try most to have you see the lies of m.a.m. [malicious animal magnetism]."[54] And she told Joseph Mann, "Calvin is invaluable to me in my work, because he would not break one of the ten commandments."[55]

Calvin certainly felt that closeness. He told colleagues at one point that although there was no blood relationship between Mrs. Eddy and himself, he had "an affection for her as a son would have for his mother in caring for her interests and in trying to promote her comfort."[56]

Mrs. Eddy gave her faithful compatriot a number of gifts over the years in gratitude for his service, and in 1903, she asked the Board of Directors of her Church to arrange for his fellow Executive Members to give him something special.

"Calvin is invaluable to me in my work,

because he would not break one of

the ten commandments."

— Mary Baker Eddy

"He has stood by my side to help <u>our Cause 21 years</u>," she wrote to the Board. "He has done more practical work in my behalf . . . than any other Student."[57] The Executive Members duly presented Calvin with a fine mahogany roll-top desk (see photo on page 52), along with a heartfelt letter of thanks.[58]

"It was the first desk Mr. Frye had ever had and his pride and delight in it was childlike," Irving Tomlinson would note.[59] Mrs. Eddy provided generously for Calvin in her will, ensuring that he had the means for a comfortable retirement. In 1912, he was elected First Reader of First Church of Christ, Scientist, Concord, New Hampshire, and in 1916, Calvin Frye became President of The Mother Church, where he served, faithfully as always, until his passing in the spring of 1917.

Daily duties

The day began early for the secretarial staff. Adam Dickey made a habit of rising at 5:00 a.m.; William Rathvon a bit before 6:00, sometimes heading outside to stretch his legs before breakfast; Irving Tomlinson recalls occasional early morning bicycle rides. After the morning meal, the men would often retire to the library to read the newspapers.[60] Frequently, there were hymns upstairs in the Pink Room, Mrs. Eddy's private sitting room on the second floor. By 9:00 or so, the secretaries would head to their respective rooms and their assigned

Adam Dickey's desk in his room at 400 Beacon Street. | Longyear Museum collection

Above: Irving Tomlinson's room.
LONGYEAR MUSEUM
COLLECTION

Right: William Rathvon's room.
LONGYEAR MUSEUM
COLLECTION

tasks, whether they were secretarial or prayerful. Like the metaphysical workers in the household, the men also had assigned shifts as "watchers" at specified times during the day (generally an hour in the morning, two in the afternoon, and one in the evening). Mrs. Eddy would usually provide direction for these watches, which focused on "handling such claims as seem to be urgent or intrusive," as Mr. Rathvon explained.[61] "We then shut our doors and get down to hard work."[62]

Answering correspondence was part of every secretary's duties, and to that end all four men had typewriters in their rooms. The mail was voluminous. Letters addressed to the house were delivered twice a day by the postman; those addressed to Mrs. Eddy's post office box were collected by her coachman.[63]

William Rathvon's title was corresponding secretary, and his primary responsibilities included handling Mrs. Eddy's appointments and answering letters. As he frankly admitted, "There was no little drudgery connected with it because the daily mail was extensive."[64] Some letters could be answered with a simple form response, while others — those from "cranks," for example, or from individuals seeking autographs or money — simply didn't merit a response at all.[65] As Adam Dickey bluntly put it in a letter to a friend, "I have a very large waste basket and make rather frequent use of it. . . ."[66]

Not that Mrs. Eddy, ever the captain of her ship, didn't keep an eagle eye on the proceedings. In October 1909, she cautioned Mr. Dickey against screening the mail he passed along to her, asking him to "be sure to give me all the letters that relate to me and the cause, that are for or against it or me and I will take the responsibility of deciding as to their publication."[67]

Correspondence needing Mrs. Eddy's reply was answered in various ways. Sometimes, Mrs. Eddy wrote responses by hand; sometimes, she drafted or dictated letters for her secretaries to type or gave a general response that she expected to be sent with an explanation, such as, "Mrs. Eddy has asked me to tell you that . . ."; and sometimes, the secretaries would respond on their own without interrupting Mrs. Eddy if they felt this action was appropriate.[68]

In the letters drafted by Mrs. Eddy herself, Adam Dickey recalls her precision with word choice. She would often delay sending a letter while she considered the exact word she wanted, sometimes consulting two or three dictionaries and frequently quoting the proverb attributed to Michelangelo, "Trifles make perfection, but perfection is no trifle."[69] Even after several passes, she might ask for a letter again for further edits. On those occasions, he noted, she would apologize and say, "Mr. Dickey, won't you forgive me if I ask you to bring that letter to me again?"[70]

He was happy to accommodate. As he'd affirmed when interviewed before joining the staff at Chestnut Hill, he was willing to serve in any way needed: "I had no higher aim in life than to be of service to Mrs. Eddy and the Cause of Christian Science, and . . . if they needed somebody to shovel the snow off her front sidewalk, I would drop everything else and give all my time to her service in any capacity whatever."[71]

Instead of having him shovel snow, however, Mrs. Eddy appointed Adam Dickey as her confidential or private secretary. In this role, he served as an intermediary between her and the executives at Church headquarters, including the Christian Science Board of Directors, as well as the press. According to William Rathvon, Adam was "the mouthpiece of our Leader in communicating with various heads of departments of the entire Christian Science movement," and as such, his office was "a gateway through which must pass all that was important, going in or coming out."[72]

Several aspects of Mrs. Eddy's writings also came under his purview, including some editing. "All the articles from our Leader which appear in our periodicals and in the newspapers pass through my hands," Adam related to a friend.[73]

At Mrs. Eddy's request, he would write the introduction to her final published work, *Poems,* and she also selected him to head up the committee for the first translation of *Science and Health* into another language (German).

In May 1909, Mrs. Eddy informed her household in a memo that, in addition to all of these responsibilities, Adam Dickey would "take the entire charge of my premises, and thus carry out my rules."[74]

Adam Dickey

A staunch lieutenant

"May I present for your consideration as Secretary the name of Mr. Adam H. Dickey, of Kansas City, Missouri?"

The letter from Daisette McKenzie on behalf of the Committee on Business arrived at Pleasant View in late January 1908, just as Mrs. Eddy was preparing to move to Boston. The recommended candidate "was and is in vigorous health," the Committee

Adam H. Dickey
LONGYEAR MUSEUM COLLECTION

reported, serving as First Reader for his branch church, and "known to be particularly successful in the healing work."[75]

Within a week, Adam Herbert Dickey was on a train to Boston.

"This man who in his massive physical build might have been a blacksmith, so powerful was his appearance," a contemporary would later note, "was called upon to use his strength in behalf of the woman who was devoting her life to the welfare of mankind."[76]

Born in 1864 in Toronto, Adam was the second of nine children in a close-knit family, headed by an Irish-born father and a mother who traced her lineage back to the Mayflower. He was raised in the Methodist faith of his paternal forebears, and attended Upper Canada College before emigrating with the rest of his family to the United States. The Dickeys settled in Kansas City, where abundant natural resources and a booming metropolis helped ensure the success of W. S. Dickey Clay Manufacturing Company.[77] Adam worked in the family business as a sales representative, and in 1887, he married Lillian Selden. A year later a son, Herbert Clayton Dickey, was born. Sadly, the boy would pass on at the age of seven.[78] The Dickeys had no other children.

It was Lillian Dickey who first became acquainted with Christian Science, turning to it for relief from sciatica. Her healing caught her husband's attention, and in 1893, when Lillian entered Primary class instruction with Henrietta Graybill, Adam accompanied her to some of the class sessions.

"Everything the teacher said about the Bible seemed right to me," recalled Mr. Dickey, who was healed of tobacco use during this time.[79]

Adam Dickey began his career working for his brother Walter's firm, whose original factory is pictured in this vintage postcard.

*Mrs. Eddy had Adam Dickey's portrait hung in the Pink Room, across from the photos of
her husband Asa Gilbert Eddy and herself.* | Longyear Museum collection

The couple joined The Mother Church the following year, and in 1896, Adam enrolled in Primary class himself.[80] The summer of 1897 would provide his first glimpse of Mary Baker Eddy, when he traveled to Boston for the Communion season. On July 4th, at the Sunday service at The Mother Church, an invitation was extended by Mrs. Eddy to her followers to come to Pleasant View. Adam Dickey joined the throng on the train to New Hampshire the next day, gathering with some 2,500 other Christian Scientists eager to hear their Leader's remarks.[81]

Back in Kansas City, Mr. Dickey flirted briefly with politics, running for alderman and losing by less than 200 votes.[82] He was still fully engaged in the family firm, which was expanding into foreign markets. Inquiries were fielded from as far away as Cuba and Mexico, where Adam traveled several times on business, reporting that "the demand for American goods is practically unlimited."[83] In November 1898, he and Lillian headed south of the border for the winter, spending time in Guadalajara and Mexico City.

This framed portrait of Mr. Dickey is visible in the historic photo on the facing page. | Longyear Museum collection

This business trip would prove a turning point in both their lives.

At a meeting with a government representative in Mexico City, Adam noticed that the man was suffering with a severe case of jaundice. He told him about Christian Science and agreed to pray for him. The swift healing that followed impressed the Dickeys so much that on their return to Kansas City in early 1899, Adam publicly announced in the local newspaper that he was retiring from the business world and "devoting his attention to Christian Science healing."[84] Both he and Lillian would begin advertising as practitioners in *The Christian Science Journal* that year.

In the beginning, requests for help were few. The Dickeys' savings account dwindled to eight dollars, and an offer to rejoin the family firm at a generous salary sounded tempting.[85] Adam accepted it initially but, after praying through the night, reversed his decision the following morning.

From that moment on, Mr. Dickey never looked back. His healing practice flourished, and for the next quarter of a century he devoted his considerable energy to furthering the Cause of Christian Science.

In 1901, Adam attended the Normal class in Boston with Edward A. Kimball, earning his C.S.B. degree.[86] He returned home to teach his first class in November of that year. For the next six years, he taught and practiced in Kansas City. It was while serving as First Reader of his branch church that he received the call to go to Chestnut Hill.

As a secretary, Adam proved himself nearly indispensable. For one thing, he typed rapidly, a valuable skill at the time.

"There was no one in the family who could handle a typewriter very efficiently and the correspondence had accumulated to such a point that Mr. Frye was utterly unable to cope with it," Irving Tomlinson recalled.[87]

Above and beyond his typing skills, however, Adam was efficient, decisive, and unswervingly loyal to Mrs. Eddy. She quickly grew to trust and love this blunt, capable former businessman, to the point that she had his photograph hung on the wall of the Pink Room near the portraits of herself and her husband, Asa Gilbert Eddy, and told Adam that he was "the best man she ever knew."[88]

Although not without shortcomings—colleague William Rathvon called the Kansas City transplant "aggressively assertive,"[89] while Irving Tomlinson noted that he "sometimes rode rough shod over others"—Adam Dickey was nevertheless respected and appreciated.

Irving also conceded, "[H]e did what he felt to be right. He had wonderful vigor and health and was able to serve Mrs. Eddy continuously and effectively."[90]

And William praised Adam's usefulness to Mrs. Eddy, describing him as "loving" and "considerate," and pointing out that "he is steadfast, not flurried, understands her, and has her confidence."[91] Adelaide Still would also point to his "tender, loving attitude towards our Leader, which I shall always remember."[92]

In May 1909, while not ceding an inch of her own authority, Mrs. Eddy turned over much of the day-to-day management of her household to Adam Dickey. Her last official communication with the officers of her Church was on November 21, 1910, when she nominated him to the Christian Science Board of Directors, a post he would hold until his passing in 1925.[93]

Starting in 1919, while serving as Chairman of the Board, Mr. Dickey played a pivotal role when a pair of lawsuits known as the "Great Litigation" threatened to split the Church. He firmly upheld Mary Baker Eddy's leadership, her *Church Manual*, and the authority of the Board under the *Manual*. Ultimately, so did the courts.[94]

Adam Dickey would also serve as Treasurer of The Mother Church, as a Trustee under the Will of Mary Baker Eddy, and as a Trustee of the Chestnut Hill Benevolent Association.[95] He wrote several significant articles for the Christian Science periodicals as well, including the one for which he is best known, "God's Law of Adjustment," beloved by generations of readers.

Adam Dickey at his desk at 400 Beacon Street.
Private collection

If Calvin Frye felt slighted by the shift in the household hierarchy, he must have taken comfort in the fact that it was he who was most often invited to sit with Mrs. Eddy in the room over the porte-cochère after supper, talking quietly in the twilight as the streetlamps came on.[96] And tellingly, it was to Calvin that Mrs. Eddy turned when several pressed her to change the *Church Manual* By-laws requiring her signature.

"She talked with them two or three times about it," wrote Adelaide Still, "and one afternoon after they left the room, she called Calvin Frye and said to him, 'Calvin, you know what they want me to do, don't you?' He replied, 'Yes, Mother.' She asked, 'Would you do it?' He replied, 'I'd keep it in my own hands, if I were you; it's giving them too much power.' She said, 'You are right.'"[97] And that's just what she did.

> ## "I'd keep it in my own hands, if I were you; it's giving them too much power."
> — Calvin Frye

All of the secretaries juggled multiple duties. Irving Tomlinson, for instance, was also given general oversight of the buildings and grounds at 400 Beacon Street—perhaps because of his well-known interest in plants and flowers.[98] In this capacity, he was responsible for maintaining "harmony among the workers and the successful fulfillment of their duties."[99]

Once, he and William Rathvon were even asked by Mrs. Eddy to ride along near her carriage in a rented buggy as a measure of protection. They were baffled by this request at the time, but later found out that the daughter of Archibald McLellan had overheard a conversation on a streetcar to the effect that a woman had been offered a large sum of money to run her automobile into Mrs. Eddy's carriage.[100] Thanks to Mrs. Eddy's alertness, nothing of this nature ever transpired.

William Rathvon

"A gentleman in every sense of the word"

"Four score and seven years ago our fathers brought forth on this continent, a new nation, conceived in Liberty, and dedicated to the proposition that all men are created equal."[101] Young William Roedel Rathvon was not quite nine years old when

William R. Rathvon

LONGYEAR MUSEUM COLLECTION

Above: President Abraham Lincoln (center, seated and hatless) at Gettysburg on November 19, 1863.
COURTESY LIBRARY OF CONGRESS

Left: This engraving of Lincoln was in the West Room at 400 Beacon Street. | LONGYEAR MUSEUM COLLECTION

he heard President Abraham Lincoln deliver his Gettysburg Address on November 19, 1863. The clash of Union and Confederate armies four and a half months earlier in Gettysburg, Pennsylvania, was a decisive battle of the Civil War,[102] and would have been well known to young William, who lived just 50 miles from the battleground in the up-and-coming town of Lancaster.[103]

Five generations of Rathvons had lived and prospered in eastern Pennsylvania by the time William was born on December 27, 1854. Like other European Protestants who came to the United States for religious freedom, his ancestors, who were French Huguenots and Germans, settled in the Lancaster area in 1721 and 1740 respectively.[104] William was baptized and confirmed in the Lutheran church, and as a young man he attended Franklin and Marshall College.[105]

After marrying Elizabeth (Lillie) Stauffer in 1877, he launched a career as a pioneering businessman and went west, traveling first to Kansas, where he and his older brother Samuel, a produce dealer, supplied the Denver & Rio Grande Railroad Company.[106] Sadly, the newlyweds enjoyed not quite three years together before Lillie passed on after the birth of their son, Martin. William eventually moved to Denver, and in 1883, he married Ella Stauffer, one of

Lillie's younger sisters. Ella became a devoted wife to William and stepmother to young Martin.[107]

A decade later, while on a business trip to Chicago, the financial panic of 1893 broke out,[108] leaving the Rathvons stranded with no funds to return home to Denver.[109]

"I was a man active in business, a believer in and follower of outdoor sports, athletics, etc.," William would recall. "To the deeper things of life I gave but little thought. . . ."[110] But "man's extremity is God's opportunity," and it was at this juncture that the Rathvons were led to look into Christian Science.[111]

"It was not that the healing had especial attraction for us, as we had fairly good health," William noted, "nor did its theology seem easy to understand and accept; but its strong claims to the practicability of bringing God—Good—into every condition of life here and now, impressed us most forcibly. . . ."[112]

After taking Primary class instruction from Mary M. W. Adams, a student of Mrs. Eddy's, in Chicago, the Rathvons joined The Mother Church and returned to Colorado, where they both began healing others.

William's business took the family to Florence, a small town sandwiched between the Rocky Mountains and the Arkansas River. In 1897, the first Christian Science service in the community was held in their rooms "under the shadow of the snow-capped Rockies . . . in the centre of an oil refinery running in full blast. . . ."[113] There were just four people present. By March 1898, the small congregation had gained in numbers and outgrown its temporary space. First Church of Christ, Scientist, Florence, with 16 committed members, a regular attendance of about 32, and a thriving Sunday School, was flourishing.

"We have a snug sum in our building fund, and in two weeks' time demonstrated enough cash to pay for a new organ," William reported in *The Christian Science Journal.* "This, too, without any solicitation or urging whatever. It was esteemed a privilege to give, and no one was made poorer thereby. This is the more significant when it is known that we are all working people—none of us being wealthy, as the world counts wealth."[114]

By 1903, the Rathvons had moved again, this time to Boulder, where

William was general manager of an oil company and also worked as a Christian Science practitioner.[115]

"My business and practitioner's offices adjoined," he explained, "so that I spent the mornings at business and afternoons at my Science work."[116]

The Rathvons' education in Christian Science continued that year, when husband and wife attended a Primary class taught in Boston by Edward Kimball.[117] Then, in December 1907, William was invited to go through Normal class with Judge Septimus J. Hanna.

The following summer, he was interviewed by the Committee on Business as a prospective worker for Mrs. Eddy's home. The Committee's report details Mr. Rathvon's age (53), good health, and willingness to leave his work at any time for Christian Science, "having made it a rule to give calls for help in Science the precedence over the demands of business."[118]

In November 1908, William did just that, leaving a job that paid a large annual salary to join the 400 Beacon Street household, where he would serve as corresponding secretary.[119]

There was much work to be done.

Mrs. Eddy received copious amounts of mail, and while she had multiple secretaries lending a hand, her correspondence was William's primary responsibility. His colleague Irving Tomlinson observed, "Mr. Rathvon had a rare gift for this work and handled the vast amount of worldwide correspondence which came to Mrs. Eddy with ease and dispatch. In this way he saved her much time and labor and rendered valuable service to her and the Cause."[120]

Mrs. Eddy valued William's excellent service. At one point in 1908, thinking that she was going to lose one of her secretaries, Mrs. Eddy wrote Archibald McLellan, "Hasten to get me a substitute as good as Mr. Rathvon. . . ."[121]

John Salchow also held him in high esteem. William "was a consecrated Christian Scientist," he would later write, "and gave me the feeling of being always ready and willing to serve his Leader. He was a gentleman in every sense of the word and his wife was a true lady."[122]

Described as "tall and straight" by another who knew him at the time, William

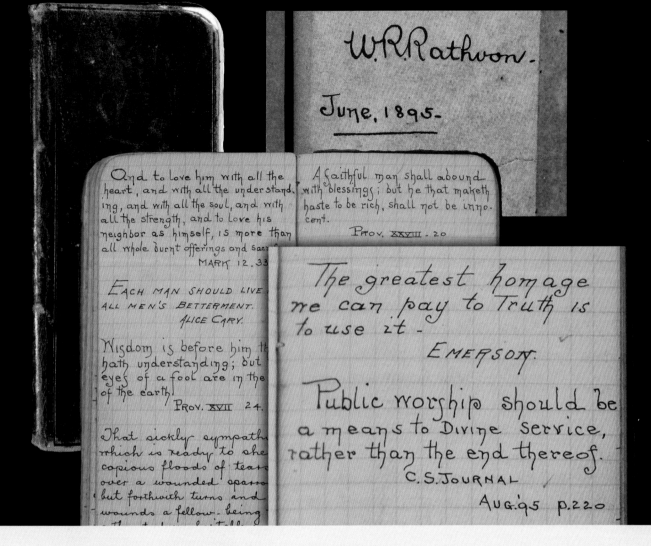

This red leather pocket journal, dated June 1895, belonged to William Rathvon. It contains nearly 200 meticulously handwritten quotations, some from the Bible and The Christian Science Journal, *others from a wide variety of authors, including Shakespeare, Emerson, Thoreau, and Henry Drummond, a number of which are cross-referenced to* Science and Health. | Longyear Museum collection

had an "innate sweetness of disposition" which "endeared him to us all...."[123]

William Rathvon's contributions to the Christian Science movement would be significant. After Mrs. Eddy's passing, he and Ella resumed their healing practices in Denver.[124] In addition to his work as a teacher and practitioner, in 1911 William would be appointed to the Christian Science Board of Lectureship,

Above: William Rathvon reading in his room at
400 Beacon Street. | Longyear Museum collection

This glazed Staffordshire tile portrait of British statesman
William Gladstone graced the mantel in Mr. Rathvon's
room and is visible in the photo above. Mr. Rathvon made
the stand for it himself. | Longyear Museum collection

traveling as far as Asia, Great Britain, and Australia, until June 1918, when he was asked to serve as Treasurer of The Mother Church.[125] Between 1898 and 1938—a span of 40 years—he wrote 43 articles for the Christian Science periodicals. In October 1918, he was elected to the Christian Science Board of Directors, a position he held until his passing in 1939.

"Art thou a Christian Scientist?"

The demands on the secretaries were many. According to Mr. Tomlinson, "Although each of us had his special hours of work, yet never was there a moment when we did not hold ourselves in readiness to assume any additional duties that might arise." This meant any recreational opportunities were mostly before 8:30 a.m., when Mrs. Eddy arrived in her study, and between 1:00 and 2:00 p.m., when she took her daily drive.[126]

Each secretary "had to be ready at all hours of the day or night to respond instantly to any request" from Mrs. Eddy, William explained.[127] That required staying within earshot of their telephones—which meant "practically staying in one's room."[128]

This could be difficult for those not accustomed to it. Mrs. Eddy was aware of this, and cautioned her Committee on Business to ask prospective candidates if they could handle "close confinement."[129] On the train to Boston for an interview with the Christian Science Board of Directors in 1908, the athletic Rathvon wrote in his diary, "I was apprehensive that the continuous confinement would be the hardest feature of the new living if I should be called to it." And when asked by the Board what he foresaw as the major challenges he would face working at Mrs. Eddy's household, he replied forthrightly that he expected it would be separation from his wife and "the confinement, for I have been a man of activity, physical as well as mental."[130]

Additionally, they would all face rebukes from their Leader. During William's very first meeting with Mrs. Eddy on the day that he arrived at 400 Beacon Street, "she prepared me for what I might expect by way of rebuke and praise at times, both of which might come to me abundantly, and they did."[131]

Mrs. Eddy was not one to let mistakes slide, whether related to lax performance, uncompleted tasks, disobedience, or other perceived errors. As she writes in *Science and Health*, "The divine demand, 'Be ye therefore perfect,' is scientific, and the human footsteps leading to perfection are indispensable."[132]

She expected to see those "human footsteps leading to perfection" demonstrated in her home, and her rebukes were meant to awaken, to rouse thought from spiritual dullness. In a word, they were meant to heal.

"You don't know what burdens I have borne through the necessity I have felt for rebuking students, but who could not receive my rebuke as coming from true love for them," Mrs. Eddy once confided to artist James Gilman. "This is the great test of the true student."[133]

To another individual she wrote: "I have so little time to consider anything but direct words and acts that I fear I am sometimes blunt and may wound when I would advise conscientiously."[134]

"I have so little time to consider anything but direct words and acts that I fear I am sometimes blunt and may wound when I would advise conscientiously."

— Mary Baker Eddy

At times, the rebukes were public.

Adelaide Still, for instance, wrote of "a student" (possibly Irving Tomlinson) who "was out gathering flowers at a time when Mrs. Eddy needed him." When the errant individual returned, Mrs. Eddy called her household together and offered a pointed lesson.

"Art thou a Christian Scientist?" she asked. "Then prove it in principle, practice, and demonstration. Is it easy to tell another his fault? Having a good time is not fighting the devil. Having a good time and dwelling in the pleasures of the senses will not bring you into heaven."[135]

At other times, the rebukes were private.

In the spring of 1908, Mr. Tomlinson was dismissed not once but twice by Mrs. Eddy, for reasons unknown. His comings and goings were quietly addressed in correspondence between the two of them (and discreetly recorded by Calvin Frye in his diary).

On June 10, 1908, for instance, after a two-week absence and a contrite letter on Irving's part ("My abiding prayer is to be in a mental state in which I can receive practically the teachings of my dear Leader. . . ."),[136] he returned to 400 Beacon Street.

A letter from Mrs. Eddy written that same day admonished, "Now you must learn by your experience and God's dear discipline your way in Christian Science." She went on to outline what that "way" entailed, including helping her, promoting peace and happiness, following the Golden Rule, and "the summing up of all: To love divine Love supremely, and be honest before God and man."[137]

Irving responded in kind, calling her "the best friend which I possess on earth," and effusively assuring her that he was grateful for her correction. "With my mistakes, she is longsuffering," he wrote. "With my errors, her loving thought is to point them out that they may be healed." He declared that he would "rather be a doorkeeper in the home of my dear Leader than to feast and frolic in the tents of mortal mind," and ended, "May this white winged messenger of peace, bearing my gratitude, witness that I have 'gained the mental state in which I will receive your teachings practically.'"[138]

This was not the case, however, as two days later, he was again dismissed. On June 20, after he'd apparently finally learned his lesson, Mrs. Eddy gave him the choice of working as a circuit lecturer or resuming his position at 400 Beacon Street. She signed her letter, "As ever your best earthly friend."[139]

Irving chose to return to serve his friend, Mary Baker Eddy, and would remain with her for the rest of her time in Chestnut Hill.

Irving Tomlinson

The unknown God made known

"For the work of the Christian ministry I was carefully prepared in college and divinity school," wrote Reverend Irving C. Tomlinson. "And yet to me Christian Science is that religion by which the unknown God is made known."[140]

Born in Perry, New York, in 1860,

Irving C. Tomlinson

LONGYEAR MUSEUM COLLECTION

Irving Clinton Tomlinson, the son of a Universalist clergyman and a devout mother who was active in social reform, grew up in a deeply Christian household.[141] Irving received his bachelor's and master's degrees from Buchtel College in Akron, Ohio (since renamed the University of Akron), in 1880 and 1883, respectively. After a brief detour into the business world, he studied theology at Tufts College near Boston.[142]

In 1888, with the ink still fresh on his diploma, Irving was granted his first ministerial post at the Universalist church in Saugus, Massachusetts. He moved on a few years later to churches in nearby Arlington and Boston, spending seven years in the pulpit before stepping away in the summer of 1895 to devote himself to philanthropic work.[143]

ARRANGING THE FLOWERS INTO BOUQUETS.

Above: Irving Tomlinson helped organize a "flower mission" to distribute blossoms to the needy in Boston tenements.
Boston Daily Globe, July 3, 1894

Below left: Sketch of Rev. Tomlinson as a young minister.
Boston Daily Globe, July 3, 1895

IRVING C. TOMLINSON.

Just a year after that, in the summer of 1896, he was enrolled in Primary class with Flavia Knapp.

It was while attending the Chicago World's Fair in 1893 that Rev. Tomlinson had first encountered Christian Science. In contrast to the sparse attendance at most of the mainstream Protestant gatherings at the exhibition's Parliament of Religions, he noted that when the Christian Scientists gathered, "the halls were not large enough to hold the throngs eager to hear Mrs. Eddy's inspiring message."[144] His curiosity was piqued.

Meanwhile, he had been growing increasingly dissatisfied

with what he felt were the shortcomings of traditional theology.

"In my pastoral work, I was instrumental in sending a drunkard to a [popular] cure," he would explain some years later in a lecture.[145] Embarrassed by the praise heaped on him by members of his congregation ("my own inability to heal the man seemed most unsatisfactory to one who was supposed to be a follower of the Master"), he was discomfited by a Bible verse he read afterward in which Jesus commanded his disciples to both preach and heal. Were material methods truly what Christ Jesus had in mind?[146]

> *"When I heard the testimonies of healing that were given, I said, 'What other people are talking about, these people are doing.'"*
> *— Irving Tomlinson*

"I wondered if there were a church which understood both commands," Tomlinson continued. "I visited churches of many denominations and finally began attending the Wednesday night meetings of the Christian Science church in Boston. When I heard the testimonies of healing that were given, I said, 'What other people are talking about, these people are doing.'"[147]

As a "doer" himself, this appealed to him.

Since assuming his first pastorate, Irving had garnered much favorable press for his enthusiastic involvement in social reform. Boston newspapers reported on his election as president of the Universalists' Social Union and his participation in interfaith groups, on his efforts with underprivileged youth and tenement improvement and other worthy causes, one calling him a "popular" pastor and "able organizer" who possessed "considerable executive ability."[148]

And yet, it wasn't enough.

Years later he would write to a friend, "One of the reasons that led me to come into Christian Science was the fact that it did not seem to me that the church was doing the work of Christ Jesus. This led me to investigate, and through this study of the Scriptures I became convinced first, that Christian Science was doing this work, and then that it was the religion of the Bible, the theology of Christ Jesus and the philosophy of common sense."[149]

As Irving continued with what he later called "a long and painstaking investigation" of Christian Science, the Bible came alive to him in a new light.[150] The first article he penned for *The Christian Science Journal*, published in June 1897, reveals some of what he was discovering:

> *If held to the light, our old bank bills disclosed a red and blue thread running through them. The red and blue threads running through the Bible are the healing of the sick, and the healing of the sinful. A banknote without those two threads was a counterfeit, and whoever holds up a Bible and does not see, running through it, those two threads of healing, has a counterfeit Bible, or rather he has a counterfeit sense of the Bible.*
>
> *Through the reading of* Science and Health *my sense of the Bible makes it no longer a counterfeit, devoid of potency, but a book so real and genuine, and so bearing the stamp of the royal mint, that it pays every human debt of sin and discharges every spurious claim of sickness. Where once the Bible served only as a fortification to attack and to defend man-made creeds, or as a catalogue of texts and pretexts for sermonizing, it is now a fountain of Divine Love, whose living waters have healing power.*[151]

Eventually "there was nothing for me to do as an honest man but to withdraw from a fellowship I dearly loved, and fully accept and strive to attain the high ideal of Christian Science."[152]

YOU ARE CORDIALLY INVITED TO ATTEND
A LECTURE ON

CHRISTIAN SCIENCE

TO BE GIVEN

WEDNESDAY, APRIL 5TH, 1899, AT 8 O'CLOCK,

IN MUSIC HALL, BOSTON.

———————

THIS LECTURE WILL BE GIVEN UNDER THE
AUSPICES OF

THE FIRST CHURCH OF CHRIST, SCIENTIST,
IN BOSTON, MASS.

BY REV. IRVING C. TOMLINSON, C. S. B.,

MEMBER OF THE

INTERNATIONAL BOARD OF LECTURESHIP OF THE
MOTHER CHURCH OF CHRISTIAN SCIENCE.

Invitation to an early Irving Tomlinson lecture.

LONGYEAR MUSEUM COLLECTION

The summer of 1897 was a momentous one for Rev. Tomlinson. On the Fourth of July, he officially became a member of The Mother Church. The next day, he traveled from Boston to Pleasant View, where he met Mrs. Eddy for the first time and was one of the featured speakers, at her request, at a gathering of some 2,500 of her followers.[153] A month later, his name appeared as a practitioner in *The Christian Science Journal*.

There would be more milestones the following year for the man whom Mrs. Eddy sometimes humorously referred to as "The Parson,"[154] including an invitation to attend her final class and appointments to the Bible Lesson Committee, the Committee on Publication,[155] and the newly-formed Christian Science Board of Lectureship.[156] In fact, it was Irving who would deliver the very first lecture by a member of that board, given in The Mother Church on September 28, 1898.[157]

Clearly, Mrs. Eddy saw great promise in this thoughtful and energetic 38-year-old former minister. His combination of deep Biblical roots, eloquence, college-educated polish, and social respectability was just what she needed in her growing church, and she quickly put him to good use. In addition to the other appointments he was given in rapid succession, in December 1898, Irving and his sister, Mary, were invited by Mrs. Eddy to become First and Second Readers of the Christian Science church in Concord, New Hampshire.[158] At the same time, Irving's passion for social causes was channeled into a subject dear to Mrs. Eddy's heart: prison reform. With her encouragement, he started a Sunday service at New Hampshire's Merrimack County jail, also serving as a practitioner for interested inmates.[159]

Mr. Tomlinson would serve his Leader directly for a dozen years in various capacities, including at times as a secretary at Pleasant View. He continued that work at Chestnut Hill, joining the household in February 1908.

After Mrs. Eddy's passing, he resumed his place on the Bible Lesson Committee, serving for over two decades in total.[160] In 1916, he

This wicker rocking chair with the cross and crown emblem was a gift from grateful inmates at the New Hampshire State Prison to Mrs. Eddy, who encouraged Irving Tomlinson to share Christian Science there and in other correctional facilities.

LONGYEAR MUSEUM COLLECTION

married Elizabeth Cadwell, a practitioner from Portland, Oregon.[161] In 1921, he was elected President of The Mother Church.[162] He wrote extensively for the Christian Science periodicals and in 1928 taught the Normal class for the Board of Education. After his initial tour of duty as a lecturer from 1898 to 1908, Irving Tomlinson lectured again from 1932 to 1935, before retiring to devote his full attention to the teaching and practice of Christian Science until his passing in 1944.[163]

Holding the fort

By and large, despite the internal disagreements and friction caused by the clash of old and new methods and viewpoints, the secretarial staff worked fairly smoothly together—in large part because they shared a common purpose: to support and defend their Leader.

"I had always imagined that Mrs. Eddy lived quietly, as any other elderly woman would live, surrounded by comforts and luxuries and by those friends whom she wished to invite to share her home with her," wrote Adam Dickey, admitting to a touch of naivete prior to his arrival in her household. "I had no idea that she was constantly besieged by all the forces of evil and that she had to be in the frontline of battle, day and night, throughout all the years of her leadership."[164]

Others agreed with this assessment. "The batteries and raids of the forces of animal magnetism were ever directed at that household," William Rathvon observed, pointing out that 400 Beacon Street was "the recognized headquarters of our Commander-in-Chief."[165]

Part of the reason that Mary Baker Eddy chose experienced practitioners for her secretaries, along with the other seasoned Christian Scientists on her staff, was to help hold the fort against such attacks. By faithfully keeping their assigned watches, by the spiritual alertness they demonstrated on a daily basis, and by their obedience, they were all learning lessons that would stand them in good stead in the years to come. Like a general preparing her troops for battle, Mrs. Eddy was ultimately preparing her household for continued service to the movement.

Mr. Rathvon recalled that she "repeatedly reminded us that while with her we were being prepared for the work of promoting and extending the Cause of Christian Science when in God's own time we should be called upon to undertake it under different conditions."[166]

Mrs. Eddy told them, "The work which you are here being prepared for will reach all over the earth. You were placed here for that purpose, and your heavenly Father is caring for you even as a material father watches over his children. It is a special God-given privilege to be in this house."[167]

Calvin Frye, Adam Dickey, William Rathvon, and Irving Tomlinson would all fulfill the trust that their "Commander-in-Chief" had placed in them, each one going on to hold a variety of responsible positions within the movement in the decades after their Leader's passing.

"The work which you are here being prepared for will reach all over the earth. You were placed here for that purpose, and your heavenly Father is caring for you even as a material father watches over his children. It is a special God-given privilege to be in this house."
— Mary Baker Eddy

"People were not invited to Mrs. Eddy's house for their own improvement," Mr. Dickey would one day write. "They were invited there to work, and what she required of them was not that they should work for themselves but that they should work for her and for the Cause of Christian Science."[168]

Chapter 4

Brightening Their Leader's Pathway

With the move to 400 Beacon Street, Mrs. Eddy traded life on a working farm for the suburbs of Boston. Where her balcony vantage point in New Hampshire took in pastoral acres of land, orchards, formal flower gardens, vegetable gardens, and grazing livestock, now she looked out on a more densely populated neighborhood, where wooded properties rolled away toward the Blue Hills. Occasionally, a train puffed by in the near distance. Still nominally in the countryside, the new house offered pleasant views of its own, as well as close proximity to her Church headquarters in Boston.

Managing the grounds and keeping up with tasks and repairs at the new estate would

John Salchow | Longyear Museum collection

require an experienced team. While the Chestnut Hill property wasn't a farm, there were still some eight and a half acres of land, a vegetable garden, a formal flower garden, horses that needed tending, and two dairy cows, along with the large house to maintain.[1]

In the seven years since he'd first joined Mrs. Eddy's household as a groundskeeper, John Salchow—or "my John" as Mrs. Eddy came to call him—had proved himself trustworthy.[2] The son of German immigrant farmers, he was healed of chronic stomach trouble after reading a few pages of *Science and Health* and in 1890 became a founding member of the Christian Science church in Junction City, Kansas.[3] Recommended to Mrs. Eddy by her student Joseph Mann,[4] Salchow received a letter at 10:00 one morning calling him to Pleasant View, and by noon he was on a train heading east.[5]

His duties in the household in Concord would echo those on the family farm he'd left behind in Kansas—arising before dawn to milk the cows and care for the livestock, tending the garden, grooming the horses, fetching ice, and so on. Good with his hands and possessed of a mechanical aptitude, Salchow also did carpentry work and made electrical and plumbing repairs around the property.[6]

"A sort of jack-of-all-trades he was, indoors and out," said Minnie Weygandt, who was on the staff with him at both Pleasant View and 400 Beacon Street.[7]

Diligent and selfless, John Salchow's sterling qualities were swiftly recognized by the other members of the household as well as by Mrs. Eddy, who early on gave him a copy of *Science and Health* with the inscription, "To our faithful John."[8] And it was Salchow whom Mrs. Eddy requested be on hand every day to hold the horses when she embarked on and returned from her carriage ride.[9]

Entrance gate to 400 Beacon Street. | Longyear Museum collection

"Mrs. Eddy was very fond of him," Miss Weygandt observed. "His trustworthiness and unquestioning obedience must have been a comfort to her."[10]

John was equally fond of his Leader. "Mrs. Eddy was always kind and gentle with me," he recalled. "If I did not get a thing just the right way, she would smile sweetly and explain it to me. There was no sense of holding me up or of condemnation. No mother could have been kinder."[11]

"No mother could have been kinder." —John Salchow

John's duties were given a new focus after the move to Chestnut Hill. At Pleasant View, he'd spent most of his time outside. Now, he would work largely indoors, where he "found much about the house to occupy my time," as he put it.[12]

"Salchow can do anything," Adam Dickey marveled to a reporter in 1909. "Why, we never so much as need to send for a plumber."[13]

Newlyweds John and Mary Salchow in 1906.
COURTESY OF THE MARY BAKER EDDY COLLECTION
ORIGINAL IN THE MARY BAKER EDDY LIBRARY

John and Mary Salchow

"Love laid the foundation"

It was a bicycle that brought the Salchows together.

John Gottleib Salchow was the Kansas-born son of German immigrants; Mary McNeil was a native Scot who came to the United States with her family as a teenager.[14] The two ended up as neighbors in Concord, New Hampshire, where John was employed at Pleasant View as a groundskeeper and maintenance man and where Mary worked in the dormitories at St. Paul's School, a prestigious boarding school that educated the elite.[15]

The McNeils shared a fence line with Pleasant View. The family kept a flock of chickens, and Flora McNeil, Mary's widowed mother, "was always very proud to fill Mrs. Eddy's orders for eggs," according to John.[16]

The McNeils were impressed by the kindness shown to them by Mrs. Eddy, whom they had never met. Once, when a severe storm knocked down many trees in the area, Mrs. Eddy sent estate manager Joseph Mann over to see if there was anything he could do to help. Another time, when "sorrow came to our home," as Mary put it, Mrs. Eddy sent flowers along with her love. "We felt if she was kind to people whom she had not come in contact with, what must it mean to know the woman herself?"[17]

Mary McNeil was learning to ride a bicycle when she met her future husband.

"In the summertime it was my custom to take my bicycle and ride up and down in front of Pleasant View in the early evening," John recalled. "This was the only recreation I had. One evening when I was out riding, I saw Miss McNeil having difficulty in keeping on her bicycle. I came to the rescue and offered to help her master it."[18]

From this encounter, a friendship blossomed. When the weather turned cold and it came time to put bicycles away for the season, John found a way to continue seeing Mary.

"On winter evenings when the furnace was banked for the night, it was necessary to let the fire run for ten or fifteen minutes before closing it up," he explained. "Often during that time I would run over to the McNeils for a brief visit, but I was always careful never to let these visits or thoughts of this friendship drive out my loyal interest in and obligations to my Leader."[19]

This continued for the next few years. At some point, Mrs. Eddy became aware of the courtship.[20] On December 30, 1906, she sent a letter to Mary's brother James, letting him know that she had spoken to John that morning about the couple's intentions. She wrote in part, "I said if you have promised to marry her, <u>do it</u>...."[21]

John did. The couple were married the following day, on New Year's Eve, 1906. John was 41, Mary was 34.

"Mrs. Eddy was very happy when she knew we were married . . . and she showed her love to us in many ways," Mary would later write — including having homemade ice cream sent over to their home.[22]

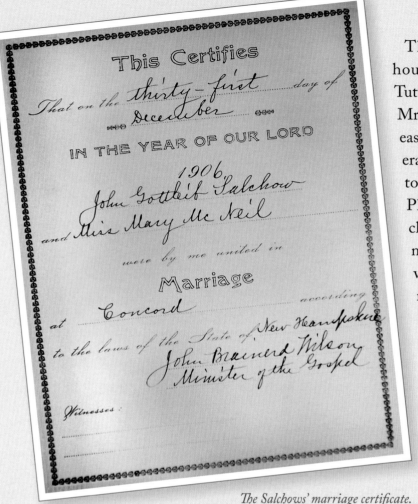

The Salchows' marriage certificate.

PRIVATE COLLECTION

The newlyweds set up housekeeping on nearby Tuttle Street, "just adjoining Mrs. Eddy's property on the east."[23] As John told it, "several things were sent down to our little home from Pleasant View—a Morris chair, bookcase, rug, etc. I never knew whether these were sent at Mrs. Eddy's request, but I always liked to think that they were an evidence of her tender, motherly interest."[24]

At some point, Mary, who was not a Christian Scientist, fell ill. Her family insisted that a physician be called in to treat her. His prognosis was grim.

"[The doctor] said she could not live twenty-four hours," John would recall. "When I got home that night, her mother said she was dying, so I then asked if she would be willing to try Christian Science."[25]

Mary was willing, and she was quickly healed.

"Mrs. Eddy never asked if I was a Christian Scientist, my husband never asked me to be one, but love laid the foundation," said Mary, who took up the study of Christian Science.[26]

In January 1908, a month after their first wedding anniversary, John Salchow moved with Mrs. Eddy and her household to 400 Beacon Street, where Mary joined him to live in the gatehouse by the main entrance to the drive.

After Mrs. Eddy's passing, the Salchows remained on the property for a couple of years, while John served as caretaker. Then in 1915, he took a job as a fruit-grower for the Swetland Packing Company, an American corporation located in Isle of Pines,

The gatehouse at 400 Beacon Street today.

Cuba.[27] Later, the couple would partner with John's brother Henry and return to Kansas to farm, but by 1927 they were back in Boston, where John worked as a utility man at The Mother Church.[28]

John Salchow's love and dedication to Mary Baker Eddy shines through all of his writings, from his recollections of her to his letters, including one that he wrote in December 1901, thanking her for her gift of a pair of warm gloves. It read in part, "When *Science and Health* came to me, I had nothing in this world but husks, and they were almost gone. God has indeed been kind to me, in that I have been permitted to come to Pleasant View to do what I can do. And when I see how kindly you appreciate even the little that I may be able to do, it almost melts my heart within me, and it is this thought that I prize infinitely higher than the gift itself."[29]

Mary Salchow also held her Leader in great esteem.

"All I have seen of Mrs. Eddy for many, many years," she would write, "both before and after becoming a Christian Scientist, has been such as to touch the heart of the hardest; and I want only to try in part to follow her teaching in love and charity to all."[30]

Mrs. Eddy's private side entrance at 400 Beacon Street.

LONGYEAR MUSEUM COLLECTION

At Chestnut Hill, the handyman's days began a little later than at Pleasant View, around 6:00 a.m. instead of 4:00, "except in the winter when I got up earlier to fire the furnaces," as he later explained.[31] One of his daily duties was making ice cream for Mrs. Eddy, who enjoyed it at lunch.

The treat "was made fresh every day by the industrious John Salchow . . . who would begin grinding the ice cream freezer under my window at eleven o'clock sharp," observed secretary William Rathvon.[32]

Another job that Salchow took upon himself was finding a way to block prying eyes when it was time for Mrs. Eddy's daily carriage ride.

"It seemed that some people, not satisfied with trying to gaze at Mrs. Eddy as she drove along the street, went so far as to enter the grounds and hide around the corner of the house so that they could spy upon her as she entered her carriage," an exasperated Salchow later recounted.[33] With characteristic ingenuity, he took a pair of wooden shutters and attached them to the wall near her private entrance, ready to be pulled out at a moment's notice to screen Mrs. Eddy from view.

Another time, Salchow's strength was called on when the electric elevator in Mrs. Eddy's study had a motor malfunction. The only way for the elevator carriage to move up and down was via a hand crank in the basement, which

Salchow and another household worker operated until the motor was functioning again two or three days later.[34]

Doing "necessary work"

With Salchow mostly occupied inside, more help was needed taking care of the grounds. One key member of the team was brought in by Jonathan Irving. Mr. Irving was employed as janitor at The First Church of Christ, Scientist, in Boston, when he was called to Pleasant View in November 1903 to act as a temporary night watchman. The position became permanent in 1907, and after the move to Chestnut Hill, when those managing the grounds needed additional help, Irving reached out to Nelson Molway, a friend he had made at The Mother Church a few years earlier.

Hired to help with carpentry work during construction of the Extension of The Mother Church, Mr. Molway was not a Christian Scientist when he first met Jonathan Irving. The two struck up occasional conversations during their work days and soon became friendly. In 1906, after the Extension was completed, Irving took Molway on to assist with the janitorial duties at the Church. He was soon promoted to overseeing the boiler room there.

"The different members of the [Christian Science] Board of Directors used to visit the boiler room quite often those days," Nelson later recorded, adding that, "we were like one family and felt that we were all working together equally shoulder to shoulder."[35]

Called up to the Board offices one day, Nelson, who was covered in soot from his work, stopped to clean up a little first. The dirt had kept him from being prompt, he told William Johnson, a member of the Board, who kindly responded, "You must not think of your work as dirty. What you have to do is as important as what I have to do. You are doing things I could not do and I am doing things you could not do. Even the man who empties garbage is doing a necessary work."[36]

Jonathan R. Irving

LONGYEAR MUSEUM COLLECTION

Jonathan Irving

"I count you one of my best friends"

"Jonathan Irving was an honest and reliable man and rendered good service," said John Salchow, who worked alongside Mr. Irving for many years at both Pleasant View and 400 Beacon Street.[37] A Canadian of Scottish descent, Jonathan traveled with Mrs. Eddy on the train from Pleasant View to Chestnut Hill when she moved in January 1908.[38] In addition to safeguarding her homes, he also regularly escorted her to her carriage — he was "usually on hand to tuck her in," as Mr. Salchow put it[39] — and at 400 Beacon Street, he was the one whom Mrs. Eddy chose to accompany her up the elevator when she returned from her daily drives.[40]

In 1898, Mrs. Eddy sent him a letter of gratitude for his janitorial services: "My dear friend," she wrote, "Please find a small check as my New Year thanks to you for your fidelity in the place that you occupy at The Mother Church."[41] She gave him other gifts as well, including an inscribed copy of *Science and Health*.

Although maintaining night security was Jonathan's main priority, Mrs. Eddy trusted him with other tasks. During the move to Chestnut Hill, for instance, his task was to keep watch over her trunk and ensure its safe arrival at the new home.[42] Additional duties included tending the furnace and occasionally filling in as coachman or gardener.[43]

"I thank you deeply for all you say to me and do for me," Mrs. Eddy wrote to him at one point, "I count you one of my best friends."[44]

Mrs. Eddy possessed a motherly gentleness—she once began a letter to Jonathan with the endearing, "Mother's good boy," and another time, concerned that he wasn't get-

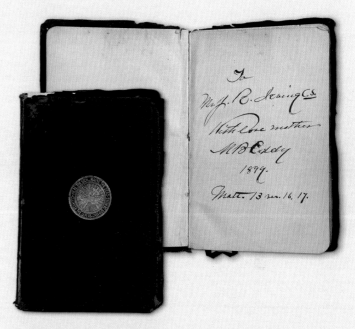

This inscribed copy of Science and Health *was given to Jonathan Irving by Mrs. Eddy. The verse she included from Matthew 13 ("Blessed are your eyes, for they see: and your ears, for they hear") seems especially appropriate for a watchman.*

LONGYEAR MUSEUM COLLECTION

ting enough to eat, she asked Elizabeth Kelly to see that he had a dish of fruit in his room.[45] When a staff member was unkind to Mr. Irving in 1908, Mrs. Eddy rebuked the individual, who tearfully vowed not to act so cruelly again. Later, in writing of this to Jonathan, she exposed the "lie of hypnotism" that would try and stir up animosity in the household, and stressed the importance of loving his fellow workers, telling him that "each one must help the other and so fulfil the law of Christ."[46]

Ever faithful at his post, Jonathan Irving would serve his Leader throughout her years at 400 Beacon Street. After her passing, he was selected to be one of the guards at the receiving vault at Mount Auburn Cemetery, watching the grounds at night for six weeks while a final resting site was prepared.[47]

The lower garden at 400 Beacon Street.

LONGYEAR MUSEUM COLLECTION

Mr. Johnson's words made a deep impression on Nelson Molway, "in such a way that I never again felt it necessary to apologize for hands soiled with the marks of honest toil."[48] Undoubtedly, the Director's comment must have come back to him when he started working on the grounds of Mrs. Eddy's home in Chestnut Hill.

His heartfelt conversations with Jonathan Irving and William Johnson also inspired Mr. Molway to join The Mother Church in November 1908. "I was very much impressed by the character of the Christian Scientists with whom I came in daily contact," he later commented, "and felt that a religion which could change people's thinking and make them so kind and happy must be a good religion and something I would like to know about myself."[49]

A few months later, Jonathan arranged an interview for Nelson at Mrs. Eddy's home, where he was soon hired. In his new work as a groundskeeper at 400 Beacon Street, Nelson's responsibilities were similar to John Salchow's at Pleasant View—he mowed the grass, planted and weeded flowerbeds and a vegetable garden, trimmed shrubbery and trees, chopped wood, shoveled snow, and more. Under the direction of coachman Frank Bowman, his overseer, Nelson Molway also purchased a workhorse for the estate—Nelly, whom he described as "a fine loveable beast, full of all kinds of tricks; it almost seemed as if she could do everything but talk."[50] With Nelly's help he plowed garden plots and mowed the lawns much more efficiently.

Nelson also made additions to the property that have lasted to the present day, helping carve out a road that led to a lower garden at the rear of the grounds so that Mrs. Eddy's carriage could take her to view the flowers in bloom.[51]

Frank and Charlotte Bowman
PRIVATE COLLECTION
LONGYEAR MUSEUM COLLECTION

Frank and Charlotte Bowman

"Good Christian people"

When Charlotte Bowman took over for Minnie Scott in the kitchen after Minnie left 400 Beacon Street, Mrs. Eddy wondered aloud one day why the crackers she enjoyed eating didn't taste the way she remembered them from earlier years. It was a small thing, perhaps, but Lottie, as she was called, was eager to help. She talked the matter over with her husband, Frank, who worked as coachman and chauffeur for the household, but who at one time had managed a general store in Essex Junction, Vermont.[52] Frank recalled a bakery in Montpelier that had been making crackers the same way for 100 years and promptly procured some.[53] After sampling them, Mrs. Eddy called Mrs. Bowman to her room and told her that they "tasted just like they used to taste, and she was very pleased."[54]

Born and bred in Vermont, the Bowmans were staunch Christians.[55] Frank was raised in the Congregational church and first took up the study of Christian Science after a relative was healed.[56] Lottie, a former schoolteacher, "did not seek the Science for physical healing," but was ever grateful that she was "ready to listen to this voice of Truth when it first spoke to me. . . ."[57] The two joined The Mother Church in 1896.

They passed their Committee on Business interview with flying colors, with the Committee's report characterizing them as "good Christian people" who "would do good, faithful service."[58] The couple, who were both in their early 50s, indeed proved an excellent fit for 400 Beacon Street, earning the respect of those who knew them. George Kinter, for instance, a Christian Science practitioner and teacher from Chicago who had served as a secretary at Pleasant View and filled in on occasion at 400 Beacon Street, called Mr. Bowman, "a gentleman and kind to the horses and the people" and complimented Mrs. Bowman as "a good and steady hand in the kitchen."[59]

Frank was first to arrive in Chestnut Hill, on December 18, 1908.[60] Lottie remained behind in Essex Junction with their son, Robert, who was a student at the University of Vermont.[61] Around this time, Mrs. Eddy sent word to Lottie through Frank: "Will you give my dear love to your dear wife. Tell her God will bless her for the good she is doing through her husband helping your Leader."[62]

Lottie's reply was likely this letter published in the *Christian Science Sentinel*: "Words cannot express my gratitude for the sweet messages of love you have sent me by my husband. We are making no sacrifice for you, dear Leader, but our hearts are filled with joy that our thought has been so lifted up that you could ask us for help. Only twice has the thought of separation suggested itself, as Robert and I sat down to breakfast, and then it was quickly banished."

She finished by relating a quick healing of a nephew, calling it her "reward."[63]

Perhaps glimpsing something of value in Mrs. Bowman's buoyantly grateful thought, Mrs. Eddy made inquiries about her through Archibald McLellan: "I wanted to know if dear Mr. Bowman's wife was as good a woman as he is a man."[64] Mr. McLellan's glowing report described Lottie as an "honest, earnest woman," noting that in the nearly 20 years that she had been a Christian Scientist, she'd healed "a number of desperate cases."[65]

The Bowmans' cottage overlooking the lower garden at 400 Beacon Street. | LONGYEAR MUSEUM COLLECTION

Mary Baker Eddy entering her carriage on July 16, 1910, the day her grandsons came to visit (see Chapter 10). Frank Bowman is at the reins. | PRIVATE COLLECTION

Mrs. Eddy was solicitous of the Bowman family's happiness. In March 1909, apparently at her invitation, Robert traveled to Chestnut Hill to visit his father.[66] A few weeks later, Lottie wrote a letter of thanks to Mrs. Eddy, both for her "great kindness" in allowing Robert to visit, as well as for the gift that Mrs. Eddy had sent to her.

"It will be very precious to me because of the 'love' which I know prompted the gift," Lottie told her, "but I prize it most of all because the books contain the Key to the Book of books,—the Word of Truth which you have toiled so long and so faithfully to give to us in all its purity of thought and diction."[67]

Perhaps Frank spoke to Mrs. Eddy about missing his family, for in June of that year she wrote him a note, telling him, "I think of you as not alone, but with God and safe and happy."[68] At some point, the decision was made to bring Mrs. Bowman to 400 Beacon Street. Although the precise date of her arrival is unclear, by August 1909 she was on the household payroll, where she would remain until after Mrs. Eddy's passing. The couple were given a cottage on the property to live in, and while Lottie worked in the kitchen, Frank drove the carriages and the household's automobiles—something he'd never attempted prior to his arrival in Chestnut Hill.[69]

He took Mrs. Eddy on her daily carriage ride at precisely 1:00 p.m.,[70] often around the Chestnut Hill reservoir, one of her favorite routes. In addition to the midday outing, Mr. Bowman also exercised the horses each morning, and members of the household would occasionally join him.[71] As Mrs. Eddy's coachman, Frank took it upon himself to be well groomed. A man who met him in the 1930s recalls an anecdote that Mr. Bowman shared. As he remembers it, "When Mr. Bowman came home one day with a new haircut, Mrs. Eddy looked at him approvingly, and turning to Mr. Frye, asked, 'Calvin, why don't you have your hair cut like Mr. Bowman's?' Calvin took the hint."[72]

Frank Bowman also oversaw mail collection and helped with the upkeep of the house and grounds.[73]

"Beloved Student," Mrs. Eddy wrote to him in September 1909, "I can never express my thanks for what you do for me but I can and do feel them."[74]

"There were beautiful flowers about Chestnut Hill, and it was arranged that a landscape gardener come … to do the best possible work in beautifying the grounds," wrote Irving Tomlinson. "It must be said, however, that despite the fact that Mrs. Eddy loved natural beauty, she had in those days neither the time nor the inclination to give attention to either the garden or the grounds. Her constant effort during those years at Chestnut Hill was to turn from the mundane and material sense of life to more spiritual views. Certainly nothing could more clearly indicate this than these words in a letter which she addressed to the gardener when he expressed a desire to do more extensive work about the estate: 'The road to heaven is not one of flowers, but it is strait and narrow, it is bearing the cross and turning away from things that lure the material senses, denying them and finding all in Spirit, in God, in good and doing good.'"[75]

"Mrs. Eddy was so appreciative of anything anyone did for her that it was a joy to work for her."

— Nelson Molway

This shift in her attention is not to say that Mrs. Eddy was oblivious to the beauty of her new estate. Far from it. In just one example of her continued interest, she sent this note to Frank Bowman in November 1909: "Can you make the left side of the walk going down the gate way as verdant as the right side? If so please do it. You are brightening my pathway."[76]

Another time, upon noticing that one of the trees on the grounds appeared to be dying and learning that it was due to be cut down, Mrs. Eddy took action, sending word to the superintendent of her grounds "to do what he could for the tree in his way, while she took the question up according to Christian Science," recalled Adam Dickey. "In a remarkably short time the tree began to grow and thrive…."[77]

Mr. Dickey also recorded an instance when Mrs. Eddy noticed exposed ironwork on the exterior of her house and requested it be painted in order to prevent rust. "Mrs. Eddy's active thought seemed to take in everything that was necessary for the protection of her home, and incidents of this nature were of more or less frequent occurrence," he wrote. "Mrs. Eddy never let down on anything."[78]

Spring tulips at 400 Beacon Street. | Longyear Museum collection

This included expressing her gratitude for the work done by those laboring on her estate. According to Nelson Molway, who was on the receiving end of numerous notes of thanks and what he called a "practical expression of gratitude" in the form of cash, "It seemed as if she was never too busy to notice the little services others rendered. . . ."[79]

John Salchow concurred. "Mrs. Eddy was quick to express her appreciation and to give loving recognition to honest effort."[80]

One day, when Nelson was asked to trim some trees that were blocking the view from Mrs. Eddy's windows, he climbed up into the branches with his saw and got to work. He remembers Mrs. Eddy sitting by the window and watching him. After he was done, she sent him an inscribed copy of *Science and Health* as a thank you.

"Mrs. Eddy was so appreciative of anything anyone did for her that it was a joy to work for her," Nelson observed. "It just made you take heart — to receive this friendly encouragement and recognition made you want to work all the harder."[81]

Opposite page, clockwise from top left: Rhododendrons in bloom in front of 400 Beacon Street; household members on a sleigh ride; splashes of summer color; formal garden in bloom; late afternoon autumn light; lone gardener labors in the snow, circa 1910.

Above, clockwise from top left: Mrs. Eddy's carriage passing a hyacinth bed; autumn twilight on the front drive; wild turkeys gather on the front lawn; after a snowfall, circa 1909; front gate in spring.

LONGYEAR MUSEUM COLLECTION

Carriages, cars, and sleighs

Also under the purview of her house and grounds staff were Mary Baker Eddy's livestock—her horses and cows—along with her carriages, automobiles, and sleighs. Mrs. Eddy purchased her first automobile, a Yale touring car, in 1902 while living at Pleasant View.[82] It was acquired not as a means of transport (for her, at least, although her staff were enamored of it), but rather to help desensitize her horses to the unaccustomed noise and smell that the advent of "horseless carriages" brought to the tranquil roads of Concord.[83]

The project had mixed results, and the Yale was retired two years later.[84]

1909 White Steam automobile advertisement from
The Saturday Evening Post.

By the fall of 1908, it was deemed time to try again, and permission was given for then-coachman Adolph Stevenson to buy another vehicle.[85] In fact, two were purchased, a White Steam Limousine for Mrs. Eddy's use, and a White Steam Touring Car for the household.[86] With its customization (including two upholstered chairs for Mrs. Eddy's comfort instead of a rear seat), the Limousine came with a price tag of $5,169.65; the Touring Car cost $2,331.25.[87]

The Leader of the Christian Science movement's maiden voyage in a motorized vehicle was apparently also her last one[88]—although the test drive wasn't without a humorous moment:

Out for a jaunt in the White Steamer: Frank Bowman (at wheel) and John Salchow; 2nd row, left to right: Jonathan Irving, Mary Salchow, Lottie Bowman, Martha Wilcox; 3rd row, left to right: Lula Phillips, Elizabeth Kelly, Katharine Retterer. | LONGYEAR MUSEUM COLLECTION

"She was somewhat dubious of enjoying the ride, and when the time came and she and Mrs. Sargent were seated in the comfortable chairs, she indicated that she would much prefer the experiment if one or two of the men were with her. There was a greater desire to comply with her request than there seemed room to carry it out, but by folding themselves up, Mr. Rathvon and Mr. Tomlinson managed to seat themselves on the semi-circular raised projection which the boiler necessitated in that make of car. It protruded from the floor like a very large cheese and as it was only about eight inches high, their knees practically touched their chins. They were oblivious to the spectacle they presented until they noticed that Mrs. Eddy was holding her tiny sunshade in front of her face to conceal her laughter. Then they all joined her and the ride ended happily, but Mrs. Eddy never wanted to go again, preferring her horses and carriage."[89]

Mrs. Eddy's horses (likely Princess and Major)
outside the carriage house.

Courtesy of The Mary Baker Eddy Collection

Original in The Mary Baker Eddy Library

Mary Baker Eddy had several horses at 400 Beacon Street, including the aforementioned "loveable beast," Nelly. Her two main carriage horses during these years were Princess and Major.[90] Growing up on a farm in Bow, New Hampshire, Mrs. Eddy had always loved horses and had fond memories of riding when she was younger.[91] She looked forward to her daily carriage rides, once referring to these outings as her "one hour cheery vacation from the desk."[92] Mrs. Eddy also famously commented, "I have uttered some of my best prayers in a carriage."[93]

Elizabeth Kelly was impressed by the way the staff looked after the animals and equipment in their charge, particularly Adolph Stevenson, who, she recalled, "took such lovely care of the horses and the carriages. He carefully washed the horses' faces, polished their hoofs, and brushed them so that not a hair was out of place."[94] Mrs. Eddy was attentive as well, though in a different sphere. She counseled Mr. Stevenson at one point, "If you treat either of our horses for the fear of an automobile — it will help them just as it heals the sick, by destroying their fear. Horses are nearly as receptive of the effects from Christian Science treatment as human beings are."[95]

The Chestnut Hill estate had a splendid carriage house. An impressive three levels, it housed the cars and cows on the lower level at the rear, the horses and carriages at street level by the front drive, and a spacious hayloft on the upper level.

As for the carriages, there were eight of them, most brought down from Pleasant View with the household during the move. Not all were in daily use, but it wasn't common practice at the time to trade in an older carriage when a newer one was purchased, and thus the "fleet" had expanded over the years.

One of Mrs. Eddy's favorite carriages was the Victoria. Known for its graceful lines and elegant style, this light two-seater, named for Queen Victoria, was a popular ladies' carriage in the 19th century. It was equipped with a "calash" top (folding hood), a convertible style that made it perfect for summer drives.[96]

The American Station Wagon, another popular and comfortable carriage of the day, was also frequently used by Mrs. Eddy. It was in this carriage that she was photographed by the press in 1909 (see page 338).

The grandest carriage she owned was the Brougham, custom built for her in 1895 by J. P. & W. H. Emond Carriage Builders of Boston. The closed two-door carriage, named for Lord Henry Brougham, a British statesman who originated the design in the early 19th century, was roughly equivalent to a limousine and served Mrs. Eddy at both Pleasant View and Chestnut Hill. Custom upgrades included windows in the rear panels, green upholstery, and quilted satin for the head lining.

Mary Baker Eddy in her Brougham carriage at Pleasant View, circa 1906.
August Mann is at the reins; Calvin Frye is seated beside him. | Longyear Museum collection

Useful for such errands as grocery shopping, a two-seated buggy was the general utility vehicle of 400 Beacon Street, while the main job of the Fringe Top Surrey was to transport visitors and members of the household to and from the train station when the weather was fine. A double-runner sleigh was pressed into service for this purpose in winter.[97]

Mrs. Eddy "was very fond of sleigh riding," John Salchow would write. "Whenever there was the least bit of snow, enough to make the roads at all passable, we used to take the wheels off of her carriage and put on the runners. We had a couple of strings of silver bells for the horses, and on a nice frosty day, it made a pretty sight to see the sleigh and hear the jingle of the bells."[98]

Right: Mrs. Eddy handwrote the words, "in sleigh," onto this typed description of a local route for her daily ride.
© THE MARY BAKER EDDY COLLECTION. ORIGINAL IN THE MARY BAKER EDDY LIBRARY. USED WITH PERMISSION.
Below: One of Mary Baker Eddy's sleighs, with coachman Frank Bowman at the reins.
LONGYEAR MUSEUM COLLECTION

083
DELIGHTFUL DRIVE. *in sleigh*

Beacon to South, to Commonwealth Ave., thence to toward Newton Centre to Grant Ave., to Beacon St., turn to Newton Centre and go around the brick School House and by the Depot on to Beacon St., and home.

Sleigh bells belonging to Mrs. Eddy's horses.

LONGYEAR MUSEUM COLLECTION

Mrs. Eddy enjoyed hearing them, too. When one of her students sent a gift of a new string of sleigh bells, she wrote him in reply, "I love to hear their silver tones over the snow. . . ."[99]

She also enjoyed watching children frolicking in the snow.

"On her drives in winter when she rode in the sleigh," said Minnie Scott, "they stopped sometimes where children were coasting and Mrs. Eddy bowed and smiled to them."[100]

A deeper purpose

Through the dedicated efforts of workers like John Salchow, Jonathan Irving, Frank Bowman, Nelson Molway, and others, Mrs. Eddy's home at 400 Beacon Street was well cared for, her livestock and automobiles properly looked after, the grounds kept lush and beautiful. But as always, their real work had a deeper purpose in supporting what Mary Baker Eddy was quietly doing upstairs in her study—leading the religious movement she had founded and had devoted so many years to cultivating.

And for at least two of the team who oversaw the house and grounds, this work didn't stop with Mrs. Eddy's passing. Nelson Molway and John Salchow continued in employment that directly supported the Christian Science movement—Molway in the stereotype department at *The Christian Science Monitor* and also, for about a year, as a watchman for the Chestnut Hill Benevolent Association, and "Faithful John" as a utility man at The Mother Church.

"Though my tasks for The Mother Church are humble," Mr. Salchow would write, "I do them now as I did when I served our Leader, with a heart full of love for Mary Baker Eddy and reverent gratitude for all the blessings which Christian Science has brought to me."[101]

Overleaf: Views of the carriage house and gatehouse today.

Chapter 5

Loving Hearts and Hands

ne Saturday in the late spring of 1905, journalist Sibyl Wilbur boarded a train in Boston and settled in for the two-hour trip north to Concord, New Hampshire. Her destination was Pleasant View, the home of Mary Baker Eddy, who had become "the object of the most intense curiosity of the public press in America," as Miss Wilbur put it.[1]

Sibyl was one of only a select number of journalists granted an interview with Mrs. Eddy at this point in time.

Furthermore, she was also offered a comprehensive tour of the Pleasant View estate, from the interior of the home itself to the gardens and outbuildings, and in her subsequent article for the *Boston Herald*, she reported that "to the last corner of this house, order, simplicity and absolute daintiness prevail."[2]

By all accounts, this was also the case at 400 Beacon Street.

Minnie Scott, who worked in both homes, noted that Mrs. Eddy "loved simplicity, accuracy, economy, order, and cleanliness in all the practical details of everyday life."[3]

"Order is essential to me," Mrs. Eddy once told a student.[4] Methodical and exact in her own life, she expected no less from her staff.

> *"Order is essential to me."*
> *— Mary Baker Eddy*

"Her capacity for work was wonderful; she always knew the right thing to do and did it," said Thomas Hatten, who in addition to his position on the Committee on Business had also witnessed his Leader's habits firsthand while serving for several months as a secretary at Pleasant View. Mrs. Eddy, he added, "was exact and did her work systematically and according to Principle. This thought was carried out in her material home and domestic relations. She was a thoroughly good housekeeper, understood domestic economy and science and demonstrated it in her home."[5]

Mrs. Eddy's insistence on order was no arbitrary directive, but rather wise counsel from an "exact metaphysician,"[6] one whose aim was not only to maintain the harmony of her home, but also to benefit those who worked in her household by bolstering their individual practice of scientific Christian healing. As she writes in *Retrospection and Introspection*, "Genuine Christian Scientists are, or should be, the most systematic and law-abiding people on earth, because their religion demands implicit adherence to fixed rules, in the orderly demonstration thereof."[7]

Mrs. Eddy knew, said housekeeper Martha Wilcox, "that if one's thought was not orderly and exact in the things that made up present consciousness, that the same thought would not be exact enough to give a treatment or to use an exact science."[8]

Martha W. Wilcox
Longyear Museum collection

Martha Wilcox

Serving in "a very practical home"

Two weeks after Mary Baker Eddy and her household moved to Chestnut Hill, Martha Wallis Wilcox arrived to join the staff as a housekeeper.

"After removing my wraps, Laura Sargent took me into Mrs. Eddy's study and introduced me as Mrs. Wilcox from Kansas City," Martha would recall. "Mrs. Eddy said to me, 'Good morning, Mrs. Wilcox, I felt your sweet presence in the house.'"[9]

Mrs. Eddy proceeded to ask her two questions: What can you do and what are you willing to do? Martha outlined her capabilities regarding general house-keeping, then affirmed that she was "willing to do anything that [Mrs. Eddy] wanted me to do."[10]

Raised in the Methodist faith on Midwestern farms in Iowa and Kansas, young Martha Meyer grew up to be a schoolteacher. Her first marriage ended tragically, when her husband of just six months was drowned. When her second husband fell gravely ill, the couple traveled to Kansas City, Missouri, in 1902 on a physician's recommendation to pursue a special course of treatment. It was at this point that Mrs. Wilcox was given a copy of *Science and Health*.

"What she read appealed to her thought and she literally devoured the truth found in its pages," her sister would later recollect. As a result, although her husband didn't express an interest in Christian Science, Martha found herself healed of a long-standing malady.

Martha immediately began to apply what she was learning, and soon was healing others. She joined Second Church of Christ, Scientist, Kansas City, and in January 1904 she had Primary class instruction.[11]

When the call came to join Mrs. Eddy's household in February 1908, "I was a very young student in Christian Science — just beginning my sixth year," Martha pointed out.[12]

Writing to a friend while living at 400 Beacon Street, she shared insights into her work there: "Many are the lessons that I have learned, none greater than the lesson of humility and that whatever comes to me to do — however small and menial it may seem — is to be done well."[13]

Committed to practicing perfection in her daily tasks, Martha Wilcox told of using a tape measure to make sure the top sheet on Mrs. Eddy's bed was folded over to Mrs. Eddy's specifications.

"I learned that in even such an inconsequential thing as turning down a sheet, I needed to be awake to exactness," she said.[14]

As others in the household had done, she would put tacks in the carpet to indicate where each piece of furniture was placed so that, after a room had been swept or vacuumed, everything could be returned to its right place. Arranging items back on the whatnot at their proper angles after dusting, however, "was almost my Waterloo," Martha admitted wryly.[15]

Her diligence helped prepare her for the day when Mrs. Eddy unexpectedly called her into her office. "I have been praying God to send someone who will stand no matter what comes up, and He has told me to call you," Mrs. Eddy told her. "Now, come in every day with the mental workers and have your lessons and do your mental work."[16]

With that, Martha joined the metaphysical workers for the next two months. It was during this time that a well-known incident occurred, in which Mrs. Eddy asked Martha to pray about something. In the morning, Mrs. Eddy asked why she had not done her work. When Martha protested that she had tried, Mrs. Eddy replied, "Well, if Jesus had just tried and failed, we would have no Science today"—and she had a card hung on the inside of Martha's door that read "Faith without works is dead."

"I looked at that for two weeks," Martha recalled with chagrin.[17]

The lesson stuck, however, and Martha's "works" earned her Mrs. Eddy's approval and support—so much so that in early November 1910, she left the household at Mrs. Eddy's direction to prepare to enter the Normal class. Later, as a newly-minted teacher of Christian Science, Martha moved back to Kansas City, where she taught and practiced Christian Science for the rest of her life.[18]

This whatnot in the Pink Room was nearly Martha's undoing. | LONGYEAR MUSEUM COLLECTION

No menial work

In charge of maintaining the sense of order that Mrs. Eddy required was the housekeeping staff, which doubled with the move to the mansion at 400 Beacon Street. Where just two or three had been able to accomplish the work at Pleasant View, five or six were needed during the Chestnut Hill years. Among those who served in this capacity were Martha Wilcox, Katharine Retterer, Anna Machacek, Frances Thatcher, and Adelaide Still. Others who assisted in addition to their regular duties were Minnie Scott, Margaret Macdonald, Elizabeth Kelly, Nellie Eveleth, and Lula Phillips. Some had been full-time practitioners, all were practicing Christian Scientists who quickly learned, if they hadn't grasped the fact ahead of their arrival, that their work went far beyond such mundane tasks as making beds, cleaning woodwork, and dusting assorted bric-a-brac.

"[Mrs. Eddy] taught us to strive for perfection in every little thing we did in attending to practical details in the home life," said Minnie Scott.[19]

As Martha Wilcox explained: "[A]lways in our thought was what [Mrs. Eddy] had given us to be demonstrated. In fact, we all were there not only to help our Leader, but to learn how to demonstrate Christian Science. From morning till night we were busy applying the instructions she gave us, to the work at hand, and trying to demonstrate the Truth of Christian Science."[20]

With a sprawling 17,000-square-foot house to care for, comprising three main floors, 30 rooms, 11 full bathrooms, and 4 lavatories, the work really did extend from "morning till night." Elizabeth Kelly and the kitchen staff were on duty as early as 5:00 a.m.; Adelaide Still's workday started before 6:00 a.m. and rarely ended before 9:30 or 10:00 at night. And that was in addition to the mental work done by the metaphysical staff, who were assigned two-hour shifts twice a day, around the clock.

There was some overlap in duties between the housekeepers and those who worked in the kitchen and dining room. While there was occasional friction, by and large the women appear to have been a close-knit group. Meals were taken together in the kitchen or the adjacent sitting room, where they had their own piano and frequently took advantage of it.[21] Evenings might find

The housekeeping staff at 400 Beacon Street enjoys a lighthearted moment in the fall of 1910. Left to right: Elizabeth Kelly, Lula Phillips, Nellie Eveleth, Martha Wilcox, Lottie Bowman, and Katharine Retterer. | Longyear Museum collection

them gathered up on the third floor in seamstress Nellie Eveleth's workroom. "I would often read aloud to Miss Nellie Eveleth while she was sewing," recalled Adelaide Still, "and quite often others would listen with her."[22]

William Rathvon described the sewing room as a "headquarters" or "club room for the 'helpers,'" noting that on the wall, Nellie posted a notice: "'No tattling allowed in this room.'"[23]

It took a certain meekness of thought to be successful in their assigned work. One busy practitioner from the Midwest, who arrived expecting to be asked to serve as a metaphysical worker, was caught off guard when Mrs. Eddy invited her to stay as a housekeeper. The astonished woman replied that she thought she had long since finished with "*menial* work." Mrs. Eddy regarded her "for a long time and just as though she could see right through her, and then said very gently, 'Why, my dear, I did not know that there was any.'"[24]

Chestnut Hill
December 11, 1908

My dear Household—

Tattling is always induced by mesmerism and it shall not go on in this house. Whatever you hear that is likely to cause a quarrel, you tell it to Mr. Dickey and tell it to no one else or I will dismiss you from my employ. The following are the rules that shall govern my whole household:

No tattling, telling something about another member of the household or one of my employees.

Take up yourself everyday for animal magnetism, that it cannot make you break this rule.

Leave me utterly out of your thoughts, except when you have something to do for me. Occupy your thought with Truth and Love, and demand of yourself to have no other mind but God, the divine Mind, and this will govern you aright and then you will love one another.[25]

This instructive letter from Mrs. Eddy likely inspired
Nellie Eveleth to post a sign in her sewing area that read
"No tattling allowed in this room."

© The Mary Baker Eddy Collection. Original in The Mary Baker Eddy Library. Used with permission.

Nellie M. Eveleth
Private collection

Nellie Eveleth

"There's sweetness in remembrance"

"Miss Eveleth, the dressmaker . . . is probably 50, white hair, Bostonese, quite capable and has her hands full with new gowns, changing old ones and making extensive alterations to bring out the desired effect."

With this vivid description, Nellie M. Eveleth makes a brief but memorable cameo in William Rathvon's reminiscence of his years serving in Mrs. Eddy's household. The vignette ends on a note of high praise—the observation that Miss Eveleth "uses her Science continually."[26]

Mr. Rathvon's words would no doubt have pleased Nellie, for,

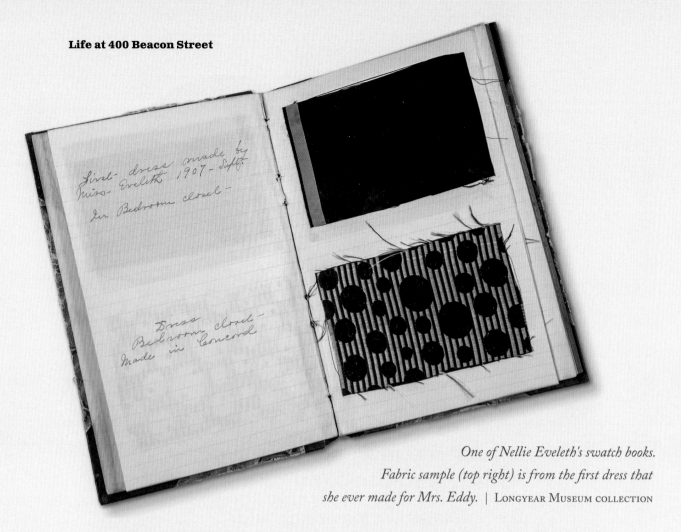

One of Nellie Eveleth's swatch books.
Fabric sample (top right) is from the first dress that
she ever made for Mrs. Eddy. | Longyear Museum collection

like nearly everyone in the household, the road that ultimately led her there began with a cherished healing.

"Why don't you try Christian Science?" a friend had suggested at a particularly low point a decade earlier, when Nellie, who had been an invalid since childhood, was told she would only live a few days longer.

Initially, she rejected the idea out of hand.

"I had been prejudiced against [Christian Science], and told her never to mention it to me again," she later recalled. But the seed was planted, and before long she sent for a minister to ask his advice. He told her of "several good cases of healing that he had seen, and after praying with me for light, said the answer he got was that it would be no harm to try it."[27]

This she did, little knowing the far-reaching effect that the quick healing that followed would have on her life.

A clergyman's daughter, Nellie was raised close to the Bible and said that she took "great comfort during my years of suffering in the sweet messages of love" she found in its pages. By the time she was introduced to Christian Science in the mid-1890s, she had become "filled with an earnest longing to know more of God to be fitted to do more for others."[28]

"Fitted" she would be, quite literally, when in the summer of 1907 she was invited to work as seamstress for the Leader of the Christian Science movement.

Adelaide Still noted, "Mrs. Eddy did not have a resident dressmaker when I went [to Pleasant View]."[29] Miss Eveleth, who was living in Boston at the time, working as a seamstress, had previously done some sewing for Mrs. Eddy, and was asked to design a dress for her.[30]

"The dress, a black satin trimmed with white satin and lace, pleased Mrs. Eddy," Adelaide explained, and Nellie was subsequently hired to do all of the sewing for Mrs. Eddy.[31]

By the time Nellie arrived in Concord in the summer of 1907, Pleasant View was literally bursting at the seams, its housing capacity stretched to the point that visiting members of the Board of Directors had to sleep on cots.[32] So she took a room in town and commuted back and forth each day, doing most of her work in Adelaide Still's room.[33] The following winter, when Mrs. Eddy moved to 400 Beacon Street, Miss Eveleth came along as a full member of the household. Her quarters in the spacious new home were situated on the third floor and included a bedroom and a workroom "equipped with all the machinery of her trade," according to William Rathvon.[34]

Photographs from Nellie's own scrapbook confirm this assessment. The state-of-the-art equipment the seamstress had at her disposal included a Singer sewing machine, an electric iron, tables for cutting and pressing, and a sleeve board. There was also a wall of cupboards and drawers for storing supplies, sources of both gas and electricity, overhead lamps, and a skylight to bring in ample daylight for her work.[35]

Shortly after she moved in, Nellie Eveleth moved out again! Mrs. Eddy was disappointed with her own accommodations. She felt that the rooms were much too large and ostentatious, compared to her cozy suite at Pleasant View, so arrangements were made to remodel them to match more closely the modest ones she'd left behind.[36] During the construction, Nellie was temporarily relocated elsewhere in the house so that her bedroom and sewing room could be turned into a suite for Mrs. Eddy.

"If you are an ordinary cook, dressmaker, or milliner, Christian Science will make you perfect in any of these lines. . . ."
— Mary Baker Eddy

Prominently displayed on the workroom wall for ready reference was the framed motto "Do Right and Fear Not." Prayer was clearly the underpinning for Nellie Eveleth's daily work, which wasn't always easy.

On one occasion, for instance, Nellie was instructed by Mrs. Eddy to let a garment out "but don't make it larger." Not knowing how to do one without the other, the dressmaker turned to God for guidance.

"She . . . was led to change the location of the dart in question," one who knew Miss Eveleth later wrote. "This proved to be satisfactory."[37]

In speaking to William Rathvon of some of the challenges of her work, the seamstress said, "[I]t has been a life-long characteristic of our Leader that it was difficult to get anything in the way of a dress to suit her. It must fit perfectly, yet she is so engrossed in other things that the usual trying on or 'fitting' is absolutely out of the question."[38]

Eventually, Nellie was able to make a paper pattern, from which a dressmaker's

Mrs. Eddy loved the view from Nellie's bedroom, which she called "the most homelike" at 400 Beacon Street. | LONGYEAR MUSEUM COLLECTION

form was created in Boston. This made fittings a little easier.

"Mrs. Eddy regarded the making of a dress as a great achievement," said Irving Tomlinson.[39]

One of Mrs. Eddy's students who worked in her household at Pleasant View described a brief talk she had with her teacher about domestic skills. Mrs. Eddy said, "If you are an ordinary cook, dressmaker, or milliner, Christian Science will make you perfect in any of these lines, and everyone should seek to perfect himself wherever he is, or whatever his calling."[40]

In addition to her duties with scissors and needle, Nellie Eveleth did the personal shopping for the household.[41] For Mrs. Eddy, that included selecting fabric samples and bringing them back for her approval.

Mary Baker Eddy "had a fondness for certain colors: her gowns, coats, hats, and accessories were for the most part soft shades of purple, lavender, and pink, or old rose — although she frequently chose gray or white," recalled Mr. Tomlinson.

Left: Close-up of a portion of Nellie Eveleth's hand-covered photo scrapbook, which bears the inscription "There's Sweetness in Remembrance."
LONGYEAR MUSEUM COLLECTION

Photos of Nellie Eveleth's workroom show a Singer sewing machine (above), which was operated by a treadle, and an electric flat iron (left, plugged into a light socket), still somewhat of a novelty at the time. Note framed motto "Do Right and Fear Not" above the decorative mantel.
LONGYEAR MUSEUM COLLECTION

He also remarked that she was "a deep lover of beauty," and had excellent taste in clothing.

"She held beauty as symbolizing the purity, the loveliness of Soul," he said. "Beauty, she felt, was a quality of divine Mind which finds expression in one's environment, in one's appearance, and in every other detail of daily life."[42]

Nellie must have been a lover of beauty, too, based on the historical evidence she left behind. As would any diligent professional, she documented the fabric samples, sketches, and notes about the garments she made for Mrs. Eddy, and a glance through a pair of her record books reveals page after page of swatches in an array of lovely colors and patterns.

While the main focus of Miss Eveleth's work was devoted to the design, construction, and maintenance of Mrs. Eddy's clothing, she probably also assisted with a variety of sewing needs for others in the household. With a staff of up to two dozen or so men and women, there would likely have been many occasions requiring her skills or expert advice, from turning of frayed collars and cuffs to reconstructive weaving or darning of tears or moth holes in woolen garments needed for cold New England winters, replacing of worn lace, trim, or garment linings, reinforcing buttons and hooks, and of course alterations.

By all accounts, Nellie did her job well. One student who knew and worked closely with Mrs. Eddy during her years at Pleasant View and 400 Beacon Street later wrote that her "attire always betokened propriety, simplicity, fitness, and good taste. . . ."[43]

These words are a tribute to Mrs. Eddy's own refinement, of course — but also, at least perhaps in part, to a humble seamstress who once prayed to be "fitted to do more for others."

In giving thanks for the healing that would bring her to the service of Mary Baker Eddy, Nellie Eveleth wrote, "My daily prayer is to be a true Christian Scientist. For darkness it has given me light; for sickness, health; in place of distress, peace; instead of perplexity, a sure guide. Whenever I go to our Leader's writings for help in any way, I find it, and I thank God for the experiences that led me to Christian Science."[44]

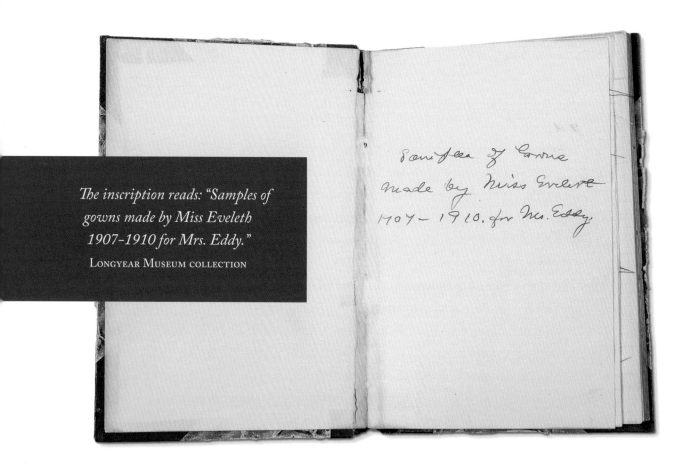

The inscription reads: *"Samples of gowns made by Miss Eveleth 1907–1910 for Mrs. Eddy."*

LONGYEAR MUSEUM COLLECTION

Wrapper Worn Out

Fall Wrapper 1910

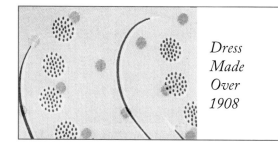

Dress Made Over 1908

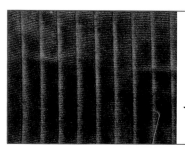

Worn as a traveling dress coming from Concord 1907

*Summer
Wrapper
1910*

*Summer
Wrapper
1910*

*Best
Wrapper
Point Lace*

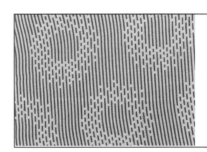

*Summer
Wrapper*

*Swatches of the fabric that
Nellie Eveleth used to make
"wrappers" (a 19th-century
term for comfortable day
dresses) for Mrs. Eddy.
Nellie's notations include
her remark at left regarding
Mrs. Eddy's quip about the
pink fabric with the circle
pattern: "Mrs. Eddy called
this her wailing dress for
it is saying 'Oh!'"*

LONGYEAR MUSEUM COLLECTION

Frances F. Thatcher
LONGYEAR MUSEUM COLLECTION

Frances Thatcher

When "homely tasks become holy tasks"

"[S]mall in stature, wiry, dark hair and eyes; pleasing in manner, accurate, competent."[45] With this succinct assessment, the Christian Science Board of Directors recommended Frances Fairlamb Thatcher to Mary Baker Eddy as a potential housekeeper.

Mrs. Thatcher's training and experience in domestic economy made her highly qualified as a candidate. A graduate of the Domestic Science course at Drexel Institute of Art, Science and Industry in Philadelphia,[46] she was employed as the cafeteria director at the prestigious Friends School in

Wilmington, Delaware, the town she grew up in and would return to after serving Mrs. Eddy.[47] In charge of feeding the school's 275 pupils, Frances also maintained a boarding house for 20 students, and since finding Christian Science had done some healing work.[48]

Unbeknownst to her, Norman John, her Christian Science Primary class teacher, had recommended her to the Committee on Business. Thus in the spring of 1908, Frances found herself invited to dinner with her teacher and his family. The actual intent of the gathering, however, was to give Daisette McKenzie the opportunity to inspect Frances's character and disposition to see if she might be suited to help in Mrs. Eddy's home.[49]

Frances passed inspection. Shortly thereafter, on just two hours' notice, she left her home and responsibilities in Wilmington to travel to Boston and meet with Church officials. Mrs. Eddy sent for her a few days later, and Frances embarked on "as wonderful a time as could come into the life of a Christian Scientist."[50]

Mrs. Thatcher was 39 when she arrived at Chestnut Hill in June 1908. Her education in the domestic sciences and subsequent employment had prepared her for the practical work involved in caring for a large house, but she soon realized that serving in Mrs. Eddy's home demanded much more than just proficiency in everyday housekeeping tasks. It required constant proof of love and humility.

"Many came and went in periods of longer or shorter duration with the greatest desire to manifest unselfed love," she would explain, "and with the greatest example before them that could be given, many could not stand the rigid proof of unselfed love required of them. . . . It was only those who could in some measure realize that homely tasks become holy tasks when the 'me' is left out, that could serve in so great a work."[51]

That blessing bore fruit within just a few years. After Frances left in January 1909, she entered the public practice of Christian Science healing. Advertising first in the *Wilmington City Directory* and later in *The Christian Science Journal*, Mrs. Thatcher would continue in the healing work until her passing at age 96.[52]

Katharine Retterer

"A good whole-souled woman"

Katharine Retterer | LONGYEAR MUSEUM COLLECTION

"I have had many proofs of the one intelligence governing all," wrote Katharine Retterer in the *Christian Science Sentinel* in 1903.[53] Those proofs may well have been a comfort to her in the summer of 1907, when Miss Retterer found herself on the return train home from Boston to Marion, Ohio, after her cousin Elizabeth Kelly was chosen to work in Mrs. Eddy's household at Pleasant View and she was not.[54]

Whatever Mrs. Eddy's reasons in her choice of candidate at that point, it's a testament to Katharine's character that she humbly and graciously accepted the call when she was asked to join the household in March of the following year, just a few weeks after Mrs. Eddy had moved to Chestnut Hill.

There's no doubt that the Committee on Business recognized her sterling qualities. They wrote several letters to Mrs. Eddy during the vetting process, describing the 50-year-old Ohioan as "a good whole-souled woman," "cheerful and capable," "bright" and "strong," a woman raised on a farm who "loves to work," and who had been practicing Christian Science healing for over a decade "with good success."[55]

Cyanotype image of Katharine Retterer reading in her room. | Longyear Museum collection

Of German descent, Katharine grew up in the Lutheran church. She initially took up the study of Christian Science "for the good reading and not for the healing. . . ."[56] Ostracized by her minister as "a disgrace to the church and my family," she sturdily persevered, despite being the only Christian Scientist in her community, traveling some ten miles each way to attend informal church services with a handful of others.[57] She joined The Mother Church in 1898, and in time, she and her cousin Elizabeth both had Primary class instruction.[58]

It was Katharine's practice to read *Science and Health* and the Christian Science periodicals aloud to her 70-year-old German-speaking mother, who wasn't able to read English. Eventually, Katharine purchased a copy of *Science and Health* for her.

"This is yours, and you must learn to read it," she told her mother. "*Science and Health* teaches there is but one Mind, and this being true, you have access to just as much as I have!"[59]

They began with lessons on recognizing the words for the synonyms of God, and within six months Katharine's mother had learned to read English. Consequently, she became a student of Christian Science, too.

Overleaf: Katharine Retterer's restored bedroom at 400 Beacon Street as it looks today.

When Katharine finally arrived at Mrs. Eddy's home in March 1908 to join the housekeeping staff, she found herself an integral part of a close-knit group of women working together to ensure that everything ran smoothly. Photographs tell part of this story, showing her gathered with her colleagues on the back lawn, seated beside them on the kitchen steps, and enjoying jaunts together in the automobile.

Most telling of all is the photograph of Katharine reading in her room at 400 Beacon Street (see page 133), her Bible and *Science and Health* close at hand, along with a Bible dictionary. She put the fruits of her study into practice both at Chestnut Hill and afterward, as she continued to prove that God, the one supreme intelligence, was indeed governing all.

Katharine returned to Ohio after Mrs. Eddy's passing, recognizing the need for dedicated Christian Scientists in her hometown. In April 1911, she wrote to Calvin Frye, "There seems very much room for improvement everywhere you go. The fields are already white to harvest but seems the laborers are few."[60]

The woman who "loved to work" waded right into those harvest fields. Two months after writing that letter, she was listed as a practitioner in *The Christian Science Journal*, and she continued in the healing work for the rest of her life.[61]

Left to right: Lula Phillips, Elizabeth Kelly (seated), unidentified woman, Katharine Retterer (seated), Mary Salchow, and another unidentified woman. | Longyear Museum collection

John Salchow beats a rug on the lawn at Pleasant View. | PRIVATE COLLECTION *Such old-fashioned methods gradually gave way to modern appliances at 400 Beacon Street, including a vacuum cleaner likely similar to the one pictured in this ad.*

Everything's up to date in Chestnut Hill

With the advent of electricity came an influx of labor-saving devices designed for the home. As a result, housework was transformed. Flat irons were replaced by electric irons; washboards were traded for washing machines; and brooms were succeeded first by carpet sweepers and then by vacuum cleaners. Martha Wilcox recalls that, several months after she arrived, the household acquired one of the first vacuum cleaners on the market. Calvin Frye's account books bear this out.[62]

At Pleasant View, rugs had been cleaned the old-fashioned way—taken outside and whacked with woven rattan carpet beaters. For fitted carpets, "we used to tear up damp newspapers into rather small pieces and scatter them on the carpets to catch the dust as it arose from the sweeping," Adelaide Still explained.[63] Now, with the acquisition of a vacuum cleaner, Mary Baker Eddy's housekeeping staff entered the 20th century. Additionally, there would be an electric iron for the seamstress, and for the laundresses, a gas-fired dryer and an electric mangle for pressing linens.[64]

A sharp-eyed reporter for the *Boston Post* who toured 400 Beacon Street in 1909 spotted one of these appliances on his tour of the basement. "An up-to-date laundry is . . . situated here," he wrote, "among the fittings of which is a large steam drying machine."[65]

The high-capacity dryer with pull-out racks on rollers would have been a boon to the laundry staff, who were kept busy with the washing generated by the large household. While Mrs. Eddy's own personal items were cared for by the house-keepers and Adelaide Still, the rest of the household depended on the efforts of day workers whose domain was the basement laundry room.

Pauline Mann (left), Minnie Weygandt (far right), and an unidentified helper clean furniture with a carpet beater and whisk broom at Pleasant View. | PRIVATE COLLECTION

Adelaide's younger sister, Laura, was one of these women.[66] Laura Still was in charge of the laundry for a good portion of the time that Mrs. Eddy lived at 400 Beacon Street, assisted in her work by a series of other helpers, two of whom were African American.[67]

Early 20th century magazine ad for the clothes dryer that was installed at 400 Beacon Street. Overleaf: The laundry room as it looks today.

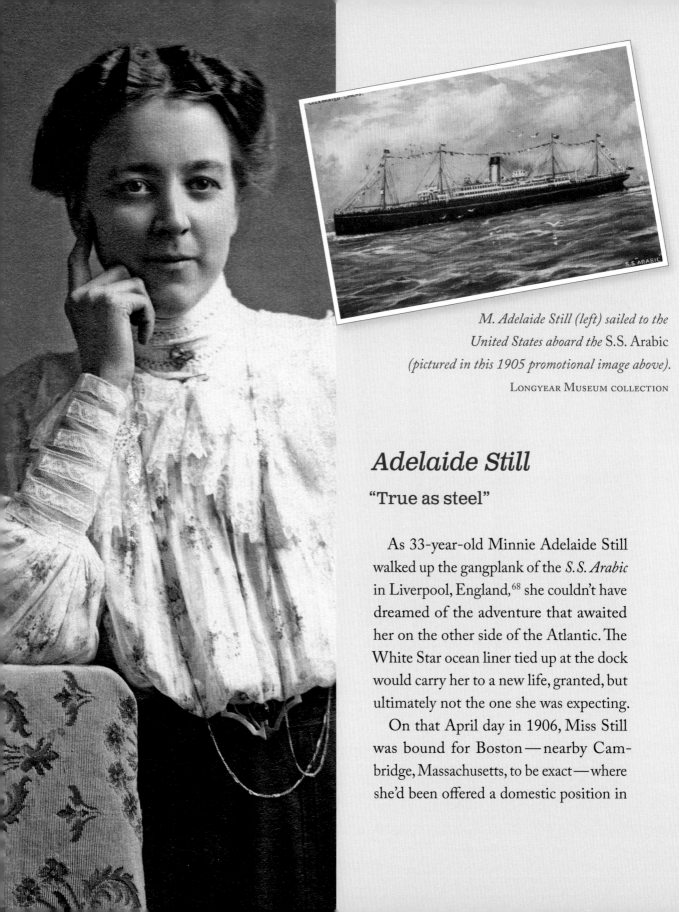

M. Adelaide Still (left) sailed to the United States aboard the S.S. Arabic *(pictured in this 1905 promotional image above).*
LONGYEAR MUSEUM COLLECTION

Adelaide Still

"True as steel"

As 33-year-old Minnie Adelaide Still walked up the gangplank of the *S. S. Arabic* in Liverpool, England,[68] she couldn't have dreamed of the adventure that awaited her on the other side of the Atlantic. The White Star ocean liner tied up at the dock would carry her to a new life, granted, but ultimately not the one she was expecting.

On that April day in 1906, Miss Still was bound for Boston — nearby Cambridge, Massachusetts, to be exact — where she'd been offered a domestic position in the household of Harvard professor James Pray and his wife, Florence.[69] Young Benjamin Pray, who was two, would be joined later that summer by a new baby sister, Frances, and Adelaide, as she would come to be called, was to be their nanny.

The *Arabic* arrived in Boston harbor on May 6, 1906, just one month before the dedication of the brand-new Extension of The Mother Church. This must have been a heady time for an enthusiastic young Christian Scientist like Adelaide, who no doubt was thrilled at suddenly being transported into the heart of the Christian Science movement. Within a year, she'd be at its very epicenter, after leaving her position with the Prays to join Mary Baker Eddy's household at Pleasant View.

Born in Banwell, England, Adelaide's early life was marked by hardship. She was raised in the Methodist Sunday School by working-class parents, and

Adelaide Still's bedroom at 400 Beacon Street. | Longyear Museum collection

was just 12 or 13 when her father became gravely ill. Adelaide had dreamed of becoming a schoolteacher, but by the following year, with three younger siblings to help support, "I was compelled to take a position in domestic service," she explained.[70]

Her father's passing a few years later "brought so much trouble, poverty and unhappiness to the family that I could not understand how God could allow it," she would write. "I passed through a number of years of doubt and darkness trying to find God, but was never satisfied."[71]

Adelaide moved to London, where in 1900 a Sunday School teacher in the Congregational church she and her sister, Laura, attended introduced Christian Science to their Bible class. "I was very much interested," Adelaide recalled.[72] She bought a copy of *Science and Health* and began to study it. Within two years, she joined The Mother Church and First Church of Christ, Scientist, London, and took Primary class instruction from E. Blanche Ward, who was also her employer at the time.[73]

> ## *"I passed through a number of years of doubt and darkness trying to find God, but was never satisfied."*
> ## *— Adelaide Still*

In the months following her move to the United States, Adelaide had a testimony of healing published in the *Christian Science Sentinel*. Her account of being freed from pain reveals both a deep well of gratitude and a sturdiness of thought notable in her willingness to persist in prayer. "I am very grateful for these and other demonstrations," she later wrote, "but they are nothing in comparison to the spiritual understanding of God and man and the Bible which I have gained from the study of Mrs. Eddy's works."[74]

Meanwhile, the Committee on Business had been searching high and low for a new maid for Mrs. Eddy. James Neal traveled to Chicago, Kansas City, "and other places in the middle west," while Daisette McKenzie went to Cleveland — all "without favorable results." There was, however, one bright note to report: "an English girl who has been a servant all her life," whom the committee recommended as "the most promising of any yet seen."[75]

Adelaide Still was "courageous, able to think for herself, and accustomed to hardships," they told Mrs. Eddy, and shared with her a passage from a letter they had received from Miss Still that very day: "I cannot begin to express the joy I feel at the thought of even a remote possibility of serving our beloved Leader. If there is any way of making myself more capable of performing the duties of maid, I will do anything in my power. I might take a few lessons in hair-dressing, or in learning to fold dresses correctly."[76]

Adelaide Still (seated) with her sister, Laura, and brother Charles, circa 1906. Laura would also work for Mrs. Eddy. | COURTESY OF THE MARY BAKER EDDY COLLECTION. ORIGINAL IN THE MARY BAKER EDDY LIBRARY.

Accompanied by Daisette McKenzie, Adelaide traveled to Pleasant View in the winter of 1907 for an interview with Mrs. Eddy.

"I was there for a few moments only and evidently was not then ready to enter her service," Adelaide later recounted with a touch of chagrin. "I had tried to do my mental work and to quiet my thought, but to sense there was still much excitement underneath, and the few questions Mrs. Eddy asked me were not what I was prepared to answer."[77]

She returned to Cambridge and her position with the Pray family. Several months later, however, she was called back to Pleasant View to assist with the housekeeping. Adelaide continued in this post for six weeks without once seeing Mrs. Eddy, and then one morning, as Miss Still would relate, "as I opened the swing-door from the kitchen she opened the one from the dining room and we stood face to face."[78]

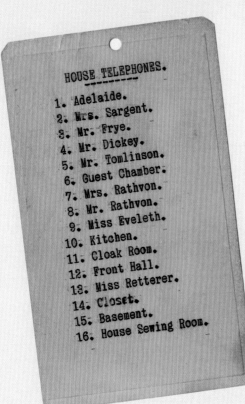

Mrs. Eddy greeted her, then placed her hand on Adelaide's arm and looked at her searchingly. A few mornings later, she asked Adelaide to be her personal maid. When Adelaide replied that she would be glad to accept the position but had never held a similar one, Mrs. Eddy reassured her with, "I know it, dear, but I'll teach you." And as Adelaide was leaving the room a few minutes later, she added, "I have been asking God to send me the right one, and I believe that He has."[79]

This, Adelaide would note, "was a great comfort in later days when things sometimes seemed difficult...."[80]

As the individual who, along with Laura Sargent, had the most daily contact with Mrs. Eddy, Adelaide was with her from morning to night. She witnessed smooth seas as well as stormy ones, periods of calm and times of turbulence. At Mrs. Eddy's

Adelaide Still's name is at the top of this 400 Beacon Street telephone list.

© THE MARY BAKER EDDY COLLECTION. ORIGINAL IN THE MARY BAKER EDDY LIBRARY. USED WITH PERMISSION.

A gift to Mary Baker Eddy from her son, George, this ring made of Black Hills gold was later given by Mrs. Eddy to Adelaide Still in 1908. | Longyear Museum collection

request, she was always near at hand, even when Mrs. Eddy had visitors, and often when she was meeting with her secretaries and Church officers. ("This was sometimes a trial to Mr. Dickey or Mr. McLellan, as they liked me out of the way when business was being transacted," Adelaide admitted.[81]) She was also present when the household's metaphysical workers came to Mrs. Eddy's study for their daily instruction, and significantly, in September 1909, Mrs. Eddy directed Calvin Frye to set Adelaide's wages at the same rate as these experienced practitioners and teachers.[82]

"[A]ll things work together for good to them that love God," the Bible promises, and this certainly proved true in Adelaide Still's case.[83] The challenges she'd surmounted in adolescence and early adulthood developed a quiet strength that was evident in her moral grit and metaphysical backbone — characteristics that would help earn her not only her Leader's affection and approval, but also the respect of her colleagues.

"[H]er understanding of Christian Science has been clear and from the first she has been an invaluable member of the household," William Rathvon would write, adding that Adelaide "is proving herself true as steel and loyal as the most faithful of the old or new."[84]

*Adelaide Still (left) on the front drive at
400 Beacon Street with an unidentified trio, possibly
her sister, Laura, or Florence Pray and Adelaide's former
charges, Frances (left) and Benjamin (right) Pray.*
© The Mary Baker Eddy Collection. Original in
The Mary Baker Eddy Library. Used with permission.

After Mrs. Eddy's passing, Miss Still remained at Chestnut Hill for a time as one of the home's caretakers. She became a U.S. citizen in 1916 and lived modestly in the Boston area for the rest of her life.[85] As one of the last surviving members of Mrs. Eddy's household, she was often sought out by those eager to hear about her time with the Discoverer and Founder of Christian Science. Ever faithful to her Leader, Adelaide always reminded them of the debt of gratitude they owed to Mary Baker Eddy "for her steadfastness in giving this great Truth to the world."[86]

"Her deep love for Mrs. Eddy was evident in all that she said, along with her clear recognition of the incomparably heavy burden of opposition and misunderstanding our Leader had to bear," wrote biographer Robert Peel, who spent many hours in Miss Still's company. "Her one thought in talking with me was always to have me recognize the magnitude of Mrs. Eddy's accomplishment in the face of the unique difficulties she faced."[87]

Caring for Mrs. Eddy

While the household's labor-saving devices may have eliminated the need for elbow grease in some areas, they didn't eliminate the need for thoughtful care.

"Everything that love could think of was done to spare Mrs. Eddy any disturbance or change from the usual routine," said Adelaide.[88]

This included looking after her suite of rooms. Some tidying was done on a daily basis — Adelaide described dusting Mrs. Eddy's study each morning while Mrs. Eddy was dressing, for instance — but once a week, usually on Wednesday afternoons, the rooms were given a thorough cleaning.[89]

As always, Mrs. Eddy's comfort was the housekeeping staff's primary concern, and thus the work was scheduled during her carriage ride.

"When she went for her daily drive there was a great bustle in the house, maids and others invaded her room with brooms, dust pan and dust cloth, and swept and cleaned as rapidly as possible while someone stood watching

Mary Baker Eddy's study at Chestnut Hill, circa 1910. | Longyear Museum collection

down the road for the reappearance of her carriage," recalled one who worked briefly at Pleasant View. "At their signal every household implement was rapidly whisked away from her room and on her return she found everything tidy."[90]

Even after the move to Chestnut Hill, when Mrs. Eddy's daily carriage rides were reduced from an hour or so to about half an hour, the housekeepers still managed this Herculean task. Minnie Scott zeroed in on the heart of what motivated their efforts. Their goal was simple, she pointed out, "that none of [Mrs. Eddy's] precious time should be wasted which was used in the interests of all mankind."[91]

Mrs. Eddy's own efforts to this end are well documented, from having her study cut down in size so that she wouldn't have to wait while her secretary walked across "all those roses" on the floral carpet, to ordering her bureau drawers so that she could find just what she needed even in the dark, to the careful arrangement of pins in her pin cushion so that she could remove exactly the one she needed.[92] Her time was precious, and she and her household knew it.

Detail from the Pink Room as it looks today.

Anna O. Machacek

LONGYEAR MUSEUM COLLECTION

Anna Machacek

"I would never have recognized her"

"When I went for the first time to a practitioner for help I spoke very little English and could not read a word," said Anna Machacek.[93]

Born Anna Olga Machacek in what was then Bohemia (now the Czech Republic), her story speaks to both the American immigrant dream and the transformative power of Christian Science on the lives of the humble men and women who served in Mary Baker Eddy's household.

In 1884, Anna fled her homeland to avoid an arranged marriage, arriving in New York at age 21.[94] From there, she made her way to Cedar Rapids, Iowa, which had a thriving Bohemian community.[95]

"She spoke broken English and looked the typical peasant girl in her long, full-skirted calico dress, with a babushka tied over her fair hair," recalled Isabelle Fleming, the daughter of Anna's employer in that city.[96]

The shy, lonely girl caught the interest of Abbie Weeks, a local Christian Science practitioner who took Anna under her wing.[97]

"[A]t this first visit to a practitioner . . . she repeated with me the Scientific Statement of Being [*Science and Health,* 468] and then let me repeat it alone. This was all of the teaching I ever had," Anna explained. "My text books were the Bohemian Bible and the English Bible. I could get nothing from dictionaries, therefore I can truly say that the Bible and *Science and Health with Key to the Scriptures* by Mary Baker Eddy have been my only teachers, my only help and inspiration."[98]

Anna, who was soon known as "C.S. Anna" to her employer's family, used part of her wages to purchase her own lamp oil so that she could study late into the night.[99] Within a year, she joined a branch church, and in 1903 she joined The Mother Church.[100]

By 1904, her friend Mrs. Weeks had moved to Chicago, where she wrote to Mrs. Eddy about Anna's domestic talents. In early 1905, following some staff turnover at Pleasant View, Mrs. Eddy sent for Anna, and in February, she found herself on a train heading East.[101]

Anna was an instant hit with the household. "She was a good, big and jolly, sound principled woman. We all liked her," said John Salchow, who worked with her at both Pleasant View and 400 Beacon Street.[102]

"Mrs. Eddy was very fond of Anna," observed Minnie Scott, who also worked with her in both homes. "She had a quaint, foreign accent which Mrs. Eddy enjoyed and used certain large words in a way that amused Mrs. Eddy, as for instance 'pomposity' when denying either audible or silent arguments of mortal mind, where I might use the term Mrs. Eddy gives us in [the *Church Manual*] Art. 8 Sect. 6, 'aggressive mental suggestion.'"[103]

Deft and accomplished in her work, Anna pitched in wherever needed, from helping out in the kitchen to caring for Mrs. Eddy's clothing to general house-keeping duties.[104]

Anna was "always ready to find a way to improve the appearance of ornaments, glass-ware, rugs, draperies & etc. as she was trained in her own country, then called Bohemia, where beautiful glass-ware was made," added Mrs. Scott, one of whose first jobs at Pleasant View was assisting Anna. She also admired her co-worker's skill with fine laundry, noting that Anna "had learned the art of cleansing laces, satin, velvet and furs, feather boas and such things so Mrs. Eddy's clothing was well cared for without sending it out of house."[105]

Anna's cheerful diligence did not go unrewarded. She was eventually promoted to the position of housekeeper, and she was serving in that capacity at the time of the move to Chestnut Hill. With the arrival of Martha Wilcox and Katharine Retterer to bolster the housekeeping staff at Mrs. Eddy's new and much larger residence, Anna asked for a leave of absence to take

Anna Machacek was adept at caring for Mrs. Eddy's fine linens, such as the monogrammed lace doily and pillowcases pictured here.

LONGYEAR MUSEUM COLLECTION

153

Left to right: Minnie Weygandt, Anna Machacek, Adelaide Still, Minnie Scott, and Jonathan Irving. Pictured here at Pleasant View, all five would go on to serve at Chestnut Hill. | PRIVATE COLLECTION

care of some urgent business back at home. She left 400 Beacon Street at the end of March 1908.[106]

Upon returning to Cedar Rapids, Anna immediately put what she'd learned under Mrs. Eddy's tutelage into action. By 1909, she was listed as a practitioner in *The Christian Science Journal*, and she would continue in the public practice of healing for the next three decades.[107] "I still turn to these books for help in every need," she later wrote, referring to her early and beloved instructors, the Bible and *Science and Health*, "pointing the same way for all who come to me for help also."[108]

Many years after their first acquaintance, the daughter of her former employer—who by this time had become a Christian Scientist herself—crossed paths with Anna in Cedar Rapids.

"I would never have recognized her," marvelled Mrs. Fleming, "trim in her tailored blue suit—smart hat, white blouse and gloves—no longer 'C.S. Anna'—but now Miss Anna Machacek, C.S., a busy practitioner"—and, she added, "a dignified and much respected member of society."[109]

This Bohemian cut glass pitcher and matching punch cups, with gold-filled leaf and lattice design, were among the elegant items that Anna Machacek cared for at Pleasant View and 400 Beacon Street. | LONGYEAR MUSEUM COLLECTION

Seated on the kitchen steps with the sun in their eyes are (left to right)
Elizabeth Kelly, Frances Thatcher, Nellie Eveleth, Minnie Scott,
Katharine Retterer, and Adelaide Still. | Longyear Museum collection

"God will bless you, dear ones"

From the refreshing homemade lemonade prepared for her each day after her carriage ride, to the heated carriage robes tucked in around her on those rides when the weather turned cool, to finding her bed warmed on wintry nights, Mrs. Eddy was touchingly grateful for the tender care and many small kindnesses shown to her by those who served in her home. On more than one occasion, she told her housekeepers, "God will bless you, dear ones, for your loving service to me."[110]

And it was service gladly given by those whose hearts overflowed with gratitude for all that Christian Science had done for them and gratitude for the one who had labored for so many years to give it to the world.

For Minnie Scott, it all came back to love.

These thoughtful acts, she said, were to Mrs. Eddy "the practical evidences of the warmth and enfolding presence of divine Love operating through the loving hearts and hands of those around her who had been taught by her precepts and example to know God as Love. The definition of Love which she has given in *Miscellaneous Writings* page 250 . . . was what she expected of the students in her home."[111]

Love is not something put upon a shelf, to be taken down on rare occasions with sugar-tongs and laid on a rose-leaf.

I make strong demands on love, call for active witnesses to prove it, and noble sacrifices and grand achievements as its results. Unless these appear, I cast aside the word as a sham and counterfeit, having no ring of the true metal. Love cannot be a mere abstraction, or goodness without activity and power. As a human quality, the glorious significance of affection is more than words: it is the tender, unselfish deed done in secret; the silent, ceaseless prayer; the self-forgetful heart that overflows; the veiled form stealing on an errand of mercy, out of a side door; the little feet tripping along the sidewalk; the gentle hand opening the door that turns toward want and woe, sickness and sorrow, and thus lighting the dark places of earth.

—*Mary Baker Eddy*

According to Minnie Scott, this passage from Miscellaneous Writings *(p. 250) epitomizes what Mrs. Eddy expected from her household workers.*

Chapter 6

Beyond the "Shadow of Frivolity"

ome years after serving in Mrs. Eddy's household, Irving Tomlinson addressed an Annual Meeting of The Mother Church as its incoming President. "To tend and water the vineyard means labor, not ease," he told his fellow members. "Mrs. Eddy knew no hours nor seasons for her labors."[1]

One of the most important things that Mary Baker Eddy modeled for her students was her work ethic. She was approaching her 90th year while living at 400 Beacon Street but was still tireless in her efforts for her Church and for mankind—"never unready to work for God," to echo her own words—and this included holidays.[2]

"When I first came to Pleasant View," wrote John Salchow, "Mrs. Eddy frequently received her followers or local friends, sometimes entertaining them on Christmas or Thanksgiving Day. . . . but her work took so much of her time and energy that

Snow softens the contours of the front gate at 400 Beacon Street on a wintry night, circa 1910. LONGYEAR MUSEUM COLLECTION

gradually even this simple pleasure of receiving her friends had to be dropped."[3]

Although there were still occasional brief visits from family and friends during the Chestnut Hill years, Mrs. Eddy no longer presided at the dinner table on holidays or any other day. The role of head of the table was now assumed by Calvin Frye. Holidays themselves held a deeper significance for the Discoverer, Founder, and Leader of Christian Science by this point in her life. As her concept of these seasons of the year deepened and ripened over the decades, she used them as fresh opportunities for further instruction, seeking to spiritualize the thought of both her immediate household and the broader field by lifting them above the outward trappings of celebration.

"Christmas respects the Christ too much to submerge itself in merely temporary means and ends," she wrote in an article for the *New York World* in 1905, counseling against "mere merry-making or needless gift-giving," and turning the reader's gaze instead beyond "the shadow of frivolity" toward "the real, the absolute and eternal."[4]

> *"The unceasing prayer that the Christ may be born in every heart is going out from this place daily, and in that way the work is blessing all mankind."*
> *— Minnie Scott*

Among the members of her household who caught the spirit of her words—and her example—and looked beyond "the shadow of frivolity" was Minnie Scott, who wrote to a friend on Christmas Day, 1908, "The unceasing prayer that the Christ may be born in every heart is going out from this place daily, and in that way the work is blessing all mankind."[5]

A gift to the whole world

A decade earlier, in an early issue of the *Christian Science Sentinel*, Mrs. Eddy had taken the opportunity publicly to request "total exemption from Christmas gifts."[6] And by 1904, a new *Church Manual* By-law required: "In the United States there shall be no special observances, festivities, nor gifts at the Easter season by members of The Mother Church."[7] As Mrs. Eddy reminded readers,

"Gratitude and love should abide in every heart each day of all the years."[8] The following year, she expanded the exemption to include "congratulatory despatches or letters to the Pastor Emeritus on Thanksgiving, Christmas, New Year, or Easter," again turning the thought of her followers away from personality.[9]

In an article preceding the announcement of this new By-law in the *Christian Science Sentinel,* she wrote,

Thinking of person implies that one is not thinking of Principle, and fifty telegrams per holiday signal such thinking. Are the holidays blest by absorbing one's time writing or reading congratulations? I cannot watch and pray reading telegrams; they only cloud the clear sky, and they give the appearance of personal worship which Christian Science annuls. Did the dear students know how much I love them, and need every hour wherein to express this love in labor for them, they would gladly give me the holidays therefor and not task themselves with mistaken means. But God will reward their kind motives and guide them every step of the way from human affection to spiritual understanding, from faith to achievement, from light to love, from sense to Soul.[10]

If holiday gift-giving had waned by the time Mrs. Eddy moved to Chestnut Hill, Thanksgiving, Christmas, Easter, and New Year's Day were not barren of normal festive elements.[11] There were still sweet exchanges of goodwill and cheer, plus traditional turkey dinners with all the trimmings at Thanksgiving and Christmas.[12] The latter prompted tips for the mail carrier and paperboys, and, on at least one occasion, a poinsettia for Mrs. Eddy's desk, complete with shiny ornaments. Too, Mrs. Eddy's natural generosity spilled over in the spontaneous sharing of her spiritual inspiration during these seasons, especially to those with whom she worked most closely.

On New Year's Day, 1909, for example, she counseled her household to "begin the New Year by doing, not talking," according to William Rathvon. "Talk is dangerous if it satisfies us and thus prevents us from going further and making our demonstration," she explained.[13]

EXTEMPORE.

Jan. 1, 1910.

I.

O BLESSINGS infinite!
O glad New Year!
Sweet sign and substance
Of God's presence here.

II.

Give us not only angels' songs,
But Science vast, to which belongs
The tongue of angels
And the song of songs.

MARY BAKER EDDY.

In addition to instruction, holidays occasionally inspired Mrs. Eddy to share her inspiration through poetry. "Extempore," written on New Year's Day, 1910, would be published in the Christian Science periodicals and later included in Miscellany *(p. 354).*

A festive poinsettia, decorated for the holidays, adorns Mrs. Eddy's desk at 400 Beacon Street. | LONGYEAR MUSEUM COLLECTION

Rear view of Mrs. Eddy's home after the 1909 Christmas snowfall.
Longyear Museum collection

On Christmas Eve, 1909, Mrs. Eddy shared another lesson with her metaphysical workers, explaining that Christmas is every day, and that it's "not so much what God does for us as what He is."[14] She urged the gathered group to express more "kind generosity and affection" in the coming year and "love God more."[15]

Mrs. Eddy's last Christmas was a "memorable day in the gray stone house on the hill," wrote Mr. Rathvon, quiet "indoors and out, serene and peaceful." Nightfall would bring the beginnings of a blizzard that would blanket the area with 18 inches of snow.[16]

Upstairs in her study that morning, a smiling Mrs. Eddy greeted her metaphysical workers with, "A cheery, holy Christ mass to you all!"—and shared insights into the holiday's significance. "A holy uplifting sense of Life, Truth and Love is the true Christmas," she told them.[17]

Later that day, she would spend the afternoon as she did every other, sorting and going over the mail. But first, she would write a greeting to the entire household, prompted by their message to her.

The message was Minnie Scott's idea. She had spearheaded an Easter greeting earlier that year, and it was she who suggested that they "write a letter to Mrs. Eddy expressing to her our love, loyalty, and appreciation and wishing her a happy Christmas," said Adelaide Still. "Mrs. Scott wrote the letter and we all signed it, and it was put on her desk for her."[18]

"A holy uplifting sense of Life, Truth and

Love is the true Christmas."

— Mary Baker Eddy

Mrs. Eddy's response was deeply appreciated by one and all. William Rathvon called it "a loving greeting to those who through feast and famine were endeavoring to uphold her hands on the mountain top of righteous endeavor."[19] Afterwards, it was sent to the editors of the periodicals, who had it printed in the *Christian Science Sentinel*, and sent a keepsake facsimile to each of Mrs. Eddy's staff members.

Irving Tomlinson framed his copy and hung it on the wall of his study.

"As this now appears in *Miscellany*," he pointed out, "it may well be said to be Mrs. Eddy's Christmas gift to the whole world."[20]

MRS. EDDY'S CHRISTMAS MESSAGE.

Mrs. Eddy's 1909 Christmas message to her household was published in the Christian Science Sentinel *on January 1, 1910, and later included in* Miscellany, *263. It reads: "Beloved: A word to the wise is sufficient. Mother wishes you all a <u>happy</u> <u>Christmas</u>, a feast of Soul, and a famine of sense. Lovingly thine, Mary Baker Eddy."*

Chapter 7

Daily Bread

t was a rare day at 400 Beacon Street that didn't begin with homemade doughnuts.

The aroma would have wafted down the hall from the kitchen, winding its way up the back stairs of the large gray stone house to where Mary Baker Eddy's staff was preparing for the morning. While a tray was brought to Mrs. Eddy, everyone else would assemble downstairs in the dining room promptly at seven.[1]

Meals were hearty for the household workers. At the breakfast table, several kinds of fruit were generally available, along with hot and cold cereal and a main entrée — eggs and bacon, for instance, or maybe chipped beef, or fish and fried potatoes. According to a menu record that Calvin Frye kept in the spring of 1909, the morning meal nearly always included hot doughnuts, often accompanied by toast, fritters, cornbread, or "gems," as muffins were called at the time.[2]

Thus fortified, the staff at 400 Beacon Street was ready for the day ahead.

A new home, a new kitchen

The move to Chestnut Hill was a significant one not only for the Leader of the Christian Science movement, but also for her household—including the cooks and kitchen helpers. Accustomed to a modest workspace in a country farmhouse, they must have been dazzled at the sight of their new domain. During the process of remodeling the home for Mrs. Eddy, a wing had been added and the decision made to relocate the kitchen from the basement to the first floor.[3] As a result, natural light streamed in through a bank of south-facing windows, affording expansive views of the estate's "sloping grounds of the most pic-

Turn-of-the-last-century doughnut cutter.
LONGYEAR MUSEUM COLLECTION

turesque kind" and the distant Blue Hills.[4] In mild weather, the tall windows ushered in abundant sunshine and passing breezes, keeping the space pleasantly airy and well ventilated. When the days grew colder, a pair of cast iron stoves ensured the room stayed snug. Along with the rest of the house, the kitchen had been equipped with electric lights, ensuring ample illumination in the evenings and in the pre-dawn hours when the staff began their work.

A reporter who toured the house enthused over the kitchen, describing it as "a very large room, 20 feet or more in length, and fitted with all the conveniences and improvements of the most up-to-date hotel's culinary department."[5]

Among the "conveniences" were not one but two stoves—a Vulcan gas range and a state-of-the-art coal or wood-fired Magee Kitchener. Pleasant View had also been equipped with a Magee, but that model paled in comparison to this "mammoth double oven range" that held court from its corner like enthroned royalty.[6]

In addition to the stoves, there was a large double sink under the windows, a separate room for the icebox, and twin pantries at opposite ends of the workspace—one for food storage and the other a butler's or serving pantry that opened onto the dining room and came complete with china cupboards, a dumbwaiter, a silver safe, and an additional pair of sinks. These latter must have come in handy making short work of the mounds of dishes that the steady stream of meals would have produced, especially considering that there was no automatic dishwasher in the home, only the willing hands of those who had come to serve their Leader.

Below: Light floods in through the restored kitchen's tall windows. Overleaf: The kitchen as it appeared, circa 1908. The Magee Double Oven Kitchener is on the right. Longyear Museum collection

Looking through the kitchen to the butler's pantry and dining room beyond. The smaller Vulcan gas range can be seen in the center. | LONGYEAR MUSEUM COLLECTION

"True and loving Scientists"

To serve, yes—but not as servants. "There were no servants," said housekeeper Frances Thatcher. Those called to Pleasant View and later Chestnut Hill were there to "bring out the harmony of the home," she explained. "Some of them may have had servants doing that work for them in their own house, but … they were doing it for the sake of our Leader and to make things comfortable and right."[7]

Cook Margaret Macdonald shed more light on the subject: "Those who took care of Mrs. Eddy's home for her had been workers in the field; they left their practice, nursing, and home duties, church work and relatives, to serve their Leader and friend who had left all for Truth and given up everything that she might give to us and to the whole world a workable knowledge of the healing Truth. And each of us was grateful for the opportunity to serve her, and wish we could have served her better."[8]

Mrs. Eddy, in turn, spoke warmly of her household as "family" and frequently expressed her gratitude for their support. "What a lovely class of students I have about me," she remarked in May 1909. "All reflecting love. Those in the kitchen as well as those here. All are true and loving Scientists."[9]

There were some half a dozen of these "true and loving Scientists" who worked in the kitchen and dining room at various times and in various capacities, including Minnie Scott, Margaret Macdonald, Lula Phillips, Martha Wilcox, and Elizabeth Kelly. Lottie Bowman, wife of coachman Frank Bowman, lent a hand when needed, as did Minnie Weygandt, who cooked at Pleasant View for nearly eight years, and who occasionally filled in at 400 Beacon Street.[10]

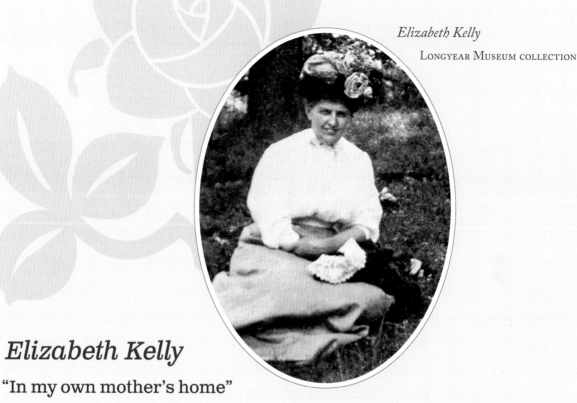

Elizabeth Kelly

LONGYEAR MUSEUM COLLECTION

Elizabeth Kelly

"In my own mother's home"

"From the very beginning of my service in Mrs. Eddy's home, I felt no sense of strangeness," Elizabeth Kelly would recall, "I felt exactly as though I were working in my own mother's home."[11]

Although she officially began her employment with Mrs. Eddy just six months prior to the move to Chestnut Hill, Mrs. Kelly's real preparation for the work started a decade or so earlier, when she'd first learned of Christian Science. After witnessing her brother-in-law's healing of severe headaches, she began to study the new religion, "not to gain healing but to know more about God."[12]

Sought or unsought, healing came.

"I was healed by reading the books," Mrs. Kelly later explained. She found that as she studied the Bible and *Science and Health,* the painful neuralgia from

Elizabeth Kelly reading in her room at 400 Beacon Street. | Longyear Museum collection

which she'd suffered for years vanished.[13] She embraced Christian Science wholeheartedly, writing to The Christian Science Publishing Society in Boston to see if they could share the names of any other students of this new religion in her hometown of Marion, Ohio.

She was put in touch with a local family, and together they began hosting informal church services in their homes. The number of attendees grew, and by 1897 a branch church in Marion was listed in *The Christian Science Journal*. Mrs. Kelly eventually served as a Reader and in the Reading Room.

Widowed in the early 1900s, at some point she also began taking practitioners' patients into her home to help with practical care while they were seeking healing.

Perhaps because of this work, she came to the attention of the Committee on Business. Thomas Hatten traveled to Ohio in the summer of 1907 to interview Mrs. Kelly and her cousin Katharine Retterer. The Committee's report to

Mrs. Eddy noted that Elizabeth, who was 50 and "accustomed to hard work," gave satisfactory answers to all of their questions, and more importantly, "says she owes all to Christian Science and would gladly serve you."[14]

Sometime in the latter part of July, Katharine came to the Reading Room to see Elizabeth. Katharine had received a letter, requesting that the two of them travel to Boston immediately.

"This was on Friday afternoon and we started for Boston Saturday," said Mrs. Kelly.[15]

After further interviews, the cousins passed muster and were sent on to Pleasant View.

"You are a perfect picture of health," Mrs. Eddy told Mrs. Kelly at their first meeting, and then quizzed her on deeper metaphysical points.[16]

The result was that Elizabeth was asked to stay, while her cousin Katharine was not (she'd join the household later). After her cousin returned to Ohio, Mrs. Kelly was left alone in her hotel room, where "the suggestion of homesickness tried to talk pretty strongly because I had never been away from home for any length of time before."

Prayer once again proved effective, however, "and during my stay in Mrs. Eddy's home I was never again troubled with that belief."[17]

Clockwise from left: Calvin Frye, Adam Dickey, Lillian Dickey, Irving Tomlinson, Elizabeth Kelly (standing), William Rathvon, and Ella Rathvon. | Longyear Museum collection

Above: The dining room as it looks today.
Inset: The dining room, circa 1909.
Left to right: Adam Dickey, William Rathvon,
Elizabeth Kelly (standing), Laura Sargent,
Ella Rathvon. | LONGYEAR MUSEUM COLLECTION

"We have missed you, Sister Kelly!"

While at Pleasant View, Mrs. Kelly had worked as the housekeeper's assistant. At 400 Beacon Street, she had new responsibilities. Instead of making beds, sweeping, and dusting, she would be overseeing the dining room.

Mrs. Kelly's workday began early, when she rose at 4:00 a.m. in order to have time to read the Bible Lesson ("never once missed a time," she would later note with satisfaction) before breakfast preparations began at 5:00 a.m. She had a few brief hours of free time in the afternoon—unless it was her turn to listen for the doorbell and the telephone—then was back on duty to help begin preparing for dinner. She and the other staff took turns shutting off the lights in the house each night.[18]

Elizabeth enjoyed her work and was clearly a favorite with her fellow house-hold members, one of whom referred to her as "the smiling Mrs. Kelly."[19] She later recalled "many pleasant memories" of mealtimes at 400 Beacon Street, and would record several pranks that were played in the dining room. Once, when the men were engulfed in loud laughter, she mockingly scolded, "I guess I shall have to send you boys into the kitchen."

William Rathvon countered, "I believe Mrs. Kelly likes the sanctimonious kind, one with a long flowing beard"—and afterward propped a picture of an old man with a flowing beard on the table for her to find.[20]

Elizabeth Kelly (center right) and her cousin Katharine Retterer flanked by chauffeur
Frank Bowman (right) and an unidentified gentleman (left, possibly Irving Tomlinson).
LONGYEAR MUSEUM COLLECTION

When Elizabeth made a month-long visit back to Ohio in the winter of 1910, her absence didn't go unnoticed by her fellow household members, who wrote her a poem:[21]

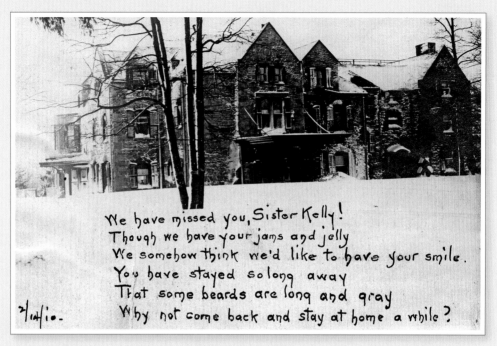

We have missed you, Sister Kelly!
Though we have your jams and jelly
We somehow think we'd like to have your smile.
You have stayed so long away
That some beards are long and gray
Why not come back and stay at home a while?

2/14/10.

Poem and photo sent to Elizabeth Kelly by her colleagues. | Longyear Museum collection

Although her assigned duties didn't bring Mrs. Kelly into daily contact with Mrs. Eddy, the times that she did see and speak with her were memorable.

"I felt such a sense of sweet motherliness and nearness with Mrs. Eddy, there was never any sense of aloofness about her."[22]

Looking back on her years of service, Mrs. Kelly would write, "Many helpful and far-reaching lessons were learned while I was a member of Mrs. Eddy's household, and it always has meant much to me to have been permitted the privilege of this experience."[23] Elizabeth would put those "helpful and far-reaching" lessons to good use when she returned home to Ohio after Mrs. Eddy's passing. Thanks to the new By-law provision that was added to the *Church Manual* in November 1908, Mrs. Kelly became a Christian Science nurse.[24]

"There is a splendid corps in the kitchen at present," noted George Kinter in October 1910, when he was filling in briefly for Adam Dickey.[25]

Most of that "corps" were experienced metaphysicians, chosen not only for their culinary and domestic skills, but also for the quality of thought they would bring to the home's mental atmosphere.

> *"Mrs. Eddy's home was a very practical home. There was nothing mysterious going on, but it was necessary to have around her those who could in a small way understand her mission to the world."*
> *— Martha Wilcox*

"Mrs. Eddy's home was a very practical home," Martha Wilcox would recall. "There was nothing mysterious going on, but it was necessary to have around her those who could in a small way understand her mission to the world."[26]

Especially since that mission often brought waves crashing down on Mrs. Eddy, whether in the form of attacks from the press, challenges to her leadership from within the movement, or resistance to her God-given work — "those things which have been marked out for me to do," as she told a reporter a few months before moving to Chestnut Hill.[27]

She needed the prayerful support of the seasoned Christian soldiers who were called to serve in her home, and in turn, the lessons they learned on the front lines of battle would serve them well in the years ahead.

Margaret Macdonald
LONGYEAR MUSEUM COLLECTION

Margaret Macdonald

"The most profitable period of my life"

"It was not for physical healing that I came to Christian Science, but to find the way out of discord, fear, and discouragement," wrote Margaret Macdonald.[28]

Born and raised in Canada by parents who were native Scots (Miss Macdonald was fluent in Gaelic), she received a strong Christian upbringing in the Presbyterian faith, and often turned to her Bible as a child, opening it at random to seek answers when troubling situations arose.[29]

At 17, she moved to the United States and worked for some years as a nurse and companion. Longing to understand the Scriptures better, she took up the study of Christian Science after a family member was healed of a severe malady by reading *Science and Health*.[30] Margaret was living in Littleton, New Hampshire, when Thomas Hatten came to call. He had been tipped off by a fellow Christian Scientist who spoke highly of Margaret, and who told Mr. Hatten that she was "a very good girl to do work at Pleasant View."[31]

Miss Macdonald was one of the only members of the household who had not had class instruction when she joined the staff in November 1907. When

Mrs. Eddy inquired about her teacher, Margaret replied that she didn't have one yet, but that she "was studying the Bible and *Science and Health,*" along with Mrs. Eddy's other works, with an eye toward that goal. Mrs. Eddy approved this course of action and told her to put what she was learning into practice so that she would "get much more out of class" when the time came.[32]

While at Pleasant View and Chestnut Hill, Miss Macdonald would have plenty of opportunity to do just that. In addition to housekeeping duties and preparing meals for the household, her role was to help the staff whenever she saw a need. Margaret worked hard to fulfill her Leader's charge that she "always demonstrate law and order" in everything that she was doing.[33]

> *"Memories of that happy household bring the assurance of companionship, home, and family, for there is only one family — the household of God, divine Love."*
> *— Margaret Macdonald*

After leaving Mrs. Eddy's employ in the spring of 1910, Margaret would have Primary class instruction and would go on to become a Christian Science practitioner.[34] Harking back to the lessons she learned during her years of service to Mrs. Eddy — years she would refer to as "the most profitable period of my life"[35] — Margaret wrote, "Many lessons learned while there, or partly learned, are still unfolding to my understanding. Often do they strengthen me in times of trouble, uplifting thought above discouragement and fear. Memories of that happy household bring the assurance of companionship, home, and family, for there is only one family — the household of God, divine Love."[36]

Top Left: Mrs. McLellan's "OK" and initials can be seen on this receipt for the Magee stove.
COURTESY OF THE MARY BAKER EDDY COLLECTION. ORIGINAL IN THE MARY BAKER EDDY LIBRARY.
Top right: Jeannette McLellan. | PORTRAIT BY ARTHUR HAZARD, LONGYEAR MUSEUM COLLECTION
Above: Meals were cooked on this Vulcan range (foreground) and a Magee Double Oven Kitchener
similar to the one in the restored kitchen today.

*The kitchen and housekeeping staff took their meals in the kitchen
and in a small sitting room adjacent.*

Feeding the "family"

The task of outfitting the new kitchen fell to Jeannette McLellan, wife of
Archibald McLellan, who, in his capacity as chairman of the Christian Science
Board of Directors, had overseen the purchase and remodeling of the property.
Mrs. McLellan consulted with Mrs. Eddy in the months leading up to the move
and "attended with rare discrimination and good judgment to the furnishing
of the house," wrote a *Boston Globe* reporter who viewed the home.[37] It's her
initials that appear on many receipts, approving such purchases as the new
Magee stove and the many items needed by the kitchen and housekeeping staff.

Page after page of some of these latter receipts give a sense of the scope of the
undertaking, listing everything from egg beaters and pudding pans to dishware,
dusters, brushes and brooms, rolling pins, tea kettles, pots and pans—in short,
everything needed to care for the house and produce the meals that appeared
on the table as regular as clockwork.

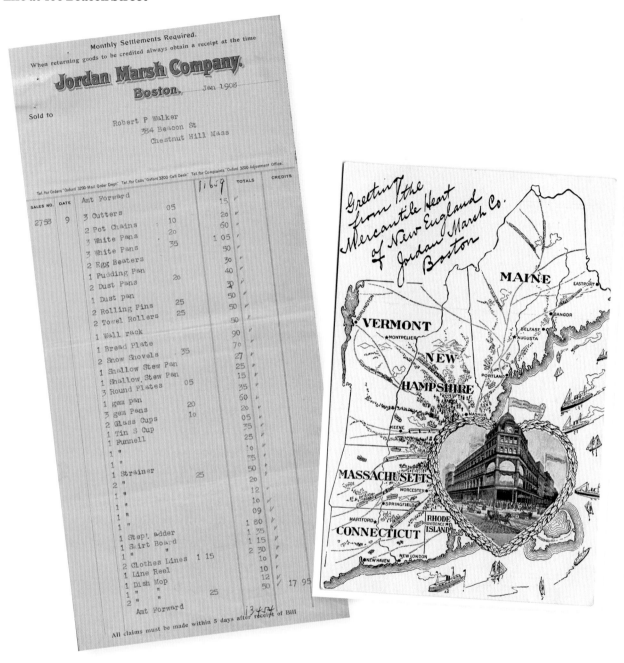

Left: One of the multiple pages of receipts for household items ordered by Mrs. McLellan.

COURTESY OF THE MARY BAKER EDDY COLLECTION. ORIGINAL IN THE MARY BAKER EDDY LIBRARY.

Right: Circa 1908 Jordan Marsh promotional Postcard. | LONGYEAR MUSEUM COLLECTION

Opposite page: Minnie Weygandt subscribed to this culinary magazine. | LONGYEAR MUSEUM COLLECTION

"Everything in the home was done by the clock," observed Lula Phillips, who at 28 was the youngest member of the kitchen staff. "[W]hen the big clock struck seven in the morning the family sat down to breakfast, and when it struck twelve at noon we had dinner, and the same at six in the evening supper was served."[38]

When needed, second seatings ensured a place for everyone at the table. Mrs. Eddy's meals were sent up in the dumbwaiter.[39] The kitchen workers themselves generally ate in the kitchen, and they also had a small sitting room adjacent, complete with a piano reserved for their use.

Lula Phillips

Longyear Museum collection

The food served at Mrs. Eddy's table was generous—"too much so at times," admitted William Rathvon, adding that the meals "tempted one to eat more than was profitable for such sedentary habits as we assumed from necessity."[40]

Mrs. Eddy herself was a good cook, and she expected her meals to be competently—and lovingly—prepared.

"[K]nowing how things ought to be done it naturally made her more particular about the way others did," said Minnie Weygandt. "In order to learn all the newest and best ways of cooking I had brought all my cookbooks with me and subscribed to the Boston Cooking-School magazine," she added, explaining how she would pore through each issue "to see if there was anything new I thought Mrs. Eddy would like."[41]

Minnie B. Weygandt at Pleasant View.
PRIVATE COLLECTION

Minnie Weygandt

"Our work was to patiently uphold her hands"

A fixture at Pleasant View, Minnie Belle Weygandt was not among the household members who traveled on the train from Concord to Chestnut Hill when Mary Baker Eddy moved in January 1908. After nearly eight years of service, she had left Mrs. Eddy's employ just a few months earlier but would return to help out at 400 Beacon Street (and to visit her friends and former colleagues) on several occasions.

First introduced to Christian Science in 1886 in her hometown of Fairfield, Iowa, Miss Weygandt was a sturdy, practical Midwesterner with a dry wit and a keen eye for detail.[42] She grew up in a Lutheran family, and as a young woman witnessed a relative's healing of consumption through Christian Science. Later, while working at a local hotel, she rebuffed her employer's talk about the new religion, declaring that she didn't need it as she was never sick.

"A few weeks after this talk I suddenly came down with about everything there was to have," Minnie commented wryly. It was at this point that she agreed to try Christian Science, "with the result that within half an hour I was absolutely healed."[43]

Minnie and her sisters Sadie and Mary began to read *Science and Health* in earnest. Mary soon began healing others and traveled to Boston in 1894 to have class instruction with Janet Colman. Minnie followed six months later, and she, too, studied with Mrs. Colman. That June, both sisters joined The Mother Church.

Before long, they found themselves working as maid and cook for Edward and Caroline Bates, "two very consecrated Christian Scientists who loved Mrs. Eddy," according to Minnie. The Bateses told her that if Mrs. Eddy ever needed her, she was to "drop everything and go." Minnie would take them at their word when the call came in January 1899 that her services were needed at Pleasant View.[44]

"I remember my sister Mary sat up all night making a new skirt for me, so that I might look my best," Minnie recalled.[45]

Two weeks later, Mary joined Minnie at Pleasant View, and both women would remain faithfully at their posts for years, Mary until her passing in 1904, and Minnie until the fall of 1907.

The Weygandt sisters' salt-of-the-earth work ethic would be put to the test at Pleasant View, where Minnie's main duties were in the kitchen, but where she also helped Mary with the washing, ironing, cleaning, serving, and even sewing.

"When the strain seemed too great and the temptation to complain came, we tried to think of our Leader as Moses, and see that our work was to

Minnie Weygandt (left)
and Adelaide Still
at 400 Beacon Street.

PRIVATE COLLECTION

patiently uphold her hands as his had been upheld," Minnie would write.[46]

After the move to Chestnut Hill in the winter of 1908, Minnie Weygandt was asked to return briefly to help with the ironing. She would be back again later that spring, when she stayed for nearly a month to help out in the kitchen.

"It was my great privilege to know Mrs. Eddy more as a woman, as the wise loving director of a constantly changing and growing household, rather than as a Leader of a great cause," Minnie said, recalling her years at Pleasant View and 400 Beacon Street. "But one could not serve in our Leader's home without comprehending in some degree her greatness, and without realizing the directness and power of her spiritual vision."[47]

Chief among Miss Weygandt's treasures was an 1871 edition of *The Young Housekeeper's Friend* that had been a gift from Mary Baker Eddy. Well-worn and peppered with marginal notations in Mrs. Eddy's handwriting, Minnie assumed it was the one she had used while "keeping house on Broad Street" in Lynn. Minnie made sure to leave it for the cooks who followed her in the Pleasant View and Chestnut Hill kitchens—but was also happy to retrieve it when she later returned to 400 Beacon Street.[48]

The food that was served earned high praise from the members of the household.

"The quality and cooking were of the very best that could be supplied," declared Mr. Rathvon, who had joined the household from his home in Denver, Colorado. "New England dishes were common, some of which were strange to Westerners like myself. I remember once when Calvin Frye, from his end of the

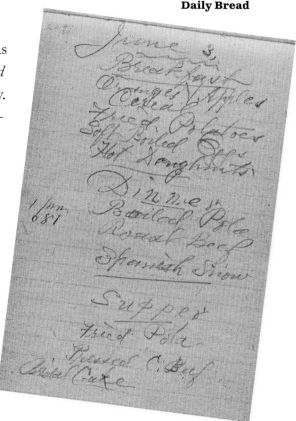

Calvin Frye's handwritten record of the household menu for June 3, 1908. | © The Mary Baker Eddy Collection.
Original in The Mary Baker Eddy Library.
Used with permission.

table, asked me for the first time if I would have some of 'the picked fish,' I replied, 'I certainly will,' though I had no idea what my plate would bring back. It proved to be cod or some other coarse-grained fish, shredded, with cream sauce, and very good."[49]

Dinner was served at noon, and it was substantial—often soup followed by meat or fish of some kind along with a variety of vegetables—and occasionally included such popular menu items of the day as potted pigeon and finnan haddie (a Scottish dish of smoked haddock poached in milk). Regional dishes, including New England boiled dinner (boiled corned beef with vegetables), a favorite of Mrs. Eddy's, also appeared on the table. Suppers tended to be lighter—cold meats, boullion, clam chowder, or perhaps other local specialties like lobster salad or that Yankee Saturday night staple, baked beans and brown bread (which would thriftily reappear on the table the next morning).[50]

"There was no excuse for anyone going hungry," quipped Minnie Weygandt.[51]

Desserts were plentiful and homemade, which must have pleased Irving Tomlinson.[52] The former minister who teasingly called himself "the parson"

"There was no excuse for anyone going hungry."
—Minnie Weygandt

was a bit of an amateur naturalist and "always looking for flowers, birds, and cake frosting," according to Margaret Macdonald, who noted with amusement that Mr. Tomlinson loved to scrape the frosting bowl with his pocket knife.[53] Others appreciated the kitchen's sweet treats as well.

Household accounts list frequent purchases from this local fish purveyor. | Longyear Museum collection

"It had been a custom at Pleasant View to treat the messenger boys bringing telegrams or special delivery letters to an orange, apple or cookie which were kept on [a] small table near [the] side door for that purpose," explained Minnie Scott, "and we continued it at Chestnut Hill to boys delivering the *Monitor* as well as messenger boys."[54]

Local grocer S. S. Pierce, circa 1906.
COURTESY BROOKLINE HISTORICAL SOCIETY

Quincy Market, looking toward Faneuil Hall, circa 1907.

Courtesy of the Bostonian Society

The steady stream of meals that flowed forth from the kitchen required carefully planning. After Minnie Weygandt left, Mrs. Scott was put in charge of ordering food and planning meals.[55] She also did some of the shopping, as is evidenced by regular entries in Calvin Frye's account books. Martha Wilcox, who was on the housekeeping staff, also helped out.

With "a family of seventeen regularly and up to twenty-five at times," according to Martha's tally, it's not surprising that she made two trips to Faneuil Hall Market in downtown Boston each week to buy meat and fish. Most of the other groceries were purchased locally, and in summer "a Greek boy came to the house with fruits and berries and vegetables each day."[56]

Other regular line items document the purchase of such kitchen staples as coal and ice, as well as provisions from Huggard & Polley, a local firm long since vanished into the mists of history, and S. S. Pierce, whose iconic storefront still graces nearby Coolidge Corner in Brookline.

A pair of Jersey cows graze on the estate's lower meadow. They provided a key ingredient in one of Mrs. Eddy's favorite desserts—ice cream!

COURTESY OF THE MARY BAKER EDDY COLLECTION

ORIGINAL IN THE MARY BAKER EDDY LIBRARY

Maple syrup also made a regular appearance in Mr. Frye's accounts, and in August 1908 there was a purchase of 30 quarts of blueberries—perhaps with an eye to preserves for the basement jam closet. Milk for the household came from nearby Wauwinet Farm—at least until early April 1908, when a pair of dairy cows were purchased for the estate.[57]

Minnie Scott

"The right idea of service"

"In my boyhood home the kitchen was a place that always had an attraction for me," wrote William Rathvon, "and so at Chestnut Hill I would often visit the spacious kitchen and pass a friendly word with the faithful workers there, who were all Christian Scientists and with the right idea of service."[58]

Minnie A. Scott was one such worker.

For Minnie, serving in Mrs. Eddy's home was a family affair. Born Mary

Minnie A. Scott | PRIVATE COLLECTION

McCalden in Northern Ireland to Scottish parents, she grew up in the Presbyterian faith and was just 17 when she arrived in Boston. She married Clarence Scott in 1892, and the two became active members of a local Baptist church.[59] Longing to understand the Bible better and curious about the new church they'd watched being built, in 1895 the young couple attended a Friday evening service at the newly-dedicated Mother Church.[60] They were reassured by the familiar Scriptural verses they saw on the walls, impressed by the practical application of some of those verses in the testimonies they heard, and intrigued by the promise of the "Key to the Scriptures" in the Christian Science textbook's title, *Science and Health with Key to the Scriptures.*

"We were both so interested that we wanted to get a copy of the text-book at once," said Mrs. Scott, recalling how an usher took them next door to The Christian Science Publishing Society, where they immediately purchased one. "[T]hree dollars ... seemed quite a little money in those days for us to spend on a book but we certainly never regretted it!"[61]

Minnie read by day; Clarence read after work until late in the evening. The Scotts found that the book did indeed contain the "Key to the Scriptures," opening to them "the promises which before we could not understand, and teaching how we might follow in the steps of our dear Master, and do the works he did."[62]

Neither Minnie nor Clarence had ever heard of people being healed simply by reading the textbook, but this is in fact exactly what happened — he of sciatica and heart trouble, she of the lingering effects of a bad fall through a trap door.

Clarence and Minnie Scott at Pleasant View.
Private collection

195

"As I read the Bible and *Science and Health,* such an abiding sense of the ever-presence of God came, that I forgot about the claims which had troubled me, and one by one they dropped off," wrote Minnie.[63]

The Scotts joined The Mother Church in 1897, and people quickly began coming to Minnie for healing.

By early 1899, she was listed as a practitioner in *The Christian Science Journal.*[64] She and Clarence rented a house near The Mother Church, subleasing several rooms to other Christian Scientists to help defray their own monthly expenses.[65] And then in May 1906, Minnie received a message asking if she could go to Pleasant View to help in Mrs. Eddy's household.[66]

She didn't hesitate.

Neither did Clarence, who put all their belongings in storage and took a furnished room to help support Minnie's efforts. She warmly praised her husband for the role he played, noting that he "did his part lovingly for which credit is due him."[67]

Unsure at first whether she was up to the household tasks assigned to her, Mrs. Scott confided her concerns to Mrs. Eddy. "I told her I had no special training but was glad to help her where I could. . . ."[68]

Mrs. Eddy reminded her that when she was establishing her home in Lynn, she'd had to learn how to run a household, too. Then, said Minnie, she "smilingly added, 'The Scotch have native abilities.'"[69]

Earnestly and lovingly Mrs. Eddy counseled her, "[M]y dear, you are in a better frame of mind to help me than if you felt more competent, and if you will lean on divine Mind as a little child you will be shown just how to do anything I may ask of you. . . ."[70]

Minnie found this to be true. "[I]deas came to me about dainty nourishing dishes that were never found in cookbooks," she wrote, adding that they "must have come to meet the need, humanly, of our beloved Leader who was giving her every moment to bless all mankind."[71]

Eventually, Minnie would go on to cook exclusively for Mrs. Eddy, while Margaret Macdonald cooked for the household. Minnie earned high praise

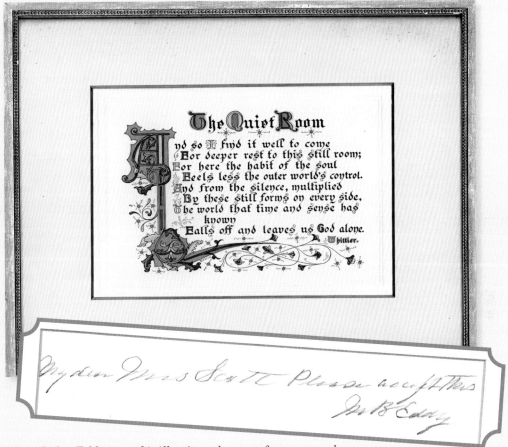

Mary Baker Eddy gave this illuminated stanza from a poem by
John Greenleaf Whittier to Minnie Scott. | LONGYEAR MUSEUM COLLECTION

from her colleagues, including Irving Tomlinson, who called her "an earnest Christian Scientist, who faithfully devoted herself to her Leader's interests."[72]

Minnie Scott was listed as a practitioner in *The Christian Science Journal* for 47 years. Thinking back on her time at Pleasant View and 400 Beacon Street, she would write that Mrs. Eddy's "lovable naturalness, her gentle, sweet appreciation of every little service rendered her, is indeed a happy memory.... To have come so closely in touch with her compassionate love for everyone, her ready forgiveness, her daily practical application of Christ's Sermon on the Mount, I count among my richest blessings."[73]

Images from the restored kitchen at 400 Beacon Street.

Striving to please God

There was more to the kitchen work than just the daily round of grocery shopping and preparing, serving, and cleaning up after meals. As with all of the work undertaken in her home, Mrs. Eddy expected everything to be approached prayerfully.

For example, she impressed upon Ella Rathvon, one of the metaphysical workers, "When ministering your daily tasks, do not think that you have done something through matter, but know that God has done it through Mind."[74]

> *"Don't try to please me, but strive to please God; and when your work is pleasing to Him it will be well done."*
> *— Mary Baker Eddy*

Qualities such as order, economy, and accuracy were prized, and long after her years in Mrs. Eddy's household, Minnie Scott would remember her Leader's "bright glance of approval" that greeted the "punctual, neat, and cheerful worker."[75]

The very first thing that young Lula Phillips learned on the job was order: "You know the saying that 'order is Heaven's first law,' and Mrs. Eddy tried to bring out order and harmony in every little detail. She taught us that bringing out perfection in small things gave us power to manifest Truth and Love and bring out harmony in the larger things of God's universe."[76]

Ultimately, the work had a higher aim. Mrs. Eddy told Margaret Macdonald, "Don't try to please me, but strive to please God; and when your work is pleasing to Him it will be well done."[77]

Haviland & Co. Limoges tableware used by the household. | LONGYEAR MUSEUM COLLECTION

The lessons learned in working for Mrs. Eddy lingered long after service in her household had come to a close.

"Many times after talking with us alone or together she would end by saying, 'now lift your thought to God as you go about your work,'" Mrs. Scott later wrote, adding that "this admonition comes to memory very often with the sound of her voice and is a continual help on the way."[78]

A gracious hostess

Mrs. Eddy delighted in hosting guests. Although they may not have been as frequent during the Chestnut Hill years, and she didn't join them in the dining room, she often invited them up to her study after their meal for a visit.

Martha Wilcox recalled Christian Science practitioner and teacher Bicknell Young being invited to dinner and to see Mrs. Eddy shortly before he taught the Normal class in December 1910. "[W]hen he told Mrs. Eddy that 'that was the best dinner I ever ate,' she expressed just as much satisfaction as any other woman would have done."[79]

Oyster stew was often on the menu when company came, according to Minnie Weygandt,[80] and Margaret Macdonald recollected that Mrs. Eddy always planned the meals for guests herself. "Her favorite was an old-fashioned turkey dinner with all the good things New Englanders used to serve with it."[81] As for dessert, guests were often treated to another of Mrs. Eddy's favorites: Homemade ice cream.

Mary Beecher Longyear

LONGYEAR MUSEUM COLLECTION

That was the case when Mary Beecher Longyear was invited to lunch at Chestnut Hill in January 1910. "If a sovereign had invited me to his house I couldn't have felt more humbly proud," she would later write. "I did not dare reveal the precious secret to any of my family. It was a festive scene that greeted my eyes as I entered. The odor of roses filled the rooms, and smiling faces greeted me. We had a delicious lunch, perfectly cooked and served: there was laughter and joy at the festive board. The luscious strawberries served with the ice cream in the midst of winter filled me with astonishment. The whole scene is impressed indelibly on thought."[82]

Others who came to 400 Beacon Street but didn't stay for a meal also went away impressed. John and Mary Salchow, who lived in the gatehouse on the estate, hosted a friend from New Hampshire one day.

Above: A luncheon guest recalled fresh strawberries served in midwinter. Right: Homemade ice cream, a favorite of Mrs. Eddy's, was made nearly every day in a freezer likely similar to the one pictured in this June 1909 advertisement. Overleaf: The restored kitchen as it appears today.

"We never thought of asking any privilege," Mrs. Salchow explained, but to her surprise and delight, Laura Sargent invited them up to the main house for a private tour. Their visitor was taken all over the house, and "the pantries and kitchen were not overlooked." This friend, "a bright, keen woman of the world, noted everything as she went along; and on coming outdoors stood on the lawn and exclaimed, 'Mary, what is in that house? I never felt anything like it. I never saw the sun shine in any home like it did there. And there seems such a calmness. What is it?'"

Mary Salchow replied that it was "harmony, ever present."[83]

Chapter 8

A "Joyful Noise"

M usic is the rhythm of head and heart," writes Mary Baker Eddy in *Science and Health with Key to the Scriptures*.[1]

By all accounts, music was dear to her heart throughout her life, and just as her writings abound with musical imagery, so Mrs. Eddy's household at 400 Beacon Street often rang with harmonies both vocal and instrumental.[2]

Growing up in rural New England long before the advent of radio or recordings, young Mary Baker lived in a world where music was nevertheless part of the fabric of life. From cradle lullabies to communal hymns at Sunday worship to homemade entertainment with family and friends, music wove through her days like a silver thread, tracing down the decades from her birthplace in Bow, New Hampshire, to her final residence on the outskirts of Boston.

Some of Mrs. Eddy's fondest memories were musical ones. Later in life, for example, she would recall the comforting verse of a hymn her mother, Abigail Baker, sang to her as a little girl before bed:

> *How can I sleep while angels sing,*
> *And hover o'er my bed;*
> *And clap their wings in joy to Him*
> *Who is their glorious Head.*[3]

There was another of her mother's songs that she would remember as well. Clara Shannon, a vocalist by training who was healed by reading *Science and Health* and left her singing career for the Christian Science practice, tells of an evening when she was working at Pleasant View and Mrs. Eddy rang for her.

"I want you to open my door half-way and stand outside," Mrs. Eddy told Clara. "I want to sing you something that my mother used to sing to me, and, knowing that your profession was singing, I feel too shy to sing while you look at me."

Clara did as she was asked.

"Then she sang so sweetly, in a high soprano voice, the old fashioned song named, *Come to My Bower Sweet Bird*. . . .That was a wonderful experience in the quiet hours of the night, and, in memory, that voice still comes back."[4]

Abigail Baker wasn't the only family member to share songs that left a deep impression on Mrs. Eddy.

"My brother [Albert] had a beautiful tenor voice and people would come miles to hear him sing," she would tell another of her students many years later. "I remember his singing in the crowded parlor, and one song especially, 'Comin' Thro' the Rye,' was a favorite. His voice is as clear in my memory now as when I heard him singing in those olden days."[5]

Right: This traditional song was sung frequently in Mrs. Eddy's household.

Courtesy Library of Congress

Nº 244
Dep. July 10. 1852
A. Fiot
Piano

COMIN' THRO' THE RYE

SCOTISH BALLAD

As Sung by MAD^{elle} JENNY LIND. Arranged for the Guitar, by F. WEILAND.

R.M. Cam. Eng?

Philadelphia, A. FIOT 196 Chesnut St

Entered according to Act of Congress, in the Year 1852, by A. Fiot in the Clerks Office of the District Court of the Eastern District of Pa.

Gin a bo_dy meet a bo_dy, Comin' thro' the rye; Gin a bo_dy kiss a bo_dy Need a bo_dy cry! Il_ka las_sie has her laddie, Nane they say ha'e I, Yet a' the lads they

Mrs. Eddy told that same student of an occasion when a composer came to visit the Bakers and heard singing in the next room. "That is beautiful music and I must have it," he said to Mary's father, Mark Baker. When the musician continued to press Mr. Baker for a copy of the melody, he explained that he couldn't give it to him, because it was his daughter Mary singing, and "she is spinning that music out of her own little self."

"Even then my entire being seemed attuned to harmony," Mrs. Eddy remarked.[6]

Later, as a young widow living in her parents' home in Tilton, New Hampshire, desperately seeking some means of supporting herself and her young son, Mary Baker Glover briefly considered giving piano lessons.

"I feel as if I must <u>begin</u> something this summer, if my health is sufficient," she wrote to her sister Martha in 1848. "I want to learn to play on a piano so that I can go south and teach. Tis all I shall ever be <u>able</u> to do, and this <u>once</u> accomplished and I am independent. . . . O how I wish I had a <u>father</u> that had been <u>ever</u> willing to let me know something."[7]

"We had a pleasant little number in last evening to sing and play the piano. . . ."
— Mary Baker Eddy

Alas, there was no money forthcoming from Mark Baker for either a piano or the lessons to learn how to play it. There was still some musical solace, however, as one biographer mentions a circle of local friends who enjoyed gathering for "sings," including Mary's brother George; Mary's friend and eventual sister-in-law, Mathy Rand; Reverend Richard Rust; and John Bartlett, to whom Mary would become engaged.[8]

It wouldn't be until decades later, possibly as early as Lynn but certainly after she moved to Columbus Avenue in Boston, that Mrs. Eddy would finally have a piano of her own. While most of her time was occupied with work at the Massachusetts Metaphysical College, there were occasional opportunities for musical entertainment.

"We had a pleasant little number in last evening to sing and play the piano, and the hours passed swiftly," she wrote to one of her students in the fall of 1882.[9]

Julia Bartlett, who worked closely with Mrs. Eddy during those years at the College, also remembered musical gatherings.

"We had very happy, restful times together when Mrs. Eddy would sometimes come with us in the parlor after the day's work and we listened to her sweet voice

This upright grand piano graced the Pink Room at Chestnut Hill.

while she sang hymns or some sacred song with Mr. Frye accompanying her on the piano."[10]

It's unclear whether Mrs. Eddy took that particular piano with her in 1889 when she left Boston for a rented house at 62 North State Street in Concord, New Hampshire, but she definitely brought along her love of music, even singing soprano in a home quartet while living there.[11]

A new piano—a fine upright grand from local Concord manufacturer Prescott

*Left: Sepia print of
Chickering Hall, circa 1890.
Christian Science services
were held in the second-floor
venue during the movement's
early days, and Lyman Foster
Brackett, editor of the first
Christian Science hymnal,
had a teaching studio here.*

LONGYEAR MUSEUM COLLECTION

The parlor grand piano was purchased from Chickering & Sons in Boston.

LONGYEAR MUSEUM COLLECTION

Piano & Organ Company—features prominently in photographs of Pleasant View. The instrument would accompany the household when Mrs. Eddy moved to Chestnut Hill.

In fact, there were three pianos at 400 Beacon Street, as well as a Victrola, a music box, and a player piano of sorts called a "pianola."

One of the pianos was in the staff sitting room off the kitchen. The Prescott was placed upstairs in the Pink Room,[12] while a brand-new six-foot "parlor grand" was purchased for the downstairs parlor. Made of mahogany with claw-and-ball feet, this handsome instrument and its matching bench were purchased for Mrs. Eddy from Chickering & Sons in Boston, widely considered one of the finest piano manufacturers of the day.

The company also operated Chickering Hall, a concert venue on the second floor of their showroom that hosted early Christian Science services (1885-1894).[13] Located on Tremont Street across from Boston Common, Chickering & Sons was part of Boston's famous "piano row," a district of leading piano makers and showrooms in the late 19th and early 20th century.[14] Steinert & Sons on Boylston Street, builder of Steinway pianos used in concert halls around the world, is the sole remaining business from that era and continues the tradition today.

When Mrs. Eddy moved back to the Boston area in January of 1908, it was the "golden age" of piano building and sales.[15] Between 1870 and 1925, increasing numbers of people looked to the piano as a form of entertainment in their homes, and many more learned how to play than do today. In addition, the player piano became popular toward the end of this era, allowing listeners to hear music that most could never master themselves.

An Aeolian pianola was purchased for the home in March 1909. Not quite a player piano, but rather a "piano player," it could be rolled up to a piano's keyboard, where its extension-like "fingers" would play tunes generated from a selection of paper rolls.[16] These selections were prime examples of music that was difficult for most individuals to play and included classical performances seldom heard outside of a concert hall.

Clockwise from above left: Mrs. Eddy's pianola in front of the keyboard of the parlor grand piano; Nellie Eveleth seated at the pianola while Irving Tomlinson looks on; Pianola roll for Benjamin Godard's "Second Mazurka, Op. 54." | LONGYEAR MUSEUM COLLECTION

In addition to the pianos and pianola, there was also a music box. Given to Mrs. Eddy in 1897 by her student Laura Lathrop and Laura's son, John, the beautiful piece made the move with the household from Pleasant View to Chestnut Hill, where it graced a corner of the dining room.[17] One of the songs it played was *Then You'll Remember Me*, later described as one of Mrs. Eddy's favorites by an acquaintance of her granddaughter, Mary Baker Glover Billings.[18]

Mrs. Eddy's music box and music disc for "Then You'll Remember Me," said to be one of her favorite melodies. Detail shows song title on disc. | Longyear Museum collection

Musical interludes

"Musicals comprise a frequent means of divertisement and entertainment," George Kinter wrote to a friend, while filling in for one of Mrs. Eddy's secretaries in October 1910. "Sometimes we are all asked to join, but oftenest it is a solo or more by one of the ladies who sings and plays well; the Victrola is now in the pink parlor and is frequently brought into requisition."[19]

Although the household's work in support of the Cause of Christian Science and its Leader was tireless and ongoing, Mrs. Eddy encouraged her staff to take time for refreshment. Music often featured prominently in this endeavor.

John Salchow described a recurring scene where some of the household's musical talents were on display: "Often after Mrs. Eddy returned from her drive, the members of the family would gather in the Pink Room and sing for Mrs. Eddy. Mrs. Rathvon with her beautiful soprano, Mrs. Sargent singing good alto, Mr. Frye with his surprisingly good tenor and Mr. Dickey's fine bass made a splendid quartet. Whenever I could get a chance, I would stop outside after Mrs. Eddy had gone upstairs and listen. Usually they sang one or more hymns."[20]

Sometimes there were musical interludes earlier in the day as well, after the morning duties were completed.

Household members would be invited into the Pink Room for a "service of song," according to

From top: Ella Rathvon, Laura Sargent, Calvin Frye, and Adam Dickey. | Longyear Museum collection

Early edition of the Christian Science Hymnal.

LONGYEAR MUSEUM COLLECTION

Irving Tomlinson. One of the group would accompany them on the piano, while the others would sing some of Mrs. Eddy's favorite hymns, ranging from well-loved gospel tunes to selections from the *Christian Science Hymnal* or other Christian hymnaries, including Moody and Sankey's.[21] According to William Rathvon, Mrs. Eddy frequently sang along, "and her voice was sweet and clear as a bell."[22]

Ella Rathvon, who joined her husband at 400 Beacon Street in the fall of 1909 as a metaphysical worker, kept a record of all the songs that were sung for Mrs. Eddy during her tenure in the home and how often each one was requested. Among the hymns topping the list were *Watchman Tell Us of the Night; Jesus, Lover of My Soul; Onward Christian Soldiers; I Love to Tell the Story;* and *Guide Me, O Thou Great Jehovah.*[23]

First translated into English in 1771, the Welsh hymn *Guide Me, O Thou Great Jehovah* was likely learned by Mrs. Eddy as a child and is particularly significant in that it was the hymn she recited aloud on her first visit to the The Mother Church.[24] It appears as Hymn 90 in today's *Christian Science Hymnal*, with two alterations by Mrs. Eddy to the original words. Always seeking to uplift traditional theology with the leaven of Christian Science, she replaced the phrase "I am weak, and Thou art mighty" with "I am Thine, and Thou are mighty"; and at the end of the first verse she chose a phrase from the *Wesleyan Hymnal*—"Feed me now and evermore"—instead of "Feed me till I want no more."[25]

Mary Baker Eddy's edits weren't confined to language—she took a keen interest in the melodies as well, especially those to which her own poems were set.[26] Mr. Rathvon recounted an illustration of this from the time of the *Hymnal* revision in 1909.

"When it was all ready to go to press, no tune was found for her poem 'Mother's Evening Prayer' that was wholly satisfactory to her," he explained. Eventually, the melody "Morecambe," today's Hymn 207, was settled upon. "As she desired to have the music of her hymn conform as far as possible to the sentiment of the words, she changed the last line of the first stanza so that the notes for the words 'on upward wing tonight' would ascend instead of descend as originally written.... This change was made, and it so appears in the present edition of the *Hymnal*."[27]

A joyful noise

Hymns weren't the only music to resound through the halls of 400 Beacon Street. The household enjoyed listening to and singing popular songs as well, and so did Mrs. Eddy.

Biographer Lyman Powell writes, "With her lovely voice often, in those later years, she joined her household in singing such old favorite songs as *Auld Lang Syne, Comin' Through the Rye, Annie Laurie,* and *The Old Oaken Bucket....*"[28]

In September 1910, Mrs. Eddy gave Ella Rathvon a compilation titled "Home Songs."

Ella Rathvon received a songbook similar to this one as a gift from Mrs. Eddy. | Longyear Museum collection

The gift had been bound in leather and included a loving inscription from Mrs. Eddy.

Many songs listed in the table of contents were sung at Chestnut Hill, and a few are still fairly well known today, including *Home Sweet Home*, *My Old Kentucky Home*, and *Way Down Upon the Swanee River*. Not as frequently sung, but interesting in that their appearance on Mrs. Rathvon's list illustrates the diversity in the household's tastes, are *Good Night Ladies*, *The Star-Spangled Banner*, and *Listen to the Mockingbird*.[29]

In addition to singing with and for Mary Baker Eddy, some of the staff also enjoyed entertaining themselves with music.

William Rathvon paints an amusing vignette of good-natured camaraderie amongst members of an otherwise serious and purposeful household, recalling evenings when "the five of us — Mrs. Hoag, Mr. Dickey, Mr. Tomlinson, my wife, and I — would go down to the sitting room adjoining the kitchen and there sing together with Mrs. Hoag or Mrs. Rathvon at the piano.

"What our voices lacked in melody, they surely made up in volume. . . . Mrs. Hoag and Mrs. Rathvon sang soprano. Mr. Dickey stumbled along under a heavy load of bass, while I clawed the scales toward the high notes, trying to contribute a

From top: Ella Hoag, Adam Dickey, Irving Tomlinson, and William and Ella Rathvon.

LONGYEAR MUSEUM COLLECTION

Above: Logo from Mrs. Eddy's Victrola.

Right: Victor record needles and needle tin.

LONGYEAR MUSEUM COLLECTION

thin tenor, and the Reverend (as we called Mr. Tomlinson) wobbled around in every direction. If we didn't make music, we certainly did produce a joyful noise."[30]

The choir invisible

Ever the teacher, at times music—both sacred and secular—prompted instruction from Mrs. Eddy. Early student Clara Choate told of one such instance back in the 1880s, after the Eddys had given up their home in Lynn and were temporarily living in Boston with Clara and her family. Music provided "a sunny vein amid the shadows" for Mrs. Eddy, who was often burdened with work for the growing Christian Science movement. As Clara recounted, "She once rebuked us all for singing 'In the sweet bye and bye' so much, and tried to have us realize the 'now' of things." Clara added that Mrs. Eddy told them, "Here and now God was, is, and ever will be."[31]

At 400 Beacon Street, such tutelage continued. In November 1909, the household's original "Victor talking machine," given to Mrs. Eddy by Mary Beecher Longyear in 1905, was traded in for a newer model.[32]

Like the pianola, the Victrola could provide a quality of music superior even to the talents of Mrs. Eddy's considerably talented household. She was quite taken with the record player, calling it the "most wonderful of inventions!"[33] Mr. Tomlinson noted that she took "keen pleasure in a few of the recordings by leading musicians."[34]

One day in February, Mrs. Eddy asked her household to sing along with a recording of *Home Sweet Home* for her. As the last strain died away, William Rathvon observed Mrs. Eddy displaying what he called her "natural playfulness" by talking back to the voice on the Victrola. What did she say? "Thank you, Mr. Singer Man, but I prefer my own choir to the choir invisible."

Mary Baker Eddy listened to this recording of "Home Sweet Home," featuring tenor Harry Macdonough.

LONGYEAR MUSEUM COLLECTION

Then, turning serious, she gave a spiritual lesson on the subject of home to those present: "Home is not a place, it is a power," she told them. "Going home is doing right. If you cannot make a home here, you cannot anywhere. I am glad all of you, so many, are going with me homeward, and we will all meet there. Blessings immortal, eternal, infinite, come not through personality, but through understanding Principle."[35]

"The home of Soul, where sense has no claims and soul is satisfied."

— Mary Baker Eddy

A couple of months later, on April 21, 1910, the same song prompted further instruction, when Mrs. Eddy told her household, "The home of Soul, where sense has no claims and soul is satisfied."[36]

For one who cherished home as "the dearest spot on earth," music, with all of its memories and meaning, appears to have played an important and unique role in contributing both to the household's happiness and her own.[37]

Singing for Mrs. Eddy

Mary Baker Eddy's household members weren't the only ones to sing with and for her. "On a few occasions," recalled Irving Tomlinson, "the soloist of The Mother Church and other Scientists who were well known singers came to Mrs. Eddy's home and sang for her enjoyment."[38]

Not everyone who was invited to perform for Mrs. Eddy was able to come—and not everyone was invited!

According to William Rathvon, "Offers to sing for our Leader have time and again been made … but as often have been declined with thanks. Why? For one or both of two reasons: our Leader has shunned the intrusion

Marcia Craft, early soloist for The Mother Church.

LONGYEAR MUSEUM COLLECTION

Frank Leonard | Courtesy of
The Mary Baker Eddy Collection
Original in The Mary Baker Eddy Library

of every outside thought, and because many of the offers have not been wholly unselfish. The advertisement would be worth much to some."[39]

One who was deemed "wholly unselfish" was Frank Leonard, who in the spring of 1909 was invited to Chestnut Hill. The son of Mrs. Eddy's student Pamelia Leonard, Mr. Leonard had been healed of a serious heart condition that had consigned him to chronic invalidism as a young man.[40]

"I well remember that first treatment!" he would later write of his "last resort" visit to a Christian Science practitioner. "I was not a believer in any sense, so that the spectacle of a woman sitting with her eyes closed for a few moments, with the idea that she could help me, seemed, at the time, farcical and absurd."

That night, though, he rested for the first time in many months, "and in the morning the ridicule had departed and I realized that I stood in the presence of a great Power."[41] The healing progressed rapidly, and within three months Frank was completely restored to health.

He would cross paths with Mrs. Eddy numerous times in the coming decades, beginning in the fall of 1884, when he accompanied his mother to the Massachusetts Metaphysical College.

"I remember . . . the wonderful tenderness of both eyes and voice as [Mrs. Eddy] greeted me, and then, too, how I felt that she had looked right through me and knew all my thoughts," he would recall. "Then she talked to some who were there about God, and I was spellbound, because I had been afraid of God, and what she said made me love Him."[42]

He would also visit her later on at Pleasant View, after his mother was called to help Mrs. Eddy. "[W]ith my maturer years, I gained some conception of the scope of the work she was inspired to do and what a tireless worker she was."[43]

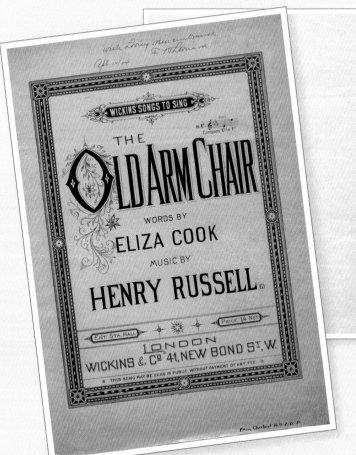

Mr. Leonard signed this sheet music,
"with loving remembrance," on April 14, 1909,
the day he sang for Mrs. Eddy.
COURTESY OF THE MARY BAKER EDDY COLLECTION
ORIGINAL IN THE MARY BAKER EDDY LIBRARY

On April 14, 1909, Mr. Leonard found himself on the doorstep of 400 Beacon Street at Mrs. Eddy's invitation. By now he was a Christian Science practitioner, teacher, and lecturer — in fact, he had just given a lecture the previous evening in Rockland, Maine.[44] The household was called in to join them in the Pink Room, and Leonard sang several selections for Mrs. Eddy, including "an old time favorite of her mother's which she had known in her childhood days, entitled *Napoleon's Grave*."[45]

At her request, he also sang *The Old Armchair, Home Sweet Home, I'm a Pilgrim and I'm a Stranger*, and *Eternity*. Then he finished with one of his own choosing: Mrs. Eddy's poem "'Feed My Sheep.'"

As he sang her poem, "Mrs. Eddy sat in rapt attention" with a smile on her face, observed Irving Tomlinson. Afterwards, she applauded, thanking her guest heartily and telling him that he "would be of great service to the world."[46]

Indeed he would. Frank Leonard would continue healing and teaching and would travel the world lecturing on Christian Science for nearly two more decades.

Marcia Craft in the organ loft of the Original Edifice of The Mother Church. Albert Conant is seated at the keyboard. | Longyear Museum collection

A "richly deserved" fame

The most well-known vocalist to sing for Mrs. Eddy was Marcia Craft, an accomplished young soprano who served as soloist at The Mother Church.[47] Mrs. Eddy called her "our sweet singer."[48]

While Mrs. Eddy was living at Pleasant View, Marcia had performed a concert with the Philharmonic Orchestra at White's Opera House in downtown Concord. Although Mrs. Eddy was unable to attend, she sent flowers, which were presented to Miss Craft across the footlights.[49]

Marcia was a friend of Laura Sargent's and, according to Mr. Rathvon, a "faithful little Scientist." When Mrs. Sargent heard that Miss Craft was leaving the country to accept a five-year contract with the Royal Opera House in Munich, Germany, she very much wished that Mrs. Eddy could have a chance to hear the young woman before she left.

On August 31, 1909, just before Marcia's ship sailed for Europe, Laura Sargent's wish was granted. An invitation was extended, and Irving Tomlinson and Adam Dickey set off in the White Steamer to whisk Miss Craft to Chestnut Hill. After a private visit with Laura, Marcia was taken to the downstairs parlor, where she sang for the household. Ella Hoag accompanied her on the piano.

"She sings artistically, earnestly, and with honesty," was William Rathvon's assessment, "and I liked her talk even better than her songs which is saying much."[50]

Finally, at three o'clock, it was time to sing for Mrs. Eddy.

"We all trooped upstairs," wrote Mr. Rathvon, "including the laundress from the basement."[51]

Calvin Frye was waiting at the head of the stairs, and after being introduced to him, Miss Craft was ushered down the hall to the Pink Room.

"I have a vivid picture of the Pink Room that day with our Leader seated in state in her new black and white gown, and Ada [Adelaide Still] standing behind her chair which was facing the piano," Rathvon continued. "Marcia was presented and soon was deep in 'Hear ye, Israel,' with Mrs. Hoag accompanying her."

Marcia Craft as Madame Butterfly.
LONGYEAR MUSEUM COLLECTION

Only Adam Dickey and Calvin Frye joined the women inside the room. The rest of the household listened and watched from the open doorway and along the hall.

"After one high sustained note our Leader applauded," Rathvon recalled, and afterward, Mrs. Eddy told the young woman, "You richly deserve all the fame you have received."

When Miss Craft left the room after finishing her song, said Rathvon, "her eyes were filled with tears." She was given a tour of the house, and on leaving, said, "I shall never forget this day."[52]

Later that year, just before Christmas, Miss Craft would write to Mrs. Eddy from Munich: "Dear Mrs. Eddy:—The day after I was at your home and had the great honor and privilege of singing for you, I left for Europe. Since arriving here I have been plunged into all manner of activity, and the days have flown by on wings. I have often wanted to write to you, but have felt that I ought not to take even one moment of your time and attention, unless in that moment I could do something for you. Now I realize that not to have sent you a written acknowledgment of the treasure you sent me—the dear copy of *Science and Health*,—was an unintentional rudeness on my part, though I feel you must have known the joy it brought to me, and the gratitude and appreciation which daily rise from my heart to you. That you should have thought of me is an honor never to be forgotten; that I could give you a moment's pleasure is a joy treasured in memory."[53]

Chapter 9

Calvin Frye's Day Off

he reader must not think that there was never anything but work of a strenuous kind at Chestnut Hill," wrote Adam Dickey. "There were days, and even weeks, when the clouds seemed to lift and the workers in the home had time for self-advancement, and even for some little recreation."[1] Irving Tomlinson agreed, noting that "the members of Mrs. Eddy's household lived a normal and happy life."[2]

That sense of normalcy included the odd hour here and there for sports and hobbies, walks and drives, a bit of self-improvement—such as a grammar class that was organized at one point for those eager to improve their English—even vacations.[3] Always at the forefront of each staff member's thought, however, was their top priority: being on hand to help Mrs. Eddy.

"[N]ever was there a moment when we did not hold ourselves in readiness to assume any additional duties that might arise," Mr. Tomlinson explained.[4]

Perhaps it was the extra hands at 400 Beacon Street making lighter work, for in a letter to a friend written in the fall of 1910, George Kinter, who was filling in as a secretary, noticed a marked change in the household routine from when he worked at Pleasant View, including "the increasing release of pressure upon those in attendance. . . . [T]he folks disport themselves in manners and fashions unknown in days of yore."[5]

Leisure time may have been more abundant during the Chestnut Hill years, but it still depended on one's given assignment. Housekeepers and kitchen workers often had a short stretch to themselves in the afternoons. Evenings might bring a quiet hour to spend with a book, or in shared conversation, or for a musical interlude. On Sunday mornings and Wednesday evenings, those whose schedules allowed were often free to attend church services, "another innovation and one much appreciated by the help," according to Mr. Kinter.[6]

For the secretarial staff, one opportunity for recreation was before Mrs. Eddy arrived in her study each morning. All of the secretaries owned bicycles, and John Salchow remembers seeing them occasionally start off on an early ride together. As a rule, however, he noted, "they, like the rest of the family, were too busy to indulge in much personal pleasure, so that these intermittent opportunities were always appreciated."[7]

Merrily we roll along

It was Mrs. Eddy herself who suggested that the household use the hour when she was on her carriage ride for their refreshment, with the provision that two would remain behind in the house ("thus we took turns," Elizabeth Kelly explained).[8]

William Rathvon described the household "scattering on their outings" after the noon meal, with one popular choice being to go "motoring," with Mrs. Eddy's blessing.[9]

A group of Mary Baker Eddy's household workers sets off on an outing in the White Steamer.
Adam Dickey is at the wheel; his wife, Lillian, is beside him. In the back (left to right) are
William Rathvon, Laura Sargent (with parasol), and Ella Rathvon. | Longyear Museum collection

"All of you go out in the automobile when I go out if you care to," she told Adam Dickey, and she conveyed a similar message to other staff members.[10]

Automobiles were still a novelty in 1908, so when one was delivered to 400 Beacon Street that May, there was keen interest in it, particularly amongst the men in the household. Their excitement was short-lived, however.

"Had engaged to buy [a] Columbia Electric car," Calvin Frye reported in his diary, "but on its arrival the 'kids' made such a fuss over trying to monopolize it . . . that I refused to take it and Mr. Neal took it away."[11]

> ## "All of you go out in the automobile when I go out if you care to."
> ## —Mary Baker Eddy

Eventually, even Calvin would relent, and by mid-September of that year, two White Steam cars had been purchased for the estate — a limousine intended for Mrs. Eddy's use, and a touring car for the household. By the following summer, the touring car was traded in for a model that seated up to seven passengers.

Coachman and chauffeur Frank Bowman had never driven an automobile before coming to work for Mrs. Eddy, but when he was interviewed by the Committee on Business, he assured them that his college-aged son, Robert, had. Presumably, some father-son driving lessons took place prior to Mr. Bowman's arrival at Chestnut Hill.[12]

Amongst the rest of the staff, John Salchow taught Adam Dickey how to drive, and Irving Tomlinson recalled William Rathvon instructing him on the smaller Ford "runabout" (Model T) that was eventually purchased for household errands.[13]

These afternoon motoring adventures were by necessity short, as all hands were due back on deck by the time Mrs. Eddy's carriage returned.

Above: Out for a spin on a fine day (left to right): Chauffeur Frank Bowman, Lula Phillips, Adelaide Still, Katharine Retterer, Elizabeth Kelly, Martha Wilcox.
Longyear Museum collection

Right: A cheerful group sets off from 400 Beacon Street. Left to right: Ella Rathvon, Irving Tomlinson, William Rathvon, Ella Hoag.
Longyear Museum collection

Take me out to the ball game

With so much of their time and effort focused on the work indoors, it's not surprising that, when it came to recreation, many in the household headed outside, again with Mrs. Eddy's approval.

"It was also her wish that each worker should go for a ride every day, or have some opportunity to be out of doors," said cook Margaret Macdonald, who noted that, in addition to the automobile outings, "some of us often went riding in the carriage when the horses were exercised."[14]

"It was also her wish that each worker should go for a ride every day, or have some opportunity to be out of doors."
— Margaret Macdonald

The staff explored the expansive grounds and neighborhood on foot, enjoyed the formal garden, and on at least one occasion played a round of golf.[15] There was even thought given to adding a tennis court to the property at one point, although nothing ever came of it.[16]

Several also participated in America's favorite pastime.

"After dinner the men would sometimes play ball on the front lawn, and the team . . . was playfully called The Chestnut Hill Doves," Margaret recalled.[17]

Ella Rathvon was a fan of the game as well and enjoyed playing catch with her husband and "running after stray balls which Irving [Tomlinson] has knocked too far" for William to catch.[18]

There were conflicting opinions as to what Mrs. Eddy thought of these household athletics. According to William Rathvon, she was interested. One evening, he and Ella and Adam Dickey made a point of playing catch by her window, after which Adam performed several stunts, including walking on his hands.

"It was an immense success," William would record in his diary. "When afterwards we went upstairs, we found our audience pleased to the point of mild excitement, and we were complimented on our nimbleness and proficiency."[19]

Calvin Frye's diary tells a completely different story. According to him, "the result was a very disturbed night and a fear she could not live!"[20] These kinds of differing viewpoints seem to reflect the old guard/new guard division in the household.

Outdoor activity continued year round. In addition to sleighing, Mr. Rathvon wrote of playing baseball "even while it snows upon us," and the hardy Coloradan and Irving Tomlinson also ventured out on skates on occasion.[21]

When the weather was fine, the local flora and fauna proved a big draw.

"Within ten minutes' walk of the Chestnut Hill residence, one worker identified one hundred and forty varieties of wild flowers," Mr. Tomlinson would recall (likely speaking of himself, as Margaret Macdonald noted that, on one

Ella Rathvon looks on as her husband, William, shows off his skating skill.

LONGYEAR MUSEUM COLLECTION

April day, he was "out for an hour and brought back seventy-five varieties of wild flowers").[22]

Birdwatching was also popular.

"Often we would look out on the rear lawn to see what new bird notes we were hearing, but to find only some of the men imitating birds which they wished to attract, and often brought them to the lawn answering their calls," said Margaret.[23]

William Rathvon was a keen birder and recorded some 60 species in 1909—including "permanent residents," "summer boarders," and "transient guests," among other categories—and Irving Tomlinson, again presumably speaking about himself, observed that one worker's vest pocket diary for 1910 topped that with 90 different birds spotted.

It was Mr. Rathvon who sent off to Pennsylvania for several birdhouses in the spring of 1910, including a large martin house that was mounted on the back lawn on a tall pole and was clearly visible from his third-floor bedroom window. In a lively correspondence with the birdhouse purveyor, William noted the winged comings and goings:

Other feathered visitors we had in abundance, but of martins, not one. Perhaps there are none in the habit of visiting this section although we have almost everything else that wears feathers. Anyway we will not call our attempt a failure for we have had quite a little diversion in watching the antics of the various little chaps with bills and claws and tails and wings, who investigated the premises with view of renting for the season. A pair of tree swallows had serious intentions and several couples of blue birds made a daily inspection of several of the apartments for nearly two weeks. Finally they chose two of the boxes bought from you, stopped flirting with the-white-house-on-the-pole and went to raising blue birds. They succeeded, and today at the close of September three of them, youngsters probably, are piping musically from the roof of the very little house their Paws and Maws rejected earlier in the season. . . .[24]

William Rathvon's bird book and 1909 list of species spotted.

LONGYEAR MUSEUM COLLECTION

Above: The birdhouse that William Rathvon ordered was a focal point in the backyard.
LONGYEAR MUSEUM COLLECTION

Camera in hand, Irving Tomlinson coaxes Spike with a treat.

LONGYEAR MUSEUM COLLECTION

In addition to feathered visitors, there was also one in a fur coat, a "disreputable looking" grey squirrel, who appeared one day begging for food, according to Margaret Macdonald. Christened "Spiketail," due to the sorry state of that appendage, she quickly became the darling of the household, who fattened her up and rejoiced when her fur grew back.[25] Duly rechristened just plain "Spike," the gentle, friendly creature loved to hunt for treats in the gentlemen's coat pockets—and to pose for photographs!

Fortunately for future generations, photography was one of the hobbies pursued by a number of staff members, including Minnie Weygandt, John Salchow, Calvin Frye, William Rathvon, and Irving Tomlinson. They photographed the house inside and out, the gardens and grounds, each other, and they even, on occasion, photographed themselves.

William Rathvon experimented with double exposure to create this photograph of himself in his room at 400 Beacon Street (note the string in his hands to activate the camera). He titled it "Rathvon talking to Rathvon!" | Longyear Museum collection

Starry nights

"The stars make night beautiful," Mary Baker Eddy writes in *Science and Health*.[26] Her household could attest to that.

On warm nights, seeking cooler air, some of them headed up the short, steep flight of stairs that led from the third floor to the cupola, and from there onto a flat part of the mansion's roof.

"As the house was on a hill they had a wide expanse of the heavens before them and on cloudless nights could clearly see the stars," said Irving Tomlinson. "This led them to become interested in the constellations and planets...."[27]

Above: Rooftop of 400 Beacon Street (note railing around viewing platform).
Longyear Museum collection

Right: Newspapers ran extensive coverage of Halley's comet in 1910. Boston Globe *(top), May 19, 1910;* Chicago Tribune, *May 27, 1910.*

Mrs. Eddy purchased a telescope, similar to the one pictured here, for the stargazers in her household. The cupola and roof, pictured above as they appear today, provided the perfect vantage spot.

Their interest was conveyed by Adam Dickey to Mrs. Eddy, who promptly purchased one of the best telescopes of the day, a four-inch Alvan Clark model.[28]

"We all became quite interested in astronomy," recalled John Salchow, listing Nellie Eveleth and Laura Sargent among those who ventured up on the roof from time to time.[29] Mr. Tomlinson added that Adelaide Still sought out books on the subject and by summer's end "could readily point out the leading constellations and the stars of larger magnitude in the heavens."[30]

Margaret Macdonald remembered trooping up to the roof "with our books and flash lights" to try and identify the constellations. Ella Rathvon spotted Jupiter's moons. Her husband looked forward to seeing Halley's comet, which stirred world-wide interest in the spring of 1910. John Salchow remembers searching for it, but says he never quite managed to spot it. [31]

Those daring young men in their flying machines

The year 1910 found the household scanning the skies for another type of star, too—those in the aviation world.

"The leading aviators declare this field the best in America," an advertisement in *The Christian Science Monitor* that September proclaimed, "and the meet the MOST IMPORTANT EVER HELD."[32]

The event was the Harvard-Boston Aero Meet, the first organized airplane competition in the eastern United States.[33] Sponsored by the Harvard Aeronautical Society, it was the talk of the town, capturing front page headlines and imaginations up and down the Eastern Seaboard. Hundreds of thousands of spectators attended the event, which was held on a 500-acre parcel of land located just south of Boston on the Squantum peninsula.[34] An estimated million more viewers flooded the streets of the city to catch a glimpse of the daring young men in their flying machines, among whom were America's own celebrated Wilbur Wright, the dashing Englishman Claude Grahame-White, and a teenager by the name of Cromwell Dixon.[35] Attendees included such notables as President William Howard Taft, local philanthropist Isabella Stewart Gardner, and a young Franklin Delano Roosevelt.[36]

Above: Advertisements like this one in the September 3, 1910,
Manchester Union [NH], *helped draw enormous crowds.*
Facing page: Promotional advertisement for the event.
Courtesy Harvard University Archives
Overleaf: Aviators prepare for the race to Boston Light.
Winner Claude Grahame-White piloted #3, a Bleriot
monoplane. | Courtesy Library of Congress

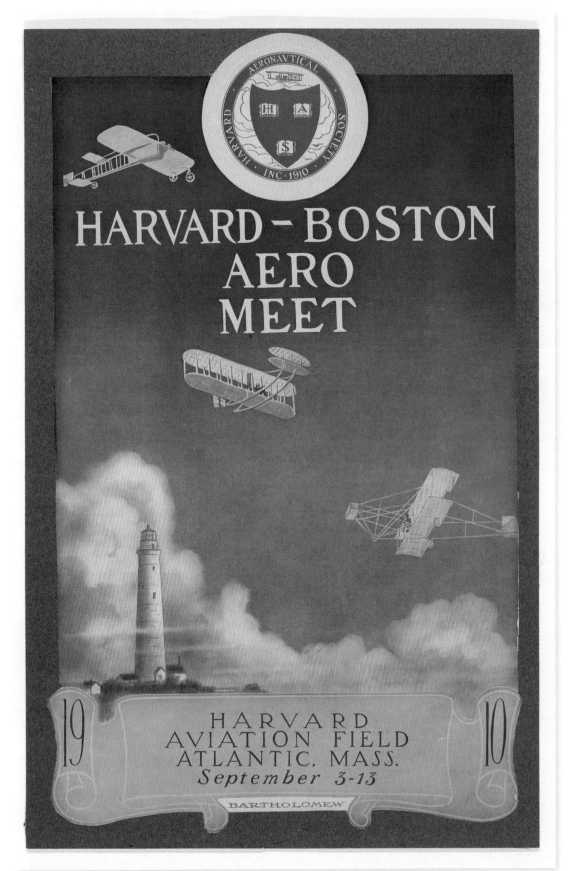

Cromwell Dixon's dirigible balloon in the field at the junction of Norway and Hemenway streets where he landed after his trip from Squantum field. The dome of the Christian Science church, which he mistook for the state house, is plainly seen in the background. Thousands of men, women and children are massed about the young aviator who sits unconcernedly on the framework of the balloon.

Top: Cromwell Dixon | Courtesy Smithsonian
National Air and Space Museum
Above: Onlookers swarm Dixon's dirigible,
which landed mistakenly near The Mother Church,
the dome of which is visible in the background.
Boston Post, September 9, 1909

Cromwell Dixon

Of the many different types of aircraft on display at the 1910 Harvard-Boston Aero Meet, there was one standout: a dirigible flown by 18-year-old Cromwell Dixon.[37]

Acclaimed as "a prodigy of the air," the teen was regarded as the next up-and-coming aviator, one who had dazzled the entire nation in 1907 after building his own pedal-powered airship.[38]

Calvin Frye and the other members of Mary Baker Eddy's household who attended the meet on September 8th may well have seen Cromwell exhibiting his dirigible, and may well have been eyewitnesses to his preparations for lift-off prior to his flight that day to Boston Common, a 50-acre public park in downtown Boston.[39]

Whether or not they saw him in person, the following day's news would surely have caught their attention! Mistaking the dome of The Mother Church Extension for the State House, his intended target, Cromwell Dixon veered off course and readied for landing. During his 1,000-foot descent, the teen realized that Boston Common was nowhere in sight, but it was too late to turn back. Instead, he skillfully navigated his aircraft to a safe landing in a vacant lot near The Mother Church.[40]

Although disappointed by his navigational misjudgment, the young aviator deemed his 372nd flight in a dirigible at the Harvard-Boston Aero Meet one of his most successful. Sadly, his promising career came to an end when he perished in a plane crash in October of the following year. Just days before that happened, however, Cromwell Dixon earned his place in aviation history by becoming the first pilot ever to cross the Continental Divide.[41]

The aeronauts dazzled onlookers with their skill as they competed in events grading speed, altitude, duration, distance—even bomb-dropping accuracy.[42] The most anticipated event was a race around the Boston Light, with a prize of $10,000 for the winner.[43]

Mrs. Eddy "was always interested in the affairs of the day, and especially was she interested in all inventions," said Martha Wilcox. "To her these things were 'expansive and promoted the growth of mortal mind out of itself.'"[44]

Back in 1901, in an interview with the *New York Herald*, Mrs. Eddy was asked how she felt about "the pursuit of modern material inventions." She replied: "Oh, we cannot oppose them. They all tend to newer, finer, more etherealized ways of living. They seek the finer essences. They light the way to the Church of Christ. We use them, we make them our figures of speech. They are preparing the way for us."[45]

When she heard about the aviation meet, Mrs. Eddy encouraged her household to attend. Normally, Martha Wilcox noted, she didn't want her staff to be away, "but on this occasion she insisted that several of us go to see these flights. . . . [T]o Mrs. Eddy it was the

Claude Grahame-White greets President Taft (top), and takes Boston Mayor John Fitzgerald (grandfather of President John F. Kennedy) on a sightseeing flight. The Christian Science Monitor, *September 9, 1909.*

appearance of an advancing thought, and she was interested in every detail of the exhibition."[46]

Over the course of several days, nearly the entire household would bundle into the White Steamer and head down to the airfield. According to Ella Rathvon, at 2:15 p.m. on the afternoon of September 8, 1910, she joined Elizabeth Kelly, Katharine Retterer, Calvin Frye, Irving Tomlinson, chauffeur Frank Bowman, and "Robert" (possibly the Bowmans' college-age son) as they set off on the first trip to Squantum.[47] A second group ventured out on the 12th, including the Dickeys, Nellie Eveleth, Lula Phillips, and William Rathvon.[48] John Salchow recalls going separately by himself.[49]

Although Mrs. Eddy didn't go, she was keenly interested in hearing all about it. "Her interest in aviation was remarkable," said William, adding that she "had a number of us go to the beach and report to her in detail just what occurred. The trip was too long for her to undertake, but she had one of her secretaries try to arrange, if possible, for a flight over the house that she might see the plane in motion; but the aviator did not deem it wise to fly so far inland."[50]

In a lecture he would give nearly a quarter of a century later, Irving Tomlinson mentioned Mrs. Eddy's broader interest in these kinds of advances in thought.

"She was keenly interested in exploration and invention in everything that meant victory over limitation," he would tell his audience. "But in all these matters everything was secondary to the spiritual."[51]

As with so many things that crossed her mental horizon, either in her own daily rounds or in the wider events of the world, Mrs. Eddy drew a metaphysical lesson from the aviation meet, which inspired an unpublished essay that she dictated to Laura Sargent in September 1910. It reads in part:

> *The present mania over flying needs to define itself. Is the flight upward that you so covet a material or a spiritual soaring? If it be the former it had better be a fall than a flight. Beloved friends and followers begin today, this hour, this moment your spiritual flight your look and your soaring heavenward. . . .*[52]

Calvin Frye's day off

Irving Tomlinson claimed that Calvin Frye's day off (really only half a day) at the Harvard-Boston Aero Meet "was the longest vacation Mr. Frye had in all his years of service — certainly a mark of devotion."[53] Although this wasn't entirely accurate, it was close.[54] Of all the household members, Calvin and Laura Sargent, the two staunchest members of the "old guard" and

Elizabeth Kelly awaits the ferry in Harpswell, Maine.
LONGYEAR MUSEUM COLLECTION

arguably the two who were closest to Mrs. Eddy, "took less time for their own affairs than any other students, although they all had to sacrifice much," said Adelaide Still.[55]

For the rest of the staff, while vacations had been almost unheard of at Pleasant View, they did occur at 400 Beacon Street, although infrequently. William Rathvon, Adam Dickey, and Martha Wilcox all made trips home during their years of service. In the summer of 1910, the Bowmans took a few days off, and John Salchow took a two-week trip to Nova Scotia. At one point, dining room worker Elizabeth Kelly and her cousin, housekeeper Katharine Retterer, enjoyed an all-expenses-paid vacation in South Harpswell, Maine, courtesy of Adam Dickey.

"We had a lovely time and came back much refreshed," a grateful Elizabeth would later recall.[56]

And what of Mrs. Eddy's own opportunities for refreshment?

As far back as 1888, she'd written to a student on the subject of vacations, "O how I want one! Twenty one years, and two weeks are the only vacations I have allowed myself. Well, God, our dear Father, and our only Mind takes no

Mary Baker Eddy on a carriage ride near 400 Beacon Street in 1909. Frank Bowman has the reins; Calvin Frye is seated beside him. | Longyear Museum collection

vacations. Let that Mind be ours and then we should want no respite from active and continual serving."[57]

If she was unable to take extended periods of time away from her work, Mrs. Eddy still made time for daily refreshment. In former years, she was an enthusiastic walker. Students from the early days of the movement tell of her heading out on foot from her home in Lynn as a break from teaching and writing, and later, after Mrs. Eddy moved to Concord in 1889, Laura Sargent recalled her taking a walk each morning at 10:00 a.m.[58] When her growing celebrity precluded such public promenades, Mrs. Eddy still found time for physical activity, perhaps making a circuit around the pond on her property, or pacing one of the covered verandas at the rear of her house for an hour.[59]

While the Chestnut Hill years were quieter ones in this regard, Mrs. Eddy still looked forward to the mental refreshment of a change of scene after spending long hours in her study. She made time each day for a carriage or sleigh ride, depending on the weather. These brief excursions provided a welcome break.

"She loved these drives in the neighborhood," Irving Tomlinson wrote.[60]

Her carriage and sleigh rides were not always pleasure outings, however, according to Adam Dickey. He contended that Mrs. Eddy went out "because she felt obligated to do so in order to refute the constant charges that she was dead or incapacitated. She knew that as long as she appeared in her carriage every day it would satisfy mortal mind and meet the charge that she had already departed and was no longer with us. There were times when it was a very severe task to take this drive. . . . [b]ut she did it nevertheless and always succeeded in meeting the attacks upon her so that she returned master of the situation."[61]

Mrs. Eddy also took time in the evenings for a bit of relaxation.

"If our Leader had any favorite hour in the day," wrote Mr. Dickey, "I think it was after the evening meal, at twilight, when she loved to sit quietly in her room and gaze from her window at the lengthening shadows. . . . We had bright electric lights installed on the gateposts where her driveway entered the street and she would sometimes make remarks about the vehicles that passed her residence."[62]

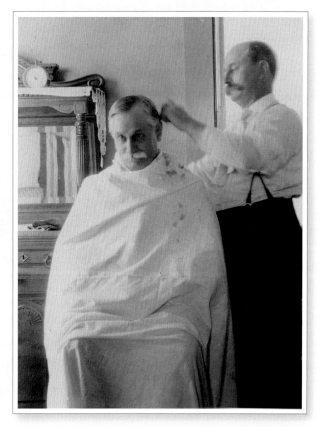

Coachman August Mann gives Calvin Frye a trim at Pleasant View. | Longyear Museum collection

A friend and colleague of Calvin Frye's once related an anecdote that highlights Mrs. Eddy's nimble wit as well as her appreciation for her long-time worker's faithfulness. Mrs. Eddy had remarked to Calvin that she'd noticed he hadn't had a vacation in a long time. When he agreed, she asked how long it had actually been. "Oh, it has been several years," came Calvin's response. To that she quipped, "Well, suppose you go down town and get your hair cut." [63]

Calvin Frye frequently joined her in the gathering darkness for conversation, as did Adam Dickey.[64] And although Mrs. Eddy didn't entertain at Chestnut Hill as often as she had at Pleasant View, there was still the occasional social call from family and old friends, including William and Daisette McKenzie, Judge Septimus and Camilla Hanna, her cousin Henry Baker, and her grandsons, among others. And on at least two occasions, Mrs. Eddy delighted in visiting with young children.

In the spring of 1910, one of Adelaide Still's former charges from the time she was a nanny came to see her with his mother. Knowing how fond Mrs. Eddy was of children, Adelaide brought now-six-year-old Benjamin Pray upstairs to Mrs. Eddy's study. Mrs. Eddy "spoke to him and kissed him," Adelaide later recalled, and gave him a gift of cherries. "When I took him outside the room, a member of the household asked him what Mrs. Eddy said to him, and he replied, 'She kissed me twice; once for me, and once for mother.'"[65]

Afterwards, Benjamin's mother observed to her son, "She is a very lovely old lady, isn't she, dear?"—to which the boy responded indignantly, "She isn't old!"[66]

In the fall of 1910, the Rathvons invited friends in town from Denver to stop by for a visit. To their surprise, they brought their baby son with them. Mrs. Eddy got wind of the little one's presence and asked to see him. Young Carol Montgomery made quite an impression.

"She held out her arms to him, and he immediately went to her," said Adelaide.[67]

Mrs. Eddy cuddled the baby on her lap, gave him a silver stamp holder to play with (and later take home with him), and enthused to her staff afterwards, "I wouldn't take a thousand dollars for this. Can't I see him every day?"[68]

Joyous moments like these, however brief or infrequent they may have been, clearly illustrate what Irving Tomlinson described as the "normal and happy life" enjoyed by all of those living at 400 Beacon Street—including Mary Baker Eddy.

Chapter 10
A Grandmother's Love

he Boston papers broke the story first: The Glover boys were in town!

The July 16, 1910, morning editions reported that Mary Baker Eddy's grandsons would be paying her a call that afternoon to commemorate her 89th birthday. By evening, details of the visit were splashed across the front pages of the late editions, and the story quickly spread nationwide in newspapers hungry for headlines about the Leader of the Christian Science movement.

Despite the scrutiny of the press, the visit itself was private and heartfelt. Some two decades in the making, its roots stretched back to the early days of the 19th century and sheds light on an aspect of Mrs. Eddy's life that is often overlooked — her role as a grandmother.

The youngest of six children, Mary Baker was born on the family farm in Bow, New Hampshire, on July 16, 1821, into a family rich with relatives and love. Her relationship with her mother, Abigail,

*Mary Baker Eddy's five grandchildren, circa 1894: At back, standing, are Mary (left)
and Evelyn. In front are George (left), Gershom (seated), and Andrew.*

LONGYEAR MUSEUM COLLECTION

was tender and close, and her paternal grandmother, who lived with the family, was also an indelible early influence. Though Mary's own life would eventually be devoted to nurturing the growth of Christian Science and her Church, she would also have a family of her own — including five grandchildren, whom she loved dearly.

A wife and mother's love

When Mary was 10, she attended the wedding of her eldest brother, Samuel, to Eliza Ann Glover of Concord, New Hampshire. There she met the bride's brother, George Washington Glover, a handsome young man of 21, who was learning the construction trade in Boston with Samuel.[1] George noticed something special about young Mary, and when she was older, struck up a correspondence.

Years later, the budding relationship blossomed into a proposal, and on Sunday, December 10, 1843, Mary Baker and George Glover were married. Sadly, after a brief, happy sojourn in the South, Mary's new husband died of yellow fever a mere six months after their wedding.[2] Mary, who was expecting a child, settled his affairs and made the long, arduous journey back to her parents' home in New Hampshire. Her son was born that autumn.[3]

Frail, grieving, and with no real means of supporting herself and little Georgy, Mary had few options. Her writing brought in a bit of money, and she tried running a school for a while, but a variety of reasons, including ill health, forced her to close it.[4] A succession of blows followed. John Bartlett, a long-time friend to whom she became engaged, went to California to join the Gold Rush and died in Sacramento just weeks after Mary's beloved mother's passing. Her father soon remarried and had little tolerance for six-year-old Georgy's boyhood exuberance. Mary moved in with her sister Abigail, but her son wasn't welcome there, either. Eventually, against Mary's wishes, the boy was sent to live with family friend and housekeeper Mahala Sanborn and her new husband,

Russell Cheney, in North Groton, New Hampshire, some 30 miles away from where Mary was living.

When itinerant dentist Daniel Patterson proposed marriage in 1853, he promised to welcome Georgy into their home. After the wedding, however, he reneged on that offer.[5] In the spring of 1855, Mary persuaded Daniel to move to North Groton, where she could be near her son, but the following year, the boy, now nearly 12, was taken to Minnesota by the Cheneys.

"A plot was consummated for keeping us apart," Mary would later write. "The family to whose care he was committed very soon removed to what was then regarded as the Far West. After his removal a letter was read to my little son, informing him that his mother was dead and buried. Without my knowledge a guardian was appointed him, and I was then informed that my son was lost. Every means within my power was employed to find him, but without success."[6]

Mary was devastated. She would have no further word from her son until October 1861, when he was 17. She received a letter from him, letting her know that he had joined the Union army.[7] Mother and son corresponded throughout the war and in the years following, when George returned to the West to make a life for himself—and soon, for his own family.

The blessing of grandchildren

On April 15, 1874, in Fargo, North Dakota, George married Ellen Bessant, the daughter of the carpenter who had helped George build his house. Nellie, as she was called, had emigrated from Southampton, England, the year before to join her father.[8]

Edward Gershom Glover, George and Nellie's son, was born in March 1875.[9] A great deal had happened to the new baby's grandmother in the intervening years. That same month, Mrs. Eddy would move into her first home of her own (in Lynn, Massachusetts), and in October of that year, she would publish the first edition of *Science and Health*. Two years later, in the fall of 1877,

Two of Mary Baker Eddy's three grandsons: George (left) and Andrew Glover, circa 1900.

LONGYEAR MUSEUM COLLECTION

Mary Baker Eddy's second grandchild, Mary Baker Glover, arrived,[10] and near the end of 1879, Mrs. Eddy's son George, now 35, traveled east alone to reunite with his mother. It was the first time they'd seen each other in 23 years.[11]

At some point during his visit, George expressed concern about his daughter Mary because she was cross-eyed. "George, you are surely mistaken," Mrs. Eddy replied. "Mary's eyes are not crossed." This made quite an impression on George. As young Mary Glover would later recall, "When he returned home late at night he told mother of this conversation with [G]randmother and insisted on seeing my eyes, though mother had just succeeded in putting us to sleep." Mary's eyes were perfectly straight—she'd been healed.[12]

Mrs. Eddy's third grandchild, Evelyn Tilton Glover, was born in January 1880, in North Dakota, while George was in Boston.[13] Nearly a decade later, she would accompany her parents and older siblings when George returned to see his mother again in the latter part of 1887. The family's extended visit would last six months.

By that time, Mrs. Eddy was living in modest quarters at the Massachusetts Metaphysical College at 571 Columbus Avenue in Boston, deeply involved with teaching and other demanding work for her Church.[14] She settled her family in nearby Chelsea and enjoyed several warm visits during their stay. Most notably, in November they joined her for Thanksgiving dinner at her home, and in February, before preaching a sermon on "Names and Baptism," Mrs. Eddy surprised the congregation by introducing her grandchildren, including them with 26 other children she christened that day.[15]

Mrs. Eddy's fourth grandchild was born in January 1889, a boy who would carry the name of his father and grandfather before him.[16] His grandmother sent him a fine present—the pocket watch that had belonged to her first husband, the original George Washington Glover. After receiving a photograph of the toddler with his present, Mrs. Eddy wrote to her son: "Give the dear

Left: Mary, George, Nellie, Evelyn, and Gershom Glover, circa 1887.

Longyear Museum collection

George Washington Glover III, circa 1890, holding the watch that belonged to his grandfather.
Above right: Close-up of the family heirloom. | LONGYEAR MUSEUM COLLECTION

little fellow who held his grandfather's watch in his little hand a sweet kiss from his Grandma."[17]

The fifth and final Glover child was born in early July 1891. His proud father would write to Mrs. Eddy: "My fourth of July boy is as fat as a pig his name is Andrew Jackson Glover."[18]

In the spring of 1893, George Glover traveled east for a third time to see his mother, now living at Pleasant View.[19] He brought his young namesake along on the trip. Little George was just four, and later in life he would recall the visit with great fondness, telling how his grandmother would walk with him down to the pond to feed the fish and ducks. He also remembered riding in the carriage with her on some of her daily drives.[20]

Laura Sargent told Irving Tomlinson that the boy "was the cutest child I ever saw,"

Andrew Jackson Glover, circa 1892. | LONGYEAR MUSEUM COLLECTION

and related this anecdote from the visit: "While he was in the room with his grandmother she said, 'Georgie now you hide under my desk and we will see if Mrs. Sargent can find you.'

"I came into the room and Mrs. E said, 'Have you seen Georgie anywhere?'

"I said, 'No, but I'll look for him.' Then he jumped laughing from under the desk where his Grandma had hidden him."[21]

"I have the great pleasure of presenting to you on this Christmas Eve a sweet home...."
— *Mary Baker Eddy*

During the summer of 1899, Mrs. Eddy, through the help of two of her students, began secretly building a home in Lead, South Dakota, as a Christmas gift for her son and his family. That December, she wrote to them from Pleasant View, informing them of her intentions.[22]

The Glover home in the Black Hills, circa 1891. Left to right: Gershom, a friend, Mary (seated), Evelyn, Nellie (seated with Andrew), George II (holding George III), more friends. The Glovers would move from this rustic log cabin to the house in town (right) that Mrs. Eddy gave them as a Christmas present in 1899. | LONGYEAR MUSEUM COLLECTION

Dec. 15, 1899

My dear Son & Grandchildren:

Through the ability and kindness of my students, Mr. Charles M. Howe and Mr. Ryan,—I have the great pleasure of presenting to you on this Christmas Eve a sweet home— the gift of Mother.

May the loving spirit of the Christ that is commemorated on this anniversary, be and abide in this house—consecrate the life of each inmate, and hallow the memory of this home.

With love Mother,
Mary Baker Eddy

© The Mary Baker Eddy Collection. Original in The Mary Baker Eddy Library.

Used with permission.

The house was the talk of the town, with the local newspaper describing it as "one of the most elegant and beautiful gifts ever made in this city … a handsome brick mansion at the head of Main Street thoroughly equipped and furnished from cellar to garret."[23]

Many years later, when he was in his 80s, Mrs. Eddy's grandson George still had vivid memories of that special surprise.

"We moved into the big house on Christmas Eve 1899. I was only ten years old and that Christmas I don't believe I'll ever forget," he mused. "To move into a big house like that, from the small house … was something for a youngster…. It was a beautiful home. We enjoyed it—the whole family enjoyed it as long as we were together and home together…. It was just beautiful. It was the most beautiful home … built in the Black Hills at that time. And I think it still is!"[24]

Provisions for her grandchildren

Throughout her life, Mrs. Eddy was keenly interested in her grandchildren's academic, moral, and religious education. Her letters to them are filled with counsel, encouragement, and love—along with occasional despair at their poor spelling and grammar. She purchased a typewriter for Mary, and repeatedly offered to bring the girls and their brothers back East to be educated, all expenses paid.[25]

Her family's lack of education was a constant source of concern to her, and in 1900, she arranged for one of her students, Charles Howe of St. Joseph, Missouri, who had been instrumental in building the new house for the Glover family, to oversee for a period the education of her grandson George and, eventually, two of his siblings as well.[26] Mrs. Eddy wrote to Mr. Howe regarding George, "Words are weak to tell my gratitude to you for taking my dear grandson … under your care till he is thoroughly prepared to enter Harvard College…. What I am most grateful for is the moral teaching and training that I know you will give him."[27]

Mary Baker Eddy's granddaughters, Mary (left) and Evelyn Glover.

LONGYEAR MUSEUM COLLECTION

Boston Sunday Post

PAGES 25 to 34

SUNDAY MORNING, JULY 17, 1910

Desire to Visit Famous Grandmother Again Cause of Visit, Say Grandsons of Mrs. Eddy

MRS. MARY BAKER G. EDDY.
Whose grandsons are visiting Boston.

GEORGE W. GLOVER, JR., AND ANDREW JACKSON GLOVER, GRANDSONS OF MRS. EDDY, NOW VISITING IN BOSTON.

George and Andrew Glover's 1910 visit with their grandmother was front-page news.

In the fall of 1906, Judge William Ewing gave a lecture on Christian Science in the branch church in Lead, South Dakota, where he met the Glover family. His letter to Mrs. Eddy about this meeting mentioned her grandchildren: "Your grandsons acted as ushers at the lecture at Lead, South Dakota, and your granddaughter seemed to be the executive head of the enterprise…. I feel that you would like to know this, and am sure it will be a great comfort to you to know that your grandchildren are so active in their devotion to the great Cause that you have brought from its hiding and given to the world."[28]

Four years later, two of those grandsons would travel to Boston and become front-page news.

The "call of relationship"

Grandsons George and Andrew traveled east by train in early July 1910 at the invitation of former United States Senator and ex-Secretary of the Navy William Chandler.[29] In 1907, in league with the *New York World* newspaper, which cooked up the scheme, Mr. Chandler had filed a lawsuit on behalf of Mrs. Eddy's son George and several other relatives, after persuading them that Mrs. Eddy was not competent to handle her own affairs. Although the lawsuit eventually collapsed after a court-directed investigation found her fully competent, the experience was a bitter one for Mrs. Eddy.[30]

Afterward, Chandler continued on as family counsel for Mrs. Eddy's son, and in 1910 he asked George if his boys Andrew, then 18, and young George, 21, could come out for a visit. Mr. Chandler's motive wasn't entirely straightforward — he wanted the young men to meet the trustees of the fund that Mrs. Eddy had set up to provide for her family. In fact, it appears he was already planning on contesting the arrangement after Mrs. Eddy's passing.[31]

George and Andrew arrived in Concord on July 8. After spending the night in a hotel, they continued on the next day to Chandler's summer home in Waterloo, New Hampshire, where they spent a week sight-seeing.[32] Chandler also put them

This photograph of Andrew (left) and George Glover was likely taken during the summer of 1910 in New Hampshire. | LONGYEAR MUSEUM COLLECTION

to work caulking his boats. While this arrangement worked to the former Senator's satisfaction — one newspaper report noted that he inspected their progress from time to time, offering "jovial comments in a most jocular manner" — the boys themselves weren't necessarily as enthused. Many years later, George in particular would complain about being taken advantage of by their host.[33]

Finally, the day of the visit with their grandmother arrived. On Saturday morning, July 16, Chandler took the boys by train to Boston. They checked into the swanky Parker House hotel — undoubtedly quite an impressive sight for two young men from rural South Dakota!

There, Chandler introduced Andrew and George to Archibald McLellan, who at this time was editor of *The Christian Science Monitor*, and Irving Tomlinson. Both men, along with attorney Frank Streeter, served as trustees for the Glover family trust fund.[34]

Boston's Parker House Hotel, circa 1910.
COURTESY LIBRARY OF CONGRESS

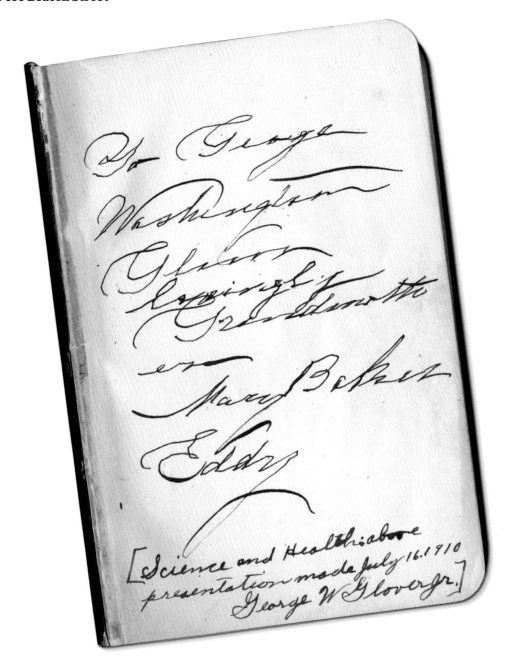

Inscription page from the copy of Science and Health *that Mrs. Eddy gave to her grandson George Washington Glover III.*

Longyear Museum collection

Mr. Tomlinson noted that the meeting with Chandler, Mrs. Eddy's former adversary, was "soon cordial." He and Mr. McLellan took the boys to The Christian Science Publishing Society for a tour. Chandler joined them afterward, and at 1:30 p.m. the group headed out to Mrs. Eddy's home.[35]

After returning from her daily carriage ride, Mrs. Eddy greeted her two grandsons. She hadn't seen George since he was four and visited her at Pleasant View; she'd never met Andrew before.

"George was a good-looking young man with auburn hair," recalled Adelaide Still who, along with Mrs. Sargent, was present during the visit. "Mrs. Eddy told him that he was very much like his grandfather, Major Glover. Andrew, the younger, was a tall, rather awkward looking lad of about seventeen."[36]

Awkward, perhaps, but in the end Andrew was the one who did most of the talking. George, said Miss Still, "just sat and smiled at [his grandmother] and answered only when a question was addressed directly to him."[37]

"She was delighted to see them. . . . "

— Irving Tomlinson

Mr. Tomlinson called the visit "most pleasing" to Mrs. Eddy.

"She was delighted to see them," he later wrote, "conversed with them, and told them she hoped they would both have a good education. She planned that George should go to Harvard College and study law at her expense. Andrew was to have a business education and to be properly equipped for the business of life."[38]

The boys presented their grandmother with a gift from their father — a piece of custom jewelry made of gold from the Glover mine.[39] Mrs. Eddy in turn gave each grandson a copy of *Science and Health*, in which she had written "Lovingly Grandmother Mary Baker Eddy."[40]

Behind the counter of the Glover family's soda fountain and store in Lead, South Dakota, are Andrew (left) and George. | Longyear Museum collection

Mrs. Eddy invited her grandsons to stay with her in Chestnut Hill for a little while, but Andrew replied, "Oh, no, we've got a store; we must get back."[41]

The brothers, Tomlinson recorded in his diary that day, were "pleased and impressed" with the visit and their gift, and left their grandmother's suite "with tears in their eyes."[42]

Downstairs, sherbet, cake, and lemonade awaited, and then George and Andrew were given a tour of the house. When it was time to leave, they were met outside by a throng of reporters and photographers.

"It was evident that they had enjoyed themselves and that their relations with their grandmother were of the pleasantest," observed the *Boston American*.[43]

As the newspapermen advanced on the brothers, Andrew "ducked to one side and walked rapidly to the other side of Senator Chandler," the newspaper reported. But not George. Mrs. Eddy likely was proud of how he handled the situation, for the report continues, "[Andrew's] older brother, however, stood his ground." When pressed for a comment, George replied, "I cannot say anything about our visit. I do not think it would please my grandmother if we went to talking about it. We have just time to catch our train and must hurry."[44]

The brothers did end up posing for a photograph, which appeared in the newspapers the next morning. Mrs. Eddy was sent a copy, "and she had it framed and always kept it in her room," according to Adelaide Still.[45]

Later, George and Andrew released a statement to the press: "Our visit to our grandmother, Mrs. Mary Baker G. Eddy, founder and head of the Christian Science faith, at her home in Chestnut Hill, Newton, is purely because we wished to see her once more. The call of relationship led us across the continent."[46]

On the very same day that her grandsons came to call, Mrs. Eddy composed a poem about their visit. It includes these lines:

> *My heart is touched with a hand unseen.*
> *My soul is stirred by a blazing beam.*
> *What joy what bliss can come to me*
> *Beyond the joy of seeing Thee.*
> *O darling grandson.*[47]

In August, Mrs. Eddy sent the boys the rest of her published writings, and George promptly wrote a sweet thank you note back.[48]

"Why — I thought she <u>loved</u> me!"

Many years later, while conducting research on the Glover family, biographer Jewel Spangler Smaus made several trips to see Mrs. Eddy's grandson George, then in his 80s and living at the old family cabin in South Dakota's Black Hills. At onc point, she asked him about that visit with his grandmother at Chestnut Hill back in 1910.

"As George recounted the experience for me, it was evident that he was

George Washington Glover III in the 1970s.

Photograph by Louis Smaus, Longyear Museum collection

quietly reliving the visit, and had done so many times," wrote Mrs. Smaus. "But he had little else to say about it. So I pressed him a bit, hoping that he might reveal more.

"'If you didn't say much, George,' I said, 'then what were you thinking?'

"As he sat there for a moment, just remembering, the sun glinted through the window on his white hair, and seemed to light up his face. I saw that his blue eyes had filled with tears. There was another moment of silence. Then Mrs. Eddy's grandson replied quietly: 'Why—I thought she <u>loved</u> me!'"[49]

In 1948, with his own children now grown, George Washington Glover III, a lifelong student of Christian Science, traveled back East with his wife for one more visit to Boston. After an early Sunday morning tour of The Christian Science Publishing Society, the Glovers attended the service in The Mother Church. They were greeted at the door and escorted down the center aisle as honored guests. That afternoon, they drove the few miles out to George's grandmother's home in Chestnut Hill where, to George's surprise and delight, they were welcomed by Adelaide Still, who was present during the birthday visit almost four decades earlier. Miss Still could not make enough of George, and after embracing both Glovers, gave them a grand tour of the home.

"I was very royally treated," George recalled.[50]

As he stepped once more into his grandmother's suite, George slowly scanned the room until his gaze fell upon her mantel. The picture taken all those years ago by the newspapermen was still there, enduring evidence of a grandmother's love.

Mrs. Eddy proudly displayed this photo of her grandsons George (left) and Andrew holding the copies of Science and Health *that she gave them.*

LONGYEAR MUSEUM COLLECTION

Chapter 11

At the Fountainhead

n the spring of 1906, as the finishing touches were being put on the Extension of The Mother Church, Minnie Scott was invited to interview with Mary Baker Eddy for a position in her household at Pleasant View. As the two of them settled in for a chat in the library, Mrs. Eddy turned to Minnie and said, "Now here you are at the fountainhead, and there is an opportunity for you to prove your gratitude by service."[1]

Being "at the fountainhead"—living and working side by side with the Discoverer, Founder, and Leader of Christian Science—was the chief benefit of employment in Mary Baker Eddy's household, and her staff was keenly aware of this advantage.

"From the day of my first interview with her," William Rathvon would later write, "I became cognizant of the unparalleled privilege and opportunity for spiritual development that was daily mine."[2]

Laura Sargent was attuned to this as well, telling reporter Sibyl Wilbur, "We who are spending our days at 'Pleasant View' have the opportunity of growing wonderfully in the tenets of the Christian Science faith."[3]

This continued to hold true at 400 Beacon Street, although there were some changes. At Pleasant View, for instance, Minnie Scott had become accustomed to seeing and hearing from Mrs. Eddy on an almost daily basis. The move to Chestnut Hill meant this was no longer always the case.

"[T]here were so many to cater for and all could not be called so I did not see her so often," said Minnie. Her colleagues kept her in the loop, however, and "someone always came to give me the key-note of her talk to know how we were to work for the cause. . . ."[4]

> *"From the day of my first interview with her, I became cognizant of the unparalleled privilege and opportunity for spiritual development that was daily mine."*
> *— William Rathvon*

Regardless of the frequency of their interaction with their Leader, everyone under Mrs. Eddy's roof was expected to put what they were learning about Christian Science into daily practice.

"We attended to her wants and necessities," noted Martha Wilcox, "but always in our mind was what she had given us to be demonstrated. . . . From morning till night, we were busy applying the instructions she gave us to the work at hand and trying to demonstrate the truth of Christian Science."[5] They were also busy refraining from talking about metaphysics. As Martha explained, "We were to live Christian Science, to be it, and not just talk the letter. This was one place in the world where the chatter about Christian Science was not heard."[6]

This steel engraving of Mary Baker Eddy is from a 1908 pen-and-ink drawing by noted artist and illustrator Jules Maurice Gaspard. | Longyear Museum collection

Laura Sargent

"A true and helpful friend"

"The world may some day know of the debt it owes this woman," wrote William Rathvon of Laura Sargent, "but it never can repay her."[7]

Second only to Calvin Frye in length of service to Mary Baker Eddy, Laura Ellen Adams was born in Wisconsin on April 26, 1858, the youngest of five girls. The year before her birth, her father, Samuel Adams, a New England sea captain turned shipbuilder (and said to be a cousin of Founding Father Samuel Adams), left the village of Bowdoinham,

Laura E. Sargent | Longyear Museum collection

Maine, with his wife, Minerva, and family in tow. They journeyed by train and horse-drawn sled to their new home in what was then the West, settling in Green Bay, Wisconsin, where Laura was born. Later, the family would move to the burgeoning pine belt of Oconto, where Captain Adams—after serving in the First Wisconsin Cavalry during the Civil War—began farming.[8]

In Oconto, Laura was enrolled in a private primary school taught by Louise Hall.[9] Laura excelled in most subjects, but Miss Hall later reported that she "despaired of teaching Laura mathematics."[10] It wasn't until many years later, while in Mrs. Eddy's employ, that Laura would again grapple with sums and prevail.

By 1870, when Laura was 12, she and her mother were boarding with Laura's older sister Victoria and her husband, lumber merchant Henry Sargent, along with two of Henry's younger brothers, Edward and James. Born and raised in New Brunswick, Canada, the Sargent brothers had emigrated to the United States, eventually making their way to Wisconsin to enter the lumber business. They chose an excellent spot.

"A strong odor of pine sawdust pervades Oconto, and with good reason," the *Chicago Herald* would later report. "Its sawmills are the glory of the town."[11]

Laura continued her studies, pursuing some advanced work at the Young Women's Academy in Green Bay. And then, in the summer of 1876, when she was 18, she married James Sargent.

James built his bride a home on Main Street, a snug single-story Victorian bungalow with a broad front porch almost directly across the street from where Henry and Victoria lived.[12] The sisters were close, and both couples enjoyed what their bustling frontier community had to offer. They were active in the local Presbyterian church, and newspaper reports of the day tell of visits to and from friends and even a camping trip by steamboat to Idlewild, a remote spot on Lake Michigan.[13]

Laura, however, was plagued with ill health, and by the early 1880s she was a semi-invalid. After learning that a friend was receiving Christian Science treatment, she traveled to Milwaukee in 1883 to join her. There, Laura engaged a practitioner, too, and returned home a month later completely healed. She also brought back a copy of *Science and Health*, the first to reach Oconto. Laura gave it to her mother, urging her to read it. Mrs. Adams duly did just that and told her daughters, "Girls, this book is of God. I have read it through and I find nothing in it that interferes with the Bible. I believe it is the 'second coming of the Christ.'"[14]

In May of the following year, 1884, Laura Sargent had her first encounter with Mary Baker Eddy in the only class that Mrs. Eddy taught in Chicago. Directly afterwards, Laura treated her first patient—her mother, who had been confined to bed with a badly injured ankle.

"Mother, you are going to be my first patient, and you will be healed," Laura reportedly told her, and this proved to be the case.[15] Laura would eventually heal another family member, too—her eldest sister Anna Heney, who had contracted typhoid fever some 16 years earlier. After years of invalidism, she had been given just six months to live.[16]

There would be more instruction for Laura over the next few years. Just six months after the Chicago class, she traveled to Boston for a second Primary class with Mrs. Eddy (not an uncommon practice in the early days of the Christian Science movement). This time, she brought along her sister Victoria, who had been healed by reading *Science and Health*. And then in May 1886, at Mrs. Eddy's invitation, Laura joined the Normal class at the College.[17]

Described by a contemporary as "a very pleasant woman, who has the hallmark of kindness and goodness stamped all over her face,"[18] Laura's serene demeanor belied an unshakeable inner strength. "[T]he meek Christian Scientist holds on to God, and goes calmly on," she would write to Mrs. Eddy a few years later—words that could well have described herself.[19]

Laura proved a sturdy pioneer, working tirelessly to establish Christian Science in her native state. She weathered the ire of her Presbyterian minister and his withering sermons against the new religion, eventually withdrawing, along with her sister Victoria and a handful of others, to found a Christian Science church in Oconto.[20]

Laura Sargent as a young woman.

LONGYEAR MUSEUM COLLECTION

This is the First Christian Science Church Built in America, Built in 1886, Oconto, Wis.

3664-29

Vintage postcard of First Church of Christ, Scientist, Oconto, Wisconsin. | Longyear Museum collection

"Give my forever-love to your dear church."
— Mary Baker Eddy

Although neither James nor Henry Sargent was interested in leaving the Presbyterian faith, Victoria's husband, Henry, donated a piece of land for the new church. With this support and the aid of a small but determined band of Christian Scientists, the first church edifice in the world built specifically for Christian Science services opened its doors on October 31,

1886. Laura would help conduct services for the next two years. In 1889, Mrs. Eddy wrote a letter to the congregation. It reads in part: "Guided by the pillar and the cloud, this little church that built the first temple for Christian Science worship shall abide steadfastly in the faith of Jesus' words: 'Fear not, little flock; for it is your Father's good pleasure to give you the kingdom.' . . . Give my forever-love to your dear church."[21]

The same month that the Oconto church began holding services, Laura's healing practice was officially recognized in *The Christian Science Journal.*[22] Her first listing cites her address as St. Paul, Minnesota, where she went briefly at the request of Mrs. Eddy. After a three-month sojourn in the Twin Cities, Laura returned to Oconto, where she would go on to report healings that included those of scarlet fever and rheumatism.[23]

Laura taught her first Primary class in 1887 in Marinette, Wisconsin.[24] She was active in the National Christian Scientist Association (an organization of Mary Baker Eddy's own students, as well as the students of all authorized teachers of Christian Science), and in 1889, she gave a public talk about Christian Science in Green Bay.[25] That year, she would also send a letter to Mrs. Eddy on behalf of the workers in Oconto.

MRS. LAURA E. SARGENT, C.S.B.,
MERCHANTS HOTEL, Room 5,
ST. PAUL, MINNESOTA.
Science and Health Mental Healing, Defence of Christian Science, Christian Science and the Bible, on sale.
Sample copies sent, and subscriptions received for *Christian Science Journal.*
Normal Course graduate of the Massachusetts Metaphysical College, practises and teaches the Practice of Mind-Healing, Christian Science.

Laura Sargent's first advertisement in
The Christian Science Journal *(October 1886).*

"This is where your students stand here," she wrote, "loyal to their Leader, firm, and brave; and will stand by her, no matter what move is made, shod only with the preparations of Love. . . ."[26]

285

"What should I have done without your dear sister?"

Laura would have further opportunity to "stand by her" the following year, when she first entered Mrs. Eddy's employment. Arriving in Concord on January 16, 1890, she joined Mrs. Eddy at her rented house at 62 North State Street. It would be an intense year, as Mrs. Eddy was working day and night to finish the landmark 50th edition of *Science and Health*. She was tremendously grateful for Laura's support.

"What should I have done without your dear sister?" Mrs. Eddy wrote to Victoria Sargent in January 1891, the same month that the new edition was published. "But God tempers the winds to the shorn lamb. I hope I shall live to see her good husband desire to be taught Christian Science, and teach him myself. I shall always love him for letting his wife stay with me so long. Oh! I wish it could be always so, and I could have her with me while I pilgrim here. She is the best, the kindest and dearest girl in all the world to me...."[27]

Although there is no record that James Sargent ever became one of her students, Mrs. Eddy's wish to have Laura at her side permanently would eventually be granted. Over the next two decades, Laura would spend the majority of her days with her Leader, returning home to Oconto or going to other posts in Boston from time to time.[28] She kept in close touch with her family ("We hear from dear Laura about every week," her sister Victoria wrote in March 1897), and to all appearances she had her husband's blessing—and his financial support in the form of an allowance for the first five years of her employment, during which time she drew no salary.[29]

In February 1898, James Sargent headed north to the Klondike to prospect for gold. After his return a year and a half later (empty-handed, alas),[30] Laura again went home to Wisconsin. She shuttled back and forth between Oconto, Concord, and Boston for the next few years. When she returned to Concord in June 1903, she would remain continuously with Mrs. Eddy for the next seven and a half years, until Mrs. Eddy's passing.

Laura Sargent's room at 400 Beacon Street. | Longyear Museum collection

"I am Mrs. Eddy's student"

Laura Sargent's role in the household defies easy categorization.

"I am neither Mrs. Eddy's companion nor her housekeeper," she told the press in 1909. "I am Mrs. Eddy's student. . . . I have always gone to her when she has sent for me, and remained a longer or shorter period as the circumstances required."[31]

Faithful student, loyal friend, household manager, right-hand woman—Laura Sargent was all of these and more to Mary Baker Eddy. Theirs was a close friendship, and Laura was keenly attuned to Mrs. Eddy's needs.

"No one was quicker to catch the meaning or spiritual intent of Mrs. Eddy's teaching and the moves she made for the Cause," said Adelaide Still, who worked closely with Laura at both Pleasant View and Chestnut Hill.[32]

Mrs. Sargent was on hand for many momentous occasions in the last two decades of Mrs. Eddy's life. Even before she joined the household, it was Laura's steady arm and reassurance that proved of inestimable value in 1888, when Mrs. Eddy was asked to give an impromptu address before a crowd of thousands in Chicago and responded with "Science and the Senses."[33] It was Laura who supervised the move to Pleasant View in the summer of 1892 and who would again be on hand for the move to Chestnut Hill in 1908.[34] She was with Mrs. Eddy as the Original Edifice of The Mother Church was built in 1894, as well as the Extension a decade later. She was at her Leader's side during much of the two long years that the Woodbury trial dragged on and for all of the Next Friends suit in 1907.[35] Mrs. Eddy once told James Gilman, illustrator of *Christ and Christmas*, "Mrs. Sargent has been with me in more trying times than any other woman," and Mr. Gilman added that Mrs. Eddy "repeated the thought that she was a true and helpful friend."[36]

Their affection for one another ran deep. Mrs. Eddy clearly treasured Laura, telling her one day, "You seem like my own daughter"—to which Laura responded, "You seem like my own mother."[37]

Despite their closeness, Laura, too, came in for her share of reprimands.

John Salchow recalled one occasion at Pleasant View when he overheard Mrs. Eddy administer a particularly severe one. Laura later returned to Mrs. Eddy's study in tears.

"'Why, Laura,' Mrs. Eddy exclaimed in gentle surprise, 'I was not speaking to you; I was speaking to the error. You should not take it to yourself.'"[38]

"You seem like my own daughter."
— Mary Baker Eddy

Like Calvin Frye, Laura Sargent was willing to do just about anything that was asked of her. She balked at bookkeeping, however — perhaps harking back to those early struggles with math — when Mrs. Eddy asked her to keep the household accounts.

"Laura," Mrs. Eddy promptly informed her, "God is a business God. He attends to the business of the universe, and you reflect His business ability."[39]

With this bracing instruction, Laura rose to the occasion and successfully kept the books. She also welcomed visitors to Mrs. Eddy's home and served as proofreader, messenger, and metaphysical worker, among other assignments.[40]

"[T]o her loving attendance much of the quiet order of that home may be attributed," Sibyl Wilbur reported after touring Pleasant View.[41]

A tower of strength

Known to be serious-minded and responsible, it was Laura whom Mrs. Eddy entrusted with the page proofs for the 50th edition of *Science and Health*, sending her from Concord to Boston to take them directly to the printer. A few years later, in 1896, Laura would reprise her role as "carrier pigeon"—Mrs. Eddy's nickname for her, because she was "a bright bearer of messages"—once again ferrying proofs to Boston, this time for *Miscellaneous Writings*.[42]

Others describe her by turn as a "tower of strength," a "steady horse," a strong metaphysician who "faithfully performed her work every day," and the one who "did much to weld the workers together as a unit so that the home ran smoothly."[43] At 400 Beacon Street, William Rathvon observed that Laura was "rarely out of sight, always within hearing" of her Leader.[44] She was on hand day and night, through mental weather both stormy and fair, rarely absent from her post. At times, when the pressure seemed intense to the point of exhaustion, she would withdraw for a few days of renewal. Mrs. Eddy was always overjoyed at her return.

"[T]he members of Mrs. Eddy's household who recall her will always think of her as the loving and devoted Laura Sargent," said Adam Dickey.[45]

"I am waiting and trusting"

On December 10, 1910—two days after Mrs. Eddy's funeral—Laura sent a letter of thanks to Mary Beecher Longyear for some unspecified "loving kindness."

"You have been such a dear sister to me through all the past years," Laura wrote. "I have some work to finish here and then I shall turn my thought to the future. I am waiting and trusting, knowing that divine Love does lead and direct."[46]

Laura's "waiting and trusting" quickly bore fruit. She would be appointed official custodian of 400 Beacon Street by the Christian Science Board of Directors and would also serve on the Committee on Business. She spent a one-year term on the Bible Lesson Committee,[47] and in 1913, she taught the Normal class—only the second woman to do so, apart from Mrs. Eddy.[48]

Adelaide Still, who along with Lula Phillips stayed on with Laura at Chestnut Hill following Mrs. Eddy's passing, worked side by side with her as she prepared.

"As was her custom with anything which she was called upon to do, she threw her whole heart and time into the task," Adelaide recalled, noting that as a complete concordance to Mrs. Eddy's writings had not then been compiled, "I gladly spent much time in looking up and typing references for her."[49] She found the experience wonderfully uplifting, adding "I think I gained almost as much as the students who were in the class."[50]

Afterwards, in a jubilant letter to Judge Septimus Hanna and his wife, Camilla, Laura vividly described the experience:

> *Well! The Normal class is born, and such a glorious birth, normal and painless. . . . From first to last a baptism of love seemed to enfold us, and the presence of the Holy Spirit "moved upon the face of the waters." I seemed to be only an instrument in Love's dear hand to use in His own way. When the moment came . . . for me to enter by the door that the Readers used to come through I waited one moment to lift my heart to our dear Father-Mother God. . . . They were expecting to see a man when lo! the door opened and your sister Laura appeared on the scene. The hush that swept over the room could be felt.*[51]

Laura Sargent made a lasting contribution to the Christian Science movement on many fronts, from her dedication and hard work as a pioneer in Wisconsin and beyond to her cheerful willingness to tackle any assignment that would help further the Cause she loved so dearly. But the friendship and unflagging support that she offered Mary Baker Eddy for the better part of two decades was her greatest gift.

"[M]y life must prove the heart's gratitude," Laura once wrote to Mrs. Eddy —and when weighed in the balance, there's little question that hers did.[52]

View of a household worker's desk as interpreted at 400 Beacon Street today.

Manna for the day

Mary Baker Eddy was a born teacher, Irving Tomlinson once wrote. "[S]he imparted the truth as naturally as the sun gives out light and heat."[53]

Her inclination in this direction blossomed early. As a teenager, she tutored a motherless neighbor boy who helped out with chores on the Baker farm, teaching him to read from the Bible.[54] As a young woman, she taught school, both at the kindergarten and secondary levels.[55] And one of the first things that occurred after her landmark healing in 1866 was that she was asked to teach the new healing method she had discovered.[56] Mrs. Eddy's work as a teacher flowered from that point on, through her years as president and chief instructor at the Massachusetts Metaphysical College, to the decades following her retirement from its classroom, during which she continued to instruct and mentor her students and followers through her writings as well as through copious correspondence. For those within the close-knit circle of her home — those whom she called her "family" — this generous tutelage occurred on a daily basis.

Sometimes it was shared one on one, sometimes in small groups, and sometimes after what the Rathvons referred to as an "Everybody Call," when Mrs. Eddy used the household bell system to ring for all the metaphysical workers and secretaries.[57]

"She <u>always</u>, without variation whatsoever,

started each day by reading the Bible."

— George Kinter

There was a pattern and a rhythm to the days at 400 Beacon Street, and just as the housekeeping and other practical work in Mrs. Eddy's home was done in a systematic, orderly fashion, so too, for the most part, instruction followed a regular routine.

"She <u>always</u>, without variation whatsoever, started each day by reading the Bible," stated George Kinter, who worked at both Pleasant View and Chestnut Hill. His colleague Irving Tomlinson elaborated, "There is a sweet picture of Mrs. Eddy . . . which comes before the eyes of those who were the members of her household. They see her, in the morning hours of each day, seated in her rocking chair beside her writing table in the bay window of her study, with the Bible and the textbook in her lap. She would first read from the Scriptures and then from *Science and Health*."[58]

Mary Baker Eddy's study at 400 Beacon Street.

LONGYEAR MUSEUM COLLECTION

Next, according to Mr. Kinter, "After her devotions, she would call one or more of her helpers, and generally would comment upon what she had read from the Scriptures. Sometimes she would read the same passages to us, and ask us to comment upon them. Again, she would ask one of us to read the text and then would ask another to explain the meaning, but always before dismissing us, she herself would deliver one of her inimitable sermonettes, that furnished the keynote for that day's work. . . ."[59]

Sometimes, Sunday mornings would find a small group gathering with Mrs. Eddy in the Pink Room for an informal service.

"Grouped around her, we listened absorbed to a short inspiring talk, perhaps on the subject of the Sunday lesson or some other topic that might come to her," recalled William Rathvon.[60]

Although glimpses of instruction from these "sermonettes" and other household talks remain in the brief notes taken afterward by some of those who were in attendance, full transcripts of her remarks don't appear to have been captured.

"I never undertook to write down their substance," Mr. Rathvon explained, "which would have been difficult even if done at once, and impossible if deferred, so rich were they in profound exposition of the deeper things of life."[61]

In addition to the morning meetings, Mrs. Eddy often took the opportunity to instruct and guide her staff at other times throughout the day, when individuals or small groups were in her presence. And while there was no formal classroom or curriculum, she also encouraged her household to ask questions, "just as if you were in my College."[62]

> "As students, you are to kindle your light to make the way clear for all travelers, and then you are to go forth bearing this light."
> — Mary Baker Eddy

Most eagerly took advantage of this invitation. During his first summer on the staff, for instance, William asked Mrs. Eddy a question about his practice work and received a helpful reply. "Why can I cure another's failures and he, mine?" he wanted to know. She told him, "Because you are afraid of what he was not afraid, and he afraid of what you were not."[63]

Mrs. Eddy's staff cherished her "pearls of wisdom," as Irving Tomlinson called them, and took pains to record them.[64] For instance, in March 1910,

Handwritten notes in a copy of Science and Health
belonging to Laura Sargent. | LONGYEAR MUSEUM COLLECTION

Mr. Rathvon wrote down the following statement that Mrs. Eddy shared: "As students, you are to kindle your light to make the way clear for all travelers, and then you are to go forth bearing this light."[65]

The subject must have been uppermost in Mrs. Eddy's thought. Mr. Tomlinson recorded another statement on light that she made that same day: "When night comes on over the city, the students of Christian Science light their lamps to banish the darkness. It is because of the gloom that they light their tapers. So you are lighting your lamps of Truth to banish the darkness of error. You are not appalled by darkness. . . . Then let this be your comfort not that you are shrouded with gloom, but that you have the light with which to overcome the darkness."[66]

Whenever and however it occurred, Mrs. Eddy's helpful instruction would strengthen the members of her household for years to come. In a letter written nearly two decades after her service, for example, Minnie Scott would recall a meaningful conversation that Mrs. Eddy had with her housekeeping staff at one point: "She thanked us for the helpful things we were doing for her and for the Cause, but 'You must save some time for God,' she said. 'You must listen for God's voice and let divine Mind tell you what to do and how to do it.' Mrs. Eddy's instruction was very precious to me on those occasions. . . ."[67]

Ella Hoag

"As if a ladder had been put in front of me"

Like many, Ella Whitaker Hoag's introduction to Christian Science came about because of a need for healing.

Born and raised in Toledo, Ohio, Ella studied piano and voice in New York after graduating from high school. Some years later—married to Frank Hoag by this time and mother to seven-year-old Florence (a second daughter, Helen, would arrive several

Ella W. Hoag | Longyear Museum collection

years later)—her health began to fail and she was unable to eat normally. After consulting physicians in Toledo, she traveled to New York to see specialists, but the help she sought wasn't forthcoming. She returned to Ohio, feeling like a "physical wreck" and "heartsick over the perpetual thought of self that the most advanced systems of medicine and hygiene constantly imposed."[68]

A friend convinced her to try Christian Science, which Ella did as a last resort in 1887.

"I found old theological enigmas solved, old doubts dispelled, the Bible illuminated...."

— Ella Hoag

"Never shall I forget my first visit to the Christian Scientist," she later wrote, "when I made the joyful discovery that there were people living on earth in this age, who believed that Jesus meant what he said; that his teachings were not largely abstractions, but were all practical truths...."[69]

Mrs. Hoag's complete recovery under Christian Science treatment was swift. "In three weeks' time I gained fifteen pounds and my whole body was renewed and strengthened.... [F]rom that day to this I have been able to obey Paul's injunction: 'Whatsoever is set before you, eat, asking no question for conscience sake.'"[70]

Ella, who had grown up in the Congregational church, immediately began studying *Science and Health*, wanting to know more about this religion that had healed her. Later, when she was a teacher of Christian Science, she told her students that she could scarcely put the book down.[71] "I found old theological enigmas solved, old doubts dispelled, the Bible illuminated, and ever since then the teachings of Christian Science have been my guide through every moment of my life."[72]

Not only herself, but also her whole family benefited from what she was learning.

"Medicine was immediately banished from our home, and neither my two children nor I have taken any since, although children's diseases of severest types have presented themselves to be overcome," she would write.[73]

Soon after her healing, Ella took Primary class instruction in Toledo from Sarah J. Clark, one of Mary Baker Eddy's students. Later that year, she made an appointment with Mrs. Eddy herself to inquire about admission to the Massachusetts Metaphysical College. Ella described the scene when Mrs. Eddy entered the Columbus Avenue parlor for the interview: "[I]t seemed that the room was filled with her presence. She appeared like a large person, although she was really dainty and small in stature. It was the sense of God's presence, which was the substance of Mrs. Eddy's consciousness, that filled the room."[74]

After taking Primary class instruction from Mrs. Eddy in 1888, Ella Hoag devoted her life to the Cause of Christian Science.[75] She continued to keep in touch with her teacher, and in the fall of 1894, she sent roses to Mrs. Eddy, whose reply read in part: "I thank you for your kind thoughts of me and beautiful roses. Oh may the blossoms of sweet peace be as odorous and beautiful in your pathway as the kind memories of your Teacher are to her.... May the Love that clothes the lily wrap you in its garments of white and give you a gracious answer to all your prayers."[76]

Mrs. Eddy signed her letter "With much love."

Mrs. Hoag's devotion to her work made a deep impression on her family. Once, when they urged her to make more time for recreation, she replied, "Let me get my work done; I have all eternity to play in."[77] And many years later, family members would include among her characteristics "love, depth of perception, clear thinking, forgiveness"—and refer to her as "a Christian woman capable of standing in the face of strong assault."[78]

These qualities of thought and single-minded devotion to her work didn't

Ella Hoag as a young woman.
Longyear Museum collection

Ella Hoag's room at 400 Beacon Street. The photographs on the table and wall may be of her husband, Frank, and daughters, Florence and Helen. | LONGYEAR MUSEUM COLLECTION

go unnoticed. In the spring of 1907, Thomas Hatten wrote to Mrs. Eddy on behalf of the Committee on Business, recommending 53-year-old Ella as a prospective worker. In his report, he described her as "an active and successful practitioner" who was well versed in handling animal magnetism. He also noted that her husband, though not a Christian Scientist, was "interested in it and willing to help her."[79]

And so it was that the following year, in April 1908, Mrs. Hoag left Toledo for Chestnut Hill to join the ranks of Mrs. Eddy's household.

"I went with deepest reverence for her in my heart and with as exalted an estimate of her as I was capable of entertaining," Ella would later recall. "To me,

Mrs. Eddy was not alone the Discoverer and Founder of Christian Science, the revered Leader of the Christian Science movement, the author of the Christian Science textbook,—she was my teacher, my example, the one whose teachings I had been endeavoring to understand and whose life I had been endeavoring to follow for over twenty-one years."[80]

At 400 Beacon Street, Ella served as a metaphysical worker. She was also a companion to Mrs. Eddy, sitting beside her on carriage rides and attending to her daily needs.

"I was often with her from early morning until late at night," Ella would write about her time with her Leader. "Never was she other than the consistent Christian, the exquisite gentlewoman, the loving friend and counselor, the faithful, loyal practitioner of the faith she professed; in other words, the perfect Christian Scientist."[81]

Ella worked intermittently in the home for two years, periodically returning to Toledo to be with her family. After one of her departures from Chestnut Hill in September 1909, her colleague William Rathvon—who often sang with Mrs. Hoag in household gatherings—recorded in his diary that the household was "very sorry to lose Ella Hoag, who is beloved on all sides."[82]

News of her return the following spring gladdened her colleagues: "Her clear thought and uncompromising attitude towards error wherever manifested will make her a valuable addition to our team," William continued. "We are all—the team I mean—looking forward to her coming with much satisfaction, for a better, clearer, stauncher Scientist does not go to church anywhere than ... Mrs. Hoag."[83]

When Ella's husband passed on in March of 1910, Mrs. Eddy wrote her a tender, comforting letter, which reads in part: "Your dear husband has not passed away from you in spirit; he never died only to your sense; he lives and loves and is immortal. Let this comfort you dear one, and you will find rest in banishing the sense of death, in cherishing the sense of life and not death. Your dear husband is as truly living to-day as he ever lived, and you can find rest and peace in this true sense of Life."[84]

At the close of her service in Mrs. Eddy's home, Ella resumed her teaching and practice in Toledo. She remained in Ohio until 1918, when she was once again called to serve the Cause of Christian Science—first, when she was appointed to the Board of Lectureship, and then in 1919, when she was named Associate Editor of the Christian Science periodicals. That same year, she taught the Normal class for the Board of Education, and then, in 1927, she was elected President of The Mother Church, the first woman ever to hold that office.

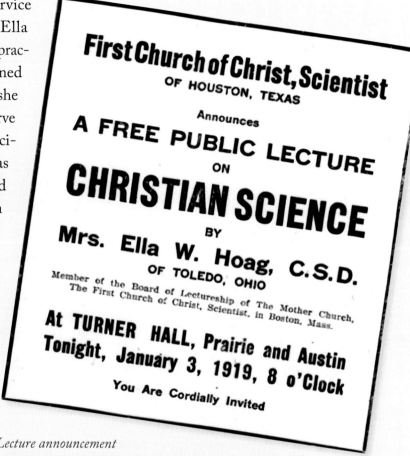

First Church of Christ, Scientist
OF HOUSTON, TEXAS

Announces

A FREE PUBLIC LECTURE
ON

CHRISTIAN SCIENCE
BY
Mrs. Ella W. Hoag, C.S.D.
OF TOLEDO, OHIO

Member of the Board of Lectureship of The Mother Church,
The First Church of Christ, Scientist, in Boston, Mass.

At TURNER HALL, Prairie and Austin
Tonight, January 3, 1919, 8 o'Clock

You Are Cordially Invited

Lecture announcement from the Houston Post, *January 3, 1919.*

"I would never have sought any of these positions," Mrs. Hoag later explained. "However when they were presented, it was as if a ladder had been put in front of me which I must climb, and this climbing has made me ever better equipped to serve the Cause and help others."[85]

Humility was a virtue Ella greatly valued and one she touched on in an address at the Annual Meeting of The Mother Church in 1927: "As members of The Mother Church it is our undoubted right to fulfill all God's wonderful promises for His own people. Protected and cared for by The Mother Church, nothing 'shall be impossible' to us. Always on guard against that egotism which would cast us outside its walls, we can through humble obedience to Christian Science assuredly know that, as Jesus said, 'the gates of hell shall not prevail against it'! Ever humbly loyal to the one Mind and His Christ, as Christian Science teaches us how to be, we shall prove, as Daniel declared, that 'the people that do know their God shall be strong, and do exploits.'"[86]

Ella Hoag was active in the Christian Science movement for nearly half a century as a practitioner, teacher, lecturer, writer, and editor. After her passing, her fellow editors wrote, "Hers was a labor of love, performed in a graciously Christian spirit; and it will never cease to fulfill its healing mission.... Her devotion to her work, uniformly done in a spirit of joy, humility, and thanksgiving, has been a constant inspiration to all with whom she has been associated. . . . To us in her daily life she symbolized true Christianity."[87]

Mrs. Eddy referred to Ella as "my dear student Mrs. Hoag," and gave her this diamond pin in appreciation for her service. | LONGYEAR MUSEUM COLLECTION

Adam Dickey reading in bed at 400 Beacon Street. | Private collection

The "tug of war"

Mrs. Eddy's staff wasn't just gathering and writing down her words as an abstract exercise, or simply to preserve them for posterity. They were striving to put into daily practice what she was teaching them. And Mrs. Eddy knew this wasn't easy. As she told Irving Tomlinson in the summer of 1908, Christian Science "is simple in its theory and simple in its explanation, but in its living, there comes the tug of war."[88] Helping her household win this tug of war by making practical what she was imparting to them appears to have been a chief aim in her ongoing instruction.

"[W]hat so impressed her instructions upon my mind," recalled Martha Wilcox, "was that she required of me immediate application and demonstration of what she taught. Without this required application and demonstration, Mrs. Eddy knew that the instructions she gave would be of little value to me."[89]

Often Mrs. Eddy requested that her workers give their prayerful treatments aloud so that she might help hone and guide their efforts.

"If there was any flaw in their work, she could instantly detect it and set the student on the right track," said Adam Dickey. "A carelessly worded treatment bespeaks a careless or indifferent thought, and any form of carelessness or inexactness of thought or expression was quickly corrected by our Leader."[90]

He cited as an example an occasion when he told her, "you cannot have a return of an old belief." She immediately corrected him, helping him understand that he should have said "diseased belief" or "an old belief of sickness." As she explained, "At one time I had a belief of excellent health, and your declaration, if carried out, would prevent me from expressing that belief of health, and that is what I am striving for."[91]

"None could be more austere and unyielding when confronting an error; none more wise and gentle in counseling and comforting the erring one."
— William Rathvon

Correction like this was a key component of Mrs. Eddy's teaching—and it often included rebuke.

"None could be more austere and unyielding when confronting an error; none more wise and gentle in counseling and comforting the erring one," observed William Rathvon.[92]

These rebukes from Mrs. Eddy weren't random, nor were they motivated by a wish to humiliate or discourage, but rather by a heartfelt yearning to support each student's spiritual progress. Mr. Tomlinson, who came in for his fair share of correction, noted that it was part and parcel of Mrs. Eddy's friendship—friendship which "was manifested not only in words of counsel and acts of love but in pointed, timely rebukes. Although occasionally they hurt at the moment, they proved to be a healing fire, destroying only the error."[93]

Teaching by example

"In our association with our Leader," said Mr. Rathvon, the members of her household "had rare opportunities for gaining invaluable instruction from what she did as well as from what she said."[94]

From their front-row seats, they were able to see for themselves how she put Christian Science into practice. One such incident that touched on the entire staff, from the mansion's upper floors to the stables, occurred during the summer of 1908, when Mrs. Eddy was fully engaged with the upcoming launch of *The Christian Science Monitor*. A neighbor girl was being particularly annoying, lingering by the front gate each day to gawk at Mrs. Eddy as she passed by on her daily drive, and, according to one staff member, actually climbing into the carriage on one occasion "to examine it."[95]

Adolph Stevenson, who was the coachman at the time, was fit to be tied, and some of the household "were voicing radical ways" in which this behavior should be stopped, recalled cook Margaret Macdonald.[96]

Coachman Adolph Stevenson at the reins of one of Mrs. Eddy's carriages. | Private collection

Mrs. Eddy on a carriage ride near her home in Chestnut Hill.

Longyear Museum collection

On one particular day, said Minnie Scott, when the girl was "quite offensive in her attitude," Adolph had finally had enough, and came in after the day's drive "very much incensed and wishing to punish that girl."[97]

Mrs. Eddy had a different plan.

Waiting upstairs on the desk in her study was a gift that had just arrived from some of her students—a basket of beautiful peaches. After penning a loving note to the girl, Mrs. Eddy gave it and the basket to her still-seething coachman, with the request that he deliver it next door.

The result of her kindness?

"The girl was overcome by this gracious act and was healed of her undue curiosity. The [coachman] had a lesson in forgiveness, and we all were blessed by Mrs. Eddy's method of overcoming ignorance and hate," said Mrs. Scott.[98] In thinking back on her Leader's actions that day, Minnie came to understand that they went deeper than just placating a rude neighbor with a present. She would later write: "[O]f course the realization of God's allness and man's unity with Him must accompany such a gift to bring out healing as it did in this case."[99]

Ella Rathvon

"Have this one come and see me"

Ella Rathvon's first glimpse of Mary Baker Eddy was a memorable one. She and her husband, William, were in Concord, New Hampshire, for the day, when Mrs. Eddy passed by in her carriage, and the pair caught a glimpse of her "gracious smile."[100]

Little did they know the time would come when they would see that smile every day!

Ella S. Rathvon | LONGYEAR MUSEUM COLLECTION

The Rathvons, who were one of the few married couples who worked on Mrs. Eddy's estate, made a great team.

"[S]he stood happily at my side through adversity and prosperity," William stated about the woman with whom he shared a 40-year marriage. Ella, he continued, was "an ideal wife and help meet and above all a consecrated Christian Scientist."[101]

Although she didn't pursue Christian Science for physical healing, Ella Rathvon was nonetheless cured of a malady that a physician had pronounced incurable, after she and her husband were introduced to the new religion while visiting Chicago in 1893.[102]

"While deeply grateful for the physical benefits received," Ella would later write, "they seem insignificant when compared to the spiritual awakening through which I begin to realize that the tormenting fears are being displaced by the 'perfect love' which 'casteth out fear.'"[103]

Ella Janet Stauffer was born in 1863 in Lancaster, Pennsylvania, as was William Rathvon, whom she wed in 1883. With their marriage, she became stepmother to William's two-and-a-half-year-old son, Martin, who was her nephew and the child of William's previous marriage to Ella's older sister, Lillie.[104] Ella was, according to her husband, "a devoted mother...."[105]

Raised in the Presbyterian church, she was swift to embrace Christian Science, as was her husband. The couple were living in Denver when they took Primary class instruction during a sojourn in Chicago, and the following year, in 1894, they returned to Colorado and immediately put into practice what they had learned.[106] By 1899, both were listed as practitioners in *The Christian Science Journal.*

The Rathvons were instrumental in bringing Christian Science to Florence, the small town where William worked in the booming oil industry, and they helped establish a church there before moving to Boulder.[107] In her practice, Ella would report healings of tumors, abscess, ankle sprain, scarlet fever, tuberculosis,

Right: Ella and William Rathvon share a laugh. | LONGYEAR MUSEUM COLLECTION

paralysis, and more over the next decade.[108] In 1903, the couple journeyed to Boston, where they were instructed in another Primary class, this one taught by Edward Kimball. Afterward, they returned once again to Colorado, and their respective healing practices.

Sometime in 1907 or early 1908, Ella caught the eye of the Committee on Business, who recommended her to Mary Baker Eddy as a prospective worker. One report described her as plump and rosy-faced, "of sturdy German stock," with a disposition that shines through in four brief words: "sunny, unselfish, fearless, strong." Ella, the report concluded, "is holding herself in readiness to respond to a call. . . ."[109]

Another letter noted that Ella had been a Christian Scientist for 15 years and in the public healing practice for 14 of them. "She has treated hundreds of cases . . . and has healed nearly all of them," it stated. Atop this page, Mrs. Eddy scribbled the words, "Have this one come and see me."[110]

Although Ella Rathvon was called to Boston on several occasions to meet Mrs. Eddy, her staff, or members of the Christian Science Board of Directors, the time was not quite ripe for her to join the household.[111] Instead, her husband was the one who was welcomed first.

The Rathvons' separation tested their dedication and commitment. When William was asked about the hardest thing he would have to face if invited to work in Mrs. Eddy's home, he responded, "Separation from the one with whom I have worked side by side in Science since the first. . . ."[112]

Ella was praying diligently about this challenge, too. In a letter to Mrs. Eddy, she wrote, "It gives me great joy to tell you that the sense of separation is being gloriously overcome. . . . Meeting this claim of separation has been the supreme test of my life, but by the grace of God and your messages of love and encouragement I have been able to stand the test. . . ."[113]

Mrs. Eddy's "messages of love and encouragement" recognized the contributions made by both husband and wife and helped them see their demonstration as a divine oblation. "[Y]ou must both know that what you are doing and giving is not a sacrifice," Mrs. Eddy counseled, "but an offering."[114]

Ella Rathvon's room at 400 Beacon Street. | Longyear Museum collection

Ella continued with her healing practice in Boulder until the spring of 1909, when she moved to an apartment in Newton Centre, Massachusetts, just down the road from Chestnut Hill so that, as William would explain, "we might be near each other and at least have a little daily companionship."[115]

> *"[Y]ou must both know that what you are doing and giving is not a sacrifice, but an offering."*
> *— Mary Baker Eddy*

On September 3, 1909, Ella Rathvon was finally invited to join Mrs. Eddy's staff. It took her exactly 40 minutes to pack up her belongings and head over to the house. As she recorded in her diary for that day: "Phone at 4:10 pm from Chestnut Hill to be there by 4:45. Packed suitcase and dressed and at Chestnut Hill by 4:50. Accepted as one of the household."[116]

Like Laura Sargent and Ella Hoag, Mrs. Rathvon served as a metaphysical worker and companion—spending her days at Mrs. Eddy's side, accompanying her on her daily carriage rides, and, at Mrs. Eddy's direction, praying for the household along with anything else she was instructed to treat. According to groundskeeper John Salchow, "Mrs. Ella Rathvon and Mrs. Laura Sargent relieved one another in the capacity of companion to Mrs. Eddy. Both were very wholesome women and served faithfully and well."[117]

Ella's colleagues and contemporaries remembered her in particular for her "joyous, youthful attitude," her devotion to Christian Science, and for her beautiful singing voice, which brought "great enjoyment and delight" to Mrs. Eddy.[118] One worker recalled Ella singing every morning to Mrs. Eddy.[119]

Once, when Ella told Mrs. Eddy how much she loved her, Mrs. Eddy responded, "I know you do, dear, your work shows it."[120]

During her time of service, Ella kept a diary in which she recorded not only the comings and goings of the household, but also a great deal of Mrs. Eddy's instruction, both to her individually as well as to the rest of the metaphysical workers and staff as a whole. It's clear that she cherished her Leader's counsel and took it to heart.

The entries range from short and sweet ("Heard our Leader read her poem 'Satisfied'—inspiring!"[121]) to more substantive, and include insights into the household's daily life. For instance, Ella's entry for New Year's Day, 1910, noted, "At ten a.m. we had a love-feast in Mother's room. Sang hymns and had a loving talk. This is my first New Year's day at Mrs. Eddy's home, Chestnut Hill. Never have I felt a greater sense of love for all mankind."[122]

From several of Ella's entries, it appears that Mrs. Eddy was working to help her staff look beyond their tenure at 400 Beacon Street to the years that lay ahead. For instance, at the end of March 1910, everyone was called to Mrs. Eddy's study for a talk. Ella jotted down the gist of it: "We have a great work to do, and are now preparing for it. When we again go out into the world [we have] a big debt to pay to God. He does not demand it all at once, but is satisfied with interest."[123]

Ella Rathvon would work hard to repay that debt. While interviewing for a position in 1908, it was her "very successful healing" work that caught her Leader's attention.[124] After leaving Chestnut Hill—her metaphysics strengthened and honed under Mrs. Eddy's close tutelage—Ella would persist in the public practice of Christian Science and support her husband as he shouldered new responsibilities for the Church until her passing in 1923.

Prepared for a high calling

Working closely with their Leader, seeing her example, learning more about Christian Science under her instruction, and putting into practice what she was imparting to them—even smarting under the sting of rebukes—all of this was counted an inestimable privilege by those chosen to serve in her household.

"To live in Mrs. Eddy's home was an education in itself and those of us who heeded the daily lessons were always blessed," said cook Minnie Weygandt.[125]

The intense training ground was designed to equip them for the work that lay ahead. In December 1909, William Rathvon recalled that "a most illuminating talk on our duties and privileges" occurred in the Pink Room, as Mrs. Eddy's staff stood grouped around her.

"You have been called here of God for the special purpose of carrying on His work," their Leader told them. "You are here to prepare yourselves for that high calling. This is a preparatory school. . . ."

She then asked, "Now what is the first thing for you to learn?" and Adam Dickey replied, "To know there is nothing but God and His idea."

"That's it, dearie," Mrs. Eddy said, "and when you really know that, then there is no sickness to heal, and no sin to destroy. Get out of your thoughts every word that suggests a belief apart from God. Every word."[126]

In the final year that she was with them, Mrs. Eddy would return to this theme on several occasions.

"You are here preparing to take a strong position before the world," she told them in March 1910. "There is a high purpose to be fulfilled by you in healing the sick and reforming the sinner, but you are now getting ready for the higher office of teaching and preaching and carrying on the Cause in other important directions."[127]

Less than a week before her passing, she reminded them, "Turn your thoughts to Principle, not to me. You lose your answer from God by looking to me for the answer."[128] Around that same time, an "Everybody Call" went out one day, and the Rathvons, Laura Sargent, Calvin Frye, Irving Tomlinson, and Adam

Dickey all came to Mrs. Eddy's study. She then proceeded to put "a long series of questions to each one as to how he might do better than he was doing, seeking to impress upon us that we must put in practice the truth we have."[129]

Like her colleagues, Minnie Scott, who would be in the public practice of Christian Science healing for nearly half a century, cherished her Leader's instruction and deeply valued all that she had been given while under her tutelage.

"Turn your thoughts to Principle, not to me.

You lose your answer from God by

looking to me for the answer."

— Mary Baker Eddy

"In July 1909," she would later recall, "I said to her, 'I wish I could remember every word you have said to me.' She said to me, 'My dear, it will all come to you just when you need it, and you will find as you go on that your experience here with me will prove invaluable to you.' I am grateful to record that I found this also to be true."[130]

Some of Mary Baker Eddy's household toward the end of their service at 400 Beacon Street. Left to right: Jonathan Irving, Calvin Frye, William Rathvon, John Salchow, Ella Rathvon, Laura Sargent, Elizabeth Kelly, Martha Wilcox, Katharine Retterer, Lula Phillips, Nellie Eveleth, Adelaide Still, Charlotte Bowman, Irving Tomlinson, and Frank Bowman. | LONGYEAR MUSEUM COLLECTION

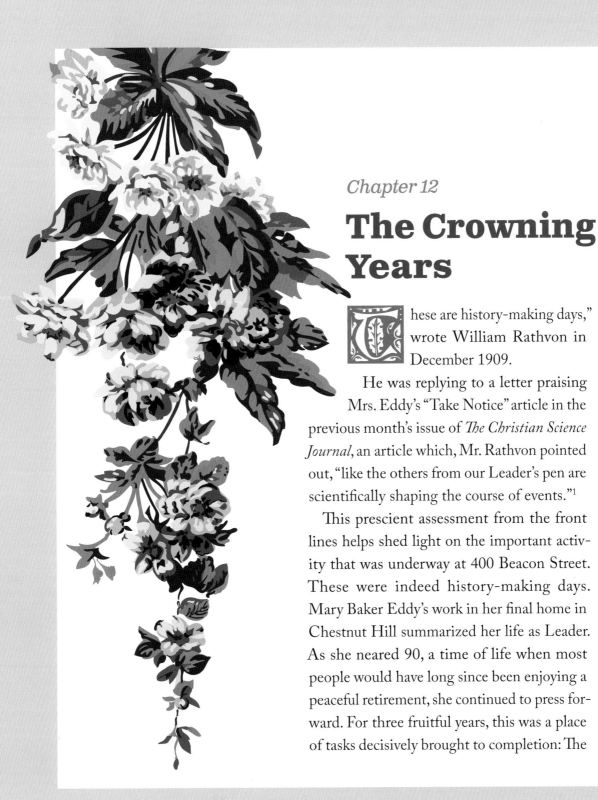

Chapter 12

The Crowning Years

hese are history-making days," wrote William Rathvon in December 1909.

He was replying to a letter praising Mrs. Eddy's "Take Notice" article in the previous month's issue of *The Christian Science Journal*, an article which, Mr. Rathvon pointed out, "like the others from our Leader's pen are scientifically shaping the course of events."[1]

This prescient assessment from the front lines helps shed light on the important activity that was underway at 400 Beacon Street. These were indeed history-making days. Mary Baker Eddy's work in her final home in Chestnut Hill summarized her life as Leader. As she neared 90, a time of life when most people would have long since been enjoying a peaceful retirement, she continued to press forward. For three fruitful years, this was a place of tasks decisively brought to completion: The

Mary Baker Eddy's study at 400 Beacon Street as interpreted today.

birth of *The Christian Science Monitor;* settling the succession question; making hundreds of revisions to her writings, including *Science and Health;* authorizing the textbook's first translation into another language; writing final By-laws for the *Church Manual;* establishing Christian Science nursing; and producing a stream of pastoral letters, articles, and messages to her Church and the world.

"Mrs. Eddy was tireless in her industry; her capacity for work was prodigious," Irving Tomlinson would tell his lecture audiences in the decades to come. "Up to the time of her passing she had oversight of all the affairs of her vast movement. Every important step awaited her decision."[2]

While Mrs. Eddy was as mentally active as ever, these were quieter years physically for her. Aside from her daily carriage ride, she spent most of her days upstairs in her suite. "I sit quietly alone in my room conversing with the world," she would write in October 1910.[3]

The "Calm, Sacred Retreat" of Christian Science Nursing

In late 1908, readers of the *Christian Science Sentinel* opened their November 21 issue to find that a new *Church Manual* By-law had been authorized by Mary Baker Eddy under Article VIII, "Guidance of Members," providing for Christian Science nurses:[4]

> ## NEW BY-LAWS.
> ### ARTICLE VIII.
>
> CHRISTIAN SCIENCE NURSE.—SECT. 31. A member of The Mother Church who represents himself or herself as a Christian Science nurse, shall be one who has a demonstrable knowledge of Christian Science practice, who thoroughly understands the practical wisdom necessary in a sick-room, and who can take proper care of the sick.
>
> The cards of such persons may be inserted in *The Christian Science Journal* under rules established by the publishers.

While the By-law itself may have come as a surprise, the impulse behind it had been ripening for some time. As early as the first edition of *Science and Health*, Mrs. Eddy had addressed the importance of the mental atmosphere of the sick room,[5] and by 1881 she was cautioning, "A cross or complaining nurse should never take charge of the sick."[6] Later editions of the textbook would begin to address necessary qualities of thought, culminating in the statement which stands today that a nurse "should be cheerful, orderly, punctual, patient, full of faith,—receptive to Truth and Love."[7]

Mrs. Eddy herself demonstrated the "practical wisdom" of which she wrote in the new By-law. For instance, while at Pleasant View in 1903 and again in 1905, cook Minnie Weygandt struggled with a physical difficulty. She was given

Above: Daisette Stocking McKenzie.
Right: Elizabeth Kelly
at Pleasant View.

LONGYEAR MUSEUM COLLECTION

time off by Mrs. Eddy, who told her, "I am going to have a place where those who <u>think</u> they need recruiting can go."[8] That vision wouldn't be realized until 1916, when preliminary steps were taken to establish The Christian Science Benevolent Association in Boston. Meanwhile, Mrs. Eddy took the practical steps necessary for Minnie, seeing to it that she was transferred by carriage to a cottage on the property to be cared for by the Mann family.[9]

Over the coming years, Mrs. Eddy continued to think about a "sanatorium" or "resort for invalids," as she described it in a 1905 letter to Mary Beecher Long-year.[10] Then, some months after enacting the By-law establishing the provision for Christian Science nurses, she submitted another By-law to the Board of Directors. This one called for "a Christian Science resort for the so-called sick." Although Mrs. Eddy would eventually ask them to shelve the idea for the time being, within a decade the seed she planted would come to fruition with the establishment of the first facility for Christian Science nursing.[11]

Unofficial nursing activity had been going on in the field for some time. There were many accounts in the Christian Science periodicals of friends, family, and even practitioners caring for patients, and some of her own students, as well as members of her household, were involved in these kinds of endeavors. Elizabeth Kelly had cared for practitioners' patients in her home back in Marion, Ohio, prior to entering Mrs. Eddy's employ. It's highly likely that Mrs. Eddy was aware of this.

She was certainly aware of a similar enterprise in Canada. Daisette Stocking, who would eventually marry William McKenzie, was living in a small house in Toronto in the mid-1890s with a friend who was a fellow Christian Science practitioner.[12] The two women opened their home to help care for female patients while they were seeking Christian Science treatment.

"We called our little home 'Sharon,' which is interpreted as 'a fold for the flocks,'" Daisette would later write.[13]

> *"Please give my love to the lady who is with you in your calm, sacred retreat...."*
> *— Mary Baker Eddy*

Mrs. Eddy approved of their efforts and sent letters of encouragement, addressing one "To the Dwellers in Sharon," and in another telling Daisette, "Please give my love to the lady who is with you in your calm, sacred retreat...."[14]

The compassionate, practical provision for the care afforded by Christian Science nurses, along with her vision of a "resort for invalids," would be a lasting accomplishment, begun while Mrs. Eddy was living at Chestnut Hill.

*William Dana Orcutt of University Press
in Cambridge, Massachusetts.*

COURTESY LIBRARY OF CONGRESS

Several years before her move to 400 Beacon Street, Mrs. Eddy told a journalist, "All that I ask of the world now is that it grant me time, time to assimilate myself to God."[15] And in June 1909, when her old friend William Johnson stepped down from the Christian Science Board of Directors, she counseled him, "Having no office work to meet in a business way will give you a better chance to attend to yourself, and we all must do this sometime or the weeds will choke the growing grain. One of the best, gladdest moments of my life would be to have more time in which to help myself...."[16]

Mary Baker Eddy herself would characterize this period of her life as "consolidating my gains, while I keep on with the building." She made this comment to her long-time printer and friend William Dana Orcutt when he came to see her in 1909. Mr. Orcutt hadn't visited for five years. "Naturally," he recalled, "I was prepared for changes." He noticed only one. "[I]t was the first time she had ever received me sitting down. But the clear voice that greeted me, the bright eyes, and the keen expression of interest belied any thought that her sitting posture was enforced." He went on to note that, during their meeting, she rose easily from her chair to reach for something on a nearby table.

Regarding her comment, he added, "What a wonderful self-analysis of those final fruitful years!"[17]

A facsimile of the first edition of The Christian Science Monitor.

The greatest step forward

Of all that Mary Baker Eddy would accomplish during this period, one of her most significant acts was founding a newspaper. As she would afterwards remark to her household, "When I established *The Christian Science Monitor,* I took the greatest step forward since I gave *Science and Health* to the world."[18]

In and of itself an accomplishment of a lifetime, the fact that Mrs. Eddy took this step at the age of 87, after decades of equally notable accomplishments, makes it all the more noteworthy.

As she'd told reporter W. T. MacIntyre of the *New York American* five months before moving to 400 Beacon Street, "I have much work to do. . . . I trust in God, and He will give me strength to accomplish those things which have been marked out for me to do."[19]

Starting a newspaper was one of those things.

She'd had the idea in mind for many years—as early as when she lived in Lynn, in fact—cherishing it quietly as she allowed it to ripen.[20] As always, she relied on God to inspire the timing, and by the summer of 1908, the timing was finally right.

A crisp note to the Board of Trustees of The Christian Science Publishing Society set the wheels in motion:

Beloved Students: *It is my request that you start a daily newspaper at once, and call it the* <u>Christian Science Monitor</u>. *Let there be no delay. The Cause demands that it be issued now.*[21]

Mrs. Eddy set an ambitious deadline for the launch: November. Conventional wisdom deemed such an undertaking impossible, but in the space of just three short months, experienced staff were hired, equipment acquired and put swiftly in place, and arrangements made for distribution. Each of the many hurdles presented was overcome; each objection answered—including objection to the newspaper's name. No one would purchase a newspaper with the name "Christian Science" on the masthead, Mrs. Eddy was told. There was too much prejudice against it. Why not simply call it *The Monitor*?

Mrs. Eddy held her ground in the face of stiff opposition.

"God gave me this name and it remains," she said in no uncertain terms when soon-to-be-editor Archibald McLellan made a last-ditch effort to persuade her otherwise.[22]

The day before Thanksgiving was publication day. When one member of the household mentioned that the weather outside was dark and foggy, Mrs. Eddy quickly responded, "Yes, but only according to sense. We know the reverse of error is true. This, in truth, is the lightest day of all days. This is the day when our daily paper goes forth to lighten mankind."[23]

"Her great hope which she had cherished so long had at last found expression."
— Daisette McKenzie

A few miles away at The Christian Science Publishing Society, the press room was abuzz with activity. As the printing equipment was fired up for its inaugural run, Trustees William McKenzie, Thomas Hatten, and Clifford Smith took off their jackets and assisted in their shirt sleeves.[24] The first copy that rolled off the press was ferried to Mrs. Eddy by maintenance man Walter Watson. "It was all securely wrapped and tied with pink ribbon," he would later record, "and I carried it as carefully as if I had been transporting the crown jewels."[25]

A delighted Mrs. Eddy "clasped it to her heart," recalled one onlooker. "Her great hope which she had cherished so long had at last found expression."[26]

Each member of the household received his or her own copy of that first issue as well. "The joyous expectation in the home far exceeded any of the preparation and festivities any of the members of the household had experienced in their homes at the Christmas season," said housekeeper Frances Thatcher.[27]

Mrs. Eddy's interest in and direction of the newspaper didn't wane after its launch.

"Mrs. Eddy conceived the idea of a clean newspaper, outlined its policy and purpose, and as long as she was here, remained in absolute command," observed Alexander Dodds, the *Monitor's* first managing editor.[28]

According to Irving Tomlinson, Mrs. Eddy read the newspaper thoroughly every day and continued to watch over its progress as carefully as a mother bird watches over her fledgling.[29]

For more than two years that followed the launch of the *Monitor*, "I had daily opportunity to note Mrs. Eddy's interest in its progress and her watchful solicitude for its permanent success," William Rathvon would recall. One of the first copies off the press continued to be brought to her each day.

> *"Where technical experience was needed she had little to say; where wisdom, vision, and a reflection of divine intelligence were requisite she alone spoke, and her word was law."*
> *— William Rathvon*

"She was specially interested in the constructive and helpful news of the day, in the metaphysical article on the Home Forum page and the editorials," he observed. "She was closely interested in the successive steps of the paper's development, outlining and directing its policies but entrusting the mechanical and business sides of it to her chosen associates. Where technical experience was needed she had little to say; where wisdom, vision, and a reflection of divine intelligence were requisite she alone spoke, and her word was law. . . . *The Christian Science Monitor* was the demonstration of the Discoverer and Founder of the religion whose name it bears. Upon her rested its creation, upon her followers rests its success."[30]

"We rise by what we demonstrate"

Mrs. Eddy's years in Chestnut Hill were not without struggle. She continued to face and surmount serious hurdles, from a press that seemed perpetually poised—even eager—to report her demise; to challenges to her leadership; to physical suffering; and so on.

"As the years advanced," said Mr. Tomlinson, "Mrs. Eddy was vigilant in working for herself, turning the truth upon whatever suggestion presented itself. . . . At times she had mighty wrestlings with error. But she was faithful in applying the truth to whatever argument assailed her, and she never swerved from the path in which her feet had been set."[31]

One morning, he said, she told her metaphysical workers, "I had a hard time last night, but I am only the better for it. Why? Because every trial of our faith lifts us higher. We rise by what we demonstrate."[32]

On another occasion, Mrs. Eddy told Mr. Rathvon, "I am struggling with the claims of old age and death, and if I undertook to handle them as presented, I could never meet them; but I just hold to the allness of God, that there is nothing else, and I want all of you to do just the same."[33]

Her household had long been aware of how closely aligned her thought was with all that transpired in her Church, and how often steps of progress seemed to be accompanied by physical discomfort.

"Those closely associated with Mrs. Eddy knew when she was giving birth, in thought, to some important decision—such as a change in the Church, the making of a new By-Law, or something in connection with her writings," Martha Wilcox recalled. "Many times there seemed to be great travail when these things were being born of the Spirit. I remember such a time when she abolished the Communion season of The Mother Church, and again when certain new By-Laws were brought out."[34]

Over the years, the sacredness of the Communion service in The Mother Church had been nearly smothered by the surrounding activities, as members flocked to Boston—and to Pleasant View.[35] And so, in 1906, Mrs. Eddy requested that members of The Mother Church not gather at her residence in Concord, New Hampshire, reminding them that "the divine and not the human should engage our attention at this sacred season of prayer and praise."[36]

Ignoring her request, some members went to Pleasant View anyway, and in the wake of this, Mrs. Eddy amended a By-law. While local members of The Mother Church would continue to observe an annual Communion, distant members would be invited to attend only once every three years.

Despite this amendment and despite a reminder issued in the *Sentinel* the following year, some 8,500 people attended the 1907 Communion. By 1908, the number swelled to 10,000.[37]

"Mrs. Eddy seemed very restless and unsettled on that Sunday," Adelaide Still would write. "At last she turned to Laura Sargent and said, 'What is it, Laura? I have always suffered for what was not right with my church.' Mrs. Sargent could not answer her. Mrs. Eddy turned away, and we knew from her attitude that she was praying and meditating. I think it was the next day that she wrote the By-Law abolishing the Communion service."[38]

Adam Dickey offered additional detail: "Our Leader had been suffering intensely for several days before this By-law came out, and even while she dictated to me the words included in it, she was lying on the lounge in her study wrestling with a malicious attack of unusual severity. I took the proposed By-law . . . to my desk, and after transcribing it, I returned with it immediately to her room and was overjoyed to find her seated at her desk, wreathed in smiles, and pursuing her regular work with her usual vigor."

Mr. Dickey, who had been in Mrs. Eddy's household only a few months at this point in time, later discussed the incident with Calvin Frye, who told him, "[W]henever any great revelation came to her, concerning that which seemed necessary for the welfare of our Cause, these struggles appeared in her body."

This made a deep impression on her private secretary. Adam went on to note that Mrs. Eddy never complained about these bouts, but "was willing to take the suffering if she could only succeed in obeying the voice of God."[39]

"Your Leader is living, loving, acting, enjoying"

In addition to weathering such private storms as these, Mrs. Eddy again found herself the object of public scrutiny. In the spring of 1908, just a few months after the move to Chestnut Hill, rumors began circulating in the press that she was ill.[40]

Alfred Farlow, in his role as Committee on Publication and Church spokesman, stepped forward to refute them.[41] His rebuttal was widely published, but even more effective in quashing the rumors was an article by Edwin Park of the *Boston Globe.*

Mr. Park was one of a handful of respected journalists to whom Mrs. Eddy had granted interviews back at Pleasant View during the Next Friends suit the previous summer, and on May 12, he stopped by 400 Beacon Street to see for himself what was going on. He found Mrs. Eddy in fine fettle.

"Her eye is as bright, her hand-clasp as strong and hearty and her voice as full and steady as when I visited with her for forty minutes on the afternoon of June 15 last year at her old home," Park reported. "If there has been any change in Mrs. Eddy's physical condition during the past eleven months it has been for the better."

The newspaperman watched her walk unaided ("with a vigorous step") from the side door to her carriage, where she bowed and smiled at him. After she returned from her drive, he enjoyed a brief visit with her upstairs in her study.

Mrs. Eddy's household told Park that they were mystified as to the reports in the *New York Herald* that she had been too ill to take her drive for the prior two weeks. Both Laura Sargent and Adam Dickey declared that she had missed her drive on only two occasions since moving to her new home, when "the streets were so icy and the weather so bad that she thought it would be cruel to take the horses out."[42]

The article that resulted from Park's visit put an end to the erroneous news, as did a trio of statements from Mrs. Eddy herself that were widely circulated—statements that one newspaper termed "direct and to the point."[43]

All three were initially published in the *Christian Science Sentinel,* the first two in the May 16, 1908, issue. Aimed at the press and the general public, this one brims with the tart wit for which Mrs. Eddy was well known:

> *Since Mrs. Eddy is watched, as one watches a criminal or sick person, she begs to say, in her own behalf, that she is neither; therefore to be criticized or judged by either a daily drive or a dignified stay at home, is superfluous. When accumulating work requires it, or because of a preference to remain within doors she omits her drive, do not strain out gnats or swallow camels over it, but try to be composed and resigned to the shocking fact that she is minding her own business, and recommends this surprising privilege to all her dear friends and enemies.*[44]

The other, titled "Nota Bene" and meant for Christian Scientists, strikes a tone that is at once tender and militant and offers a rousing rebuke to the world's expectations about aging, with all its accompanying retrenchment and decline. It begins:

> Beloved Students:— *Rest assured that your Leader is living, loving, acting, enjoying. She is neither dead nor plucked up by the roots, but she is keenly alive to the reality of living, and safely, soulfully founded upon the Rock, Christ Jesus, even the spiritual idea of Life with its abounding, increasing, advancing footsteps of progress, primeval faith, hope, love.*[45]

The third, her letter to the editor of the *New York Herald,* was reprinted the following week, in the May 23 issue of the *Sentinel.* It begins:

> My Dear Editor: — *Permit me to say the report that I am sick (and I*
> *trust the desire thereof) is dead, and should be buried. Whereas the fact*
> *that I am well and keenly alive to the truth of being — the Love that*
> *is Life — is sure and steadfast. I go out in my carriage daily, and have*
> *omitted my drive but twice since I came to Massachusetts. Either work,*
> *the demands upon my time at home, or the weather is all that prevents*
> *my daily drive. Working and praying for my dear friends' and my dear*
> *enemies' health, happiness, and holiness, the true sense of being goes on.*[46]

Further erroneous reports of this nature would crop up again from time to time while Mrs. Eddy was living at 400 Beacon Street, including the night before she requested that the Christian Science Board of Directors start a daily newspaper.[47] Shortly after midnight on July 28, 1908, as Calvin Frye recorded in his diary, an editor from the *Boston Herald* called to ask at what hour Mrs. Eddy had died.

"She had been having a series of attacks for over a week which kept her in bed and on the lounge almost the entire time," Calvin wrote. He went on to say that, when the telephone call was received, it revealed the malpractice at the root of her discomfort, and she was able to gain relief.[48]

"When these things cease to bless they will cease to occur"

Mrs. Eddy would again find herself in the headlines the following year, with a pair of challenges to her leadership. The more serious of the two was from the formidably ambitious Augusta Stetson; the lesser from a flamboyant minor character by the name of Della Gilbert. Both women were from New York.

On April 10, 1909, Mrs. Gilbert made the front page of the *New York Times*, in an article revealing her plans to hold Christian Science services in the grand ballroom of Manhattan's fashionable Plaza Hotel. The article indicated that this undertaking had the full approval of Mrs. Eddy and that the Plaza orchestra would accompany the hymns in a bid to recruit "people well known in society."[49]

The same day that this article appeared, Mrs. Eddy wrote a rousing letter to the Christian Science Board of Directors. "Awake! and Arise!" it began. "Read the awful reports from New York relative to the leasing of a hotel ball-room for Christian Science services." She urged them to alert members of The Mother Church to address the situation prayerfully. "Know that animal magnetism and unrighteous prayers are powerless, and they cannot overthrow the institution of Christian Science, nor retard its growth."[50]

The following day, both the *Times* and the *New York Sun* published corrections. Alfred Farlow informed the *Sun* that no application for a new church organization in New York had been received and that Mrs. Eddy had not given her consent to the proposed lavish services. John Dittemore, Committee on Publication for New York, assured the *Times* that "Christian Science services are always conducted in a modest and quiet manner, without ostentation. Music by an orchestra or other special features intended to attract large congregations are never indulged in. An effort to gain converts among the residents of Fifth Avenue or to proselyte any other particular class of people would be entirely foreign to the methods of Christian Science."[51]

Claiming that her motives had been misunderstood, Della told those who arrived at the hotel on Easter Sunday only to find the service called off, that she was postponing the launch until she'd had a chance to "confer with headquarters and . . . let the authorities there know that all this notoriety has been totally unfounded."[52]

By April 19, however, the *Sun's* headline read "Mrs. Gilbert Gives Up."[53] In May, a disgruntled Della sent a letter to Adam Dickey containing threats against Mrs. Eddy.[54] And then, on June 5, 1909, the *New York World*, which had unleashed the attacks on Mrs. Eddy three years earlier that eventually led to the Next Friends suit, published an open letter from Della, who claimed that the Christian Science church was "without a spiritual leader in the flesh," painting 400 Beacon Street as "that house of mystery in Brookline" (a direct echo of a charge the *World* made earlier about Pleasant View); and asserting that "Mrs. Eddy is either dead or a helpless, mindless puppet in the hands of conscienceless men."[55]

She insisted that what she was claiming about Mrs. Eddy had been revealed to her by God, and called on Christian Scientists to join her in what she termed, "a purification of our church." She ended her letter, "There must be a living spiritual head"—not so subtly positioning herself as that individual.

"Now that [Mrs. Eddy] has ruled her church for 40 years, the time has come when, as Moses did, she must step down and yield leadership to some other one," Della told another reporter a few days later—adding that she was only too happy to serve in that role "if it is the will of divine love."[56]

The volley caused another sensation in the press. Once again, Alfred Farlow stepped forward to issue a rebuttal: "Mrs. Della M. Gilbert's statement is but a reiteration of the oft-repeated and oft-refuted claim that Mary Baker Eddy is no longer the head of the Christian Science church," he stated. "In fact, Mrs. Eddy has never relinquished the active supervision of the Christian Science movement. She is in good health and mentally alert."

"Mrs. Eddy has never relinquished the active supervision of the Christian Science movement. She is in good health and mentally alert." — Alfred Farlow

Mr. Farlow also revealed that Della had expressed the desire that "Divine Love" would "send, give, or loan" her $5,000. If the funds weren't forthcoming [presumably from The Mother Church], she'd warned, "I can by following my original plan [of starting a church at the Plaza] secure a much larger sum of money."[57]

On June 7, the day after this revelation, reporters "besieged" 400 Beacon Street, as Calvin Frye put it, to get to the bottom of things.[58] They were greeted cordially and shown through the house, from the kitchen to Mrs. Eddy's own suite of rooms ("a privilege never before extended to journalistic visitors," noted

Mrs. Eddy in her carriage on June 7, 1909. Laura Sargent is seated beside her;
Frank Bowman is at the reins; Calvin Frye is next to him. | Longyear Museum collection

The Christian Science Monitor).[59] They also had the opportunity to see Mrs. Eddy, who smiled and waved at them as she passed by in her carriage.[60] One of the newsmen—A.B. Reed of the *Boston Traveler*—snapped a photo.[61]

Once again, Mrs. Eddy came to her own defense with a written statement:

To Whom It May Concern:—*I have the pleasure to report to one and all of my beloved friends and followers that I exist in the flesh, and am seen daily by the members of my household and by those with whom I have appointments. Above all this fustian of either denying or asserting the personality and presence of Mary Baker Eddy, stands the eternal fact of Christian Science and the honest history of its Discoverer and Founder. It is self-evident that the discoverer of an eternal truth cannot be a temporal fraud. The Cause of Christian Science is prospering throughout the world and stands forever as an eternal and demonstrable Science, and I do not regard this attack upon me as a trial, for when these things cease to bless they will cease to occur.*[62]

The *San Francisco Examiner* spoke for many when it opined, "Mrs. Gilbert seems to have overshot the mark this time. The public is tired of the hue and cry against Christian Science and not a little sympathetic with the dignified old lady who presides over the counsels of that church. The letter which Mrs. Gilbert wrote . . . may be couched, as she says, in the language of Christian Science, but it was the kind of letter not unfamiliar to public prosecutors, despite the disguise."[63]

Della Gilbert insisted that her motives weren't mercenary and vowed to continue her battle. "If those who are guarding [Mrs.] Eddy wish to make a Sherlock Holmes mystery of her existence, I will try to be a Sherlock Holmes," she declared.[64] In the end these proved to be empty threats, and Mrs. Gilbert quickly faded from the public eye, public interest, and posterity.[65]

Even as her challenge to Mrs. Eddy's leadership fizzled, however, a much more serious one was heating up.

Front-page story about Della Gilbert from the June 7, 1909, Boston Post.

MRS. GILBERT'S SECRETS WORTH $5000, SHE SAID

Letter Asked Christian Scientists to Pay Her That Sum and She Would Remain Silent

Mrs. Eddy's carriage passes the reservoir near her home in Chestnut Hill. | Longyear Museum collection

A Sweet Interlude

If the summer of 1909 brought challenges for Mrs. Eddy, it also brought sweeter interludes.

One occurred on Friday, July 30. It was the kind of day New Englanders call "a scorcher," with soaring temperatures prompting the *Boston Post* to report that "the downtown streets fairly sizzled."[66] Shortly after lunchtime, eleven taxicabs carrying more than 50 men and women—Christian Science Committees on Publication who were meeting in Boston from all parts of the United States and Canada, along with a few from Great Britain—set off from The Mother Church towards Chestnut Hill. Their destination? 400 Beacon Street. As they rounded the reservoir, one of Mrs. Eddy's favorite routes for her daily drive, they met their hostess heading in the opposite direction in her carriage.[67]

"Mr. Frye was on the box with the driver," one of the Committees would recall, "and Laura Sargent accompanied Mrs. Eddy. As we passed her carriage, we tipped our hats to her and she bowed to us."[68]

The invitation to visit Mary Baker Eddy's home had come as a surprise to the group, and they'd jumped at the chance to accept it. When they arrived at their destination, Irving Tomlinson was waiting at the door to greet them. A tour of the first floor followed, along with an opportunity to talk with several other members of the household. After Mrs. Eddy returned from her carriage ride, the Committees trooped back outside to the front drive, where their Leader greeted them, waving from an upstairs window. The visit was capped off with refreshments.[69]

Before her guests left Chestnut Hill that day, Mrs. Eddy sent Adam Dickey downstairs to the front parlor to deliver the following message: "Tell them they cannot know me in my personality, but in my books and my writings and in my love for them and all mankind."[70]

A thank-you letter from the Committees was published the next month in the *Christian Science Sentinel.* In addition to sharing their appreciation for the kind hospitality Mrs. Eddy had shown them, her visitors expressed gratitude "for the opportunity thus afforded to see you in your home, and . . . to observe our Father's loving care of you manifested in such evident good health, and to know that you are daily about His business."

The Committees also thanked Mrs. Eddy for her message to them, and told her, "In response to your loving admonition . . . we answer that the test of our fidelity shall be the fruits of our labors in obedience to your precepts and example."[71]

The "Defender of Christian Science"

Few players on the stage of early Christian Science history loom as large as Augusta Stetson. Gifted, ambitious, volatile—she was one of Mrs. Eddy's most promising students, as well as a significant thorn in her Leader's side.

"You have always been the most troublesome student that I call loyal," Mrs. Eddy wrote to Augusta in 1897.[72]

Little changed in the decade that followed. In fact, Augusta grew even more troublesome and substantially less loyal as she angled to position herself as the successor to Mary Baker Eddy. By the summer of 1909, events would come to a head.

Born Augusta Emma Simmons in 1842, "Gussie," as she was nicknamed, grew up in Damariscotta, Maine. A bright child ("she always was smarter'n lightning," a neighbor would tell a reporter many years later),[73] she was well-educated for a girl of her day and known for her singing voice and her ability to play the organ—something she did at the local Methodist church as a teenager.[74] It was likely there that she met Frederick Stetson, the Civil War veteran whom she would marry in the summer of 1866.[75] The newlyweds spent the first few years of their marriage sailing to the far corners of the world with Frederick's business as a ship-broker.[76] Their globe-trotting lifestyle came to an abrupt end, however, when a lingering ailment, contracted during his wartime incarceration in Andersonville Prison, forced Frederick to retire in 1870 and apply for a government disability pension.[77] He and Augusta moved in with her parents, and by the mid-1870s they were all living near Boston. In 1882, Augusta enrolled in the Blish School of Oratory in hopes of earning a living on the speaking circuit.[78] It was at this juncture that she first encountered Christian Science.

In the spring of 1884, Augusta attended a parlor talk given by Mrs. Eddy in Charlestown, Massachusetts. The experience would prove transformative.

"I went . . . weighted with care and nearly prostrated with the effects of watching for one year in the room of an invalid husband," Augusta recalled. "During this lecture I lost all sense of grief, physical weakness, and prostration."[79]

World travelers Augusta and Frederick Stetson pose for a photographer in Cardiff, Wales.

PRIVATE COLLECTION

Afterward, she was introduced to Mrs. Eddy, and in November she entered a Primary class at the Massachusetts Metaphysical College. An apt student, Augusta immediately put into practice what she had learned, and by July 1885 was able to report a list of substantial healings in *The Christian Science Journal*.[80]

While Mrs. Eddy recognized Mrs. Stetson's potential (at one point she nicknamed her "my war horse"), she was also keenly aware of her promising pupil's shortcomings.[81] Yes, Augusta was well educated, well traveled, and well spoken. Her polish and skills as a trained elocutionist could and did prove helpful in the pulpit and in presenting Christian Science to the public, and she would soon display impressive executive ability.[82] But Augusta was also willful, materialistic, domineering, manipulative, and possessed of a combative nature that helped earn her the nickname "Fighting Gus" within Boston's Christian Science community.[83] In short, she was both a formidable ally and a formidable foe.

For the next 25 years, Mrs. Eddy let the tares grow among the wheat as she patiently (and sometimes not so patiently) mentored Augusta, by turns guiding and chiding her, ever hopeful that her often wayward pupil could be kept within the fold, her talents and abilities steered into productive channels.

"She is a worker capable of doing great good and that is why I have held on to her because I loved that in her and still love it," Mrs. Eddy explained to one student.[84] To another, while complaining of "the madness of her ambition," she also pointed out, "She has her good qualities."[85]

> *"She is a worker capable of doing great good and that is why I have held on to her because I loved that in her and still love it."*
> *— Mary Baker Eddy*

Some months after completing the Normal class of February 1886, Augusta was sent to New York to help establish Christian Science alongside Laura Lathrop, Pamelia Leonard, and other pioneering workers.[86] There was friction from the start. Augusta was quick to quarrel and didn't hesitate to meddle with the students of her fellow teachers.[87] Mrs. Eddy frequently admonished her, in one letter warning, "There are dangerous schisms rising up in your midst," and scolding her for childish squabbling and jockeying for position.[88]

In 1888, Mrs. Stetson was appointed pastor of the newly-formed First Church of Christ, Scientist, New York. Over the next seven years she preached in a succession of rented venues before finally settling uptown near Central Park.[89]

In December 1894, Mrs. Eddy ended personal preaching in The Mother Church and established the Bible and *Science and Health* as Pastor. By April, that directive would apply to branch churches as well.[90] Mrs. Stetson duly traded her title of pastor for First Reader, a position she then maintained for an additional seven years.

Although they would have a much broader impact and application, numerous *Church Manual* By-laws were initially sparked by Mrs. Eddy's efforts to rein in Augusta.

"Almost all of my rules in the Manual have been made to prevent her injuring my students and causing me trouble in my church," Mrs. Eddy wrote to Laura Lathrop in 1897.[91]

In 1902, she enacted a By-law setting term limits for readers. Augusta relinquished her position—albeit somewhat reluctantly—but her influence continued virtually unabated.[92] There was continued friction, as she repeatedly sparred with other local Christian Scientists, claiming to be the only true teacher of Christian Science in New York City and closer to Mrs. Eddy spiritually than anyone else. Mrs. Eddy had warned her repeatedly about this.[93]

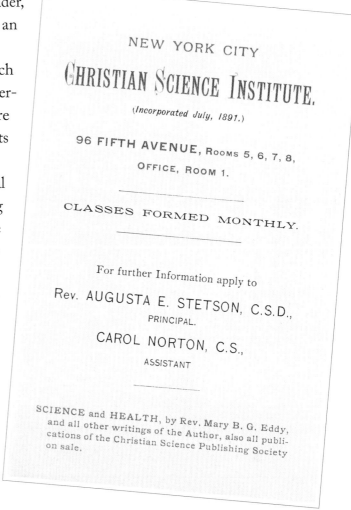

Advertisement for Augusta Stetson's teaching institute. | Longyear Museum collection

"Do not claim that you are my chosen one for you are not," Mrs. Eddy told her in no uncertain terms, in just one of many letters over the years rebuking this behavior.[94]

As was her habit, Augusta would swiftly express her contrition and then turn right around and repeat her misdeeds.

Top: First Church of Christ, Scientist, New York, circa 1912. | Courtesy Library of Congress
Above: Third floor Reading Room and practitioners' offices, pictured in Broadway *magazine (May 1907).*
Longyear Museum collection

On November 30, 1899, First Church broke ground at 96th and Central Park West.[95] Initial construction estimates of $300,000 quickly swelled to nearly $1.25 million.[96] The church's auditorium boasted seating for 2,500, one of the largest and most expensive organs in the U.S., gold-plated light fixtures, and chandeliers that echoed those at Versailles.[97] Elevators in the lobby (a first for a New York City church) whisked visitors to the sky-lit third floor that housed the Sunday School, an expansive Reading Room, and opulent practitioners' offices that Mrs. Stetson assigned to a coterie of her loyal students. Augusta's own office on the mezzanine overlooked Central Park.

A highlight of the dedication service four years later was a message from Mary Baker Eddy, which was read aloud to the congregation. One passage in particular must have given at least some listeners pause amidst all the pomp and circumstance: "The letter of your work dies, as do all things material, but the spirit thereof is immortal. Remember that a temple but foreshadows the idea of God—the 'house not made with hands, eternal in the heavens,' while a silent grand man or woman healing sickness and destroying sin builds a heaven-reacher. Only that group of men and women gain greatness who gain themselves, in a complete subordination of self."[98]

Subordinating self was hardly Augusta's *modus operandi.* The most conspicuous object in the church, one newspaper reported, was a "magnificent life-size portrait of Mrs. Stetson."[99] The *New York Times* noted that her photograph was displayed in each of the practitioners' offices, prints of which were also on sale in the Reading Room, along with copies of

In 1905, Augusta Stetson built this brick-and-marble mansion for herself next door to First Church of Christ, Scientist, New York. A covered passageway connected the edifice to her home, whose luxurious furnishings were paid for by her students.
Architecture *magazine (September 1906).* | Private collection

her book of poems.[100] Each day at noon, dressed in one of her signature gowns of flowing white,[101] Augusta held court in the board room in compulsory closed-door meetings for "her" practitioners, designed to keep them all in a firm grip.[102] Fashionable carriages and automobiles drew up to the new edifice every Sunday and Wednesday, their well-dressed occupants filing inside to join a congregation "overflowing with people highly representative of the intelligence, activity, fashion and wealth of New York."[103] A dazzled press began painting Augusta as Mrs. Eddy's heir apparent, a view that Augusta publicly denounced but privately encouraged.

Beneath the church's prosperous veneer, however, ran a strong undercurrent of discontent. "It has been a case of too much Stetson right along," one disgruntled fellow church member told a reporter.[104]

Irving Tomlinson offered a clear-eyed assessment of the whole situation. "Mrs. Stetson did not know what to do with power," he said, "and unfortunately used those with whom she came in contact largely for her own ends, thus bringing about her own downfall."[105]

And by 1908, her downfall was right around the corner.

Just days after the first issue of *The Christian Science Monitor* rolled off the press came the stunning news that, with church services drawing capacity crowds, Mrs. Stetson was planning to build a satellite edifice.[106] Rivaling The Mother Church Extension in grandeur and size, it would serve as a branch of First Church of Christ, Scientist, New York, which would then be positioned "literally to be the mother church of [Mrs. Stetson's] following," as Mr. Tomlinson put it, "though she was careful not to state this."[107]

This was no small threat, and there was serious concern as to the future of the movement if Mrs. Stetson tried to wrest control before or after Mrs. Eddy's passing, or foment a split in the Church.[108]

Mrs. Eddy took swift and decisive action, dictating an editorial titled "Consistency," which was published at her request in the December 5 *Christian Science Sentinel* under Archibald McLellan's byline. It posed a series of pointed questions, including, "Are you striving, in Christian Science, to be the best Christian on earth, or are you striving to have the most costly edifice on the earth?" Mr. McLellan's byline appeared on an additional editorial in that issue, "One Mother Church in Christian Science," which was actually written by Irving Tomlinson under Mrs. Eddy's supervision.[109]

Next, Mrs. Eddy invited Mrs. Stetson to visit her in Chestnut Hill. Augusta arrived at the appointed time on Thursday, December 9, joining Mrs. Eddy on her afternoon carriage ride.[110] It was the last time the two women would meet face to face.

Mrs. Eddy was solicitous of Augusta's comfort, sharing her lamb's-wool lap robe with her and instructing the coachman, "Be sure and go by the Reservoir and then return by the prettiest route you can. . . ."[111]

The end result of the outing was that Augusta abandoned plans for expansion.

"When she returned from that drive Mrs. Stetson was, for the time being, quite another woman," recalled Mr. Tomlinson. "Mrs. Eddy had pointed out her error and had convinced her that it was not wise to build such a church."[112]

Mrs. Eddy finally weighed in publicly with "The Way of Wisdom," published in the January 16 *Sentinel.* It included this passage, with its unmistakable rebuke to Phariseeism embedded in the phrase "enlarge their phylacteries":

> *I have crowned The Mother Church building with the spiritual modesty of Christian Science, which is its jewel. When my dear brethren in New York desire to build higher, — to enlarge their phylacteries and demonstrate Christian Science to a higher extent, — they must begin on a wholly spiritual foundation, than which there is no other, and proportionably estimate their success and glory of achievement only as they build upon the rock of Christ, the spiritual foundation. This will open the way, widely and impartially, to their never-ending success, — to salvation and eternal Christian Science.*[113]

Although Augusta may have shelved her scheme to create a rival mother church, "spiritual modesty" was not on her agenda. She continued to meet with her band of practitioners daily, and disturbing reports continued reaching Boston about her peculiar teachings, which among other things included a new trinity, with Mrs. Eddy as God, Augusta as the Christ or "First Born," and her inner circle of practitioners at First Church, New York, as the Holy Ghost.[114]

The tipping point came that summer, when Augusta forwarded to Mrs. Eddy a gift of gold her students had given her, along with a composite letter from them in which they virtually deified Mrs. Stetson.[115]

Again, Mrs. Eddy took immediate action. Her July 12 reply to Mrs. Stetson was published in the next issue of the *Christian Science Sentinel,* and she sent a new By-law to the Board of Directors to approve, forbidding teachers and practitioners from having offices in branch churches or Reading Rooms.[116]

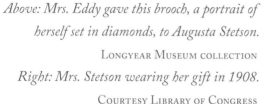

Above: Mrs. Eddy gave this brooch, a portrait of
herself set in diamonds, to Augusta Stetson.
LONGYEAR MUSEUM COLLECTION
Right: Mrs. Stetson wearing her gift in 1908.
COURTESY LIBRARY OF CONGRESS

"There is a very great need of putting a stop to Mrs. Stetson's present move-ments," she told them, adding "and in doing it in a manner, if possible, that will not sever her from our Church relations, or make her our enemy."[117]

To Augusta herself Mrs. Eddy wrote, "My Dear Student: awake, and arise from this temptation produced by animal magnetism upon yourself, allowing your students to deify you and me. . . ."[118]

At Mrs. Eddy's direction, Mrs. Stetson was summoned to Boston to meet with the Board.[119] Although the matter was ultimately referred to her branch church in accordance with the *Church Manual,* Augusta wasn't off the hook. She still needed to obey the new By-law regarding practitioners' offices.[120] After it appeared in the *Christian Science Sentinel,* the press reported on a mass exodus at First Church, New York, as Mrs. Stetson and her inner circle decamped from their plush quarters.[121]

From that point on, the situation unraveled quickly.

One of the members of the Christian Science Board of Directors traveled to New York at First Reader Virgil O. Strickler's request to see the detailed diary Virgil had been keeping of Augusta's daily meetings.[122] Other evidence of her misconduct had been flowing unsolicited to Boston as well, prompting the Board to write to Mrs. Eddy a summary of a state of affairs "almost beyond belief."[123]

Mrs. Eddy lost no time in replying.

"I now ask that you act upon this information," she instructed them the following day, "as becomes [T]he Mother Church, when called upon to act upon such impious conduct."[124]

> *"My Dear Student: awake, and arise from this temptation produced by animal magnetism upon yourself, allowing your students to deify you and me. . . ."*
> *— Mary Baker Eddy*

Over the next few weeks, some two dozen practitioners—Mrs. Stetson's "bodyguard," as the Board described them in their letter to Mrs. Eddy—were summoned to Boston for questioning.[125] As was so often the case involving momentous events in her Church, Mrs. Eddy struggled physically during this time, and all of the metaphysical workers in her home staunchly endeavored to support her.[126] In the end, the Board's decision was unanimous: Augusta Stetson's authorization to teach and practice Christian Science was revoked, and her card removed from *The Christian Science Journal.*[127]

The press had a field day in the weeks that followed. There was rampant speculation about what would happen next. Some predicted a schism in the movement, with Augusta splitting off to start a church of her own; others predicted her ouster.

Mrs. Eddy issued a flurry of new and amended By-laws, clearly directed at Mrs. Stetson and her followers but also firmly establishing boundaries for the future, should this type of behavior ever be repeated.[128] First, she required branch churches to "acknowledge as such all other Christian Science churches and societies . . . and to maintain toward them an attitude of Christian fellow-ship"—a direct response to Mrs. Stetson's actions toward her fellow New York churches and their members.

Next, Mrs. Eddy served up a trio of amendments including "A teacher shall not assume personal control of, or attempt to dominate his pupils"; "Teachers shall not call their pupils together, or assemble a selected number of them, for more frequent meetings"; "each student occupies only his own field of labor."[129]

Mrs. Eddy also came out in vigorous support of the structure she had put in place for governing her Church, issuing a statement in both the *Sentinel* and *Journal* titled "Take Notice":

I approve the By-laws of The Mother Church, and require the Christian Science Board of Directors maintain them and sustain them. These Directors do not act contrary to the rules of the Church Manual, neither do they trouble me with their difficulties with individuals in their own church or with the members of branch churches. My province as a Leader—as the Discoverer and Founder of Christian Science—is not to interfere in cases of discipline, and I hereby publicly declare that I am not personally involved in the affairs of the church in any other way than through my written and published rules, all of which can be read by the individual who desires to inform himself of the facts.[130]

Augusta Stetson had been put on notice, and so had the entire movement. The future of the Church would rest on law, not on personality.

Meanwhile, in New York, at "the most tumultuous meeting ever held in a Christian Science church in this city," according to the *New York Times*, the trustees of First Church presented the results of a full inquiry of their own that exonerated Augusta on all points.[131]

"Mrs. Stetson, the storm centre of the proceedings, was not present," noted the *Boston Post*. "Dressed in white she sat at a window in her house next door to the church and received frequent bulletins from supporters...."[132]

The meeting lasted for six hours.[133] By a narrow margin and with a dwindling quorum, a vote was passed, formally expressing loyalty to Mrs. Stetson. "The members of the First Church," the newspaper report concluded dramatically, had "placed themselves squarely against the directors of the Mother Church in Boston."[134]

The following day's issue of the *New York Times* revealed that a second admonition had been issued to Augusta from the Christian Science Board of Directors a few days earlier, this time for her "contumacious" attitude and stubborn persistence in continuing to hold daily practitioners' meetings in her home.[135]

A tense stand-off between the trustees of First Church, New York City, and the Christian Science Board of Directors played out in the periodicals in the following weeks, as their correspondence was published for all to read, along with Mrs. Eddy's July 23 "Awake and arise" letter to Augusta.[136]

A brief note in Ella Rathvon's diary offers a glimpse of what was going on back at 400 Beacon Street: "Eventful times, error being uncovered," she wrote. "'Keep it uncovered.'"[137]

The 15th of November was a momentous day. Augusta was back in Boston again, scheduled to appear before the Board of Directors for the first of what would be three full days of examination.[138] Some 200 miles away in New York, another meeting was slated at First Church.[139]

Given the tenor of the branch's previous meeting, along with Mrs. Stetson's own combative disposition, fireworks were expected in both locations. The press was poised and ready: "Mrs. Stetson Here to Fight Expulsion," the

Boston Post reported. Excommunication was a "foregone conclusion," the *New York Times* declared.[140]

An article in the *New York Sun*, under the headline "Civil War in the Church," detailed the "hostile factions" that would be squaring off at First Church that Monday afternoon.[141]

Instead, something extraordinary happened.

Taking up her pen, Mary Baker Eddy wrote a letter to the congregation — a "marvelously brave and loving" letter, as one Christian Scientist put it.[142]

When their Leader's words were read aloud, the results were immediate.

"The instantaneous effect of your 'Peace, be still' upon the troubled waters of our church . . . was a never-to-be-forgotten proof of the love and esteem in which your words are held by the entire membership," wrote one who had been part of Augusta's inner circle. "I know that I am expressing the sentiment of our church in thanking you from the bottom of my heart for having shown us 'how good and how pleasant it is for brethren to dwell together in unity!'"[143]

First Reader Virgil Strickler entertained a motion to adjourn, which passed unanimously, and the meeting ended with the singing of Mrs. Eddy's hymn "'Feed My Sheep.'"

"Mrs. Eddy's words were so potent that a meeting which was expected to split the church lasted only 14 minutes and ended in a song," one newspaper reported.[144]

A LETTER BY MRS. EDDY.

Brookline, Mass., Nov. 13, 1909.
To the Board of Trustees, First Church of Christ, Scientist, New York City.

Beloved Brethren:—In consideration of the present momentous question at issue in First Church of Christ, Scientist, New York city, I am constrained to say, if I can settle this church difficulty amicably by a few words, as many students think I can, I herewith cheerfully subscribe these words of love:—

My beloved brethren in First Church of Christ, Scientist, New York city, I advise you with all my soul to support the Directors of The Mother Church, and unite with those in your church who are supporting The Mother Church Directors. Abide in fellowship with and obedience to The Mother Church, and in this way God will bless and prosper you. This I know, for He has proved it to me for forty years in succession.

Lovingly yours,
MARY BAKER EDDY.

Mrs. Eddy's letter to First Church of Christ, Scientist, New York, was reprinted in both the November 20 and December 4, 1909 issues of the Christian Science Sentinel.

In Boston, meanwhile, after the second full day of examination, Augusta called a press conference at her hotel. Perhaps in a last-ditch effort to avoid expulsion, she released a statement reiterating "her loyalty to Mrs. Eddy and the church, saying she was obeying and would continue to obey the judgment carrying punishment of suspension issued against her. . . ."[145]

> *"Thus the Defender of Christian Science, Mary Baker Eddy, once more protected her followers and firmly entrenched her Cause under the leadership of divine Principle."*
> *—Irving Tomlinson*

Her efforts were in vain. On Wednesday, the Board came to its decision, which was made public the following day. The verdict was unanimous, Alfred Farlow told the press. Augusta Stetson's name had been dropped from the membership rolls of The Mother Church.[146]

"Thus the Defender of Christian Science, Mary Baker Eddy, once more protected her followers and firmly entrenched her Cause under the leadership of divine Principle," wrote Irving Tomlinson.[147]

With Augusta Stetson's excommunication, the threat to the future of the Christian Science movement was successfully averted. There would be no schism, no split. Mrs. Eddy had surmounted one of the most serious challenges she faced during her final years, decisively settling the succession question for her Church once and for all. The authority of the *Manual* and the Christian Science Board of Directors would stand.

"It is a work of eternity"

"I am glad you called," Mrs. Eddy told *Boston Globe* reporter Edwin Park when he stopped by one spring afternoon to see her. "I would ask you to sit down, but this is my time for work. It is a work of eternity. The hours do not give me time enough."[148]

Above the ongoing fray in the field and in the press, above the ebbing and flowing tides of public opinion — above "all this fustian,"[149] as she put it — Mrs. Eddy continued to press on with her God-given mission. She gave much thought to the future of her Church during the Chestnut Hill years, shoring up its structure and ensuring that all the elements were in place to carry the movement forward when she was no longer personally at its helm.

"It was her child, her offspring, and her constant concern, day and night, was what was to become of this Cause," Adam Dickey would later recall. "Her constant anxiety was for its preservation and future unfoldment."[150]

Increasingly, Mrs. Eddy turned her Church officers and followers to the *Manual* as the governing document of her Church, as well as to her other writings, and ultimately to divine Mind for direction and guidance.

"Although she continued, during those years, to grant interviews to the various officials of the Church," said Irving Tomlinson, "yet she endeavored to turn them away from her human personality, and gently to lead them to God, who would guide, care for, and lead both their individual lives and the Cause for which they labored."[151]

Mrs. Eddy continued to revise and expand the *Manual* while living at 400 Beacon Street, adding a dozen new By-laws in 1908 and 1909 and amending many more.[152] In March 1910, in a forward-looking move that underscored the growing worldwide reach of Christian Science, she authorized the first translation of *Science and Health* — into German.[153]

And, as always, she was writing.

Mrs. Eddy, Laura Sargent told Mr. Park on that day of his visit, "always plunges right into her work of writing as soon as she returns from her drive."[154]

Above: The German translation committee, circa 1911.
Clockwise from left: Ulla Schultz Oldenbourg,
Helmuth von Moltke, Adam H. Dickey,
Renate Hermes King, Dorothy von Moltke,
Theodor Stanger. *Right: Early edition of*
Wissenschaft und Gesundheit.

Longyear Museum collection

And sure enough, after the reporter had
finished his conversation with Mrs. Eddy and
was turning to go, he saw that she had already "resumed her seat
to take up her pen and a writing pad. . . ."[155]

Writing had always been Mrs. Eddy's main means of communication, and
the words continued to flow from her pen unabated at Chestnut Hill.

"We editors are in constant communication with her," Annie Knott, an associate
editor of the Christian Science periodicals, told the *Detroit Free Press*, "and there
is scarcely a day that she does not send us communications or corrections."[156]

Not only did Mrs. Eddy keep a close watch on the periodicals, but she also scrutinized her own writings, making scores of revisions to *Science and Health* and her other books during these years. Some were minor adjustments and grammatical clarifications, some were more substantial changes, and others, which might at first glance have seemed minor, held great significance. For example, in the spring of 1910, she revised two chapter headings in *Science and Health:* "Christian Science and Spiritualism" became "Christian Science vs. Spiritualism," and "Animal Magnetism" became "Animal Magnetism Unmasked."

"I wish to express my deep appreciation of the recent changes in the titles of two chapters in *Science and Health*," Mrs. Knott wrote after the revisions appeared. "These changes are not only of importance to inquirers, in setting forth more clearly the topics discussed in the chapters named, but to older students they indicate the widening of the gulf between the real and the unreal, the false and the true."[157]

Such editorial painstaking was entirely characteristic of Mrs. Eddy, and the effort she put into both writing and revising was noted by many in her household.

"I was very much impressed with the time and care which she gave to anything intended for publication," said Adelaide Still, recalling that Mrs. Eddy "spared neither time nor labor in the endeavor to prevent anything from going out that could be misunderstood or misinterpreted."[158]

In addition to corresponding with Church and Publishing Society officials, Mrs. Eddy also wrote letters to family and friends, mentored her students and followers, and occasionally addressed the general public. In the spring of 1908, for instance, as national controversy swirled around President Theodore Roosevelt's address to Congress urging an increased naval appropriations bill, Mrs. Eddy published a statement titled "War."[159]

Reprinted in newspapers nationwide, Mrs. Eddy's thoughts on the subject were shared with Teddy Roosevelt, who declared, "I wish that all other religious leaders showed as much good sense."[160]

Mrs. Eddy had always used the Christian Science periodicals to communicate with those who would never know her personally. In later years, she

> "I wish that all other religious leaders showed as much good sense."
> — Teddy Roosevelt

THE CHRISTIAN SCIENCE JOURNAL

"For the weapons of our warfare are not carnal, but mighty through God to the pulling down of strong holds"

Volume XXVI	MAY, 1908	Number 2

WAR.

MARY BAKER G. EDDY.

FOR many years I have prayed daily that there be no more war, no more barbarous slaughtering of our fellow-beings; prayed that all the peoples on earth and the islands of the sea have one God, one Mind; love God supremely, and love their neighbor as themselves.

National disagreements can be, and should be, arbitrated wisely, fairly; and fully settled.

It is unquestionable, however, that at this hour the armament of navies is necessary, for the purpose of preventing war and preserving peace among nations.

Mrs. Eddy's statement on war was shared with President Theodore Roosevelt, shown here at his desk, circa 1906.

Courtesy Library of Congress

even shared private correspondence—both to her and from her. In February 1903, the *Sentinel* introduced "Letters to Our Leader," which became a regular feature through September 1910. Some letters that Mrs. Eddy received were published with her reply; others were published without it. Some were from branch churches and well-known workers in the field; others from relative unknowns. A few were even from children.

A pair of such letters was published in May 1910, and Mrs. Eddy's responses offer a glimpse of the affection she had always felt for the young.

"Well done, my good, faithful little Christian Scientist," she told eleven-year-old Julia McFall, who had written to tell her of family healings and thank her for writing *Science and Health* (Julia also sent mayflowers). And to eight-year-old Margaret Waddles, who wrote of her love for Sunday School and proudly announced, "I have not been sick once since I have been in Christian Science," Mrs. Eddy responded, "God bless my little Christian Science girl, as He does all good girls."[161]

Aside from a collection of her poetry, Mrs. Eddy published no new books while she was living at 400 Beacon Street. She did produce a number of articles, however, including several in the latter half of 1910 that make it abundantly evident there had been no diminishment of vigor in her thought or expression.

In September, around the same time that her staff visited the Harvard-Boston aviation meet, Mrs. Eddy wrote two articles on flight: "Soaring," dictated to Adam Dickey, and an untitled one dictated to Laura Sargent. Neither would ever be polished or published, but both contain penetrating insights as they lift thought above "the present mania over flying," as Mrs. Eddy put it, to a more spiritual altitude.[162]

"The elevation desirable worth obtaining or possible to obtain in Science is spiritual ascent," she wrote in the former, "thought soaring above matter—soul overcoming mortal and material sense, holiness discounting sin and destroying the love of sin and the capacity to sin. This elevation is not manifested by kiting the skies or kicking the earth. It is something first felt, second seen, third acted."[163]

"More Personal Than Prose"

"Oh, you have put my pink roses on my poems."[164]

Mary Baker Eddy's face lit up as William Dana Orcutt, head of the University Press in Cambridge, Massachusetts, placed a slim volume in her hands.

In the spring of 1910, University Press had been commissioned to create a collection of some of Mrs. Eddy's poems, and recalling her fondness for pink roses, Mr. Orcutt asked the artist to incorporate them into the book's design. Bound in white, the cover of the sample volume he'd brought along to show her bore an elegant

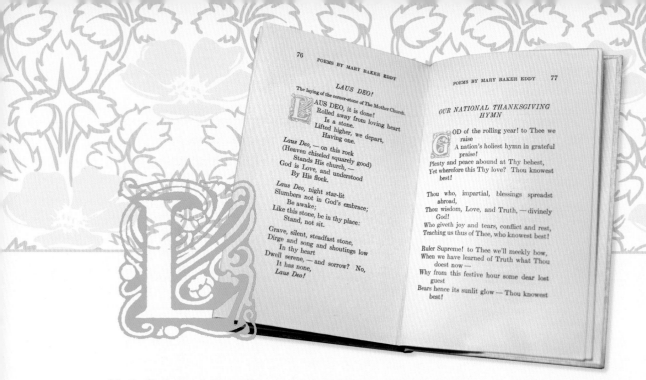

The book's design features illuminated capital letters intertwined with roses. | Longyear Museum collection

floral motif stamped in green and pink and gold. Inside, mocked-up pages in a substantial cream stock showed off the attractive typeface and layout, which would include an illuminated capital letter intertwined with more roses at the beginning of each poem.

In addition to her obvious delight with the book's design, Mrs. Eddy displayed another emotion that day, which Orcutt had never seen in their nearly two decades of working together: A hint of shyness.

"Somehow poems seem more personal than prose," she told him as they discussed publication plans.[165] The original intent had been a 100-copy presentation edition for private distribution, but Mrs. Eddy was being encouraged by her staff to approve another edition for the general public.

As a collection of what Adam Dickey would describe in the book's foreword as "the spontaneous outpouring of a deeply poetic nature,"[166] the volume that Mrs. Eddy held in her hands *was* personal—as much so as an album of candid snapshots. The poems spanned nearly her whole life, stretching back to girlhood with such early efforts as "Autumn" and "Resolutions for the Day." Some had been published in newspapers and magazines; others had appeared in the

Christian Science periodicals. They touched on moments both public and private, triumphant and tender. For example, "Laus Deo!" was written to mark the laying of the cornerstone of The Mother Church in 1894, and "I'm Sitting Alone," written decades earlier, reveals the depth of loneliness she'd felt missing her mother and her first husband, who had both passed away, and her son, who had been taken from her when young.[167]

Before Mrs. Eddy could decide whether or not to approve a general edition, though, she had work to do. As Orcutt watched, she reached for her pencil and began to edit.

Poetry had always come naturally to Mary Baker Eddy. In fact, she told one of her secretaries that as a child "it was easier for me to write in poetry than in prose," and that she even wrote some school compositions in verse.[168] To another household worker, she recalled writing "Mother's Evening Prayer," one of seven of her poems that would later be set to music as hymns, "without conscious effort, the words slipping off her pen fast as she could form them."[169]

If Mrs. Eddy wrote poetry with ease, the end result nevertheless came under the same close scrutiny as her prose. Just as with *Science and Health* and her other writings, she expended much effort in editing and revising her poems, always striving to clarify her message.

"Mother's Evening Prayer," for instance, originally ended with the phrase "mother finds her home and far-off rest." At one point during the time she lived at 400 Beacon Street, Mrs. Eddy changed the final words to "heavenly rest" and asked Mr. Dickey what he thought of the change.

"I told her that to me it conveyed a much better thought," he would later recall. "I said that 'her home and far-off rest' carried the impression that she had a long and toilsome way ahead of her."

"That is just the thing I want to get rid of," Mrs. Eddy replied.[170]

"Christ My Refuge," another of her poems that would become a hymn, was first published in the *Lynn Reporter* in February of 1868. Mrs. Eddy would return to these verses again and again over the next 40 years, making both major and minor revisions. The final edit also occurred while she was living at Chestnut

MEETING OF MY DEPARTED
MOTHER AND HUSBAND

JOY for thee, happy friend! thy bark is past
The dangerous sea, and safely moored at
last —

Beyond rough foam
Soft gales celestial, in sweet music bore, —
~~Mortal~~ emancipate for this far shore, —
Thee to thy home.

Spirit

*Mrs. Eddy's handwritten edits are visible on
this and other pages of the sample volume.*
LONGYEAR MUSEUM COLLECTION

Hill, when she changed the last stanza of the third verse from "I kiss the cross, and wait to know a world more bright" to "I kiss the cross, and wake to know a world more bright."[171] Just one word, but what a world of difference!

During their meeting in her study that day in 1910, William Dana Orcutt witnessed this same close attention to detail as Mrs. Eddy took her editing pencil to one of the poems in the mocked-up volume — the first verse of "Meeting of My Departed Mother and Husband," which at that point read:

JOY for thee, happy friend! thy bark is past
The dangerous sea, and safely moored at
last —

Beyond rough foam
Soft gales celestial, in sweet music bore, —
Mortal emancipate for this far shore, —
Thee to thy home.

As Orcutt recalls, Mrs. Eddy read the verse aloud twice, emphasizing the next to the last line.

"*Mortal* is not the right word," she concluded, and with a decisive swipe of her pencil she changed the phrase to read, "Spirit emancipate for this far shore."[172]

In the end, Mrs. Eddy gave her consent to publish two editions of the poetry collection. The first was the presentation edition, printed in September 1910. Later that fall, notices in the Christian Science periodicals announced an edition for the general public, cherishing the hope that "the opportunity now presented to secure these rare gems of true inspiration, which tell of God's kingdom ever with those who have eyes to see and ears to hear its message, will be eagerly welcomed."[173]

Messages to the field

In October 1910, Mrs. Eddy wrote a pithy (and unpublished) article that begins, "The deepest hallowed intoned thought is the leader of our lives, and when it is found out people know us in reality and not until then. The surface of the sweetest nut is often a burr, and the thought that guides our life and expresses our being is unseen, except in the outward expressions and actions thereof." Further on, she continues, "The wisdom of this hour and the proper labor of this hour is to know of a certainty the quality of the seed which takes root in our thought and understanding, and by their fruits this can only be known; in short, the moral life's history is be good, do good, speak good and God infinite good cares for all that is and seems to be."[174]

At some point that fall, Mrs. Eddy dictated what would be her last published article—although it wouldn't appear until 1917, when it ran as the lead editorial in the *Christian Science Sentinel* just a few months after the United States entered the First World War. A brief introduction by the editors at the time noted that the article's message "is of vital importance to every Christian Scientist today." Titled "Principle and Practice," it sheds light on what Mrs. Eddy may have been pondering during the autumn when it was written and her great yearning to impress upon her followers the yawning chasm between understanding and belief, between genuine Christian Science healing and what she calls "faith-cure."

Christian Science requires understanding instead of belief; it is based on a fixed eternal and divine Principle wholly apart from mortal conjecture, and it must be understood, otherwise it cannot be correctly accepted and demonstrated. . . . It is the healer's understanding of the operation of the divine Principle, and his application thereof, which heals the sick, just as it is one's understanding of the principle of mathematics which enables him to demonstrate its rules.

She concludes the brief article with a solemn warning:

> *Christian Science is not a faith-cure, and unless human faith be distinguished from scientific healing, Christian Science will again be lost from the practice of religion as it was soon after the period of our great Master's scientific teaching and practice. Preaching without practice of the divine Principle of man's being has not, in nineteen hundred years, resulted in demonstrating this Principle. Preaching without the truthful and consistent practice of your statements will destroy the success of Christian Science.*[175]

Mrs. Eddy's final communications with her followers occurred in September and October. In the September 3, 1910 *Sentinel,* she would answer one last question from a reader. In part of her reply to one who had been taken to task by a practitioner for referring to himself or herself as "an immortal idea of the one divine Mind," Mrs. Eddy told the questioner that the statement was "scientifically correct," adding "In practising Christian Science you must state its Principle correctly, or you forfeit your ability to demonstrate it."[176]

The September 17, 1910 *Sentinel* would carry the first of two concluding messages to the field, a brief "Take Notice" about Blanche Hersey Hogue's article "The Church Manual." Published in the previous week's edition of the *Sentinel,* Mrs. Hogue's article began: "Christian Scientists have for their instruction the Scriptures, the writings of Mrs. Eddy, which open to them the Scriptures, and the Church Manual, the rules of which help them to apply what they have been taught."[177] Mrs. Eddy heartily approved of this article, and her endorsement of it would be repeated in the October *Journal.*[178]

TAKE NOTICE

THE article on the Church Manual by Blanche Hersey Hogue, in the *Sentinel* of Sept. 10, is practical and scientific, and I recommend its careful study to all Christian Scientists.

MARY BAKER EDDY.

The second of Mrs. Eddy's final messages to the field came in the form of an announcement written on September 28, 1910. It would run in the October 1, 8, and 15 issues of the *Sentinel*, as well as in the November *Journal*. In it, Mrs. Eddy stated that she was not to be consulted about matters "relating to Christian Science practice, to publication committee work, reading-room work, or to Mother Church membership," and that all such inquiries should be sent to the Christian Science Board of Directors.[179]

With that, Mary Baker Eddy put away her public pen. She had done all that she could for her Church and followers, pointing them back to the *Manual* and to the governing structure that she had put in place for their future guidance. The rest would be up to them.

Keeping her memory green

Mary Baker Eddy, Irving Tomlinson once wrote to an acquaintance, "was just the kind of Leader that one would like to have."[180] Fearless, strong, and unfailingly tender, she was, he would tell his lecture audiences, "obedient to the revelation that God had given her."[181]

Minnie Scott, who had "intimate knowledge of her daily life," would attest that, "in the line from a hymn, 'she lived the precepts that she taught.'"[182]

In the years that followed Mrs. Eddy's passing in December 1910, nearly everyone who served in her Chestnut Hill household would try and articulate, in some fashion, what they witnessed while living there, from the importance of the work their Leader had undertaken to the lasting impact her example and instruction had made on their individual lives. They recorded their impressions in diaries, wrote reminiscences and books, and shared publicly and privately with friends, family, fellow church members, and students through letters, articles, lectures, and addresses. At least one even testified about their Leader under oath.

"Mrs. Eddy was the most remarkable character I ever became acquainted with," Adam Dickey told the Massachusetts Supreme Court in July 1919.[183]

Collectively, the words of those who stood shoulder to shoulder with Mary Baker Eddy during these crowning years of her fruitful life ring not only with deep affection and respect, but also with a sense of urgency in what is clearly a heartfelt desire to preserve an accurate record for future generations. Perhaps they foresaw the danger in the years to come for those who wouldn't have known Mrs. Eddy personally, who wouldn't have worked side by side with her and thus gained that "intimate knowledge of her daily life," who wouldn't have been on hand to witness for themselves her selfless labor and sacrifice. Perhaps they sensed how easily a life could be erased, forgotten, or marginalized.

In 1914, a mere four years after Mrs. Eddy's passing, William Rathvon would tell his students, "It has been your privilege to share in the trials and triumphs of our Leader, while her mission kept her here on earth. You were Christian Scientists while she was. You read her words as they were originally given to the world through our periodicals. You have worked with those who have worked with her; you have been given words of hers that have never been publicly imparted or recorded. Never again can such experience fall to the lot of mankind."

However, he warned, "It will not be so many years before a new generation of Christian Scientists will be active in our Cause. The days and doings of our Leader may seem to them but a shade less remote than the times of our Master, if we do not awaken to the part we have mentally and materially in keeping her memory green and her achievements fresh in the minds of those who follow."

The importance of "keeping her memory green" cannot be overstated, he continued.

"Now that we no longer see her face, or hear her kindly messages . . . too many of our people seem to be content to drink the healing draught without

Mary Baker Eddy in her final years. | © The Mary Baker Eddy Collection.
Original in The Mary Baker Eddy Library. Used with permission.

"It will not be so many years before a new generation of Christian Scientists will be active in our Cause. The days and doings of our Leader may seem to them but a shade less remote than the times of our Master, if we do not awaken to the part we have mentally and materially in keeping her memory green and her achievements fresh in the minds of those who follow."

—William Rathvon

a thought of her who fashioned the cup and showed us how to find the spring from which to fill it."

The solution?

"First: we can see that her place in our own thought is always garlanded with gratitude and love, and second: we must pass no opportunity to let our patients and friends know that whatever blessings they have derived or can derive from Christian Science, are largely due to the spirituality and goodness and selflessness of her whom we love to refer to as our revered Leader."[184]

That garland of gratitude and love of which Mr. Rathvon speaks appears to have been uppermost in Irving Tomlinson's thought at the Annual Meeting of The Mother Church in 1921. In his remarks as incoming president, he reminded his fellow members, "There is need on the part of all of us for greater love for our revered Leader. There should be more intelligent appreciation not only for her revelation, but for her untiring devotion and sacrifice. A proper sense of love for her will bring us nearer to her work. Knowing her rightly, we can know her revelation rightly."[185]

And as Mrs. Eddy herself pointed out to the visiting Committees on Publication who gathered at her home in the summer of 1909, the way to "know her rightly" was through her books, and her love for mankind.[186] Through her timeless published writings, she would continue to lead and mentor her Church and impart Christian Science to her followers, as well as to "honest seekers for Truth."[187]

The last word belongs to a member of the household who spent as much time as anyone with Mary Baker Eddy during her three years at 400 Beacon Street: Adelaide Still, erstwhile nanny turned personal maid to the Discoverer, Founder, and Leader of Christian Science. She wrote: "That Mrs. Eddy should have stayed with us for so many years after her discovery; that she should have accomplished such a great work as establishing and founding the Cause of Christian Science, manifesting so much wisdom in organizing and building up the Church, and in giving its By-laws for the guidance and protection of its members, is a marvel for which we can never be grateful enough, and which should prove an inspiration to each and every one of her followers."[188]

Acknowledgments

Behind every book stands a team, and here at Longyear Museum I am fortunate to work with the very best team that a historian could ask for. First and foremost, I am indebted to President and Executive Director Sandra Houston for her unwavering enthusiasm and encouragement every step of the way—and for her keen editorial eye. Heartfelt thanks are owed to Longyear's Board of Trustees as well, who stood firmly behind the project from the very beginning, and to the Longyear members whose generous support of the Museum helped us see it through.

A number of my colleagues contributed to early drafts of portions of this book, including John Alioto ("A Grandmother's Love"), William O. Bisbee (Ella Hoag profile), Susan E. Kilborn (Nellie Eveleth profile), and Deborah Slade Pierce ("A 'Joyful Noise'"). Chief among them is Kelly Byquist, who served as my research assistant and who contributed to numerous profiles, including Minnie Scott, Margaret Macdonald, Jonathan Irving, Frank and Charlotte Bowman, Frances Thatcher, Katharine Retterer, William Rathvon, Laura Sargent, Ella Rathvon, and Cromwell Dixon. Kelly's invaluable assistance and cheerful readiness to tackle any assignment has been a tremendous help. I'm also grateful to Leslie Vollnogle for her genealogical research skills, and to

Longyear staff photographer Andrew Parsons and former staff photographer Nathan Wright for their fine work.

Looking further afield, I salute the spirit of fellowship in which Ralph Byron Copper and Keith McNeil shared their private collections—and their historical knowledge. The end result is immeasurably richer for their contributions.

Those on whose professional services we relied include our stellar book designer, Sarah Nichols, whose artistry is evident on every page, and Lark Smith, whose diligent fact-checking kept our scholarship on its toes. Editorial reviewer Marjorie Kehe shared exactly the honest, forthright feedback we knew she would; proofreader Sukey Barthelmess took on a Herculean task with patience and grace; Derek Dibble and Stefanie Milligan offered valuable insights and eagle-eyed corrections; and Kristin and Mark Palkoner of inGRACE Photography provided several lovely images of the interior of the house. James Spencer provided editorial guidance and invaluable support throughout.

No research involving Christian Science history would have been complete without a visit to The Mary Baker Eddy Library—and there were many! Our friends and colleagues Michael Hamilton, Judy Huenneke, Carl Sheasley, Dorothy Rivera, Shanna Smith, Mark Montgomery, Kurt Morris, Dan Bullman, and Terra Cutaia welcomed us warmly on numerous occasions, helped us navigate to the material we needed, and unstintingly shared their time, expertise, and resources. We're also grateful for the Library's generosity in granting us permission to use a number of letters and images from The Mary Baker Eddy Collection.

A final note of gratitude to Mary Baker Eddy herself and to each of the men and women profiled in these pages. Without her, and without the dedication of these early Christian Scientists, who so carefully recorded their experiences serving in her household and whose quiet labors behind the scenes often went unsung, this book would not have been possible.

Endnotes

Abbreviations used in Endnotes

Manuscript Collections:

LMC   Longyear Museum Collection, Chestnut Hill, Massachusetts

MBEL   The Mary Baker Eddy Collection, The Mary Baker Eddy Library, Boston, Massachusetts

Published Works by Mary Baker Eddy:

Church Manual	*Church Manual of The First Church of Christ, Scientist, in Boston, Massachusetts*
Message 1901	*Message to The Mother Church for 1901*
Miscellaneous	*Miscellaneous Writings 1883-1896*
Miscellany	*The First Church of Christ, Scientist, and Miscellany*
Retrospection	*Retrospection and Introspection*
Science and Health	*Science and Health with Key to the Scriptures*

Other Frequently Cited Works:

Baxter, *Mr. Dickey/Chestnut Hill Album*	Nancy Niblack Baxter, *Mr. Dickey: Secretary to Mary Baker Eddy with a Chestnut Hill Album*, Second Edition
Canham, *Commitment*	Erwin D. Canham, *Commitment to Freedom: The Story of The Christian Science Monitor*
Dickey, *Memoirs*	Adam H. Dickey, *Memoirs of Mary Baker Eddy*
Proceedings in Equity	*Proceedings in Equity 1919-1921: Concerning Deed of Trust of January 25, 1898*
Ferguson and Frederick, *A World More Bright*	Isabel Ferguson and Heather Vogel Frederick, *A World More Bright: The Life of Mary Baker Eddy*
Gottschalk, *Rolling Away*	Stephen Gottschalk, *Rolling Away the Stone: Mary Baker Eddy's Challenge to Materialism*
Meehan, *Late Suit in Equity*	Michael Meehan, *Mrs. Eddy and the Late Suit in Equity*
Orcutt, *Mary Baker Eddy and Her Books*	William Dana Orcutt, *Mary Baker Eddy and Her Books*
Painting a Poem	*Painting a Poem: Mary Baker Eddy and James F. Gilman Illustrate Christ and Christmas*
Peel, *Discovery*	Robert Peel, *Mary Baker Eddy: The Years of Discovery*
Peel, *Trial*	Robert Peel, *Mary Baker Eddy: The Years of Trial*
Peel, *Authority*	Robert Peel, *Mary Baker Eddy: The Years of Authority*
Powell, *Portrait*	Lyman P. Powell, *Mary Baker Eddy: A Life Size Portrait*
Smaus, *Golden Days*	Jewel Spangler Smaus, *Mary Baker Eddy: The Golden Days*
Tomlinson, *Twelve Years*	Irving C. Tomlinson, *Twelve Years with Mary Baker Eddy*, Amplified Edition
Wilbur, *Mary Baker Eddy*	Sibyl Wilbur, *The Life of Mary Baker Eddy*
WKMBE Vol. I	*We Knew Mary Baker Eddy*, Expanded Edition, Vol. I
WKMBE Vol. II	*We Knew Mary Baker Eddy*, Expanded Edition, Vol. II

References

Chapter 1: A New Home for Mary Baker Eddy

1. John C. Lathrop, "Recollections of Mary Baker Eddy," *We Knew Mary Baker Eddy,* Expanded Edition, Vol. I (Boston: The Christian Science Publishing Society, 2011), 268, hereafter referenced as *WKMBE* Vol. I. For more on Mrs. Eddy's departure from Concord, see "Mrs. Eddy's Farewell," *Concord Evening Monitor,* January 27, 1908; "In Hurried Trip on 'Special' Mrs. Eddy Quits Concord for New Brookline Home," *Boston Post,* January 27, 1908; Edwin J. Park, "Estate at Chestnut Hill New Home of Mrs. Eddy," *Boston Daily Globe,* January 27, 1908, reprinted in the *Christian Science Sentinel* 10 (February 1, 1908): 423; Margaret Macdonald, "Reminiscences," 4, The Mary Baker Eddy Collection, The Mary Baker Eddy Library, Boston, Massachusetts, hereafter referenced as MBEL; Rev. Irving C. Tomlinson, "Reminiscences of Rev. Irving C. Tomlinson, C.S.B.," 760-763, MBEL; Rev. Irving C. Tomlinson, *Twelve Years with Mary Baker Eddy,* Amplified Edition (Boston: The Christian Science Publishing Society, 1994), 265-266, hereafter referenced as Tomlinson, *Twelve Years.* To see a photograph of a fabric sample of the gray velvet that Mrs. Eddy wore on her journey, see page 128.

2. *WKMBE* Vol. I, 268.

3. *Boston Post,* January 27, 1908.

4. Viola Rodgers, "Christian Science Most Potent Factor in Religious Life, Says Clara Barton," *Boston American,* January 6, 1908. Miss Barton added, "Love permeates all the teachings of this great woman — so great, I believe, that at this perspective we can scarcely realize how great—and looking into her life history we see nothing but self-sacrifice and unselfishness."

5. Sibyl Wilbur, "The Story of the Real Mrs. Eddy," *Human Life,* February 1907.

6. W. T. MacIntyre, "'I Hold No Enmity,' Says Mrs. Eddy To The American In Long Interview," *New York American,* August 26, 1907. This interview with Mrs. Eddy was reprinted in the *Christian Science Sentinel* 9 (August 31, 1907): 1003-1004.

7. Thomas W. Hatten, "Some Reminiscences of Our Revered Leader—Mary Baker Eddy," 6, MBEL.

8. *WKMBE* Vol. I, 268. See also "Mrs. Eddy Moves Home," *Baltimore Sun,* January 27, 1908.

9. *Concord Evening Monitor,* January 27, 1908.

10. *Boston Post,* January 27, 1908. Alfred Farlow served as the first Manager of the Christian Science Committee on Publication for The Mother Church. The *Boston Globe* caught wind of the move but was persuaded by Mr. Farlow and Archibald McLellan to embargo the news in exchange for an exclusive story. "The kindness of the *Globe* made it possible for Mrs. Eddy to make the trip from Concord to Boston free from unusual excitement and curiosity." Tomlinson reminiscences, 761-762, MBEL. See also M. Adelaide Still, "My Years in Mrs. Eddy's Home," *We Knew Mary Baker Eddy,* Expanded Edition, Vol. II (Boston: The Christian Science Publishing Society, 2013), 476, hereafter referenced as *WKMBE* Vol. II.

11. Mary Baker Eddy to Archibald McLellan, September 24, 1907, L07056, MBEL. Mrs. Eddy may have been contemplating a move as early as the fall of 1906. See Mary Baker Eddy to Joseph Armstrong, November 28, 1906, V00718, MBEL.

12. Tomlinson reminiscences, 758, MBEL. Chestnut Hill, which is not an incorporated municipal entity, encompasses parts of neighboring Brookline and is one of 13 "villages" that comprise the City of Newton, Massachusetts.

13. Renowned Boston architectural firm Peabody & Stearns designed the house for William Dupee and his family. Annie Robinson, *Peabody & Stearns: Country Houses and Seaside Cottages* (New York: W. W. Norton & Company, 2010), 156. The residence was later owned by Boston banker R. Ashton Lawrence, before being purchased by Robert Walker, an agent for Mary Baker Eddy, in October 1907. At the time that Mrs. Eddy lived in the house, the street address was 384 Beacon Street, but this was changed by the City of Newton to 400 Beacon Street in 1933.

14. City of Newton, Massachusetts, "Real Estate, 1908," 25, line 5, entry for Eddy, Mary Baker G., 384 Beacon; Newton City Archives, Newton Free Library, Newton, Massachusetts.

15. Coffin & Taber to Robert P. Walker, September 30, 1907, IC 658a.70.014, MBEL. Ultimately, the house was sold to Mrs. Eddy for $68,250 (roughly $1.9 million in 2018 dollars). IA Box 419, Box 7, Folder 9, MBEL. One newspaper of the day estimated that construction and remodeling costs would double that price. "300 Men Work Day and Night Upon Supposed Eddy College," *Boston Herald*, January 7, 1908.

16. "I think you had better let Mr. Beman come up & see the arrangements of rooms in this house to pattern after it, & Mrs. Eddy thinks so too." Calvin A. Frye to Archibald McLellan, October 15, 1907, L07089, MBEL. Mr. Beman traveled to Pleasant View twice in October and once in November to discuss plans for the remodel. Stephen R. Howard, *Homeward Part II: Chestnut Hill* (Chestnut Hill, Mass.: Longyear Museum Press, 2008), 12. Reporting after the fact, one journalist noted that "since the property was bought for Mrs. Eddy the house has been doubled in size by an addition built to it, the original structure has been remodeled, and the entire establishment brought right up to date in the matter of modern improvements and conveniences, including an electric elevator, and the house is splendidly furnished throughout." *Boston Daily Globe*, January 27, 1908; reprinted in the *Christian Science Sentinel* 10 (February 1, 1908): 423.

17. *Boston Herald*, January 7, 1908.

18. Ibid.

19. Ibid. In this article, which included a photo of one of the vaults, the *Herald* also noted, "The entire house has been fire-proofed and reinforced to a degree uncommon even in public buildings."

20. "Fund to Educate Healers," *Boston Post*, December 28, 1907. After a copy of Mrs. Eddy's December 14, 1907, letter to Archibald McLellan announcing her desire to fund an institution "for the special benefit of the poor and the general good of all mankind" was printed in the *Sentinel* [*Christian Science Sentinel* 10 (December 21, 1907): 310], the *Post* and other newspapers reported that the $1 million gift was "in the nature of an endowment for a college of Christian Science." Apparently nothing ever came of this idea.

21. "General Streeter Sheds No Light," *Boston Globe*, January 7, 1908; "Purchase of an Estate in Newton Can't be Identified with Christian Scientists," *Boston Globe*, January 8, 1908.

22. "Not 'House of Mystery,'" *Boston Post*, January 8, 1908.

23. "Mrs. Eddy Moves," *Washington Post*, January 27, 1908; *Boston Herald*, January 7, 1908.

24. *Washington Post*, January 27, 1908. The *Boston Post* would dub the train "the Eddy Special." *Boston Post*, January 27, 1908.

25. "Such precautions were never known before in this section of the country, not even on the occasion of visits by Presidents." "Mrs. Eddy Moves Home," *Baltimore Sun*, January 27, 1908.

26. *Boston Post*, January 27, 1908.

27. Irving Tomlinson described the weather as "gray and cloudy." Tomlinson reminiscences, 760, MBEL. John Lathrop called it "beautiful, calm, and glorious." *WKMBE* Vol. I, 268. John Salchow noted that the air "was mild and quiet, with no hint of the terrific snowstorm which was to follow that night." John G. Salchow, "Reminiscences of Mr. John G. Salchow," 89, MBEL.

28. Hatten reminiscences, 5, MBEL. The private coach contained a separate compartment in which Mrs. Eddy rested during part of the trip. M. Adelaide Still, "Reminiscences of The Time I Spent in Mrs. Eddy's Home," 25, MBEL.

29. *Baltimore Sun*, January 27, 1908.

30. *Boston Daily Globe*, January 27, 1908.

31. The other household staff members included secretaries John Lathrop and Arthur Vosburgh (shortly to be replaced by Irving Tomlinson, who was also on the train), metaphysical worker Sarah Clark, groundskeeper and handyman John Salchow, night watchman Jonathan Irving (and possibly a second watchman, William Lloyd), seamstress Nellie Eveleth, and kitchen and housekeeping staff members Minnie Scott, Anna Machacek, Elizabeth Kelly, and Margaret Macdonald. The porter was Willis Whiting, private porter to the president of the Boston & Maine Railroad, whose car Mrs. Eddy was using. The ticket agent who had arranged the charter was W. R. Babcock, a Christian Scientist who worked at South Station in Boston.

32. Minnie A. Scott, "Reminiscences of Mrs. Mary Baker Eddy," 8, MBEL. Minnie was one of the cooks at both Pleasant View and Chestnut Hill. A homeopathic physician, Dr. Morrill had not been invited to join Mrs. Eddy in his professional capacity, but rather simply because he was the closest relative at hand. In fact, he didn't even see her on the short trip. One newspaper reported that as the train neared its destination on that chilly January night, Dr. Morrill did make one contribution—by warming Mrs. Eddy's outer garments, including gloves and overshoes, "before the range in the [train] car kitchen." *Boston Post*, January 27, 1908. Morrill would spend the night at 400 Beacon Street and return home the next day. Tomlinson reminiscences, 760, MBEL.

33. Elizabeth Kelly, "Reminiscences of Mrs. Elizabeth Kelly," 8, MBEL.

34. *WKMBE* Vol. II, 476.

35. *Boston Post*, January 27, 1908; *WKMBE* Vol. II, 476; Robert Peel, *Mary Baker Eddy: The Years of Authority* (New York: Holt, Rinehart and Winston, 1977), 299, 492n21, hereafter

referenced as Peel, A*uthority*.

36. Calvin C. Hill, "Reminiscences," 233, MBEL.

37. *WKMBE* Vol. I, 403. By July, Mrs. Eddy had quietly reached out to Alfred Farlow to begin unofficially looking for a property. H. Cornell Wilson and Alfred Farlow to Mary Baker Eddy, July 22, 1907, L16812, MBEL. In mid-September, she would officially give Archibald McLellan the assignment. Mary Baker Eddy to Archibald McLellan, September 24, 1907, L07056, MBEL.

38. *Boston Post*, January 27, 1908.

39. Hatten reminiscences, 5, MBEL. For more on the reasons behind this move, see Peel, *Authority*, 297; and Stephen Gottschalk, *Rolling Away the Stone: Mary Baker Eddy's Challenge to Materialism* (Bloomington, Ind.: Indiana University Press, 2006), 361-362, hereafter referenced as Gottschalk, *Rolling Away*.

40. Minnie A. Scott, "Record of Acquaintance with Mary Baker Eddy," 9, LMC, hereafter referenced as Scott, "Record of Acquaintance."

41. At Pleasant View, "we had only one bathroom for the entire household," cook Minnie Weygandt explained, adding that it was "awkwardly located" on the first floor. "In order to use the bathroom, everyone had to come down one or two flights of stairs from his room and go through the kitchen. After laboring under such disadvantages, it is not surprising that at Chestnut Hill arrangements were made for a bathroom for almost every room." Minnie B. Weygandt, "Reminiscences of Miss Minnie Belle Weygandt and of Miss Mary Ellen Weygandt," 72, MBEL. There was also an additional half bath at Pleasant View. At 400 Beacon Street, there would be a total of 11 full bathrooms and four lavatories.

42. *Boston Post*, January 27, 1908.

43. William O. Bisbee, "Furnishing Mrs. Eddy's New Home," www.longyear.org/learn/research-archive/furnishing-mrs-eddys-new-home/

44. Macdonald reminiscences, 3, MBEL; *WKMBE* Vol. II, 474.

45. *WKMBE* Vol. II, 477. Paraphrasing Thomas Jefferson's famous quote on the Presidency, Mrs. Eddy also lamented, *"Oh splendid misery, splendid misery!"* Ibid.

46. Still reminiscences, 27-28, MBEL.

47. *WKMBE* Vol. I, 471. Minnie Scott addressed the topic of friction in the household when she wrote: "Miss Havergal writes: 'We look on another's path/ as a far off mountain scene/ seeing only the outlined hills/ but never the vales between.' So while some thought it a wonderful privilege to serve Mrs. Eddy, they did not see the 'vales between' that we had to travel, due to jealousy and mistaken thinking, but God was ever near, more near indeed when error tried to scream. Love was my defense and my helper at all times." Minnie A. Scott to her family, 1945, 21, LMC.

48. *WKMBE* Vol. II, 376.

49. Mary Baker G. Eddy, "Significant Questions," *Christian Science Sentinel* 5 (April 25, 1903): 540. This article was later reprinted in the May 2, 1903, *Sentinel*, the May issue of *The Christian Science Journal*, and *The First Church of Christ, Scientist, and Miscellany*, by Mary Baker Eddy, 229, hereafter referenced as *Miscellany*.

Chapter 2: Help Wanted

1. *WKMBE* Vol. I, 350.

2. Hill reminiscences, 47, MBEL. He also noted: "Mrs. Eddy commended me when, in one of my interviews with her, I said: 'Mother, in looking for helpers for you, I am not trying to find a pleasant personality. I am looking for a quality of thought that reflects the great revelation you have given to the world.'" *WKMBE* Vol. I, 352.

3. Ibid., 350-351.

4. *WKMBE* Vol. II, 8-9.

5. Edwin J. Park, "Mrs. Eddy is Keen, Alert," *Boston Globe,* June 16, 1907. This article was reprinted in the *Christian Science Sentinel* 9 (June 22, 1907): 803 and *The Christian Science Journal* 25 (July 1907): 193.

6. Mary Baker Eddy to Calvin C. Hill, October 13, 1905, L15551, MBEL. In another letter, Mrs. Eddy would also write: "I must have better help and none leaving me when they are most needed here." Mary Baker Eddy to Archibald McLellan, July 7, 1908, L03185, MBEL.

7. Calvin Hill called Daisette McKenzie, who was added to the Committee in June 1907, "a fine worker." Hill reminiscences, 52, MBEL. Others who later served on the Committee on Business included Ida Stewart, wife of Christian Science Board Director Allison V. Stewart; George Shaw Cook; and Hermann Hering. Ibid.

8. Mary Baker Eddy, *Message to The Mother Church for 1901,* 28-29, hereafter referenced as *Message 1901.*

9. *WKMBE* Vol. II, 457.

10. "Four Congregations Heard the Message," *Boston Post,* June 24, 1901. Services were held at 9 a.m., noon, 3 p.m., and 7 p.m. John W. Reeder, who was serving as First Reader at First Church of Christ, Scientist, in Roxbury, Massachusetts, was selected to deliver Mrs. Eddy's message at each service. Although it reportedly took over an hour and a half to read aloud, his audiences were "very attentive." "Message Inspired Christian Scientists," *Boston Globe,* June 24, 1901.

11. Scott, "Record of Acquaintance," 6, LMC.

12. *Message 1901,* 29.

13. *WKMBE* Vol. I, 351-352.

14. *Proceedings in Equity 1919-1921: Concerning Deed of Trust of January 25, 1898* (Boston: The Christian Science Publishing Society, 1922), 491, hereafter referenced as *Proceedings in Equity.*

15. Hill reminiscences, 57, MBEL.

16. *WKMBE* Vol. I, 352.

17. Romans 8:7. As Adam Dickey explains, "Our Leader was very strict in her requirements. For instance, if one had formerly suffered from a belief that had incapacitated him, even though he had been healed and restored apparently to perfect health, she did not want such a person in her house. Her reason for this has already been alluded to,—that as

soon as the individual entered Mrs. Eddy's employ he came under a certain malicious mental malpractice that he had never encountered before, and our Leader was unwilling to subject anybody to this trial, who might be liable to a relapse or a return of a diseased belief." Adam H. Dickey, *Memoirs of Mary Baker Eddy* (Brookline, Mass.: Lillian S. Dickey, C.S.B., 1927), 5, hereafter referenced as Dickey, *Memoirs*.

18. Hill reminiscences, 41, MBEL.

19. The Christian Science Board of Directors/Committee on Business to Mary Baker Eddy, May 29, 1908, IC 002cP2.03.044, MBEL.

20. James A. Neal/Committee on Business to Mary Baker Eddy, July 30, 1907, IC 179a.31.024, MBEL, and Thomas W. Hatten/Committee on Business to Mary Baker Eddy, March 18, 1908, IC 179b.31.005, MBEL.

21. "Mrs. Ella Rathvon," Committee on Business to Mary Baker Eddy, June 12, 1908, Allison V. and Ida G. Stewart Subject File, MBEL.

22. Hill reminiscences, 41, MBEL.

23. Thomas W. Hatten/Committee on Business to Mary Baker Eddy, March 18, 1908, IC 179b.31.005, MBEL; "Mrs. Ella Rathvon," Committee on Business to Mary Baker Eddy, June 12, 1908, Allison V. and Ida G. Stewart Subject File, MBEL; William R. Rathvon, "Reminiscences of William R. Rathvon, C.S.B.," 16-17, MBEL.

24. Mary Baker Eddy to William B. Johnson, March 18, 1906, L03351, MBEL.

25. Hill reminiscences, 47, MBEL.

26. *WKMBE* Vol. I, 397.

27. John Salchow to Bertha Salchow, undated letter from Pleasant View, private collection.

28. Ella W. Hoag, "Reminiscences," 1, MBEL.

29. Peel, *Authority*, 499n92.

30. Mary Baker Eddy, *Science and Health with Key to the Scriptures*, 58, hereafter referenced as *Science and Health*.

31. Mary Baker Eddy to Augusta E. Stetson, December 11, 1894, H00029, MBEL.

32. Tomlinson, *Twelve Years*, 213.

33. Elizabeth Kelly was one of six household workers who wrote a joint letter to Calvin Frye, thanking him for arranging for the chairs. Nellie Eveleth, Martha Wilcox, Margaret Macdonald, Adelaide Still, Elizabeth Kelly, and Katharine Retterer to Calvin A. Frye, December 24, 1909, L18088, MBEL. Macdonald reminiscences, 6, MBEL.

34. *WKMBE* Vol. II, 547.

35. Weygandt reminiscences, 102, MBEL. Minnie also noted, "Mrs. Eddy was naturally friendly and kind-hearted and often went out of her way to do nice things for others. I have seen many evidences of her consideration and loving interest…." Ibid., 95.

36. Irving C. Tomlinson note, June 29, 1909, A12081, MBEL.

Chapter 3: Serving Their Commander-in-Chief

1. Dickey, *Memoirs*, 25.

2. Ibid., 29.

3. Adam H. Dickey diary entry, February 20, 1908, Nancy Niblack Baxter, *Mr. Dickey: Secretary to Mary Baker Eddy with A Chestnut Hill Album,* Second Edition (Carmel, Indiana: Hawthorne Publishing, 2005), 11, hereafter referenced as Baxter, *Mr. Dickey* when quoting from main text, or Baxter, *Chestnut Hill Album* when quoting from the appendix.

4. Mary Baker Eddy to Lillian S. Dickey, February 20, 1908, L04310, MBEL. Like William Rathvon, Adam Dickey would find separation from his wife difficult. Within two weeks of his arrival, he wrote to his friend Hermann Hering, thanking him for his "cheering letter," which he forwarded to Lillian. "It was so helpful I thought she would get lots of comfort out of it," he told Mr. Hering. "She has been very brave in parting with me but still she needs all the little boosts of love she can get." Adam H. Dickey to Hermann S. Hering, February 16, 1908, L12398, MBEL. As was the case with Ella Rathvon, Lillian Dickey would eventually move to Boston to be near her husband.

5. Dickey diary entry, February 21, 1908, Baxter, *Chestnut Hill Album*, 13. Mrs. Eddy's secretaries and metaphysical workers all had regular assigned shifts, or "watches," during which they would pray to support Mrs. Eddy and whatever else she directed them to prayerfully address.

6. The invention of the typewriter opened the ranks of the previously male-dominated secretarial profession to women. Tony Allan, *Typewriter* (New York: Shelter Harbor Press, 2015), 65. Mrs. Eddy's household, however, hewed to the tradition of male secretaries. John Lathrop and Arthur Vosburgh also served brief stints as secretaries, and George Kinter filled in on occasion in 1909 and 1910 for William Rathvon and Adam Dickey.

7. For a more in-depth look at the "old guard/new guard" divide, see Gottschalk, *Rolling Away,* 400-402.

8. Calvin Frye grew up in Andover, Massachusetts, and later worked as a machinist in Lawrence, Massachusetts; Irving Tomlinson was from upstate New York, earned Bachelor and Master of Arts degrees from Akron University, then received his Bachelor of Divinity degree from Tufts College (which later became Tufts University) near Boston. By the time Irving moved to 400 Beacon Street, he had lived and worked in the Boston area and in Concord, New Hampshire, for 20 years.

9. Calvin Frye had Primary class instruction with Mrs. Eddy in the fall of 1881. She would later grant him the advanced designation C.S.D., as she would a number of those who either studied with her at the Massachusetts Metaphysical College or who worked in her home and received private instruction from her there.

10. Tomlinson, *Twelve Years*, 223.

11. Ibid.

12. Peel, *Authority*, 316.

13. Mary Baker Eddy to Adam H. Dickey, March 1, 1908, L10867, MBEL.

14. William Rathvon reminiscences, 196, MBEL.

15. Mrs. Eddy herself commented on this inseparability in a letter to a student: "People seem to understand C[hristian] S[cience] in the exact ratio that they know me and vice versa. It sometimes astonishes me to see the invariableness of this rule." Mary Baker Eddy to Julia Field-King, November 26, 1897, LMC. Other members of her household would note this as well. For instance, as Martha Wilcox points out, "Those closely associated with Mrs. Eddy knew when she was giving birth, in thought, to some important decision — such as a change in the Church, the making of a new By-Law, or something in connection with her writings. Many times there seemed to be great travail when these things were being born of the Spirit. I remember such a time when she abolished the Communion season of The Mother Church, and again when certain new By-Laws were brought out." *WKMBE* Vol. I, 475-476.

16. Mary Baker Eddy to Editor, *New York Herald*, May 20, 1908, L13215, MBEL.

17. *Science and Health,* 107.

18. Today, Frye Village is part of the town of Andover, Massachusetts.

19. *Human Life,* November 1907.

20. Enoch Osgood Frye, a private in the Massachusetts 1st Heavy Artillery Regiment (Company K), died on October 29, 1861, accidentally killed at Fort Albany, Virginia, by a falling tree. U.S. Civil War Soldier Records and Profiles, 1861-1865; Massachusetts Death Records, 1841-1915. Thomas Roaf, Lydia Frye's husband, was also a private in the Massachusetts 1st Heavy Artillery (Company B). He died of typhoid fever on November 17, 1862 at Fort Warren in Boston Harbor. U.S. Civil War Soldier Records and Profiles, 1861-1865; Massachusetts Death Records, 1841-1915.

21. William Lyman Johnson, "Calvin A. Frye, C.S.D.," 12, LMC.

22. Sibyl Wilbur, *The Life of Mary Baker Eddy* (Boston: The Christian Science Publishing Society, 1966), 277, hereafter referenced as Wilbur, *Mary Baker Eddy.*

23. The two were married October 19, 1871. Massachusetts, Town and Vital Records, 1620-1988. In what may well have been a mark of deep devotion, Calvin would keep a trunk of his wife Ada's clothing for some three decades after her passing until finally disposing of them while living at Pleasant View. Weygandt reminiscences, 62, MBEL. Calvin is buried beside Ada at the West Parish Garden Cemetery in Andover, Massachusetts.

24. Clara Choate, one of Mrs. Eddy's early students, was the practitioner on the case, according to Wilbur, *Mary Baker Eddy,* 277.

25. Calvin's sister, Lydia Roaf, would study with Mrs. Eddy in 1883.

26. According to Sibyl Wilbur, "The Rev. Joshua Coit, Mr. Frye's pastor in the Congregational Church, had so spoken of Mr. Frye that Mr. Eddy recommended him to his wife as a man to be trusted with her intimate affairs." Wilbur, *Mary Baker Eddy,* 276.

27. Mary Baker Eddy to George W. Glover II, April 7, 1903, L02136, MBEL.

28. In a 1906 letter to Mrs. Eddy, Calvin Frye estimates that he had been away only four nights in all the years he was in her service. Calvin A. Frye to Mary Baker Eddy, August 17, 1906, L17856, MBEL.

29. Carolyn Armstrong, "Reminiscences," 1, MBEL.

30. Wilbur, *Mary Baker Eddy*, 278.

31. Still reminiscences, 57, MBEL. Calvin Frye's faithfulness came at no little cost to himself, as is evident in a letter he wrote to his friend Septimus Hanna at one point. It reads in part, "O my brother, you little know the agonies I endure in trying to wisely meet the demands upon me in this position. Gladly would I have given place to some other, and have repeatedly said so, long ago had there been such an one ready to fill the place acceptably to Mother. The way grows harder and harder, until it sometimes seems I can endure it no longer without a respite, a vacation even of a few days, where I could go away and be at rest. But just as I seem ready to drop there comes a renewed sense of courage and the thought 'How can you leave the Mother unprovided for and desert her?' and I gather up the little courage I can and try again." Calvin A. Frye to Septimus J. Hanna, September 27, 1899, LMC.

32. In January 1881, Mrs. Eddy obtained a charter from the Commonwealth of Massachusetts for a college to teach Christian Science. The Massachusetts Metaphysical College opened in May 1882 at 569 Columbus Avenue in Boston (and moved next door to 571 Columbus Avenue in 1884). Mrs. Eddy closed the College in 1889. As she explains in the preface to *Science and Health* (xii), "She retained her charter, and as its President, reopened the College in 1899 as auxiliary to her church." It continues its work today under the Board of Education.

33. Johnson, "Calvin A. Frye," 14-15, LMC.

34. Still reminiscences, 57, MBEL.

35. "Closest Friend of Mrs. Eddy, in Denver, Tells of Her Life," *Denver Republican*, December 24, 1912.

36. *Human Life*, November 1907.

37. "They answered the call: Calvin A. Frye," *The Christian Science Journal* 107 (February 1989): 17.

38. *Denver Republican*, December 24, 1912.

39. Calvin's 1912 passport application lists his height as 5'5" and his eyes as brown. U.S. Passport Applications, 1795-1925. "Mrs. Eddy loved his wit." Tomlinson reminiscences, 649, MBEL. "He had a keen sense of wit which Mrs. Eddy enjoyed and appreciated." Still reminiscences, 57, MBEL. Carolyn Armstrong, who visited Calvin Frye in 1916, noted: "His eyes twinkle, and a few minutes talk show his tendency to fun and jokes." Armstrong reminiscences, 1, MBEL. Adam Dickey recalled that Calvin "possessed a keen sense of humor and he was a man who liked his little joke quite as well as did others of a more mirthful disposition." Dickey, *Memoirs*, 22.

40. "Mrs. Eddy In Good Health," *The Christian Science Journal* 23 (April 1905): 65. Sibyl Wilbur would write: "His eyes have a smile lurking in them, for he is not without a gentle mirthfulness in conversation," adding that this made him "an agreeable companion." *Human Life*, November 1907; Wilbur, *Mary Baker Eddy*, 278.

41. Michael Meehan, *Mrs. Eddy and the Late Suit in Equity* (Concord, N.H.: Michael Meehan,

1908), 339, hereafter referenced as Meehan, *Late Suit in Equity.*

42. *WKMBE* Vol. I, 67, 387, 422.

43. Weygandt reminiscences, 64, MBEL. "I always liked Mr. Frye and felt that he deserved a great deal of credit for all the loyal service he so willingly gave to his Leader, and I was glad to do little things for him when I could." Ibid., 63-64.

44. "His education was broadened by the habit of reading." Wilbur, *Mary Baker Eddy,* 278.

45. Calvin A. Frye Library Finding Aid, MBEL.

46. *Human Life*, November 1907.

47. In addition to Primary class instruction in 1881, Calvin was in the Normal class of August 1884 and the Obstetrics class of October 1888.

48. Hill reminiscences, 175, MBEL. That "someone else" would be Adam Dickey, according to Hill.

49. Ibid., 155.

50. William R. Rathvon to Charles G. Baldwin, December 8, 1909, V04660, MBEL.

51. Hill reminiscences, 164, MBEL.

52. Peel, *Authority,* 244.

53. Tomlinson reminiscences, 649, MBEL.

54. Mary Baker Eddy to Calvin A. Frye, January 20, 1908, L17974, MBEL.

55. Johnson, "Calvin A. Frye," 23, LMC. One of Mrs. Eddy's early students, Joseph Mann heard of the need for additional helpers at Pleasant View and volunteered his services to Mrs. Eddy "in whatever capacity she might see fit to use" him. *WKMBE* Vol. II, 149. Stepping aside from his healing practice, he became superintendent of the Pleasant View estate for several years.

56. Lewis C. Strang and Calvin C. Hill statement, November 2, 1906, A11532, MBEL.

57. Mary Baker Eddy to the Christian Science Board of Directors, August 30, 1903, L00352, MBEL. In 1903, in addition to encouraging the Executive Members to give Calvin a gift, Mrs. Eddy gave him $1,000 (nearly $30,000 in 2018 dollars), with which he bought a municipal bond. Mary Baker Eddy to Calvin A. Frye, August 15, 1903, L09524, MBEL.

58. In their letter to Calvin Frye accompanying the gift, the Executive Members praised him for his "work for God and man which has been beyond price," adding "we cannot but marvel at the unselfed love which enabled you to sever all other ties and so consecrate yourself to the service of your fellow-men." "In Recognition of Faithful Service," *Christian Science Sentinel* 6 (October 3, 1903): 73. In his response (published in the same issue) Calvin replied in part, "I assure you that in comparison with the infinite blessings received while in this blessed service I have sacrificed nothing in leaving my former associations to serve God and our Leader...."

59. Tomlinson reminiscences, 648, MBEL.

60. Dickey diary entry, February 21, 1908, Baxter, *Chestnut Hill Album,* 13. William Rathvon reminiscences, 238, MBEL; Tomlinson, *Twelve Years,* 267; George H. Kinter to John

Carroll Lathrop, October 13, 1910, L15721, MBEL.

61. William Rathvon reminiscences, 170, MBEL.

62. *WKMBE* Vol. II, 525.

63. William Rathvon reminiscences, 33-34, MBEL.

64. Ibid., 146.

65. Ibid., 147.

66. Adam H. Dickey to Mrs. [Addie Wentz] Veazey, July 13, 1908, LMC.

67. Mary Baker Eddy to Adam H. Dickey, October 8, 1909, private collection. As late as August 1910, Mrs. Eddy wrote to her son, George, "My secretary opens only those letters of mine that he is instructed to." Mary Baker Eddy to George W. Glover II, August 26, 1910, V03141, MBEL.

68. Peel, *Authority*, 501n107.

69. Dickey, *Memoirs*, 84. Mrs. Eddy also quotes part of this phrase in *Miscellany*, 123.

70. *WKMBE* Vol. II, 427.

71. Dickey, *Memoirs*, 12-13. Although he wasn't put to work shoveling snow, soon after Adam arrived at Chestnut Hill, Mrs. Eddy's carriage driver passed on unexpectedly. As Mr. Dickey was accustomed to driving horses and sleighs, he was able to fill in for a few weeks while a new driver was found. Ibid., 36.

72. William Rathvon reminiscences, 147-148, MBEL.

73. Adam H. Dickey to Mrs. [Addie Wentz] Veazey, July 13, 1908, LMC.

74. Mary Baker Eddy to Mary Baker Eddy Household, May 27, 1909, L10877, MBEL.

75. Daisette McKenzie to Mary Baker Eddy, January 24, 1908, L07009, MBEL.

76. William D. McCracken, "Adam H. Dickey," Adam H. Dickey Subject File, 2, MBEL. Mr. McCracken was serving as a Trustee of the The Christian Science Publishing Society when Adam Dickey arrived at 400 Beacon Street, and in later years had frequent contact with him.

77. The company manufactured pipes for wastewater and sewage. For more information on the Dickey family's history and business in Kansas City, see Baxter, *Mr. Dickey*, 1-22.

78. The Dickeys' son was born October 24, 1888, and passed on December 11, 1895.

79. Susan J. Rockefeller, "Historical Sketch of Adam H. Dickey, C.S.D." January 8, 1948, Adam H. Dickey Subject File, 1, MBEL.

80. As had his wife, Lillian, Adam received instruction from Henrietta Graybill.

81. For more about this Fourth of July gathering, see James R. Suber, "'For Our Dear Cause': The 1897 Visit to Pleasant View," *Longyear Museum Report to Members*, Spring/Summer 2013, 4-11.

82. "Sawyer Elected in the Seventh," *Kansas City Journal*, April 6, 1898; Baxter, *Mr. Dickey*, 18.

83. "Price Lists in Spanish," *Kansas City Journal*, November 27, 1898; "Trip Through Old Mexico," *Kansas City Journal*, July 30, 1898.

84. *Kansas City Journal,* March 14, 1899. Rockefeller, "Historical Sketch," 2-3, MBEL; Baxter, *Mr. Dickey,* 18-19. The healing sparked interest in Christian Science, and before they left Mexico, the Dickeys were leading informal church services at their hotel, serving as First and Second Readers. From this seed would eventually grow First Church of Christ, Scientist, Mexico City, one of the first Christian Science churches outside the United States. "Among the Churches," *Christian Science Sentinel* 2 (January 11, 1900): 301.

85. Dickey was offered an annual salary of $5,000, which is about $154,000 in 2018.

86. Adam Dickey also attended the Normal class of 1900, but because of a limit at the time on the number of teachers awarded C.S.B. degrees, he deferred to a colleague from Kansas City with seniority. His graciousness was rewarded with a second invitation to the 1901 class. Lillian was a member of that Normal class as well, earning her C.S.B. degree, but only Adam would go on to teach. Mr. Dickey probably became acquainted with Edward Kimball when Mr. Kimball lectured in Kansas City in the fall of 1900. Dickey was a member of the joint committee of Kansas City churches that hosted the lecture, held on September 30, 1900, in Convention Hall. "[T]he audience," Kimball wrote to Mrs. Eddy afterward, "was *enormous.*" Newspaper estimates put attendance at 10,000; Kimball suggests 8,000. Either way, it was impressive. "Mr. Kimball at Kansas City," *The Christian Science Journal* 18 (November 1900): 520-522. See also "At Kansas City, Mo.," *Christian Science Sentinel* 3 (October 11, 1900): 88-89.

87. Tomlinson reminiscences, 764, MBEL.

88. Dickey diary entry, December 25, 1908, Baxter, *Chestnut Hill Album,* 99. For the hanging of the portrait in the Pink Room, see Baxter, *Mr. Dickey,* 58, and Gertrude Farmer's account in "Historical Sketch of Adam H. Dickey, C.S.D., Part III: Addenda," Adam H. Dickey Subject File, 1, MBEL. According to Mrs. Farmer (a former Second Reader of The Mother Church), Mrs. Eddy said the picture "should never be removed, that he stood for the Cause as Daniel stood."

89. William Rathvon reminiscences, 206-207, MBEL.

90. Tomlinson reminiscences, 765, MBEL.

91. William Rathvon reminiscences, 207, MBEL.

92. Still reminiscences, 65, MBEL.

93. Mary Baker Eddy to the Christian Science Board of Directors, November 21, 1910, L00635, MBEL.

94. For more information on Eustace vs. Dickey and Dittemore vs. Dickey, see *WKMBE* Vol. I, 502; Clifford P. Smith, *Historical Sketches from the Life of Mary Baker Eddy and the History of Christian Science* (Boston: The Christian Science Publishing Society, 1969), 219; Peel, *Authority,* 346-347; and www.marybakereddylibrary.org/research/the-great-litigation/

95. The Chestnut Hill Benevolent Association is a Christian Science nursing facility located near Boston. Adam Dickey served as Treasurer of The Mother Church from 1912 to 1917, and as a Trustee under the Will of Mary Baker G. Eddy from 1913 to his passing in 1925.

96. The two would often chat about events or news of the day, Adelaide Still notes, adding that "Mr. Dickey sometimes took turns with Mr. Frye in sitting with her." Still reminiscences,

17, MBEL.

97. *WKMBE* Vol. II, 499. For more information, see Gottschalk, *Rolling Away*, 402, and Peel, *Authority*, 346-347.

98. Irving Tomlinson's colleague Margaret Macdonald would write: "One day in early April, Mr. Tomlinson was out for an hour and brought back seventy-five varieties of wild flowers. He was always looking for flowers. . . ." Macdonald reminiscences, 9, MBEL. And Mrs. Eddy once told Irving, "You do love the flowers and a flower is the expression of infinite Good." Irving C. Tomlinson note, July 5, 1910, A11997, MBEL.

99. Tomlinson reminiscences, 766, MBEL.

100. *WKMBE* Vol. II, 565-566.

101. The opening sentence of Abraham Lincoln's Gettysburg Address, delivered in Gettysburg, Pennsylvania, on November 19, 1863, alludes to the year 1776, when the American colonies declared their independence from Great Britain. In his speech, President Lincoln dedicated the Soldiers' National Cemetery, a site that honors the Union soldiers who died at the Battle of Gettysburg in July 1863. Quoted is the same version inscribed on the Lincoln Memorial in Washington, D.C.

102. The battle was referred to as "the turning-point of the war between the States." Samuel Adams Drake, *The Battle of Gettysburg, 1863* (Boston: Lee & Shepard, 1892), 160. In an audio recording many years later, William Rathvon said that the battle was "one of the fiercest conflicts of internecine warfare that [the] modern world has ever known." "I Heard Lincoln that Day," recorded on February 12, 1938, on the Boston radio station WRUL. Despite the high casualty toll for both armies, the battle of Gettysburg was a major victory for the Union.

103. Lancaster was the capital of Pennsylvania from 1799 to 1813. The 1834 arrival of the railroad stimulated the development of factories and manufacturing systems. See *City of Lancaster, Pennsylvania: A City Authentic, 2017,* www.cityoflancasterpa.com/business/lancaster-previous-decades. Young William was acutely aware of the Civil War. In his recording, "I Heard Lincoln That Day," he recalls that in July 1863, "shortly after the battle, I wandered over the battlefield with two other lads gathering gruesome mementos of the fearful three days' carnage."

104. The earliest settlers in the Lancaster area, Mennonites from Switzerland and present-day Germany, came in 1709. French Huguenots and Scotch-Irish Presbyterians came over during the following decade. Franklin Ellis and Samuel Evans, *History of Lancaster County, Pennsylvania, with Biographical Sketches of Many of Its Pioneers and Prominent Men* (Philadelphia: Everts & Peck, 1883), 19. According to the U.S. and Canada Passenger and Immigration Lists Index, 1500s-1900s, William's maternal ancestors immigrated in 1721, and Friedrich Rathvon, William's paternal great-great-great grandfather, arrived in the United States in 1740.

105. The first coeducational and bilingual (English and German) institution in the country, Franklin College was launched in 1787 by leaders of the Lutheran and Reformed churches. In 1853, Marshall College moved from Mercersburg to Lancaster, and the two colleges merged, forming Franklin and Marshall College.

106. James H. Baker and Leroy R. Haven, editors, *History of Colorado,* Vol. V (Denver: Linderman Co., Inc., 1927), 582-583. Samuel would eventually move the store to Bonanza, Colorado, a mining town where William presumably joined him before moving to Denver. William would later work for Samuel's oil company.

107. Martin named his daughter Ella, perhaps as testament to the love he felt for his stepmother, who was also his aunt.

108. The Panic of 1893 was an economic depression from 1893 to 1897 that affected both national and international markets. In the United States, the New York Stock Market collapsed, and stock values fell significantly.

109. "William and Ella Rathvon," *Longyear Quarterly News*, Winter 1977-78. See also W. R. Rathvon, "Christian Scientists' Cards," *The Christian Science Journal* 16 (September 1898): 420.

110. Ibid., 419.

111. *Science and Health*, 266.

112. *The Christian Science Journal* 16 (September 1898): 420.

113. W. R. Rathvon, "Notes from the Field," *The Christian Science Journal* 16 (October 1898): 497-498.

114. Ibid.

115. William was listed as manager of the United Oil Company in the *Boulder City Directory,* April 1903. He also served on the Commercial Association committee of the Boulder city council, which initiated fundraising efforts to build the Hotel Boulderado. The hotel still stands today and has early guest registers on display in the lobby. Ella Rathvon, the honorary first guest, signed the register on opening day, January 1, 1909. Silvia Pettem, *Legend of a Landmark: A History of the Hotel Boulderado* (Missoula, Montana: Pictorial Histories Publishing Co., 1997), 15, 22-24.

116. William Rathvon reminiscences, 15, MBEL.

117. In the early years of the Christian Science movement, it wasn't unusual for people to take Primary class instruction more than once.

118. Committee on Business to Mary Baker Eddy, July 21, 1908, IC 179b.31.019, MBEL.

119. Rathvon's job at the time paid $6,000 a year, approximately $170,000 in 2018 dollars. Although Rathvon says he earned "one-tenth" of that amount working in Mrs. Eddy's household (he was exaggerating slightly—his annual salary at Chestnut Hill, adjusted to 2018 dollars, was about $55,000, in addition to room and board), he adds that he and his wife "never doubted the wisdom of the move for one moment.... [W]e never felt the loss." When he told Mrs. Eddy as much, she replied, "No, for you gained heaven and your business will prosper all the more because of it." William Rathvon reminiscences, 158, MBEL.

120. Tomlinson reminiscences, 765, MBEL.

121. Mary Baker Eddy to Archibald McLellan, December 28, 1908, L08773, MBEL.

122. John Salchow reminiscences, 115-116, MBEL.

123. William D. McCracken, "William R. Rathvon," William R. Rathvon Subject File, 1, 4, MBEL.

124. When her husband went to work for Mrs. Eddy, Ella Rathvon continued her Christian Science practice, first in Boulder and later in an apartment near Chestnut Hill, until September 1909, when she also was called to serve at 400 Beacon Street. Remarking on the work ethic of the Rathvons, one observer reported, "Mr. <u>and</u> <u>Mrs.</u> Rathvon were a real find; they have made good in all that that implies and signifies." George H. Kinter to John Carroll Lathrop, October 13, 1910, L15721, MBEL. Ella Rathvon passed on in 1923. In 1925, William married Lora Maude Carney Woodbury, who also became a staunch worker in the Christian Science movement.

125. Rathvon once listed his lecture destinations as: China, Japan, Australia, South Africa, Philippines, New Zealand, Hawaii, Alaska, Great Britain, Ireland, and Scotland. *Proceedings in Equity*, 635.

126. Tomlinson, *Twelve Years*, 267.

127. William Rathvon reminiscences, 147, MBEL.

128. *WKMBE* Vol. II, 524.

129. Hill reminiscences, 41, MBEL.

130. William Rathvon reminiscences, 17, 20, MBEL.

131. He also noted: "But I had in large measure learned to evaluate such things properly and was not unduly affected by either. Inability to impersonalize these extremes was the reason so many who were summoned to her side, and who seemed promising, could not stand after a brief stay and had to return to their homes. They took her praise to themselves as a heavenly benediction and her rebukes as personal condemnation." *WKMBE* Vol. II, 523.

132. *Science and Health*, 253-254.

133. *Painting a Poem: Mary Baker Eddy and James F. Gilman Illustrate Christ and Christmas* (Boston: The Christian Science Publishing Society, 1998), 114, hereafter referenced as *Painting a Poem*. Mrs. Eddy continued, "If they are found unwilling to bear this test, they are not worthy to be found in this work. It is the resentment that rebuke uncovers or excites that makes up the burden—the *terrible burden* that I have had, and still have to bear in this pioneer work of Christian Science." Hermann Hering also recalled: "When anyone did anything wrong, or did not carry out some of Mrs. Eddy's instructions or failed in any way to do what she wanted done, it was usual that he or she justified it or gave some reason. Mrs. Eddy was very severe on this question of self-justification, and she kept on talking and talking. A stranger might call it scolding, but it wasn't scolding; it was righteously rebuking, and she continued this until the person gave in and admitted, 'Yes, error made me do that.'" *WKMBE* Vol. I, 454.

134. Mary Baker Eddy to Willard S. Mattox, February 28, 1908, LMC.

135. *WKMBE* Vol. II, 468. Laura Sargent records a slightly different version of the same quote. *WKMBE* Vol. I, 109.

136. Irving C. Tomlinson to Mary Baker Eddy, June 8, 1908, L18194, MBEL.

137. Mary Baker Eddy to Irving C. Tomlinson, June 10, 1908, V03657, MBEL.

138. Irving C. Tomlinson to Mary Baker Eddy, June 10, 1908, IC 177c.31.024, MBEL.

139. Mary Baker Eddy to Irving C. Tomlinson, June 20, 1908, L03882, MBEL.

140. Rev. Irving C. Tomlinson, "The Unknown God Made Known," *The Christian Science Journal* 18 (May 1900): 67.

141. Among other endeavors, Emeline Tomlinson, Irving Tomlinson's mother, was also one of the founders of the Woman's Christian Temperance Union in America. E. R. Hanson, *Our Woman Workers* (Chicago: The Star and Covenant Office, 1882), 274-275.

142. A Bachelor of Divinity degree from Tufts was conferred on Irving Tomlinson on June 20, 1888. "Tufts College Commencement," *Boston Post,* June 21, 1888.

143. "They Justify Their Belief," *Boston Globe,* July 2, 1903. Tomlinson reminiscences, iv, MBEL.

144. Tomlinson reminiscences, ii, MBEL.

145. "Christian Science Is A Practical Religion," delivered February 5, 1934, at Second Church of Christ, Scientist, New York, and published in the *Brooklyn Daily Eagle,* February 6, 1934, under the heading "Christian Science Is Practical Religion." Tomlinson referenced the "gold cure," also known as the Keeley Cure, a popular medical treatment of the day for alcoholism.

146. Tomlinson, *Twelve Years,* xv-xvi.

147. *Brooklyn Daily Eagle,* February 6, 1934.

148. "Universalists Ready," *Boston Daily Globe,* July 3, 1895. Some of the other reports on Tomlinson's efforts in social reform include: "They Counsel Together," *Boston Daily Globe,* December 16, 1890; "Universalists at Work," *Boston Daily Globe,* January 25, 1894; "Mutual Helpers' Work," *Boston Daily Globe,* October 10, 1894; "Universalists Dine," *Boston Post,* May 26, 1896; "Reception to Irving C. Tomlinson," *Boston Daily Globe,* March 10, 1896. In his work with the interfaith Boston Mutual Helpers, Tomlinson helped organize a "flower mission," supervising children as they turned donated blossoms into bouquets to distribute to the elderly, indigent, and infirm living in tenements. "Posies Fresh and Fair," *Boston Daily Globe,* July 3, 1894.

149. Irving C. Tomlinson to Maurine Campbell, November 7, 1919, LMC.

150. Irving C. Tomlinson, "Christian Science, What It Is and What It Is Not," *The Christian Science Journal* 16 (March 1899): 814.

151. Irving C. Tomlinson, "The Religion of the Bible a Religion of Healing," *The Christian Science Journal* 15 (June 1897): 138-139. In a letter written several months after their first meeting, Mrs. Eddy praised this debut article as "par excellence," and asked, "What first turned your gaze toward [Christian Science], was it the head or the heart? Was it in sorrow or in joy, in health or its decline? Whatever it was, or whenever, God did it, and that's enough for me." Mary Baker Eddy to Irving C. Tomlinson, October 29, 1897, L03637, MBEL.

152. *The Christian Science Journal* 16 (March 1899): 814. Shortly after class instruction, Tomlinson resigned from the Universalist church. "By then I had found it impossible to ride

two horses going in opposite directions." Tomlinson, *Twelve Years*, xvii.

153. *Brooklyn Daily Eagle*, February 6, 1934. From the moment he first met Mrs. Eddy, Tomlinson recognized her spiritual strength and leadership: "I shall never forget my first interview with her, in her home at Concord, New Hampshire. She had just given the 'Address on the Fourth of July at Pleasant View . . .' [Mary Baker Eddy, *Miscellaneous Writings 1883-1896*, 251, hereafter referenced as *Miscellaneous*]. Mary Baker Eddy was in her seventy-sixth year. She had not only spoken at length, but had listened attentively to many speakers, had served as hostess to the throng, had interviewed many of her followers, but when I took her hand in greeting, though the day was one of the hottest of summer days, she was cool and peaceful, unruffled in outward appearance, and aglow with spiritual strength. She greeted me with a loving smile. Every look, word, gesture, showed her a born leader and a true woman. This was a picture of Mrs. Eddy's sense of service (mind you in her seventy-sixth year), and this was the way I found her during my twelve years of happy service with her, always unselfed love, expressed." "Christian Science Lecture by Irving C. Tomlinson, C.S.B.," *The Christian Science Monitor*, October 3, 1933.

154. Still reminiscences, 64, MBEL.

155. A new By-law in December 1898 established the Committee on Publication, but it "did not appear in the Church Manual. On January 16, 1900 it was repealed and shortly thereafter a new By-law took its place which first appeared in the 14th edition [1900] of the Manual." Tomlinson reminiscences, 408, MBEL. Originally, the Committee consisted of three members: Irving Tomlinson, Alfred Farlow, and Judge Septimus J. Hanna. In January 1900, an amended By-law provided for just a single member, who would at first be Alfred Farlow.

156. Tomlinson, *Twelve Years*, xvii. Irving Tomlinson was one of the original five members appointed by Mrs. Eddy to the Board of Lectureship. The others were William McKenzie, Edward Kimball, George Tomkins, and Carol Norton. Peel, *Authority*, 122-123.

157. "As To Christian Science," *Boston Globe*, September 29, 1898. The newspaper account included Judge Septimus Hanna's introductory remarks, in which he noted that Tomlinson, "though young in membership with our church and movement, has well proved himself old in understanding, fidelity and loyalty."

158. Tomlinson, *Twelve Years*, xviii. Brother and sister would continue as Readers for seven years, resigning at the end of their terms in January 1906, following publication of the amended By-law limiting Readers' terms to three years. Tomlinson reminiscences, 274, 280, MBEL.

159. "I am glad you have begun the C.S. Mission with faith that you can open the prison doors and set free the captive," Mrs. Eddy wrote. "God will bless you in this way of His appointing." Mary Baker Eddy to Irving C. Tomlinson, May 12, 1900, L03728, MBEL. Tomlinson read on Sunday afternoons at 2 p.m. from 1900 through 1906. For more information on Mrs. Eddy's interest in this subject, see "'Set free the Captive': Mary Baker Eddy and Prison Reform," March 1, 2014, www.marybakereddylibrary.org/research/prison-reform/

160. "Irving C. Tomlinson," *The Christian Science Monitor*, October 2, 1944.

161. Elizabeth Cadwell Tomlinson served as President of The Mother Church in 1936.

162. He had served previously as President in 1903.

163. *The Christian Science Monitor,* October 2, 1944.

164. *WKMBE* Vol. II, 391.

165. William Rathvon reminiscences, 97, MBEL.

166. Ibid., 86-87.

167. *WKMBE* Vol. II, 566.

168. Ibid., 389.

Chapter 4: Brightening Their Leader's Pathway

1. A line item for the purchase of the cows appears in Calvin Frye's ledger. Calvin A. Frye, Account Books, Boxes OS#27-29, MBEL.

2. John Salchow began working at Pleasant View on January 27, 1901, and remained in Mrs. Eddy's household until after her passing in December 1910. Weygandt reminiscences, 69, MBEL.

3. *WKMBE* Vol. I, 367-370.

4. Joseph Mann was John Salchow's Christian Science Primary class teacher.

5. *WKMBE* Vol. I, 371. Years later, Salchow was introduced as the man "who left his plough in the field and came to serve his Leader." Ibid.

6. Ibid., 376. Minnie Weygandt, who was one of the cooks at Pleasant View and occasionally filled in at 400 Beacon Street, noted, "John worked so hard all day that many times he did not get at watering the lawn until nearly midnight." Weygandt reminiscences, 68. After a break-in at Pleasant View in 1903, Salchow also served as the night watchman for a short time, and during that period worked nearly round the clock because of his various responsibilities. *WKMBE* Vol. I, 395-397.

7. Weygandt reminiscences, 67, MBEL.

8. *WKMBE* Vol. I, 372.

9. Ibid., 375. Homemade lemonade was customarily on hand for Mrs. Eddy to enjoy after her carriage ride, and Salchow recalls her thoughtfulness in always wanting him to have a glass, too. Ibid., 385.

10. Weygandt reminiscences, 68-69, MBEL.

11. *WKMBE* Vol. I, 398.

12. Ibid., 419.

13. "Mrs. Eddy's New Home Shown for First Time," *Boston Post,* March 15, 1909. Describing his tour of the cellars, the reporter noted, "One of the interesting places down below is the workshop of John Salchow, who attends to all the mechanical needs of the household…. Here are collected all sorts of tools and appliances from an anvil to fine implements for wood carving." Possibly there was also a darkroom, as Salchow, among others in the household, was an avid amateur photographer.

14. According to her passport application, Mary McNeil was born July 15, 1872, in Greenock, Scotland. The 1910 U.S. Federal Census cites her immigration year as 1888, and in the 1920 census Mary listed her native tongue as "Scotch." National Archives and Records Administration.

15. *WKMBE* Vol. I, 404; *Concord City Directory,* 1904.

16. *WKMBE* Vol. I, 377.

17. Mary McNeil Salchow, "My Ponderings of Our Great Leader Mary Baker Eddy," 4-5, MBEL, hereafter referenced as Mary Salchow reminiscences. The "sorrow" she mentions may have been the death of her brother William in 1898. "Death Records 1654-1949," Bureau of Vital Records, Concord, N.H.

18. *WKMBE* Vol. I, 404. Walter Watson, whose wife, Ada, also worked at Pleasant View on occasion, confirmed this account. Walter W. Watson, "Reminiscences of Mr. Walter W. Watson," 84, MBEL.

19. *WKMBE* Vol. I, 404.

20. John and Mary Salchow's accounts of how this came about differ, as does Minnie Weygandt's.

21. Mary Baker Eddy to James McNeil, December 30, 1906, V00732, MBEL.

22. Mary Salchow reminiscences, 5, MBEL.

23. John Salchow reminiscences, 80, MBEL.

24. *WKMBE* Vol. I, 406.

25. Ibid., 405.

26. Mary Salchow reminiscences, 9, MBEL.

27. John Salchow's passport application shows that he worked in Cuba from October 1, 1915, through November 1917. According to Mary's passport application, she joined him for at least part of his time there. National Archives and Records Administration.

28. 1920 U.S. Federal Census; *Boston City Directory,* 1927.

29. John G. Salchow to Mary Baker Eddy, December 31, 1901, IC 235.38.001, MBEL.

30. Mary Salchow reminiscences, 9, MBEL.

31. *WKMBE* Vol. I, 419.

32. William Rathvon reminiscences, 97, MBEL. This daily task began while Mrs. Eddy was living at Pleasant View. Minnie Weygandt noted that whatever ice cream was left over would be shared with others in the household to enjoy—although "John had usually had his portion, cleaning off the dasher." Weygandt reminiscences, 48, MBEL.

33. *WKMBE* Vol. I, 419.

34. Nelson Molway was the other man who helped run the elevator. Nelson J. Molway, "Reminiscences of Mr. Nelson J. Molway," 13, MBEL.

35. Ibid., 4.

36. Ibid., 5.

37. John Salchow reminiscences, 43, MBEL.

38. In the 1910 U.S. Federal Census, Jonathan Irving listed his birthplace as Canada and his age as 60. Both of his parents were from Scotland.

39. *WKMBE* Vol. I, 421.

40. Mary Baker Eddy to Jonathan R. Irving, undated letter, L10949, MBEL.

41. Mary Baker Eddy to Jonathan R. Irving, January 8, 1898, L08713, MBEL.

42. Unknown author to Jonathan R. Irving, January 1908, L09244, MBEL.

43. Adam H. Dickey to Alfred Farlow, April 1, 1908, L18336, MBEL. A reporter noted that Mr. Irving's quarters were in the basement, which would have given him handy access to the furnace room for this work. *Boston Post,* March 15, 1909. Tomlinson reminiscences, 763-764, MBEL.

44. Mary Baker Eddy to Jonathan R. Irving/Jonathan R. Irving to Mary Baker Eddy, undated, L10959, MBEL.

45. Mary Baker Eddy to Jonathan R. Irving, March 9, 1908, L10954, MBEL. In another expression of motherly concern, Mrs. Eddy also gave Jonathan money to buy himself a new cap at one point, noting, "I want to give it to you who are doing so much for me day and night." She signed her letter "with love." Mary Baker Eddy to Jonathan R. Irving, February 24, 1908, L08728, MBEL. See also Kelly reminiscences, 12, MBEL.

46. Mary Baker Eddy to Jonathan R. Irving, March 9, 1908, L10954, MBEL.

47. William Rathvon reminiscences, 143, MBEL.

48. Molway reminiscences, 5-6, MBEL.

49. Ibid., 6-7.

50. Ibid., 8.

51. Finished in the summer of 1910 under the direction of a landscape gardener and with the help of four day laborers, the road went past the large formal garden and looped around a second garden, which Molway made, also under the direction of a landscape gardener. Ibid., 11-12.

52. *Genealogy of the Wheatley or Wheatleigh Family (*Farmington, N.H.: E. H. Thomas, 1902), 109.

53. The iconic "Montpelier crackers," sold by the barrel in country stores across New England and beyond, were originally made by Cross Baking Company in Montpelier, Vermont. According to the Bowmans, Mrs. Eddy liked them toasted and served in milk, a traditional light supper dish in New England at that time. Memorandum, Lucia C. Warren to file, August 8, 1932, Frank E. and Lottie Bowman Reminiscence File, MBEL. Still available today, they're marketed as "Vermont common crackers." Paul Heller, "Montpelier crackers are a staple of history," *Rutland Herald*, May 6, 2015. Candace Page, "Coming to the Rescue of Vermont Common Crackers," *Burlington Free Press,* February 7, 2016.

54. Memorandum, Lucia C. Warren to file, August 8, 1932, Frank E. and Lottie Bowman Reminiscence File, MBEL.

55. Frank Elliot Bowman was born in March 1856 in Westford, Vermont. *Genealogy of the Wheatley or Wheatleigh Family*, 66. Charlotte Julia Williams Bowman was born in January 1857 in Royalton, Vermont. They were married in July 1886. Vermont Vital Records, 1720-1908. 1900 U.S. Federal Census.

56. Committee on Business to Mary Baker Eddy, undated, IC 179b.31.070, MBEL.

57. Charlotte W. Bowman, "Testimonies of Healing," *Christian Science Sentinel* 10 (September 14, 1907): 36. Before marrying Frank, Charlotte studied at the University of Vermont. She would have been in the class of 1883 but left to teach school in Essex Junction and Morrisville, Vermont. *General Catalogue of the University of Vermont and State Agricultural College* (Burlington, Vermont: Free Press Association, 1901), 150.

58. Committee on Business to Mary Baker Eddy, undated, IC 179b.31.070, MBEL.

59. George H. Kinter to John Carroll Lathrop, October 13, 1910, L15721, MBEL. Additionally, notes *Genealogy of the Wheatley or Wheatleigh Family* (109), Frank was "obliging and cordial, and is a great favorite with old and young."

60. Calvin A. Frye diary entry, December 18, 1908, EF81, 353, MBEL.

61. The University of Vermont yearbook notes that, as a freshman, Robert Elliot Bowman was awarded an entrance examination prize in Greek. *The Ariel* Vol. XXI (University of Vermont, 1908). He graduated in 1911. *The Ariel* Vol. XXIV (University of Vermont, 1911).

62. Mary Baker Eddy to Frank E. Bowman, undated, L12675, MBEL.

63. Charlotte W. Bowman, "Letters to Our Leader," *Christian Science Sentinel* 11 (January 16, 1909): 391.

64. Mary Baker Eddy to Archibald McLellan, January 18, 1909, L03211, MBEL.

65. Archibald McLellan/Committee on Business to Mary Baker Eddy, January 18, 1909, IC 179b.31.030, MBEL. Frank and Lottie Bowman both had Primary class instruction from Mrs. Alma S. Metcalf, a Christian Science practitioner and teacher from Normal, Illinois. They may have been living in the area at the time, as their son, Robert, was born in March 1889 in nearby Bloomington. 1900 U.S. Federal Census.

66. Mary Baker Eddy to Frank E. Bowman, March 29, 1909, L12678, MBEL.

67. Charlotte W. Bowman to Mary Baker Eddy, April 12, 1909, IC 649b.67.032, MBEL.

68. Mary Baker Eddy to Frank E. Bowman, June 10, 1909, L12679, MBEL.

69. The Committee on Business report notes that, although Frank has "never run an automobile," his college-age son had! Committee on Business to Mary Baker Eddy, undated, IC 179b.31.070, MBEL.

70. *WKMBE* Vol. I, 383.

71. "Take out the horses every morning and exercise them not too much but enough to keep down their spirits." Mary Baker Eddy to Frank E. Bowman, April 12, 1910, L12684, MBEL. "Now we take walks morning, noon, and night, we ride into Brookline with Bowman every morning if we like. . . ." William Rathvon reminiscences, 15, MBEL.

72. Peter V. Ross, "The Printed Page," *Christian Science Sentinel* 44 (August 15, 1942): 1446.

73. John Salchow reminiscences, 110, MBEL.

74. Mary Baker Eddy to Frank E. Bowman, September 28, 1909, L12681, MBEL. At some point after Lottie's passing in 1912, Mr. Bowman married Christine McCallum, who had worked in Mrs. Eddy's household for a few brief weeks in 1909. Frank and his second wife lived in Minnesota for a number of years before moving to Los Angeles, California. Frank passed on in 1944, and he and Lottie are buried in the Bowman family plot in the Essex Junction Village Cemetery. Christine McCallum Bowman passed on in Los Angeles in 1954.

75. Tomlinson, *Twelve Years*, 274-275.

76. Mary Baker Eddy to Frank E. Bowman, November 4, 1909, L12683, MBEL.

77. Dickey, *Memoirs*, 68.

78. Ibid., 70.

79. Molway reminiscences, 9, MBEL. He adds: "One day when I had been doing something that specially pleased her, she sent me these words in her own handwriting on her note-paper: 'Mother's thanks and dear love. M. B. Eddy Oct 9, 1909.'" Ibid., 10.

80. *WKMBE* Vol. I, 416. In his reminiscences, Salchow mentions a number of generous gifts that Mrs. Eddy gave him, including $500 as a wedding present. Frank Bowman was given a pair of gold coins, which he later made into cufflinks. Memorandum, Lucia C. Warren to file, August 8, 1932, Frank E. and Lottie Bowman Reminiscence File, MBEL.

81. Molway reminiscences, 9, MBEL.

82. Mary Baker Eddy to Calvin C. Hill, April 6, 1902, L15533, MBEL. She wrote, "I want an Automobile to use not to ride in but to drive my teams up to and take away their scare of it."

83. According to John Salchow, Mrs. Eddy "saw the signs of the times and knew that if her horses did not become accustomed to these strange machines, her daily drives might become hazardous." *WKMBE* Vol. I, 382.

84. For more on this topic, see "Yale Automobile," *From the Collections*, November 1, 2011, The Mary Baker Eddy Library, www.marybakereddylibrary.org/research/yale-automobile/

85. Mary Baker Eddy/Adam H. Dickey to Adolph H. Stevenson, September 16, 1908, private collection. Mr. Stevenson, a young man of Norwegian descent, succeeded Byron S. Burt of St. Johnsbury, Vermont, who passed on suddenly in his sleep on February 8, 1908. It was after his passing that Mrs. Eddy added this line to *Science and Health* (442): "Christian Scientists, be a law to yourselves that mental malpractice cannot harm you either when asleep or when awake." Dickey, *Memoirs*, 37. Mr. Dickey took over as coachman for a brief period until Mr. Stevenson's arrival a few days later. Stevenson didn't prove a good fit for 400 Beacon Street and was replaced on December 18, 1908, by Frank Bowman.

86. One destination for the household was The Mother Church. Elizabeth Kelly recalls someone's surprise on seeing her in the foyer, having been under the impression that members of Mrs. Eddy's household were not allowed to attend church. "I replied that we could always come if we cared to and that Mrs. Eddy provided an automobile for us." Kelly reminiscences, 7, MBEL.

87. $145,000 and $66,000 in 2018 dollars, respectively. Mrs. Eddy's purchase pre-dated the purchase of the first United States presidential limousine, a 1909 White Steam Model M owned by William Howard Taft. To watch a short video about the president and his limousine, visit www.historicvehicle.org/car-matters-1909-white-model-m-steam-car/. Today, Taft's automobile is on display at the Heritage Museums & Gardens in Sandwich, Massachusetts. Mrs. Eddy also eventually owned a smaller Ford Runabout (Model T) available for the household's use. George H. Kinter to John Carroll Lathrop, October 13, 1910, L15721, MBEL; John Salchow reminiscences, 110, MBEL. For more information about Mrs. Eddy's vehicles, see "The White Steam Automobiles," *From the Collections*, August 1, 2012, The Mary Baker Eddy Library, www.marybakereddylibrary.org/research/the-white-steam-automobiles/

88. There are conflicting accounts about the number of times that Mrs. Eddy rode in a car. Adelaide Still said "once or twice." Still reminiscences, 20, MBEL. Calvin Frye recorded two instances in his diaries. Irving Tomlinson recalled, "Mrs. Eddy did not enjoy the experience and never expressed any desire to ride in an automobile again." Tomlinson reminiscences, 772, MBEL.

89. William Rathvon reminiscences, 11, MBEL.

90. John Salchow reminiscences, 22, MBEL.

91. Jewel Spangler Smaus, *Mary Baker Eddy: The Golden Days* (Boston: The Christian Science Publishing Society, 1966), 23, hereafter referenced as Smaus, *Golden Days*.

92. Mary Baker Eddy to Gilbert C. Carpenter, December 21, 1902, L14133, MBEL.

93. William Rathvon reminiscences, 81, MBEL.

94. Kelly reminiscences, 11, MBEL.

95. Mary Baker Eddy to Adolph H. Stevenson, March 19, 1908, L08957, MBEL.

96. This was the carriage in which Mrs. Eddy was photographed at the 1900 State Fair in Concord, New Hampshire.

97. Adelaide Still, for instance, remembered being picked up at the station in a sleigh when she arrived in Concord for an interview at Pleasant View. *WKMBE* Vol. II, 459.

98. *WKMBE* Vol. I, 383.

99. Mary Baker Eddy to Gilbert C. Carpenter, December 21, 1902, L14133, MBEL.

100. Minnie A. Scott to the Christian Science Board of Directors, May 30, 1935, Minnie A. Scott Reminiscence File, MBEL.

101. *WKMBE* Vol. I, 427.

Chapter 5: Loving Hearts and Hands

1. Sibyl Wilbur, "Mrs. Eddy's Views on Vital Questions," *Boston Herald*, June 11, 1905. The article was reprinted in the *Christian Science Sentinel* 7 (June 17, 1905): 667-671.

2. Ibid.

3. Minnie A. Scott, "Testimonies of Healing," *Christian Science Sentinel* 21 (December 28,

1918): 334. Adelaide Still echoed this, adding that "simplicity, exactness and economy were Mrs. Eddy's rules for her household." M. Adelaide Still, "Reminiscences Foreword," 2, LMC.

4. *WKMBE* Vol. I, 360.

5. Hatten reminiscences, 3, MBEL. Like typical New England girls of her day, Mrs. Eddy learned homemaking skills at her mother's knee, and in earlier years she had put these skills to good use. By this point in her life, however, the demands of the important work she was engaged in were such that she relied on others for domestic chores. With an eye to explaining this progression and providing a metaphysical lesson, she once shared an anecdote with a student about the time a "famous author" (likely Bronson Alcott) knocked on her door in Lynn, looking for the author of *Science and Health*, and found her doing housework. "Mrs. Eddy related this historic incident in her early life with a view of awakening us to the fact that a true Christian Scientist begins patiently at the foot of the ladder which reaches from earth to heaven, but does not remain there. Inspiration indicates the need of legitimate progress and justifies its hope and expectation. Mrs. Eddy said of the experience that it was no disgrace for the author of Science and Health to be discovered wearing a dust cap and with broom in hand, but it would not have been in keeping with the inevitability of the law of progress for her to remain where her distinguished literary caller found her." Joseph G. Mann, "Reminiscences of Mary Baker Eddy," 50, MBEL.

6. William McKenzie used this term at the Annual Meeting of The Mother Church, June 12, 1906; see *Miscellany,* 40.

7. Mary Baker Eddy, *Retrospection and Introspection*, 87, hereafter referenced as *Retrospection*.

8. Martha W. Wilcox, "My Experiences in Mrs. Eddy's Home," 9, MBEL, hereafter referenced as Wilcox reminiscences.

9. *WKMBE* Vol. I, 470.

10. Ibid. Mrs. Wilcox worked for Mrs. Eddy from February 10, 1908, to December 1910.

11. Martha Wilcox had Primary class instruction from Amanda J. Baird. *The Life Story of Martha W. Wilcox, C.S.B.* (compiled and privately published by her sister, Alta M. Meyer), 5-6, LMC. Sadly, Martha's husband passed on later that year.

12. *WKMBE* Vol. I, 470. Martha was 37 at the time she joined the household.

13. Martha W. Wilcox to Luella Van Buren, July 8, 1908, LMC. Martha also once remarked: "There is no material activity. To Mary Baker Eddy, whatever was necessary to be done, even though it were mending stockings or writing a letter, if well done, it was scientific activity. We have been given a Science, which is to be made practical in every aspect of daily living." Meyer, *Life Story of Martha W. Wilcox*, 11, LMC.

14. Wilcox reminiscences, 10, MBEL.

15. Ibid.

16. Ibid., 24.

17. *WKMBE* Vol. I, 477.

18. Mrs. Wilcox's name first appeared in *The Christian Science Journal* in April 1911 and

remained there until her passing in September 1948.

19. Minnie A. Scott to the Christian Science Board of Directors, May 15, 1931, Minnie A. Scott Reminiscence File, MBEL.

20. Wilcox reminiscences, 2, MBEL.

21. William Rathvon reminiscences, 35, MBEL.

22. *WKMBE* Vol. II, 495.

23. William Rathvon reminiscences, 215, MBEL.

24. Caroline Foss Gyger, "Reminiscences," 11, MBEL. This occurred at Pleasant View. Stephen Gottschalk adds that the woman in question "repented of her less than humble attitude and stayed." Gottschalk, *Rolling Away*, 296.

25. Mary Baker Eddy to Household of Mary Baker Eddy, December 11, 1908, L13679, MBEL. Mrs. Eddy condemned gossip, reminding one student of the biblical admonition, "Where the talebearer is not the strife ceases," and "God gives us love for one another and aught that is not love is not from Him." Mary Baker Eddy to Lida W. Fitzpatrick, April 25, 1904, V00547, MBEL. To another she wrote: "I abhor gossip, idle or malicious." Mary Baker Eddy to John F. Linscott, May 21, 1887, L11011, MBEL.

26. William Rathvon reminiscences, 215, MBEL.

27. Nellie M. Eveleth, "Testimonies from the Field," *The Christian Science Journal* 22 (December 1904): 578.

28. Ibid.

29. Still reminiscences, 18, MBEL.

30. The 1906 *Boston City Directory* lists a Nellie M. Eveleth, dressmaker, living at 44 Batavia Street (now Symphony Road); Miss Eveleth's testimony in the December 1904 *Journal* also lists Boston as her place of residence. Nellie Eveleth may have been brought to Mrs. Eddy's attention—or to the attention of the Committee on Business—by Minnie Scott, in whose home Nellie was a lodger. 1900 U.S. Federal Census.

31. Still reminiscences, 18, MBEL. Nellie Eveleth was a member of Mrs. Eddy's household from August 1907 through December 1910.

32. Ibid., 10.

33. Ibid., 18; William Rathvon reminiscences, 215, MBEL.

34. Ibid.

35. George Constable and Bob Somerville, *A Century of Innovation* (Washington: Joseph Henry Press, 2003), 178. Electric irons were first patented in the early 1880s but not in wide use until the introduction of the Hotpoint Electric Iron in 1905, which was the first commercially successful model. The iron pictured in Nellie Eveleth's workroom may be this very model. The electrical system at 400 Beacon Street was expanded as part of the renovations prior to Mrs. Eddy's occupancy in January 1908.

36. *WKMBE* Vol. II, 477-478.

37. Cordelia Helms, "Information regarding Miss Eveleth," June 1986, Nellie M. Eveleth

Reminiscence File, MBEL.

38. William Rathvon reminiscences, 215, MBEL.

39. Tomlinson, *Twelve Years,* 213.

40. Lyman P. Powell, *Mary Baker Eddy: A Life Size Portrait* (Boston: The Christian Science Publishing Society, 1991), 199, hereafter referenced as Powell, *Portrait.*

41. Still reminiscences, 18, MBEL; William Rathvon reminiscences, 215, MBEL. Tomlinson, *Twelve Years,* 213. Others in the household concurred, including Adelaide Still, who notes that with her delicate complexion, Mrs. Eddy looked "very beautiful" in the soft pastel shades she preferred. Still reminiscences, 18, MBEL.

42. Tomlinson, *Twelve Years,* 213.

43. Annie M. Knott, "Apparel," *Christian Science Sentinel* 16 (October 4, 1913): 91. Although Mrs. Eddy expressed her unhappiness with Nellie's work at one point in a May 9, 1909, letter to Archibald McLellan, the fact that Miss Eveleth remained at her post an additional year and a half would indicate that the issue was resolved to Mrs. Eddy's satisfaction. Mary Baker Eddy to Archibald McLellan, May 9, 1909, L17864, MBEL.

44. *The Christian Science Journal* 22 (December 1904): 578.

45. The Christian Science Board of Directors to Mary Baker Eddy, May 29, 1908, IC 002cP2.03.044, MBEL. The report also notes that Frances Thatcher was divorced.

46. The Drexel Institute offered two tracks in their Department of Domestic Science and Arts: the Science course covered cookery and household economics; the Arts course focused on sewing, dressmaking, and millinery. Drexel Institute yearbook 1900. Frances Thatcher appears to have taken the former, given her work history and the fact that her obituary lists her as a "graduate dietitian of Drexel Institute." "Mrs. Frances Thatcher," *Wilmington Morning News,* December 27, 1963.

47. The oldest school in Delaware, the Friends School was founded in 1748. Grace Powers Thomas, *Where to Educate* (Boston: Brown and Company, 1898), 41.

48. *Wilmington Morning News,* December 27, 1963. The Christian Science Board of Directors to Mary Baker Eddy, May 29, 1908, IC 002cP2.03.044, MBEL.

49. Frances Thatcher, "Some of the Experiences of a Student who had the Privilege of Serving in our Leader's Home at Chestnut Hill, Mass.," 1, MBEL, hereafter referenced as Thatcher reminiscences.

50. Ibid.

51. Talk given by Frances F. Thatcher, October 11, 1941, 1, Frances F. Thatcher Reminiscence File, MBEL. Reflecting back on her own service at 400 Beacon Street, Frances Thatcher recalled Mrs. Eddy telling her that "a greater blessing will come to you through serving me, than could ever come to you in any other way on this earth." Thatcher reminiscences, 6, MBEL.

52. By 1917 (and possibly earlier—Wilmington city directories are unavailable for 1914-1916), Frances listed herself as a "Christian Scientist," then as a "practitioner" in the 1920 census. Her card first appeared in *The Christian Science Journal* in 1917. *Wilmington City*

Directory, 1917. 1920 U.S. Federal Census. *Wilmington Morning News,* December 27, 1963.

53. Katharine Retterer, "Testimonies of Healing," *Christian Science Sentinel* 5 (August 29, 1903): 833.

54. Whether she was at peace about this decision or not may never be known, but surely her expectations had been raised. Calvin Frye himself had told her that she had the better recommendation of the two, while her cousin Elizabeth Kelly admitted, "I felt that my cousin, Katharine Retterer, was well prepared and could do anything but I was not so well equipped." Kelly reminiscences, 3, MBEL. Both women were recommended to the Committee on Business by Mrs. Martha J. Scofield of Marion, Ohio, whom Thomas Hatten reported was a student of Lida Stocking Stone, sister to Daisette Stocking McKenzie and a student of Mrs. Eddy's. Thomas W. Hatten/Committee on Business to Mary Baker Eddy, August 7, 1907, IC 179a.31.027, MBEL.

55. James A. Neal/Committee on Business to Mary Baker Eddy, July 30, 1907, IC 179a.31.024, MBEL. Thomas W. Hatten/Committee on Business to Mary Baker Eddy, March 18, 1908, IC 179b.31.005, MBEL. Thomas W. Hatten/Committee on Business to Mary Baker Eddy, July 25, 1907, IC 179a.31.023, MBEL.

56. K. R., "Notes from the Field," *The Christian Science Journal* 13 (November 1895): 344-345.

57. Ibid.

58. Their teacher was Jeannette Quick. Thomas W. Hatten/Committee on Business to Mary Baker Eddy, August 7, 1907, IC 179a.31.027, MBEL. Elizabeth Kelly was dissatisfied with her teaching, and later, with the approval of the Christian Science Board of Directors, she was given permission to be re-taught. Her new teacher was Ella W. Hoag, whom she had come to know while working in Mrs. Eddy's household. Kelly reminiscences, 2-3, MBEL.

59. *Christian Science Sentinel* 5 (August 29, 1903): 833.

60. Katharine Retterer to Calvin A. Frye, April 25, 1911, Katharine Retterer Subject File, MBEL.

61. Katharine Retterer passed on in February 1917. *Marion Star,* February 26, 1917.

62. For instance, there's an entry for vacuum cleaner repairs on November 17, 1908. Calvin A. Frye Account Books, Boxes OS#27-29, MBEL.

63. *WKMBE* Vol. II, 461.

64. The household may also have had a Thor electric washing machine, which was listed in the 1917 inventory of 400 Beacon Street.

65. "Mrs. Eddy's New Home Shown for First Time," *Boston Post,* March 15, 1909. The laundry room's modern facilities didn't entirely rule out clotheslines, evidently, as historic photographs show laundry hanging on a line in the yard.

66. According to Calvin Frye's account books, Laura Still was employed at 400 Beacon Street from December 1908 through August 1910. Calvin A. Frye Account Books, Boxes OS#27-29, MBEL.

67. John Salchow reminiscences, 111, MBEL. Martha Wilcox said the women were students of Christian Science. Wilcox reminiscences, 22, MBEL. Careful cross-referencing of

Calvin Frye's account books with genealogical databases has helped identify the two African-American women as Christina Gordon, originally from Jamaica, and Jennie Loundes, from Charleston, South Carolina.

68. According to the passenger manifest for the *S.S. Arabic*, Adelaide Still traveled second class to Boston from Liverpool. According to her naturalization records, she was born April 12, 1873, and she was tall (5'8 ½") and slender, with gray eyes and brown hair. Declaration of Intention, U.S. Department of Labor Naturalization Service, November 20, 1911.

69. James Pray succeeded Frederick Law Olmsted (for whom he once worked) as chairman of the School of Landscape Architecture at Harvard.

70. *WKMBE* Vol. II, 457-458. Adelaide had one younger sister, Laura, and two younger brothers, William and Charles. County of Gloucester, England, census records, undated. Laura and Charles eventually emigrated to Boston with their widowed mother, Maria Still. 1910 U.S. Census.

71. *WKMBE* Vol. II, 458.

72. Ibid.

73. Ibid.

74. Minnie A[delaide] Still, "Testimonies of Healing," *Christian Science Sentinel* 9 (October 6, 1906): 92-93.

75. Thomas W. Hatten/Committee on Business to Mary Baker Eddy, January 1, 1907, IC 179a.31.009, MBEL.

76. Daisette McKenzie to Mary Baker Eddy, January 1, 1907, IC 013d.08.026, MBEL. Daisette McKenzie and Florence Pray, Adelaide's employer at the time, were both members of the same branch church and would have become acquainted there. Church records, First Church of Christ, Scientist, Cambridge, Massachusetts.

77. *WKMBE* Vol. II, 459-460.

78. Still, "Reminiscences Foreword," 3, LMC.

79. *WKMBE* Vol. II, 465-466.

80. Ibid., 466.

81. Ibid., 479.

82. Calvin A. Frye diary entry, September 11, 1909, EF85, 250, MBEL.

83. Romans 8:28.

84. William Rathvon reminiscences, 216, MBEL.

85. The Christian Science community in Boston at that time was closely knit—Adelaide Still's petition for naturalization was signed by Charles Welch, Clerk of The Mother Church, and by Minnie Scott's husband, Clarence. U.S. Department of Labor Petition for Naturalization, November 11, 1915.

86. M. Adelaide Still letter to Guy Parkhurst Estes, quoted in "They answered the call: M. Adelaide Still," *The Christian Science Journal* 105 (October 1987): 32-33.

87. Robert Peel, Note on Adelaide Still, September 12, 1979, private collection.

88. *WKMBE* Vol. II, 461.

89. This cleaning took place "regularly as clockwork," according to Minnie Weygandt. Weygandt reminiscences, 24, MBEL.

90. Harriet L. Betts, "Reminiscences of Mrs. Eddy," 11, MBEL.

91. Minnie A. Scott to the Christian Science Board of Directors, May 15, 1931, Minnie A. Scott Reminiscence File, MBEL. Still reminiscences, 9, MBEL.

92. Peel, *Authority*, 300. Weygandt reminiscences, 24-25, MBEL. *WKMBE* Vol. I, 473.

93. Anna O. Machacek to the Christian Science Board of Directors, February 27, 1931, Anna O. Machacek Reminiscence File, MBEL.

94. In her naturalization records, Anna listed her birthdate as September 28, 1862. She became a U.S. citizen in March 1929. Iowa, Federal Naturalization Records, 1856-1937. U.S. Naturalization Record Indexes, 1791-1992.

95. Dave Rasdal, *Czech Village & New Bohemia: History in the Heartland* (Charleston, S.C.: The History Press, 2016), 13-18.

96. Isabelle J. Fleming, "Serving Our Leader," undated, Anna O. Machacek Subject File, MBEL.

97. Ibid. See also Anna O. Machacek to Calvin C. Hill, June 30, 1930, Anna O. Machacek Subject File, MBEL.

98. Anna O. Machacek to the Christian Science Board of Directors, February 27, 1931, Anna O. Machacek Reminiscence File, MBEL. Miss Machacek's Primary class teacher was Mary H. Philbrick of Cedar Rapids, who had been taught by Mrs. Eddy at the Massachusetts Metaphysical College.

99. Anna O. Machacek to Calvin C. Hill, June 30, 1930, Anna O. Machacek Subject File, MBEL.

100. Fleming, "Serving Our Leader," MBEL.

101. Mary Baker Eddy to Anna O. Machacek, January 31, 1905, L04779, MBEL. In a letter to Mrs. Longyear, Anna said that Mrs. Weeks's letter of recommendation was approved by Edward Kimball. Anna O. Machacek to Mary Beecher Longyear, March 24, 1919, LMC. In this letter, Anna also graciously declined Mrs. Longyear's offer of financial assistance with a spirited, "to my sense it is a poor practitioner that does not demonstrate her own supply," and informed her proudly, "I bought me a little home…." According to her husband, Abbie Weeks traveled from Chicago to Cedar Rapids to help Anna with the arrangements for the trip, "as she is unaccustomed to travel." Charles B. Weeks to Calvin A. Frye, February 4, 1905, 722a.89.036, MBEL.

102. John Salchow reminiscences, 44, MBEL.

103. Minnie A. Scott to the Christian Science Board of Directors, May 15, 1931, Minnie A. Scott Reminiscence File, MBEL. In a note to Anna, which perhaps indicates Anna's eagerness to improve her English and Mrs. Eddy's willingness to help in this endeavor, Mrs. Eddy wrote, "The name of that I put on the Whatnot in the drawing room is trowel." Mary Baker Eddy to Anna O. Machacek, undated, L04786, MBEL.

104. Weygandt reminiscences, 67, MBEL. Minnie A. Scott to the Christian Science Board of Directors, May 15, 1931, Minnie A. Scott Reminiscence File, MBEL.

105. Ibid.

106. Anna fully intended to return to 400 Beacon Street after what was expected to be a three-month leave of absence, promising Mrs. Eddy that she would "leave everything and come" the minute she was called back, but apparently there was some misunderstanding about Miss Machacek's health, among other things, which Anna lamented as having "deprived our Leader of my services." Anna O. Machacek to Calvin C. Hill, November 26, 1926, Anna O. Machacek Subject File, MBEL.

107. New Hampshire Death and Disinterment Records, 1754-1947. Several months before her passing in 1940, Anna moved to Concord, New Hampshire, to live at the Christian Science Pleasant View Home. Completed in 1927 on the grounds where Mrs. Eddy's home once stood (that structure had been taken down in 1917), this establishment was maintained by The First Church of Christ, Scientist, in Boston, Massachusetts, as a home for long-time workers in the Christian Science movement until the property's sale in 1975. "Board of Directors confirms sale of Pleasant View property," *The Christian Science Monitor*, August 29, 1975.

108. Anna O. Machacek to the Christian Science Board of Directors, February 27, 1931, Anna O. Machacek Reminiscence File, MBEL.

109. Fleming, "Serving Our Leader," MBEL.

110. *WKMBE* Vol. II, 490. Weygandt reminiscences, 39, 108, MBEL. Minnie A. Scott to the Christian Science Board of Directors, ca. April 1926, and Minnie A. Scott to the Christian Science Board of Directors, May 15, 1931, Minnie A. Scott Reminiscence File, MBEL.

111. Minnie A. Scott to the Christian Science Board of Directors, ca. April 1926, Minnie A. Scott Reminiscence File, MBEL.

Chapter 6: Beyond the "Shadow of Frivolity"

1. "Annual Meeting of The Mother Church," *Christian Science Sentinel* 23 (June 18, 1921): 784.

2. *Miscellaneous*, 116.

3. *WKMBE* Vol. I, 390.

4. Originally written for the December 10, 1905, issue of the *New York World*, "Christmas as in Christian Science" was reprinted under the title "The Significance of Christmas" in the *Christian Science Sentinel* 8 (December 16, 1905): 248. The article would later be included in *Miscellany*, 259-260.

5. Minnie A. Scott to Ethel P. Reid (Curtis), December 25, 1908, Minnie A. Scott Subject File, MBEL. Offering a glimpse of the demands of her work, Minnie added, "Were it not for this consciousness one might grow weary in well-doing."

6. Mary Baker Eddy, "Early Chimes," *Christian Science Sentinel* 1 (November 10, 1898): 4; reprinted in *Miscellany*, 256.

7. Mary Baker Eddy, *Church Manual of The First Church of Christ, Scientist, in Boston,*

Massachusetts, 60, hereafter referenced as *Church Manual*.

8. Ibid.

9. "Church By-law," *Christian Science Sentinel* 8 (December 16, 1905): 248. This would be codified in the *Church Manual*, Article XXII ("Relation and Duties of Members to Pastor Emeritus"), Section 10, "Duty to God."

10. Mary Baker G. Eddy, "A Question," *Christian Science Sentinel* 8 (December 16, 1905): 248. A slightly edited version of this article would later appear under the heading "Principle or Person?" in *Miscellany*, 233-234.

11. "In later years she sent out no Christmas gifts during the Christmas season." Irving Tomlinson reminiscences, 561, MBEL. Mrs. Eddy continued to delight in giving gifts at other times, however, and so did her staff. Minnie Scott recalled neighborhood children coming to the side door on Halloween, dressed in their costumes. The young trick-or-treaters "were treated to Huntley & Palmer's biscuits which we had on hand to show our kind interest in their fun." Minnie A. Scott to the Christian Science Board of Directors, May 30, 1935, Minnie A. Scott Reminiscence File, MBEL.

12. William Rathvon described "a jovial family gathering" at the dinner table for Christmas 1909, for instance, where he did the honors carving the traditional turkey. William Rathvon reminiscences, 87, MBEL.

13. Mrs. Eddy continued, "If it does not prevent, it may hinder. The tongue may lie, but healing the sick is no lie. Wrong thought leads to wrong action and vice versa. If one is done, the other will do itself, just as the little boy in school who whistled and, when spoken to by his teacher, said, 'I did not whistle. It whistled itself.'" *WKMBE* Vol. II, 530.

14. Ella Rathvon reminiscences, MBEL.

15. William Rathvon reminiscences, 87, MBEL.

16. Ibid., 85, 87.

17. Ibid., 86.

18. *WKMBE* Vol. II, 497-498. When her household sent her a loving message on Easter 1909, Mrs. Eddy replied with one of her own in return, which concluded, "May this glad Easter morn find you all happy and blest in the understanding of Christian Science." Mary Baker Eddy to Mary Baker Eddy Household, April 11, 1909, L07363, MBEL.

19. William Rathvon reminiscences, 87, MBEL.

20. Tomlinson reminiscences, 561, MBEL.

Chapter 7: Daily Bread

1. Mrs. Eddy preferred simple meals at this point in her life, and her breakfast most often consisted of hot cereal—a bowl of cornmeal mush served with milk—or sometimes just a glass of fresh milk. Still reminiscences, 10, MBEL. "Our Leader always took her meals in her study, and they were of the simplest kind but were prepared with the greatest care," recalls William Rathvon, who also noted that Laura Sargent joined Mrs. Eddy for breakfast most mornings. William Rathvon reminiscences, 96-97, 117-118, 155, MBEL.

2. Calvin A. Frye menu notepad, Mary Baker Eddy—Household Miscellaneous, Box 61, MBEL.

3. Placing kitchens in the basement was typical of many Victorian-era homes, especially those with servants and staff. Judith Flanders, *Inside the Victorian Home* (New York: W. W. Norton & Company, 2004), 35.

4. "300 Men Work Day and Night Upon Supposed Eddy College," *Boston Herald*, January 7, 1908.

5. "Mrs. Eddy's New Home Shown for First Time," *Boston Post,* March 15, 1909. Another observer would also single out the kitchen for praise, noting, "The culinary department of the establishment is a model of convenience and cleanliness." George Shaw Cook, "The Home of Mary Baker Eddy," *Illinois Illustrated Review,* November 1909, 130. Chicago architect Solon Spencer Beman's plans for the house show the kitchen measurements as roughly 23 feet by 17 feet, the butler's pantry 12 feet square, the food pantry nine by seven, with the refrigerator room about the same size.

6. "Stove Trade Notes," *The Metal Worker* (September 5, 1896): 62.

7. Transcription, talk by Thatcher, October 11, 1941, Frances F. Thatcher Reminiscence File, MBEL.

8. Macdonald reminiscences, 11-12, MBEL.

9. Irving C. Tomlinson note, May 5, 1909, A11953, MBEL.

10. Minnie Weygandt served from January 1899 to September 1907 and for several weeks during the Chestnut Hill years; Minnie Scott from May 1906 to July 1909; Margaret Macdonald from November 1907 to May 1910; Lula Phillips from May through December 1910; Elizabeth Kelly from August 1907 through December 1910; Martha Wilcox from February 1908 to July 1908, again from February 1909 to November 1910, and again in December 1910. There was some overlap in duties—Minnie Weygandt, for instance, also did some sewing and laundry work for Mrs. Eddy at Pleasant View, and Margaret Macdonald helped out with housekeeping, which was Martha Wilcox's main duty.

11. Kelly reminiscences, 5-6, MBEL.

12. Ibid., 1-3.

13. Ibid., 2.

14. James A. Neal/Committee on Business to Mary Baker Eddy, July 30, 1907, IC 179a.31.024, MBEL.

15. Kelly reminiscences, 4, MBEL.

16. Ibid.

17. Ibid., 5.

18. Ibid.

19. William Rathvon reminiscences, 34, MBEL.

20. Kelly reminiscences, 9, MBEL.

21. The poem mentions her "jams and jelly"—a reporter who toured 400 Beacon Street noted

a "jam closet" in the basement—perhaps filled with the fruits of Elizabeth Kelly's labor! *Boston Post*, March 15, 1909.

22. Kelly reminiscences, 11, MBEL.

23. Ibid., 14.

24. Like most others in the household, Mrs. Kelly left 400 Beacon Street two weeks after Mrs. Eddy's passing. Elizabeth Kelly was first listed as a Christian Science nurse in *The Christian Science Journal* of November 1915. For more on the establishment of Christian Science nursing see pages 323-325.

25. George H. Kinter to John Carroll Lathrop, October 13, 1910, L15721, MBEL.

26. *WKMBE* Vol. I, 481.

27. "I have much work to do. . . . I trust in God, and He will give me strength to accomplish those things which have been marked out for me to do." "'I Hold No Enmity,' Says Mrs. Eddy To The American In Long Interview," *New York American*, August 26, 1907. Reprinted in the *Christian Science Sentinel* 9 (August 31, 1907): 1003-1004.

28. Margaret Macdonald, "Testimonies of Healing," *Christian Science Sentinel* 28 (May 29, 1926): 776. In her testimony, Miss Macdonald records her healing of a speech impediment.

29. Margaret Macdonald, "Recollections in Connection with Article XXVII, Section 5, of the Manual of The Mother Church," June 21, 1938, 2, MBEL.

30. *Christian Science Sentinel* 28 (May 29, 1926): 776.

31. Thomas Hatten/Committee on Business to Calvin A. Frye, December 10, 1907, IC 179a.31.032, MBEL. Emile Rounsevel, who was known to both Calvin Frye and Mrs. Eddy, was Mr. Hatten's contact in Littleton. Mrs. Rounsevel (Emile) was the sister of Janette Weller, a student of Mrs. Eddy's. Emile and her husband, Royal, owned the White Mountain House in Fabyan, New Hampshire, which was a favorite vacation destination for numerous early Christian Scientists, including Mrs. Eddy, who stayed there in the summer of 1888.

32. Macdonald, "Recollections," 2, MBEL.

33. Macdonald reminiscences, 3, MBEL.

34. Frances T. Hill, addendum to Minnie Scott reminiscences, 4, MBEL. Miss Macdonald's Primary class teacher was John Lathrop, who served in the household as a secretary from September 1907 through February 1908, returning to 400 Beacon Street to fill in for a week in May 1908.

35. Margaret Macdonald to the Christian Science Board of Directors, October 24, 1930, Margaret Macdonald Reminiscence File, MBEL.

36. Macdonald, "Recollections," 3, MBEL.

37. Edwin J. Park, "Estate at Chestnut Hill New Home of Mrs. Eddy," *Boston Globe*, January 27, 1908. Another reporter observed, "The impression one receives from a tour of the house is that comfort, rather than splendor, has been the aim of the furnishers, and that the decorators had in mind simplicity rather than ornate display." *Boston Post*, March 15, 1909. Celebrated journalist Arthur Brisbane was of the same opinion. "It would seem

that the designer and decorator, knowing Mrs. Eddy's love of peace and quiet, had chosen the furnishings with this idea in mind," he would write, "and the result is delightful and restful such as must be pleasing to her." Arthur Brisbane, *Mary Baker G. Eddy* (Boston: The Ball Publishing Company, 1908), 56.

38. Lula Phillips Bradshaw, "Reminiscences," 2, MBEL. Lula Phillips began work as assistant cook in May 1910. "Most of the helpers were middle aged, but in 1910 there was a younger girl in the kitchen," recalled Adelaide Still. "Once when Mrs. Eddy had called them in, she noticed her, and as she was leaving the room, said to her, 'Why, you're a pretty one, aren't you. Where did you come from?'" Still reminiscences, 46, MBEL. Lula Phillips returned to the Midwest after Mrs. Eddy's passing and married John Bradshaw in 1916, settling in Kansas City, Missouri. Missouri, Jackson County Marriage Records, 1840-1985.

39. William Rathvon reminiscences, 117-118, MBEL. According to Adelaide Still, Mrs. Eddy "ate simple food, never seeming to tire of home-made ice cream and custard pudding which were served twice a day; also, she had a cup of soup both for dinner and supper, cream of tomato being her favorite for some years. Sometimes a little meat for dinner, such as liver or squab; for supper, fish hash, creamed toast or cereal." Still reminiscences, 17, MBEL.

40. William Rathvon reminiscences, 93, MBEL. Case in point: "We could have pie for breakfast any time we wanted it, according to the New England custom." Ibid., 95. Rathvon wasn't the only one to indulge in this custom. Minnie Weygandt recalled that "there was a member of the family who liked mince pie and that was Calvin Frye. He could have eaten it for breakfast if it was around—and sometimes he did!" Weygandt reminiscences, 38, MBEL.

41. Weygandt reminiscences, 37, MBEL. Love was an important ingredient in Mrs. Eddy's kitchen. Mrs. Horace Boutwell, who served for a time as the household cook at Pleasant View, related that at one point Mrs. Eddy had a new cook "who had the reputation of being a fine cook and . . . was very proud of her cooking. One day, after the main meal, she served a dessert. Mrs. Eddy tasted of it and said that there was something lacking. Everybody else thought it was all right, but Mrs. Eddy insisted, and they finally called in the cook, who felt very positive that everything had gone into the dessert that should, and she was very upset because Mrs. Eddy had criticized it. Mrs. Eddy said, there is something lacking, it needs a little more love." Charles A. Blake, "Recollections of Mr. Charles A. Blake," 15, MBEL.

42. Minnie Weygandt was born in Pennsylvania in November 1864, but moved to Iowa with her family shortly thereafter. 1900 U.S. Federal Census; 1885 Iowa State Census Collection. She had a keen eye as a photographer as well and pursued that hobby enthusiastically while in Mrs. Eddy's employ. Weygandt reminiscences, 88, MBEL.

43. Weygandt reminiscences, 3-4, MBEL.

44. Ibid., 5, 13, 37.

45. Ibid., 13. According to Federal census reports, Minnie was 34 when she went to work for Mrs. Eddy. Her sister Mary was 32.

46. Weygandt reminiscences, 69, MBEL.

47. Ibid., 2, 116.

48. Ibid., 30-31.

49. William Rathvon reminiscences, 93-94, MBEL.

50. Calvin A. Frye menu notepad, Mary Baker Eddy—Household Miscellaneous, Box 61, MBEL.

51. Weygandt reminiscences, 34, MBEL.

52. Minnie Weygandt baked a cake every Saturday. Ibid., 101. Calvin Frye's menus for the spring of 1909 make note of a variety of cakes, including gingerbread, nut cake, coconut cake, strawberry shortcake, sponge cake, bridal cake, and marble cake. Additionally, he recorded a variety of puddings, pies, custards, ice cream, and such exotic-sounding confections of the era as "Spanish snow" and "Blancmange." Calvin A. Frye menu notepad, Mary Baker Eddy—Household Miscellaneous, Box 61, MBEL.

53. Macdonald reminiscences, 9, MBEL. In recalling their time at Pleasant View, Minnie Weygandt wrote: "Whenever Mr. Tomlinson came to the house, he would announce himself at the side door and say to me, 'Tell Mr. Frye the parson is here.'" Weygandt reminscences, 57, MBEL.

54. Minnie A. Scott to the Christian Science Board of Directors, May 30, 1935, Minnie A. Scott Reminiscence File, MBEL.

55. Scott, "Record of Acquaintance," 7, LMC.

56. *WKMBE* Vol. I, 480-481.

57. According to Calvin Frye's account book, the cows were purchased on April 8, 1908, for $100. Milk and eggs were also purchased for a time from one H. B. Knowles. Minnie A. Scott to the Christian Science Board of Directors, May 30, 1935, Minnie A. Scott Reminiscence File, MBEL. Calvin A. Frye Account Books, Boxes OS#27-29, MBEL.

58. William Rathvon reminiscences, 95, MBEL.

59. Clarence and Minnie were married on September 1, 1892, in Boston. Massachusetts Marriage Records, 1840-1915.

60. At Mrs. Eddy's request, testimony meetings were changed from Friday to Wednesday evenings in June 1898.

61. Scott, "Record of Acquaintance," 3, LMC.

62. Minnie A. Scott, "Notes from the Field," *The Christian Science Journal* 15 (March 1898): 788-789.

63. Ibid.

64. Minnie noted that "the only time my name was not in [the] *Journal* was when I was serving our beloved Leader…." Scott, "Record of Acquaintance," 4, LMC.

65. The Scotts lived on Batavia Street, later renamed Symphony Road. One of those who rented a room was Nellie Eveleth, who would later serve alongside Minnie at Pleasant View and Chestnut Hill as Mrs. Eddy's dressmaker. 1900 U.S. Federal Census.

66. Calvin Hill may have been the instrument through which Minnie went to Pleasant View.

According to census records, among the Scotts' neighbors were a number of early workers in the Christian Science movement, including Mr. Hill, Ira Knapp and his family, and Janette Weller. Records also show that Minnie Scott was in her mid-30s when she started working for Mrs. Eddy.

67. Scott, "Record of Acquaintance," 6, LMC.

68. Ibid., 7.

69. *WKMBE* Vol. II, 376.

70. Scott, "Record of Acquaintance," 7, LMC.

71. Minnie A. Scott to the Christian Science Board of Directors, April 1, 1933, Reminiscence File, MBEL.

72. Tomlinson reminiscences, 739, 763, MBEL. William Rathvon called Mrs. Scott "a clear metaphysician" and noted that she had a busy practice in Boston in the years after Chestnut Hill. William Rathvon reminiscences, 95-96, MBEL.

73. Minnie A. Scott, "Testimonies of Healing," *Christian Science Sentinel* 21 (December 28, 1918): 334. As just one example of Mrs. Eddy's appreciation of Minnie's service, she gave her an illuminated stanza from a poem by John Greenleaf Whittier entitled "The Meeting" (see image on page 197). This stanza ("The Quiet Room") also appeared on a bookmark given to Mrs. Eddy by two little girls and kept in the Mother's Room in the Original Edifice of The Mother Church. Joseph Armstrong and Margaret Williamson, *Building of The Mother Church* (Boston: The Christian Science Publishing Society, 1980), 69.

74. *WKMBE* Vol. I, 551.

75. *Christian Science Sentinel* 21 (December 28, 1918): 334.

76. Bradshaw reminiscences, 1-2, MBEL.

77. Macdonald reminiscences, 11, MBEL.

78. Scott, "Record of Acquaintance," 11, LMC.

79. *WKMBE* Vol. I, 479.

80. Weygandt reminiscences, 36, MBEL.

81. Macdonald reminiscences, 7, MBEL. Ice cream was made daily at 400 Beacon Street, and Minnie Scott recalled how John Salchow "was always ready to help about the ice cream freezer—not in [the] cellar but in [the] kitchen or back porch—and we laughed about 'licking the dasher' or sharing it with some workmen, electricians or others who might be around…." Scott, "Record of Acquaintance," 9, LMC.

82. Mary Beecher Longyear, "Reminiscences of Mary Baker Eddy," 11, LMC. Mrs. Longyear would record the event in her diary as well: "January 25. Tuesday—I take time to realize the blessing I had today. Went to Mrs. Eddy's house to lunch and had a lovely visit with her. The greatest blessing on earth." Mary Beecher Longyear diaries, January 25, 1910, LMC.

83. Mary Salchow reminiscences, 8, MBEL.

Chapter 8: A "Joyful Noise"

1. *Science and Health,* 213.

2. Irving Tomlinson observed that "Mrs. Eddy had always been a lover of music." Tomlinson, *Twelve Years,* 216. Others in the Chestnut Hill household concurred, including John Salchow, who said "she loved music." *WKMBE* Vol. I, 422.

3. Smaus, *Golden Days,* 37.

4. Clara M. S. Shannon, *Golden Memories,* 37-38, LMC.

5. Tomlinson, *Twelve Years,* 9.

6. Tomlinson reminiscences, 807-808, MBEL.

7. Mary Baker Glover and Abigail Ambrose Baker to Martha Baker Pilsbury, March 5, 1848, L11150, MBEL.

8. Smaus, *Golden Days,* 111. Sadly, John Bartlett would pass on before he and Mary could wed. Isabel Ferguson and Heather Vogel Frederick, *A World More Bright: The Life of Mary Baker Eddy* (Boston: The Christian Science Publishing Society, 2013), 36-37, hereafter referenced as Ferguson and Frederick, *A World More Bright.*

9. Mary Baker Eddy to Emily M. Meader, October 25, 1882, L04885, MBEL.

10. *WKMBE* Vol.I, 67.

11. Tomlinson, *Twelve Years,* 216. Elsewhere, Tomlinson named the other members of the quartet: Calvin Frye (tenor), Ebenezer Foster Eddy (bass), and Laura Sargent (alto). Tomlinson reminiscences, 805-806, MBEL.

12. Various members of the household also occasionally referred to it as the "Rose Room" or "Pink Parlor."

13. Peter J. Hodgson, *A Most Agreeable Man: Lyman Foster Brackett, Performer, Composer and Hymnal Editor for the Church of Christ, Scientist* (Chestnut Hill, Mass.: Longyear Museum Press, 2003), 13.

14. "Tremont St., towards Boylston, for some years has been called Piano Row, for a long row of piano agencies occupied a good portion of the block; but of late most of these have migrated to Boylston Street. Chickering Hall, at 152 Tremont St., was for many years a favorite place for fashionable musicales, and the headquarters of the musical profession." *How to See Boston: A Trustworthy Guide Book* (Boston: Macullar, Parker & Company, 1895), 101.

15. The American Golden Age of piano manufacturing ran from approximately 1875 to 1932. For more information, see forum.pianoworld.com/ubbthreads.php/topics/908682/Re:_Golden_Age_American_Pianos.html

16. For more information about pianolas, see www.pianola.org/history/history.cfm

17. "My precious Student and beloved disciple," Mrs. Eddy wrote to the Lathrops, thanking them for their gift. "How kind, thoughtful, tender to send me such a beautiful music box!" Mary Baker Eddy to Laura Lathrop and John Carroll Lathrop, October 28, 1897, L02426, MBEL. In his reminiscences, William Rathvon noted, "There was a fine old-fashioned

music box in one corner of the dining room, which was in Calvin Frye's special charge, and is still there." William Rathvon reminiscences, 94, MBEL.

18. Hugo Weel, Addendum to Mary Baker Glover Billings, "Memories of my Grandmother," MBEL. Hugo Weel recalled the song title as "Will You Remember Me," but Longyear Museum has the disc in its collection, and the correct title is "Then You'll Remember Me."

19. George H. Kinter to John Carroll Lathrop, October 13, 1910, L15721, MBEL. Mr. Kinter was living at Pleasant View when the first Victrola arrived in the household, a gift to Mrs. Eddy from Mary Beecher Longyear.

20. *WKMBE* Vol. I, 422.

21. Tomlinson, *Twelve Years,* 274. *Sacred Songs and Solos* was an 1877 hymn collection by the evangelical duo Ira David Sankey and Dwight Lyman Moody.

22. William Rathvon reminiscences, 105, MBEL.

23. Ella Rathvon listed the songs and hymns most frequently sung in the household on her calendar. Ella Rathvon reminiscences, MBEL.

24. Mrs. Eddy's first visit to her newly-built Church occurred on April 1, 1895. Clara Shannon described the event in detail, including Mrs. Eddy's recitation of the hymn "Guide Me, O Thou Great Jehovah." *WKMBE* Vol. II, 198-203.

25. Ibid. *Concordance to Christian Science Hymnal and Hymnal Notes* (Boston: The Christian Science Publishing Society, 1961), 215-216.

26. "God give you the inspiration of a Mozart to sing, and the vision of a revelator to utter my thoughts in harmony," Mrs. Eddy wrote to William Lyman Johnson when he was working on setting several of her poems to music. Mary Baker Eddy to William Lyman Johnson, December 11, 1904, L03372, MBEL.

27. *WKMBE* Vol. II, 556.

28. Powell, *Portrait,* 236.

29. Mrs. Eddy gave "Home Songs" to Ella Rathvon on September 10, 1910. Ella Rathvon reminiscences, MBEL. Written on September 14, 1814, by Francis Scott Key, "The Star-Spangled Banner" officially became the United States national anthem by a congressional resolution on March 3, 1931.

30. *WKMBE* Vol. II, 552.

31. Clara E. Choate, "Patience Under Tribulation," 4, LMC.

32. "The Victor talking machine that you sent to me is indeed a rare specimen of modern art," Mrs. Eddy wrote to Mrs. Longyear in thanks for the original Victrola. "I thank you and think of you in the midst of its discoursing music." Mary Baker Eddy to Mary Beecher Longyear, January 30, 1905, LMC. William Rathvon dated the arrival of the new Victrola as November 1909. William Rathvon reminiscences, 102, MBEL. Calvin Frye's check register lists payment for the Victrola to Boston's Steinert & Sons on December 6, 1909. Calvin A. Frye Checkbook and Banking Records, Box OS# 27A, MBEL.

33. According to Rathvon, this occurred on August 5, 1910. William Rathvon reminiscences, 77-78, MBEL.

34. Tomlinson, *Twelve Years*, 217.

35. William Rathvon reminiscences, 102, MBEL; *WKMBE* Vol. II, 544.

36. Ella Rathvon recorded this statement in her diary on April 21, 1910. Ella Rathvon reminiscences, MBEL.

37. *Science and Health*, 58.

38. Tomlinson reminiscences, 806, MBEL.

39. William Rathvon reminiscences, 227, MBEL.

40. Raised in the Congregational church, Pamelia Leonard first encountered Christian Science after being stricken with a paralytic condition in 1879. According to her son, Frank, all it took was five minutes with a practitioner for his mother to say, "I have *found* my God." Frank H. Leonard to Mary Beecher Longyear, January 2, 1918, LMC. The healing was hard-won, taking three years to complete, but afterward Mrs. Leonard had both Primary and Normal class instruction with Mrs. Eddy at the Massachusetts Metaphysical College in 1886, as well as the Obstetrics course in 1888. She moved to Brooklyn, New York, at Mrs. Eddy's request to help establish Christian Science there, and in addition to her work as a practitioner and teacher, she would later serve on several occasions at Pleasant View as a metaphysical worker and companion to Mrs. Eddy.

41. Frank H. Leonard, "Testimonies of Healing," *Christian Science Sentinel* 2 (September 7, 1899): 13.

42. Frank H. Leonard to Mary Beecher Longyear, March 6, 1918, LMC. Leonard added that, as a frequent visitor at Mrs. Eddy's home on Commonwealth Avenue in Boston, he "began to see that while she was loving in all her ways, it was a militant love and that she never lacked the moral courage to rebuke and destroy the slightest evidence of an attempt to personalize any work done and so lessen the glory given to God. I was impressed with the feeling that she was never asleep, never in a hurry and yet never off guard."

43. Ibid. Mrs. Eddy appreciated Mr. Leonard's work, too, and in the summer of 1902, made him a First Member of The Mother Church. "He has earned the place in doing much for our cause in various ways," she told the Church directors. Mary Baker Eddy to the Christian Science Board of Directors, August 3, 1902, L00314, MBEL. In 1904, Mrs. Eddy recommended that Frank be elected to The Christian Science Board of Lectureship. Mary Baker Eddy to the Christian Science Board of Directors, January 19, 1904, L00373, MBEL.

44. Tomlinson reminiscences, 806-807, MBEL.

45. Frank H. Leonard to Mary Beecher Longyear, March 6, 1918, LMC. In his letter, Leonard would also write that Mary Baker Eddy "showed her divine inspiration in all things connected with our beloved Cause. A sense of love beyond our or my ability to understand, an unselfed sense of the mission God had intrusted her with—an untiring willingness to be led of Him and an obedience, faithfulness and patience beyond human ken. Surrounded by doubt, she never doubted—by fear, she never feared—by hate, she always loved, until it radiated in noontide glory to all who had the blessed privilege to know her as a woman and were willing to follow her so far as she 'followed Christ.'"

46. Irving C. Tomlinson note, April 14, 1909, A11944, MBEL. Tomlinson reminiscences, 806, MBEL.

47. Marcia Craft was soloist at The Mother Church from approximately 1897 through 1900. She studied voice in Boston with noted tenor and singing instructor Charles R. Adams, before traveling to Italy in 1900 for more training. Some of Adams's other students included celebrated Australian soprano Dame Nellie Melba and American soprano Emma Eames.

48. When Marcia Craft wrote to Mrs. Eddy, informing her of her intentions to leave her post as soloist and study abroad, Mrs. Eddy replied in part: "While I deeply regret the necessity to part with our sweet singer, I honor your motives to complete a musical education." Mary Baker Eddy to Marcella [Marcia] Craft, September 14, 1900, L10812, MBEL.

49. Mrs. Eddy's calling card, on the back of which Marcia Craft recorded information about the concert and the flowers, has been carefully preserved by The Mary Baker Eddy Library (L10811 and L10811.02). The concert took place on the evening of January 25, 1900. Local papers praised the young soprano, calling her a "vocalist of charming voice, and if possible, more charming manner" ("Evening of Music," *Daily People and Patriot,* January 26, 1900), and one who "sings with a warmth and expression that win her instant favor"—the latter noting that the audience demanded two encores. "A Great Success," *Concord Evening Monitor,* January 26, 1900.

50. William Rathvon reminiscences, 227, MBEL. Calvin Frye recorded the date as August 31, 1909: "Miss Marcia Craft came and sang to Mrs. Eddy today…" Calvin A. Frye diary entry, August 31, 1909, EF81, 244, MBEL.

51. William Rathvon reminiscences, 228, MBEL.

52. Ibid., 227-229.

53. Marcia Craft, "Letters to Our Leader," *Christian Science Sentinel* 12 (January 29, 1910): 432. William Rathvon wrote a reply, in which he noted how pleased Mrs. Eddy was to hear from her, adding, "Our Leader has several times referred to your singing for her on the day of your visit here—a day so pleasurably remembered by all of us." William R. Rathvon to Marcia Craft, January 4, 1910, L13990, MBEL. Marcia would eventually change her name to Marcella, and she would go on to have a stellar international career. She sang with Enrico Caruso, was coached by Puccini, and Richard Strauss rewrote part of the leading role in *Salome* to better suit her range. Back in the United States, she settled in California and performed with numerous opera companies and symphonies in major cities across the country, even singing for Woodrow Wilson at the White House. Hal Durian, *True Stories of Riverside and the Inland Empire* (Charleston, South Carolina: The History Press, 2013), 219. Deane Wylie, "Friends Hear of Marcella Craft's Career," *The INNsider* (April-June 2015).

Chapter 9: Calvin Frye's Day Off

1. Dickey, *Memoirs*, 80. Adelaide Still agreed with this assessment: "It is not my intention to give the impression that we were so continually on duty that there was no recreation for us." *WKMBE* Vol. II, 495. Another observer pointed to the house itself, with its "cozy

library," multiple pianos, and "modern 'talking machine,'" as indications "that recreation and innocent amusement are not entirely lost sight of." George Shaw Cook, "The Home of Mary Baker Eddy," *Illinois Illustrated Review,* November 1909, 130.

2. Tomlinson, *Twelve Years,* 267.

3. *WKMBE* Vol. II, 495.

4. Tomlinson, *Twelve Years*, 267.

5. George H. Kinter to John Carroll Lathrop, October 13, 1910, L15721, MBEL.

6. Ibid. Elizabeth Kelly told of spotting an acquaintance in the foyer of The Mother Church, who asked how it was that she happened to be at church. "I replied that we could always come if we cared to and that Mrs. Eddy provided an automobile for us." Her friend was surprised to hear this, as it was his understanding that the members of Mrs. Eddy's household were not allowed to go to church. "That rumor had no foundation whatever as Mrs. Eddy was very willing that anyone should go who cared to go." Kelly reminiscences, 7, MBEL. And in January 1910, Mrs. Eddy told her secretaries and metaphysical workers, "I want it to be known that I approve of my household going to church, so once each month I want one fellow among you to go to church. If you make any contribution I will make it good to you." William Rathvon reminiscences, 124, MBEL.

7. John Salchow reminiscences, 116, MBEL.

8. Kelly reminiscences, 11, MBEL.

9. William Rathvon reminiscences, 170, MBEL.

10. Mary Baker Eddy to Adam H. Dickey, July 27, 1909, L10871, MBEL. Irving Tomlinson noted, "While Mrs. Eddy was having her afternoon outing during the customary hour, the Ford car was apt to be in active use." Tomlinson reminiscences, 772, MBEL. Elizabeth Kelly recalled Mrs. Eddy calling her staff to her study at another time and encouraging them to use the automobile when she was out for her carriage drives. Kelly reminiscences, 11, MBEL. William Rathvon's diary entry for May 9, 1909, echoed this. William Rathvon reminiscences, 59, MBEL.

11. Calvin A. Frye diary entry, May 26, 1908, EF081, 147, MBEL. Later that year, Mrs. Eddy would try and settle a dispute amongst the household about driving, hinted at in a letter to John Salchow in which she told him to "let but one person run the automobile. Unless I can have peace among my employees I shall dismiss each one that causes the trouble." Mary Baker Eddy to John Salchow, December 12, 1908, L13514, MBEL.

12. Committee on Business to Mary Baker Eddy, undated, IC 179b.31.070, MBEL.

13. Tomlinson reminiscences, 772, MBEL. According to John Salchow, the Ford runabout (Model T) "was much easier to handle than the steam touring car." John Salchow reminiscences, 110, MBEL. The Model T was first manufactured in the fall of 1908, so it would have been a relatively new automobile on the market at the time that Mrs. Eddy's household acquired it. For more information about the White Steam automobiles, see www.marybakereddylibrary.org/research/the-white-steam-automobiles/

14. Macdonald reminiscences, 8, MBEL.

15. George H. Kinter to John Carroll Lathrop, October 13, 1910, L15721, MBEL.

16. While working with a landscape gardener for the estate, said John Salchow, "Mr. Dickey arranged to have a tennis court laid out near the garden, but nothing ever came of it." John Salchow reminiscences, 115, MBEL.

17. Macdonald reminiscences, 9, MBEL.

18. George H. Kinter to John Carroll Lathrop, October 13, 1910, L15721, MBEL. William Rathvon reminiscences, 170, MBEL.

19. *WKMBE* Vol. II, 571-572.

20. Calvin A. Frye diary entry, August 21, 1910, EF85, 233, MBEL.

21. William Rathvon reminiscences, 171, MBEL. In late December 1909, for instance, the two headed to nearby Hammond Pond for some skating. On the whole, said Rathvon, "I got along fairly well, not falling and doing one or two little stunts well as I ever did." Ibid., 163. Irving Tomlinson played on baseball and football teams in college. Tomlinson reminiscences, 768-769, MBEL. As a younger man, he once climbed to the summit of Mount Washington with a group of other Christian Scientists, an adventure chronicled in the Boston newspapers after adverse weather stranded the party for several hours. "Caught in Mountains," *Boston Daily Globe,* August 29, 1896; "In Mountain Storm," *Boston Sunday Post,* August 30, 1896.

22. Tomlinson, *Twelve Years,* 267; Macdonald reminiscences, 9, MBEL.

23. Ibid.

24. William R. Rathvon to J. Warren Jacobs, September 29, 1910, V04344, MBEL.

25. Macdonald reminiscences, 9-10, MBEL.

26. *Science and Health,* 240.

27. Tomlinson reminiscences, 770, MBEL.

28. Ibid. William Rathvon reminiscences, 282, MBEL.

29. *WKMBE* Vol. I, 423.

30. Tomlinson reminiscences, 770-771, MBEL.

31. Macdonald reminiscences, 10, MBEL; Ella Rathvon reminiscences, April 1, 1910, MBEL; William Rathvon reminiscences, 282, MBEL; *WKMBE* Vol. I, 423.

32. "See the World's Most Famous Bird-Men Fly," advertisement in *The Christian Science Monitor*, September 3, 1910.

33. The Los Angeles International Air Meet, held on January 10-20, 1910, was the first major air show in the United States. The Harvard Aeronautical Society, organized in November 1909 as "an educational and scientific group dedicated to aeronautics," would host the Harvard-Boston Aero Meet on September 3-13, 1910, and again in 1911. The program for the 1911 meet would be printed with the compliments of *The Christian Science Monitor.* "Squantum, 1910: Turning Point in Aviation," *Quincy History,* Quincy Historical Society, Spring 1981. John Lenger, "Conquest of the Air," *Harvard Magazine,* May-June 2003, 32-37; Records of the Harvard Aeronautical Society (HUD 3123) at

the Harvard University Archives.

34. Present-day Squantum Point Park is located in Quincy, Massachusetts.

35. "Early Flight Over Boston Light," *The Bostonian Society News,* Spring 1997.

36. Ibid.

37. Cromwell Dixon was born July 9, 1892. His dirigible was one of some "17 different types of flying machines" competing in the meet. *The Christian Science Monitor,* September 3, 1910. Monoplanes, biplanes, and triplanes were some of the most common types of aircraft in the early 20th century. A dirigible, also known as an airship, aerostat, or dirigible balloon, is a power-driven, lighter-than-air aircraft. It takes flight as lifting gas, typically hydrogen in the early years, and more recently helium, is pumped into the gas bag.

38. "Boy Aeronaut Hopes to Win in St. Louis Race," *St. Louis Post-Dispatch*, October 2, 1907. Cromwell's dirigible, dubbed the "Skycycle," measured 32 by 15 feet and was crafted from a gas-filled silk balloon that his mother had sewn by hand, propellers, a cogwheel, and bicycle pedals. Cromwell controlled the steering through bicycle handlebars attached by cords to a bamboo and silk rudder, while propelling the machine forward by cycling, which activated the propellers. Cromwell would later become the 43rd registered pilot and youngest licensed aviator in the country, and on September 30, 1911, he would be the first to fly across the Continental Divide. "Young Hero Wins in Bicycle Airship," *The New York Times*, August 11, 1907; "Ohio Lad Invents a Unique Airship," *Daily Oregon Statesman*, August 25, 1907; Martin J. Kidston, *Cromwell Dixon: A Boy and His Plane* (Helena, Montana: Farcountry Press, 2007), 97, 145-152.

39. Cromwell exhibited his flying machine daily at the meet. He launched into the air at 5:48 p.m. on September 8, 1910, and landed in a field behind the Hotel Trafalgar on the corner of Norway and Hemenway Streets. *The Christian Science Monitor*, September 3 and 9, 1910. "Cromwell Dixon Flies to Boston in Dirigible, but Mistakes Christian Science Church for State House…," *Boston Post*, September 9, 1910.

40. Despite the misguided flight, Dixon was praised for his successful performance: "The young man's feat is looked upon as one of the greatest ever performed with a dirigible, for not only did he float with success through the air, propelling his great balloon at will, but when it became apparent to him that he must make a landing or else continue into the swamps and trees of the Fenway, he picked out the little field, and without assistance came safely to the ground, sitting nonchalantly upon the framework of the dirigible, waiting for the arrival of his mechanicians." *Boston Post*, September 9, 1910.

41. Kidston, *Cromwell Dixon,* 146-147, 157-159.

42. The bomb-dropping maneuvers were an exploration into the possibility of using the airplane as a weapon of war and were closely watched by representatives of the armed forces. The Secretary of the Navy was in attendance, as was the Russian Ambassador, among others. "Thousands Watch Altitude and Bomb-Throwing Events at Harvard-Boston Meet," *The Christian Science Monitor,* September 3, 1910; *Harvard Magazine*, May-June 2003, 32-37; *Quincy History,* Quincy Historical Society, Spring 1981.

43. The $10,000 prize, worth more than $270,000 in 2018, was donated by Gen. Charles H.

Taylor, founder and publisher of the *Boston Globe*. Flying twice around Boston Light, a lighthouse located on Little Brewster Island, Claude Grahame-White qualified on September 7 with a time slightly over 40 minutes. This event was considered an extremely hazardous flight, as is evident by the refusal of several fliers to compete in the race, even after being offered $1,000 as an incentive. On September 12, when Mr. Grahame-White bettered his qualifying time to clinch the prize (a new record at 34 minutes, 1.2 seconds), the band struck up "God Save the King" as he landed, and tens of thousands of spectators applauded his safe return. "English Airman Flies to Light," *Burlington Free Press* [Burlington, VT], September 8, 1910; "White Betters Time for $10,000," *Burlington Free Press*, September 13, 1910; *Harvard Magazine*, May-June 2003, 32-37; *Quincy History*, Quincy Historical Society, Spring 1981. Grahame-White would go on to sweep first place in speed, landing accuracy, shortest takeoff, and bombing hits (with dummy bombs). *The Bostonian Society News,* Spring 1997.

44. *WKMBE* Vol. I, 480.

45. "Mrs. Eddy Talks," *New York Herald,* May 1, 1901. Extracts from the interview were later reprinted in *Miscellany,* 345.

46. *WKMBE* Vol. I, 480.

47. Ella Rathvon reminiscences, MBEL.

48. Ibid. It's possible that this group witnessed Grahame-White's prize-winning flight to Boston Light. See also Albert Forbes, "Some details of the Squantum visit," Squantum Air Meet 1910 Subject File, MBEL.

49. *WKMBE* Vol. I, 423.

50. William R. and Ella S. Rathvon, "Reminiscences of Mary Baker Eddy at Chestnut Hill," 19, MBEL.

51. Irving C. Tomlinson, "Christian Science Is Practical Religion," *Brooklyn Daily Eagle,* February 6, 1934.

52. Mary Baker Eddy/M. Adelaide Still, September 1910, A10352, MBEL.

53. Tomlinson reminiscences, 650, MBEL.

54. In a letter to Mrs. Eddy in 1906, Calvin Frye calculated that in 24 years of service, he'd been away for only four nights. Calvin A. Frye to Mary Baker Eddy, August 17, 1906, L17856, MBEL. His diaries also record brief daytime visits to family members in later years, including on June 21, 1910 and September 11, 1910. Calvin Frye diaries, EF85, 172, and EF85, 250, MBEL.

55. Still reminiscences, 58, MBEL. In his diary entry for March 27, 1910, William Rathvon recorded that Laura Sargent had "not been on a city pavement for seven years, nor indeed outside the yard; rarely does her foot leave a carpet." William Rathvon reminiscences, 204, MBEL.

56. The two women were gone for a week. Kelly reminiscences, 12, MBEL.

57. Mary Baker Eddy to Silas J. Sawyer, May 16, 1888, LMC.

58. Julia Bartlett, for instance, wrote of walking with Mrs. Eddy to Red Rock ("where

Mrs. Eddy loved to go") at the shore in Lynn, while she was attending class. Julia Bartlett scrapbook, 159, LMC. See also *WKMBE* Vol. I, 48; Still reminiscences, 59, MBEL.

59. Wilbur, *Mary Baker Eddy,* 334; Peel, *Authority,* 22.

60. Tomlinson reminiscences, 772, MBEL.

61. Dickey, *Memoirs,* 72-73.

62. Ibid., 106.

63. Hill reminiscences, 164, MBEL.

64. "When I returned from supper," wrote Adelaide Still, "I often found Mr. Frye chatting with her about events or news of the day. At Chestnut Hill Mr. Dickey sometimes took turns with Mr. Frye in sitting with her." *WKMBE* Vol. II, 470.

65. Still reminiscences, 45, MBEL. Benjamin S. Pray Subject File, MBEL. Benjamin Sturgis Pray would grow up to become a *Journal*-listed Christian Science practitioner and an accomplished poet. A number of his poems and articles, including "The Democracy of Prayer," were published in the Christian Science periodicals, and one of his poems was chosen as a hymn (number 185 — "Master and Lord, 'tis good to be here") for the *Christian Science Hymnal.*

66. Benjamin S. Pray Subject File, MBEL.

67. Still reminiscences, 45, MBEL.

68. Irving C. Tomlinson note, October 1, 1910, A12005, MBEL. William Rathvon noted, "I never saw our Leader more genuinely pleased than she was with the little fellow's sweetness." William Rathvon reminiscences, 134, MBEL. Carol Montgomery was the son of Gray and Katherine Montgomery, Christian Science practitioners from Denver, Colorado. Gray was also Committee on Publication for Colorado.

Chapter 10: A Grandmother's Love

1. Robert Peel, *Mary Baker Eddy: The Years of Discovery* (New York: Holt, Rinehart and Winston, 1966), 30, hereafter referenced as Peel, *Discovery.*

2. Ibid., 67-72. For more about the Glovers' sojourn in the South, see Jewel Spangler Smaus's six-part series, "'Family': The Carolina Glovers," *Longyear Quarterly News,* Spring/Summer 1987, Autumn 1987, Summer 1989, Winter/Fall 1989-90, Spring/Summer 1990, Winter/Spring 1990-91.

3. George Washington Glover II was born on September 12, 1844.

4. Peel, *Discovery,* 81-84; Ferguson and Frederick, *A World More Bright,* 35.

5. Mary Baker Glover and Daniel Patterson were married on June 21, 1853. Patterson won her affections with his persistence, but Mrs. Eddy would also later write: "My dominant thought in marrying again was to get back my child, but after our marriage his stepfather was not willing he should have a home with me." *Retrospection,* 20. For more about Daniel Patterson and the issue of guardianship for young George, see Jewel Spangler Smaus, "An important historical discovery," *The Christian Science Journal* 101 (May 1983): 284-288.

6. *Retrospection,* 20-21.

7. Although it's unclear exactly how George learned that his mother was still alive, there is evidence that David Hall, who was in the same regiment, wrote letters home for his fellow soldiers who were illiterate, George among them. Peel, *Discovery*, 144, 335n68.

8. For more comprehensive information about Mrs. Eddy's son, George, and his life in the West, see Jewel Spangler Smaus's eight-part series "'Family': From New England to the Black Hills," *Longyear Quarterly News*, Autumn 1982, Winter 1982-83, Spring 1983, Autumn 1983, Winter 1983-84, Spring 1984, Summer 1984, Autumn 1984.

9. Gershom was born on March 8, 1875.

10. Mary was born on October 7, 1877.

11. Mrs. Eddy's son arrived in Boston in November 1879 and stayed for three months, living with his mother and new step-father, Asa Gilbert Eddy, in a series of boardinghouses.

12. Mary Baker Glover Billings reminiscences, 2, MBEL. Mary Billings also mentions a family photograph of her as a baby that shows her with crossed eyes.

13. Evelyn was born on January 12, 1880.

14. When she learned of his intention to bring his family to Boston at that particular time, Mrs. Eddy wrote to George: "...I live in a Schoolhouse and have no room I can let even a boarder into.... Besides this, I have all I can meet without receiving company. I must have quiet in my house...." Mary Baker Eddy to George W. Glover II, October 31, 1887, L02085, MBEL. George came anyway. For more about this family visit, see Robert Peel, *Mary Baker Eddy: The Years of Trial* (New York: Holt, Rinehart and Winston, 1971), 217-218, hereafter referenced as Peel, *Trial,* and Ferguson and Frederick, *A World More Bright,* 111, 115-116.

15. The christening service took place at Chickering Hall in Boston on Sunday, February 26, 1888. Mary Baker Glover Billings reminiscences, 2, MBEL. See also "Christening Service," *The Christian Science Journal* 5 (March 1888): 629. Peel comments: "It was an experimental concession to orthodoxy that was really anomalous in view of [Mary Baker Eddy's] definition of baptism." Peel, *Trial,* 236. Mrs. Eddy's definition of baptism may be found on page 581 of *Science and Health.*

16. George Washington Glover III was born on January 4, 1889.

17. Mary Baker Eddy to George W. Glover II, December 8, 1890, N00050, MBEL.

18. George W. Glover II to Mary Baker Eddy, December 16, 1891, IC 197.32.016, MBEL. Andrew Jackson Glover was born on either July 3 or July 4, 1891.

19. Peel, *Authority,* 385n51.

20. Smaus, *Longyear Quarterly News,* Autumn 1984, 331-332.

21. Tomlinson reminiscences, 656, MBEL.

22. Mary Baker Eddy to George W. Glover II, December 15, 1899, LMC. Mrs. Eddy took the time to hand write the letter and addressed it to "Mr. Geo. W. Glover, Mining Engineer."

23. "A Beautiful Christmas Gift," *Christian Science Sentinel* 2 (January 11, 1900): 300.

24. Smaus, *Longyear Quarterly News,* Spring 1984, 323.

25. Mrs. Eddy wrote to her son, George, repeatedly about his children's education. For instance, in 1892 she offered to pay all expenses for Mary and Evelyn to come to Boston to be privately tutored and given music lessons (Mary Baker Eddy to George W. Glover II, July 27, 1892, L02103, MBEL), and in 1900 she expressed her wish that her grandson George would be prepared for either Harvard or Dartmouth, offering to foot the bill for both his high school and college expenses. In this same letter she also wrote, "I never have given up the hope that I may sometime teach my own grandchildren Christian Science." Mary Baker Eddy to George W. Glover II, January 13, 1900, L02129, MBEL. Alas, that was not to be. Her granddaughter Mary, however, later had class instruction with Emma Easton Newman, whom Mrs. Eddy had taught at the Massachusetts Metaphysical College.

26. Richard A. Nenneman, *Persistent Pilgrim: The Life of Mary Baker Eddy* (Etna, New Hampshire: Nebbadoon Press, 1997), 282-283. Peel, *Authority,* 275. Charles M. Howe was a Christian Science practitioner and teacher who was taught by Mrs. Eddy at the Massachusetts Metaphysical College.

27. Mary Baker Eddy to Charles M. Howe, February 12, 1900, L05319, MBEL.

28. The letter from Judge Ewing to Mrs. Eddy of October 23, 1906, was reprinted in "Letters to Our Leader," *Christian Science Sentinel* 9 (November 17, 1906): 194-195. Mr. Ewing mentioned "granddaughter" in the singular, as Evelyn Glover had passed on in 1903.

29. William E. Chandler was Secretary of the Navy from 1882-1885 and served in the United States Senate from 1887 to 1901. For further details about his political career, see his Congressional bio: bioguide.congress.gov/scripts/biodisplay.pl?index=c000298

30. Filed on March 1, 1907, the litigation would come to be known as the Next Friends suit. More information may be found in Peel, *Authority,* 275-291, and Ferguson and Frederick, *A World More Bright,* 172-192.

31. After the collapse of the lawsuit in August 1907, a financial settlement was eventually agreed on by all parties involved, and in November 1909 Mrs. Eddy's son George received $245,000 (nearly $6.5 million in 2018 dollars), $125,000 of which was in a trust, under the condition that he not contest her will—a condition he would not honor, thanks in large part to William Chandler's counsel. Peel, *Authority,* 291, 489n126. Gillian Gill, *Mary Baker Eddy* (Reading, Mass.: Perseus Books, 1998), 498, 553-554. At her passing in December 1910, Mrs. Eddy also left each of her grandchildren $10,000 ($250,000 in 2018 dollars).

32. "Desire to Visit Famous Grandmother Again Cause of Visit, Say Grandsons of Mrs. Eddy," *Boston Sunday Post,* July 17, 1910. "Visited Their Grandmother: Grandsons of Mrs. Eddy Received at Her Newton Home," *Concord Evening Monitor,* July 18, 1910. Waterloo is now Warner, New Hampshire. George and Andrew's sight-seeing trips included a visit to Pleasant View, their grandmother's home in Concord, New Hampshire.

33. *Boston Sunday Post,* July 17, 1910. Smaus, *Longyear Quarterly News,* Autumn 1984, 331.

34. Tomlinson reminiscences, 655, MBEL. See also "A Birthday Gift and a Special Visit," www.marybakereddylibrary.org/research/birthday-gift/

35. Tomlinson reminiscences, 655, MBEL. It's unclear where exactly Chandler waited while

the boys were talking with their grandmother. He told reporters that he wasn't present while they were visiting, so he may have been downstairs or outside. He could hardly have been a welcome presence at 400 Beacon Street that day, given his hostility during the Next Friends suit a few years earlier. What is clear is that he held forth to the press at some point that afternoon, sharing inaccurate remarks about Mrs. Eddy and the Next Friends suit. "Mrs. Eddy Passes 89th Year: Meets Grandsons From West," *Boston American,* July 17, 1910.

36. Still reminiscences, 43, MBEL. Tomlinson, in his reminiscences, puts Mrs. Eddy's grandsons' respective heights at roughly 5'11" (George) and 6'5" (Andrew). Tomlinson reminiscences, 655, MBEL.

37. Still reminiscences, 43, MBEL.

38. Tomlinson reminiscences, 655, MBEL. In the end, Mrs. Eddy's hopes for seeing her grandsons educated would be dashed. George went to work in the South Dakota mines, and Andrew on the family farm.

39. The bar pin depicted a miner's pan atop a crossed pick and shovel, complete with a gold nugget on the tip of the pick and some gold flakes in the pan. The delicate piece was decorated with grapes, grape leaves, and vines, motifs symbolic of the Black Hills. The inscription on the box read: "From your son in Truth and Love, George W. Glover." For more about this gift (and a lovely photo), see "A Birthday Gift and a Special Visit," www.marybakereddylibrary.org/research/birthday-gift/

40. Still reminiscences, 43, MBEL.

41. Ibid. According to George Glover III, his father put him in charge of the store and his brother Andrew in charge of the family farm outside of town. Purchased around the time that the trust was settled in 1909 (and likely with part of the proceeds), the store was the "largest soda fountain and confectionary in the Black Hills — an area that had a good many more saloons than ice cream parlors." Smaus, *Longyear Quarterly News,* Autumn 1984, 331.

42. Tomlinson reminiscences, 655, MBEL. Irving C. Tomlinson note, July 16, 1910, A12000, MBEL.

43. *Boston American,* July 17, 1910.

44. Ibid.

45. Still reminiscences, 43, MBEL. Mrs. Eddy also had a picture of her granddaughter Evelyn on display on one of the shelves of her whatnot. "She treasured this picture," Miss Still recalled, "and had written on the back of it, 'My darling granddaughter, passed on.'"

46. *Boston Sunday Post,* July 17, 1910.

47. This fragmentary poem, written on July 16, 1910, was never published. See A10057, MBEL.

48. "All the family join in sending our love to you," George added in his thank you to his grandmother. George W. Glover III to Mary Baker Eddy, August 20, 1910, V03140, MBEL.

49. Smaus, *Longyear Quarterly News,* Autumn 1984, 332.

50. Jewel Spangler Smaus interview with George W. Glover III, September 3, 1970, Oral History tapes, Daystar Foundation and Library, Oklahoma City, Oklahoma.

Chapter 11: At the Fountainhead

1. *WKMBE* Vol. II, 375-376.

2. William and Ella Rathvon reminiscences, 2, MBEL. See also *Miscellany,* 228-229.

3. Sibyl Wilbur, "Mrs. Eddy's Views on Vital Questions," *Boston Herald*, June 11, 1905, reprinted in the *Christian Science Sentinel* 7 (June 17, 1905): 667-671.

4. Scott, "Record of Acquaintance," 7, LMC.

5. *WKMBE* Vol. I, 469.

6. Ibid., 470.

7. William Rathvon reminiscences, 202, MBEL.

8. *A Biographical Sketch of Victoria H. Sargent, C.S.D., and Laura E. Sargent, C.S.D.* (Green Bay, Wisconsin: Reliance Publishing, 1953), 11-14, hereafter referenced as Sargent, *Biographical Sketch. Commemorative Biographical Record of the West Shore of Green Bay, Wisconsin* (Chicago: J.H. Beers & Co., 1896), 540-541. Samuel Adams enlisted as a private in October 1863, and was mustered out in July 1865 at the close of the war. National Park Service, U.S. Civil War Soldiers, 1861-1865. Although the Commemorative Biographical Record says that after the war he "engaged in farming until his death," he may actually have returned to active duty on behalf of the armed forces at some point. Samuel Adams passed on in or near Philadelphia in 1883, and his remains were returned to Oconto for burial. His death certificate lists his occupation as Sea Captain, and his address as Bristol Pike, W[ard] 23, in Philadelphia. Philadelphia is home to the Philadelphia Naval Asylum complex, which at times during the 19th century served as a hospital, naval school, and home for retired sailors. When Minerva Adams filed to obtain a widow's pension in 1894, there was added to his service in the "Wis Cav & Navy," "Sea Captain," a number of naval vessels, and reference to Navy files.

9. Laura's older sisters, Clarentine (called Clara), Hannah (called Anna), Victoria, and Arvesta (called Vesta), attended public schools in Green Bay, but Laura was too young to do so. In 1866, Louise Hall married and closed her school. This year ended tragically for the Adams family. Vesta died in mid-November, and Clara at the end of December, just six weeks apart. They were about 15 and 20 years old. Laura was only eight. 1850 U.S. Federal Census; 1860 U.S. Federal Census; 1870 U.S. Federal Census.

10. "Notes from Mrs. Alice Bartels," April 26, 1965, LMC. Mrs. Bartels was a student of Victoria Sargent and daughter-in-law of Louise Hall, Laura Sargent's primary school teacher in Oconto.

11. Quoted in George E. Hall, *A History of Oconto, Wisconsin,* Second Edition (Oconto, Wisconsin: The Oconto County Historical Society, 2009), 140.

12. Henry and Victoria were married in 1866; Henry built their house in about 1867. James built a house for Laura in 1878. The two homes were sited catty-corner from each other on Main Street in Oconto. *Commemorative Biographical Record,* 540. Wisconsin Marriage Index, 1820-1907. Katherine E. Hundt and David A. Donath, State Historical Society of Wisconsin, "National Register of Historic Places Inventory," U.S. Department of the Interior, National Park Service, Item 7, 4-6.

13. *Green Bay Advocate,* August 20, 1885.

14. Sargent, *Biographical Sketch,* 18-19. "First Christian Science Edifice—50th Anniversary," *The Christian Science Monitor,* October 31, 1936.

15. Sargent, "Additions and Corrections," *Biographical Sketch.*

16. Jane E. Skinner to Ann Holliday Webb, March 11, 1966, LMC. Jane Skinner was Anna Adams Heney's granddaughter and grand-niece of Laura and Victoria Sargent. Anna eventually took Primary class instruction from her sister Laura, and went on to introduce Christian Science to Duluth. By 1900 she was *Journal*-listed, and remained in the practice until her passing in 1914.

17. Laura's sister Victoria Sargent would become a member of the October 1886 Normal class. Laura's final class would be an obstetrical course in December 1887.

18. W. F. Smith, "My Meeting with Mrs. Mary B. G. Eddy," *Human Life,* June 1907. William Smith, publisher of *Human Life* magazine, which ran Sibyl Wilbur's year-long series of articles on Mrs. Eddy, traveled to Pleasant View himself in May 1907. The following month, he described his visit in an article that included this incisive assessment of Laura.

19. "Extracts from Letters to Our Teacher," *The Christian Science Journal* 7 (May 1889): 78.

20. Sargent, *Biographical Sketch,* 22-23; Victoria H. Sargent, C.S.D., and Laura E. Sargent, C.S.D., Subject Files, MBEL.

21. *Miscellaneous,* 149-150.

22. *The Christian Science Journal* 4 (October 1886): 185.

23. Laura E. Sargent, "Healing," *The Christian Science Journal* 5 (December 1887): 474.

24. Laura Sargent maintained ties with Marinette and would be on hand 12 years later, in July 1899, to preside over the laying of the cornerstone for the community's first Christian Science church. "Marinette Christian Science Church," *Oconto County Reporter,* July 7, 1899. See also "A Corner-Stone," *Christian Science Sentinel* 1 (August 10, 1899): 7. Laura would teach her second and last Primary class in 1892 in Oconto. At Mrs. Eddy's request, her students and those of her sister Victoria were eventually joined into one Association, presided over by Victoria. Sargent, *Biographical Sketch,* 9. Victoria H. Sargent, C.S.D and Laura E. Sargent, C.S.D. Subject Files, MBEL.

25. "Official Minutes of Fourth Annual Meeting, N.C.S. Association," *The Christian Science Journal* 7 (July 1889): 182; *Green Bay Press-Gazette,* December 27, 1889.

26. *The Christian Science Journal* 7 (May 1889): 78.

27. Mary Baker Eddy to Victoria H. Sargent, January 3, 1891, L07855, MBEL.

28. For instance, in 1902 and 1903, Laura Sargent assisted Albert Conant with compiling the first concordance to *Science and Health,* and in 1905 she was elected to a one-year term as custodian of the "Mother's Room" in the Original Edifice of The Mother Church. "Victoria H. Sargent, C.S.D., and Laura E. Sargent, C.S.D.," Laura E. Sargent and Victoria H. Sargent Subject File, Folder 1, MBEL. Laura Sargent's listings in *The Christian Science Journal* also show that she maintained an office in Boston from 1896 through 1904.

29. "Letters to Mrs. Eddy," *The Christian Science Journal* 15 (June 1897): 160. Still reminiscences,

58, MBEL.

30. James Sargent traveled to the Klondike as a representative of an Oconto syndicate (the "Lucky Jim" Mining Club), setting off with a colleague in February 1898. "Ocontoites to Alaska," *Oconto County Reporter,* February 18, 1898; "From Klondike: Former Oconto Man Writes Home from the Gold Fields," *Watertown Republican,* June 22, 1898; "Gold Not Abundant," *Oconto County Reporter,* October 14, 1898. On his return in the fall of 1899, the local newspaper interviewed James about his journey in a report that gives some hints as to his physical appearance and character: "He says he was not sick a day, but the rigors of the climate have reduced his weight thirty pounds. He is changed in general appearance—somewhat thinner in features—and recognition in many instances was retarded until one heard his cheery voice or beheld his accustomed smile. He is welcome home." "Not Burdened by Gold: A Year and a Half in the Klondike," *Oconto County Reporter,* September 29, 1899; "Back from Gold Fields: James Sargent of Oconto Returns Without a Fortune," *Watertown Republican,* October 3, 1899. James Sargent appears to have been a bit of a peripatetic businessman, as he also traveled to Arizona in the winter of 1893-1894 to supervise "his landed interest" in a 160-acre ranch. *Oconto County Reporter,* December 9, 1893; *Oconto County Reporter,* March 10, 1894. He would eventually move to Santa Cruz, California, to live with his older brother, Thomas, and his family. James passed on in Santa Cruz in April 1927.

31. "Mrs. Sargent Is Not Mrs. Eddy's Servant," *Boston American,* June 18, 1909; "Not Companion of Mrs. Eddy," *Boston Post,* June 18, 1909.

32. Still reminiscences, 58, MBEL.

33. Ibid., 61. "Science and the Senses" would be published in *The Christian Science Journal* 6 (August 1888): 217-223, and subsequently reprinted in *Miscellaneous,* 98-106.

34. Laura E. Sargent, "Reminiscences," 20, MBEL.

35. Josephine Woodbury, a disaffected student, sued Mrs. Eddy for libel in the summer of 1899. The case would be ruled decisively in Mrs. Eddy's favor in April 1902. For more information on this lawsuit, see Peel, *Authority,* 143-171.

36. *Painting a Poem,* 49.

37. "Notes from Mrs. Alice Bartels," LMC. Adelaide Still observes: "Mrs. Sargent told me many times that she loved Mrs. Eddy more than her own mother … although she always spoke very lovingly and tenderly of her parents, especially her mother." Still reminiscences, 58, MBEL.

38. Peel, *Authority,* 319.

39. Sargent, *Biographical Sketch,* 32-33; "Notes from Mrs. Alice Bartels," LMC.

40. According to Frances Thatcher, who later took over the task of answering the front door, the doorbell at 400 Beacon Street was connected to a spot just above Laura's door frame. Thatcher reminiscences, 2, MBEL.

41. Wilbur, *Mary Baker Eddy,* 326.

42. Still reminiscences, 58, MBEL. Mary Baker Eddy to Laura E. Sargent, July 18, 1896, L05990, MBEL. Sargent, *Biographical Sketch,* 27-28.

43. Hill reminiscences, 53, MBEL. George H. Kinter to John Carroll Lathrop, October 13, 1910, L15721, MBEL. Tomlinson reminiscences, 778, MBEL. "They answered the call: Laura Sargent," *The Christian Science Journal* 107 (August 1989): 18.

44. William Rathvon reminiscences, 202, MBEL.

45. Dickey, *Memoirs*, 22. Mr. Dickey adds: "Her engaging manner and pleasant disposition made such a deep impression upon us then that we always thought of her as particularly amiable and loving. I found her devoted to Mrs. Eddy. She seemed to have but one thought and that was to serve. . . ."

46. Laura E. Sargent to Mary Beecher Longyear, December 10, 1910, LMC.

47. Laura was appointed to a one-year term beginning in July 1914. "Victoria H. Sargent, C.S.D., and Laura E. Sargent, C.S.D.," Laura E. Sargent and Victoria H. Sargent Subject File, Folder 1, MBEL.

48. Laura Lathrop, who taught in 1899, was the other woman. "I am still at the post of duty," Laura wrote to Mrs. Longyear a few months before that class commenced. "Our present sense of duty is only the sweet prelude to that diviner service whose bliss no human tongue can utter." Laura E. Sargent to Mary Beecher Longyear, September 3, 1913, LMC.

49. Still reminiscences, 63, MBEL.

50. *WKMBE* Vol. II, 453.

51. Laura E. Sargent to Septimus and Camilla Hanna, December 16, 1913, LMC.

52. Laura E. Sargent, "Letters and Telegrams to Our Leader," *Christian Science Sentinel* 6 (July 23, 1904): 747.

53. Tomlinson, *Twelve Years*, 79.

54. The story of Lyman Durgin is a touching one. Mary Baker worked with the boy for four years, after which he left the Baker farm and went on to have a successful career as a master mechanic for a Western railroad. Smaus, *Golden Days*, 89-90. See also George H. Kinter, C.S.B., "Memoirs," 48, LMC, and Tomlinson, *Twelve Years*, 79.

55. For further information on Mrs. Eddy's teaching positions as a young woman, see Peel, *Discovery*, 81-82; Tomlinson, *Twelve Years*, 24; Ferguson and Frederick, *A World More Bright*, 34-35; Smaus, *Golden Days*, 111-112.

56. Mary Baker Eddy would teach her first student, shoemaker Hiram Crafts, in the latter part of 1866 and early 1867, within a year of her healing. *In My True Light and Life* (Boston: The Writings of Mary Baker Eddy and The Mary Baker Eddy Library for the Betterment of Humanity, 2002), 202-203; Ferguson and Frederick, *A World More Bright*, 67.

57. William Rathvon reminiscences, 12, MBEL; *WKMBE* Vol. II, 560.

58. George H. Kinter, "Autobiographical Sketch of George H. Kinter, C.S.B.," 61, LMC, hereafter referenced as Kinter, Autobiographical Sketch. "Annual Meeting of The Mother Church," *Christian Science Sentinel* 23 (June 18, 1921): 784. Tomlinson's remarks were part of his address as incoming President of The Mother Church.

59. Kinter, Autobiographical Sketch, 62, LMC. Another student would also recall the way Mrs. Eddy opened her Bible at random and read aloud to them: "She would give the spiritual

interpretation of it, which flowed from her lips as freely as if she had written it out. This was her bread from heaven, her inspiration and revelation, the manna for the day, which she shared with the members of her household." *WKMBE* Vol. I, 466.

60. William Rathvon reminiscences, 83, MBEL.

61. Ibid. Elsewhere in his reminiscences (131), William Rathvon offered another example of how difficult it would have been to record all that Mrs. Eddy was sharing. On Saturday, April 9, 1910, "for forty minutes our Leader held forth in most remarkable fashion at her very best. She took high ground and held it; she thrust and parried and had everybody on the run, yet it was all straight Science. I wish I could reproduce it, but it came so fast that I can only set down this: 'When the fear of lying awake is overcome, you will sleep.'"

62. Ibid., 62.

63. Ibid.

64. Tomlinson reminiscences, 95, MBEL. Irving would also write: "Scarcely one of these visits passed that his teacher did not awaken his thought, strengthen his purpose and encourage his right endeavors. These words of instruction were so precious to him that he sometimes recorded them. . . ." Ibid.

65. Mrs. Eddy made this statement on March 13, 1910. *WKMBE* Vol. II, 569.

66. Tomlinson, *Twelve Years*, 106. See also Irving C. Tomlinson, March 13, 1910, A11859, MBEL.

67. Minnie A. Scott to the Christian Science Board of Directors, May 15, 1931, Minnie A. Scott Reminiscence File, MBEL.

68. Ella W. Hoag, "Testimonies From the Field," *The Christian Science Journal* 21 (February 1904): 687-688. Born Ella Whitaker in May 1854, she would marry Frank J. Hoag on November 22, 1876.

69. Ibid.

70. Ibid.; I Corinthians 10:27.

71. *Ella W. Hoag, C.S.D.: A Brief History of her life as a Christian Scientist*, 1, LMC, hereafter referenced as Hoag, *A Brief History*.

72. *The Christian Science Journal* 21 (February 1904): 687-688.

73. Ibid.

74. Hoag, *A Brief History*, 1, LMC.

75. Mrs. Eddy conferred on her the degree C.S.B. in 1888. She would later designate her C.S.D. Ibid., 2.

76. Mary Baker Eddy to Ella W. Hoag, October 3, 1894, L04722, MBEL.

77. Hoag, *A Brief History*, 2, LMC.

78. "Some Impressions of the Members of the Hoag Family," January 1966, LMC.

79. Thomas W. Hatten to Mary Baker Eddy, May 27, 1907, L16948, MBEL.

80. Ella W. Hoag to the Christian Science Board of Directors, May 13, 1926, Ella W. Hoag Reminiscence File, MBEL.

81. Ibid.

82. *WKMBE* Vol. II, 562. When she left Chestnut Hill for the final time, on May 14, 1910, William Rathvon wrote, on behalf of the staff, "We miss her strong and scientific work." William Rathvon reminiscences, 214, MBEL.

83. Ibid., 213. Mrs. Hoag returned in April 1910.

84. Mary Baker Eddy to Ella W. Hoag, March 30, 1910, L04726, MBEL.

85. Hoag, *A Brief History,* 3, LMC.

86. "Annual Meeting of The Mother Church," *The Christian Science Journal* 45 (July 1927): 177-178.

87. Albert F. Gilmore and Duncan Sinclair, "Mrs. Ella W. Hoag," *Christian Science Sentinel* 31 (November 10, 1928): 210; *The Christian Science Journal* 46 (January 1929): 555-556.

88. Irving C. Tomlinson note, August 28, 1908, A11915, MBEL.

89. *WKMBE* Vol. I, 477.

90. Dickey, *Memoirs,* 89.

91. Ibid., 89-90.

92. William and Ella Rathvon reminiscences, 16, MBEL.

93. Tomlinson, *Twelve Years,* 225. In one conversation with Mrs. Eddy, Irving recalled her sharing the Biblical basis for her rebukes, telling him, "Jesus never spoke in commendation to his students that he did not also point out the consequences of failure. He now says, 'But and if,' etc. [Matt. 24:48-51]. So it is the work of Mother not only to encourage but to rebuke the error. Those who accept go higher. Those who are full of resentment and justify self fall by the way." Tomlinson reminiscences, 97, MBEL.

94. William Rathvon and Ella Rathvon reminiscences, 20, MBEL.

95. Macdonald reminiscences, 11, MBEL.

96. Ibid.

97. *WKMBE* Vol. II, 380-381. Stevenson's temper may have contributed to his eventual dismissal. In an interesting postscript, on the day following his dismissal, Mrs. Eddy was speaking of him to Laura Sargent and Adelaide Still, when Laura told Mrs. Eddy that Stevenson had wanted to marry Miss Still. Adelaide wrote, "She looked at me with a twinkle in her eye and said, 'why don't you take pity on him, Adelaide?' Then, lest I should take it seriously, she said, 'You know I don't mean that, don't you?'" Still reminiscences, 36, MBEL.

98. *WKMBE* Vol. II, 381. Margaret Macdonald added this to the outcome of the story: "The girl burst into tears and said she would never annoy her again. And she kept her promise." Macdonald reminiscences, 11, MBEL. Frances Thatcher noted that Adolph Stevenson "and any who had entertained any thoughts the opposite of Love, were conscious of the impersonal rebuke." Thatcher reminiscences, 7, MBEL.

99. Scott, "Record of Acquaintance," 11, LMC.

100. William and Ella Rathvon reminiscences, 1, MBEL.

101. William Rathvon reminiscences, 14, MBEL.

102. Ella S. Rathvon, "Cases of Healing," *The Christian Science Journal* 20 (August 1902): 287.

103. Ibid. Of their introduction to Christian Science, William wrote, "without resistance it entered our lives, ever to remain." William Rathvon reminiscences, 14, MBEL.

104. Lillie Stauffer died in October 1880, just a month after the birth of their son, Martin Trueheart Rathvon.

105. William Rathvon reminiscences, 14, MBEL. Born on September 12, 1880, the boy was two and a half when William and Ella were married in April 1883. Martin named his firstborn daughter after his stepmother (Ella Josephine Rathvon was born in April 1911).

106. William and Ella Rathvon were taught in Chicago by Mary W. Adams, a student of Mrs. Eddy.

107. W. R. Rathvon, "Notes from the Field," *The Christian Science Journal* 16 (October 1898): 497-498.

108. *The Christian Science Journal* 20 (August 1902): 287-289.

109. Ida G. Stewart/Committee on Business to Mary Baker Eddy, June 12, 1908, Allison V. and Ida G. Stewart Subject File, MBEL.

110. Archibald McLellan to Mary Baker Eddy, undated, L16952, MBEL. Although the document is undated, this recommendation is nearly identical to the Business Committee letter recorded by Ida Stewart on June 12, 1908.

111. Interviewed as a possible candidate for work in Mrs. Eddy's home, Ella would travel to and from Boston three times before finally joining the household on September 3, 1909. See William Rathvon reminiscences, 15-26, MBEL.

112. Ibid., 20.

113. Ella S. Rathvon, "Letters to Our Leader," *Christian Science Sentinel* 11 (January 30, 1909): 431.

114. *WKMBE* Vol. II, 525-526.

115. William Rathvon reminiscences, 174, MBEL.

116. Ella Rathvon reminiscences, MBEL.

117. *WKMBE* Vol. I, 425-426.

118. Lora Carney Rathvon, introduction to Ella Rathvon reminiscences, MBEL; Tomlinson reminiscences, 765, MBEL. Lora was William Rathvon's third wife.

119. Tomlinson reminiscences, 806, MBEL. John Salchow described Ella as an "accomplished musician." *WKMBE* Vol. I, 422.

120. According to Ella's diary, this occurred on December 14, 1909. Ella Rathvon reminiscences, MBEL.

121. Ibid., August 26, 1910.

122. Ibid., January 1, 1910.

123. Ibid., March 20, 1910.

124. Archibald McLellan to Mary Baker Eddy, undated, L16952, MBEL.

125. Weygandt reminiscences, 104, MBEL.

126. William Rathvon reminiscences, 69, MBEL.

127. Ibid., 71.

128. *WKMBE* Vol. II, 551.

129. Irving Tomlinson recorded this in his diary on November 19, 1910. Tomlinson reminiscences, 108, MBEL. He noted that Mrs. Eddy was "much pleased with the answer which someone quoted from page 323 of *Science and Health:* 'In order to apprehend more, we must put into practice what we already know.'" Tomlinson, *Twelve Years,* 94.

130. *WKMBE* Vol. II, 382.

Chapter 12 : The Crowning Years

1. William R. Rathvon to Charles G. Baldwin, December 8, 1909, V04660, MBEL. In his letter to Mrs. Eddy, Mr. Baldwin called the article, which begins "I approve the By-laws of The Mother Church" and was later reprinted in full in *Miscellany* (358), "a declaration of independence for yourself and for humanity. It is at once the proclamation of the dearly bought liberty of the Sons of God, and the elimination of the license of mortal mind." Charles G. Baldwin to Mary Baker Eddy, December 2, 1909, IC 644b.66.012, MBEL.

2. Irving C. Tomlinson, "Christian Science Is Practical Religion," *Brooklyn Daily Eagle,* February 6, 1934.

3. Peel, *Authority,* 356.

4. "New By-laws," *Christian Science Sentinel* 11 (November 21, 1908): 230; *Church Manual,* 49.

5. In the first edition of *Science and Health*, Mrs. Eddy counseled readers to request that "a nurse or the friends of the sick" who may not think highly of metaphysical healing "leave the patient out of their thoughts as much as possible, that the influence one mind holds over another may be obviated." *Science and Health*, 1875 edition, 427-428.

6. *Science and Health,* 1881 edition, 187.

7. *Science and Health*, 395. The 50th edition first addressed specific qualities of thought necessary: "The nurse should be full of cheerfulness, faith, light,—a believer in God, Truth." *Science and Health*, 1891 edition, 394.

8. Ruth Colman to Mary Beecher Longyear, undated, LMC. A common usage of the word "recruiting" at the time meant repairing or strengthening. See also Weygandt reminiscences, 65-67, MBEL.

9. The Mann family included Joseph Mann; his sister Pauline; Joseph's brother August, who served as coachman; August's wife, Amanda, and their son, Frederick.

10. Mary Baker Eddy to Mary Beecher Longyear, January 15, 1905, quoted in "The Christian Science Benevolent Association," *Christian Science Sentinel* 19 (October 7, 1916): 110.

11. Ibid. As the *Sentinel* article explains, just a few weeks after submitting the new By-law, Mrs. Eddy noted that she was "willing to let this matter rest for the present. . . ." and

suggested they repeal it, which they did. In 1916, the Board of Directors would move forward with plans for the "resort for the so-called sick" that Mrs. Eddy had envisioned, with a gift from Mrs. Longyear of 20 acres of land near Boston.

12. Daisette and William McKenzie both attended Mrs. Eddy's final class in 1898. William was a practitioner and teacher, and would go on to become one of the first Christian Science lecturers. He would also serve as Editor of the Christian Science periodicals, a Trustee of The Christian Science Publishing Society, and a member of the Christian Science Board of Directors.

13. Daisette McKenzie, "Reminiscences of Daisette Stocking McKenzie, C.S.B., and William Patrick McKenzie, C.S.B.," 33, MBEL. Daisette recorded several inspiring healings that occurred at "Sharon," including an account of a woman who wore a neck brace to stabilize her head, and a girl who needed leg braces in order to stand erect. "Each of these dear friends were entirely healed, and one bright summer morning we took the two steel braces and buried them in the garden. They were no longer needed. We followed this simple incident with a thanksgiving service." Ibid., 35.

14. Mary Baker Eddy to Daisette Stocking [McKenzie] and Emily B. F. Shanklin, March 30, 1894, L13075, MBEL. Mary Baker Eddy to Daisette Stocking [McKenzie], March 13, 1894, L13018, MBEL.

15. Sibyl Wilbur, "Mrs. Eddy's Views on Vital Questions," *Boston Herald,* June 11, 1905. The article was reprinted in the *Christian Science Sentinel* 7 (June 17, 1905): 667-671.

16. Mary Baker Eddy to William B. Johnson, June 1, 1909, L14031, MBEL.

17. William Dana Orcutt, *Mary Baker Eddy and Her Books* (Boston: The Christian Science Publishing Society, 1978), 122-124, hereafter referenced as Orcutt, *Mary Baker Eddy and Her Books.*

18. Peel, *Authority,* 311, 496n66.

19. "'I Hold No Enmity,' Says Mrs. Eddy To The American In Long Interview," *New York American,* August 26, 1907, reprinted in the *Christian Science Sentinel* 9 (August 31, 1907): 1003-1004.

20. For more comprehensive information on the establishment of the *Monitor,* see Peel, *Authority,* 307-314; Ferguson and Frederick, *A World More Bright,* 197-205; as well as Longyear Museum's most recent historical documentary film, *"Follow and Rejoice"—Mary Baker Eddy: The Chestnut Hill Years.*

21. Mary Baker Eddy to the Board of Trustees of The Christian Science Publishing Society, August 8, 1908, L07268, MBEL. She concluded the letter, "You may consult with the Board of Directors. I have notified them of my intention." (She notified them on July 28, 1908.)

22. Tomlinson, *Twelve Years,* 125.

23. Ibid., 125-126.

24. Clifford P. Smith, "As I Recall It: Reminiscences of Clifford P. Smith, C.S.B.," 25, MBEL.

25. Watson reminiscences, 96, MBEL.

26. Erwin D. Canham, *Commitment to Freedom: The Story of The Christian Science Monitor*

(Boston: Houghton Mifflin, 1958), 54, hereafter referenced as Canham, *Commitment*. The November 21 *Sentinel* would carry this message from Mrs. Eddy: *"Beloved Christian Scientists:*—Accept my thanks for your successful plans for the first issue of *The Christian Science Monitor.* My desire is that every Christian Scientist, and as many others as possible, subscribe for and read our daily newspaper." "Mrs. Eddy's Thanks," *Christian Science Sentinel* 11 (November 21, 1908): 230.

27. Thatcher reminiscences, 7, MBEL.

28. Alexander Dodds, *Autobiography and Story of the Founding of the Monitor,* 74, LMC.

29. *Brooklyn Daily Eagle,* February 6, 1934.

30. William and Ella Rathvon reminiscences, 40-41, 43, MBEL.

31. Tomlinson, *Twelve Years,* 270-271. As an example, Mr. Tomlinson cited a morning when the metaphysical workers were gathered in Mrs. Eddy's study, and she told them she'd been praying about sight, and opening to Luke 18:42, "had realized the true significance of Jesus' words, 'Receive thy sight.'" She asked Tomlinson to pass her the newspaper, and proceeded to read aloud without hesitation—and without glasses—one of the editorials.

32. Ibid.

33. *WKMBE* Vol. II, 531. A few months earlier, she had also told Mr. Rathvon, "When I have demonstrated over old age and the other things that are trying to assail me, then I'm a Christian Scientist; until then I'm only trying to be." William Rathvon reminiscences, 68, MBEL.

34. *WKMBE* Vol. I, 475-476.

35. For a more comprehensive view of this subject, see "'Expressive Silence': Communion and the Communion Season," by Stephen R. Howard, *Longyear Museum Report to Members,* Spring/Summer 2012.

36. Mary Baker G. Eddy, "Notice," *Christian Science Sentinel* 8 (April 28, 1906): 552; later republished in *Miscellany,* 27.

37. "Under the By-law of The Mother Church which has been in force for almost a year, there will be no large gathering of Christian Scientists in Boston this year." "No Large Gathering in Boston This Year," *Christian Science Sentinel* 9 (May 18, 1907): 702.

38. *WKMBE* Vol. II, 486. Mrs. Eddy herself would address this step in several letters published in the Christian Science periodicals (and later edited and reprinted in *Miscellany,* 140-142). In one, which originally appeared in the *Boston Globe,* she assured her followers: "Take courage. God is leading you onward and upward. Relinquishing a material form of Communion advances it spiritually. The material form is a 'Suffer it to be so now' . . . Dropping the Communion of The Mother Church does not prevent its distant members from occasionally attending this church." "Letter from Mrs. Eddy," *Christian Science Sentinel* 10 (June 27, 1908): 850. In another, she wrote, "The Mother Church Communion season was literally a Communion of branch church communicants which might in time lose its sacredness and merge into a meeting for greetings. My beloved brethren may some time learn this and rejoice with me, as they so often have done over a step higher in their passage from sense to Soul." "A Letter and Its Reply," *Christian Science*

Sentinel 10 (June 27, 1908): 850. Tellingly, at the same time that Mrs. Eddy abolished the Communion season, she also added the By-law "Numbering the People" (*Church Manual,* 48), which prohibits the reporting of numbers of church members. As she had earlier stated in *Retrospection* (45), "… Christianity has withstood less the temptation of popularity than of persecution."

39. Dickey, *Memoirs,* 45-47, 118. Adam Dickey also cited the disbanding of the Executive Members of The Mother Church as another instance where this occurred. "She suffered greatly in both these instances, but the moment she arrived at a decision and framed the By-laws which treated with these two conditions, her relief was instantaneous and she arose immediately, healed." Ibid., 46.

40. The report apparently first ran in the *New York Herald,* since it was to the editor of that paper whom Mrs. Eddy issued a rebuttal on May 15, 1908, later reprinted in the *Sentinel.* "Mrs. Eddy's Own Denial That She is Ill," *Christian Science Sentinel* 10 (May 23, 1908): 750. This statement would later be reprinted in *Miscellany,* 275.

41. "Mrs. Eddy Reported to Be Ill Again: Alfred Farlow Denies the Rumors Started by Neighbors," *Times Recorder* [Zanesville, Ohio], May 12, 1908.

42. Edwin J. Park, "Mrs. Eddy Is Not Ill," *Boston Daily Globe,* May 13, 1908. The bulk of Mr. Park's article was reprinted in the *Christian Science Sentinel* 10 (May 16, 1908): 723-724.

43. "She Is Neither Sick nor a Criminal," *Morning News* (Wilmington, Delaware), May 19, 1908.

44. Mary Baker G. Eddy, "To Whom It May Concern," *Christian Science Sentinel* 10 (May 16, 1908): 730. This would later be reprinted in *Miscellany,* 276.

45. Mary Baker G. Eddy, "Nota Bene," *Christian Science Sentinel* 10 (May 16, 1908), 730. This would later be reprinted in *Miscellany,* 139. It concludes: "Like the verdure and evergreen that flourish when trampled upon, the Christian Scientist thrives in adversity; his is a life-lease of hope, home, heaven; his idea is nearing the Way, the Truth, and the Life, when misrepresented, belied, and trodden upon. Justice, honesty, cannot be abjured; their vitality involves Life,—calm, irresistible, eternal."

46. *Christian Science Sentinel* 10 (May 23, 1908): 750.

47. Mrs. Eddy had drafted earlier directives to Archibald McLellan on May 3 and July 3, 1910. Neither was sent. In response to the July 28 letter that she did send, the Christian Science Board of Directors suggested that the Board of Trustees of The Christian Science Publishing Society was the proper avenue for carrying out her orders for founding a newspaper. Consequently, on August 8, she duly sent a letter to the Trustees: "Beloved Students: It is my request that you start a daily newspaper at once, and call it the Christian Science Monitor. Let there be no delay. The Cause demands that it be issued now. You may consult with the Board of Directors, I have notified them of my intention. Lovingly yours, Mary B. G. Eddy." Mary Baker Eddy to the Board of Trustees of The Christian Science Publishing Society, August 8, 1908, L07268, MBEL. For more detail on this sequence of directives, see Canham, *Commitment,* 18-24.

48. Calvin A. Frye diary entry, July 28, 1908, EF81, 210, MBEL.

49. "Science Church in Hotel Plaza," *New York Times,* April 10, 1909. The *Times* also noted that, although there were already half a dozen Christian Science churches in New York City, "the officials feel that they can establish another one among the more influential people in the Fifth Avenue neighborhood if the doctrines of the Church are properly presented to them and are made attractive as are Sunday afternoon entertainments in the large hotels of the city." It would later be reported that Mrs. Gilbert had recently resigned as a Reader at First Church, Brooklyn, and taken up residence at the Plaza to help further her plans. "Plaza Science Service Off," *New York Times,* April 12, 1909.

50. Mary Baker Eddy to the Christian Science Board of Directors, April 10, 1909, L00604, MBEL.

51. "Plaza Services 'Unofficial,'" *New York Times,* April 11, 1909. "Mother Eddy May Frown," *New York Sun,* April 11, 1909.

52. "Plaza Services Called Off," *New York Sun,* April 12, 1909.

53. "Mrs. Gilbert Gives Up," *New York Sun,* April 19, 1909.

54. Calvin A. Frye diary entry, May 21, 1909, EF81, 142, MBEL.

55. "Woman Reports Mrs. Eddy Dead or Mere Dupe: World Prints Appeal of Christian Scientist to Members of Church," *Denver Post,* June 6, 1909.

56. "Mrs. Eddy on View," *Washington Post,* June 8, 1909.

57. "Exposed," *Los Angeles Times,* June 7, 1909; "X-Science Refused $5,000 to Accuser," *New York Times,* June 7, 1909. Clifford Smith, who was then First Reader of The Mother Church and at the time charged with Church discipline, was sent to see Mrs. Gilbert.

58. Calvin A. Frye diary entry, June 7, 1909, EF81, 159, MBEL.

59. "Mrs. Eddy Sees Reporters Who Visit Her Home Today," *The Christian Science Monitor,* June 7, 1909.

60. "Mrs. Eddy Shown in Carriage," *Boston Post,* June 8, 1909; *Washington Post,* June 8, 1909.

61. The photo would be featured above the fold on the front page, accompanying a lengthy article. "Mrs. Eddy, in Her Carriage, Is Shown to Newspaper Men," *Boston Traveler,* June 7, 1909.

62. Her statement would appear in the *Christian Science Sentinel* 11 (June 12, 1909): 810, and be widely circulated in the press. It would also be reprinted in *Miscellany*, 143. She ended it with a quote from the Bible: "And we know that all things work together for good to them that love God, to them who are the called according to His purpose. . . . What shall we then say to these things? If God be for us, who can be against us?" Romans 8:28, 31.

63. "Attacks on Christian Science," *Madera Mercury,* June 26, 1909, quoting the *San Francisco Examiner.* Celebrated journalist Arthur Brisbane, who, like the *Globe's* Edwin Park, had interviewed Mrs. Eddy at Pleasant View during the Next Friends suit, would also come to Mrs. Eddy's defense, vouching for her handwritten signature in a recent communication and championing her in a ringing editorial: "It is surprising and rather shameful that any newspaper could be persuaded thus to encourage the hounding of a woman who has brought happiness into the lives of hundreds of thousands of human beings, who has

certainly harmed nobody, and who has the devoted affection of an enormous following," Brisbane wrote in part. "She is entitled to, and she has, the respect and admiration of millions of human beings who, like this writer, do not share the belief in Christian Science, yet render the tribute of profound respect to the leader of that belief. . . . Christian Scientists may rest assured that they have in their leader an actual, living person, energetic, determined, and marvelous in her apparent defiance of great age." "A Truly Wonderful Woman Is Mrs. Mary Baker Eddy," *Boston American,* June 11, 1909.

64. *Washington Post,* June 8, 1909; "Woman Asks $5,000," *Inter Ocean* [Chicago], June 7, 1909. Perhaps in an attempt to fulfill her Holmesian boast, Della Gilbert hired detectives to surveil Clifford Smith and his family. Clifford Smith reminiscences, 35, MBEL. In July, Della was spotted by Calvin Frye outside the gate at 400 Beacon Street as Mrs. Eddy drove off on her carriage ride. Calvin A. Frye diary entry, July 14, 1909, EF81, 196, MBEL.

65. Della Gilbert would resurface briefly in October 1909, when it was reported that she had leased the ballroom of the Hotel Gotham and would again attempt to hold services — this time for "The New Church," of which she pronounced herself leader. She drew only a small crowd the first Sunday, however, and faded entirely from the news thereafter. "Mrs. Gilbert Goes Ahead Now," *New York Times,* October 3, 1909; "Slow to 'Purge' X-Science," *New York Sun,* October 11, 1909.

66. Boston missed out on the title of hottest spot in the United States that day by a single degree. (The honor went to Abilene, Texas.) "Heat Record for Year Is Smashed with 95 Degrees," *Boston Post,* July 31, 1909.

67. In his account of a visit with Mrs. Eddy the previous year, reporter Edwin Park noted that the reservoir circuit was one of Mrs. Eddy's favorite drives. *Boston Daily Globe,* May 13, 1908.

68. William Curtis Coffman, "Memoirs of a Christian Scientist," 31, MBEL.

69. Tomlinson reminiscences, 119, MBEL. See also Calvin A. Frye diary entry for July 30, 1909, EF81, 212, MBEL.

70. George Shaw Cook to the Christian Science Board of Directors, November 10, 1927, George Shaw Cook Subject File, MBEL. A Christian Science practitioner (and later teacher) from Chicago, Mr. Cook was serving as Committee on Publication for Illinois at the time of this visit. He would also serve on the Committee on Business at one point, helping find staff for Mrs. Eddy's household.

71. "Letters to Our Leader," *Christian Science Sentinel* 11 (August 7, 1909): 971.

72. Mary Baker Eddy to Augusta E. Stetson, October 26, 1897, V01549, MBEL.

73. Grace Duffie Boylan, "Saw 'Divine Plan' As Child," *Chicago Daily Journal,* July 30, 1914.

74. Augusta attended the local high school as well as nearby Lincoln Academy. She was 14 when she joined the Methodist church.

75. Frederick J. Stetson joined the Union Army at age 15, enlisting in Maine's Fourth Regiment on June 15, 1861. (His father, Abner, had been a drummer boy in the War of 1812, which may have inspired Frederick's own underage enlistment.) U.S. Civil War Soldier Records and Profiles, 1861-1865.

76. Seafaring was the Stetson family business. Abner Stetson was a well-known shipbuilder, and Frederick was one of five sons who became ships' captains. Frederick piloted one of his father's ships, the *J. H. Stetson* (named for Frederick's older brother) for Baring Bros. of London, before starting his own firm based in Havre, France. *Stetson Kindred of America* (Medford, Mass.: Press of J. C. Miller, Jr., 1907); "Mrs. Stetson Explains," *Lincoln Journal Star,* March 4, 1901.

77. Captured just over a month later during the first battle of Bull Run, Frederick spent about a year in Andersonville Prison (he may have been in Libby Prison as well) before he was released, returning home "almost a total wreck." *Stetson Kindred of America.* U.S. National Archives Administration, compiled Military Service File for Frederick J. Stetson. He later applied for a pension as an invalid. U.S. Civil War Pension Index, 1861-1934; *Lincoln Journal Star,* March 4, 1901.

78. Just three years later she would display her skills at the Point of Pines picnic, a festive occasion held July 16, 1885, on the ninth anniversary of the founding of the Christian Scientist Association. "Mrs. Stetson added largely to the interest of the occasion by two recitations," reported the *Boston Traveler,* quoted in *The Christian Science Journal* 3 (August 1885): 96.

79. Augusta E. Stetson, *Reminiscences, Sermons, and Correspondence* (New York: G. P. Putnam's Sons, 1917), 1.

80. "Letters and Cases of Healing," *The Christian Science Journal* 3 (July 1885): 79.

81. Mary Baker Eddy to Augusta E. Stetson, December 10, 1893, H00026, MBEL.

82. Along with other students, Augusta substituted for Mrs. Eddy on occasion at services in Boston, including at Chickering Hall, before filling a pulpit of her own at First Church of Christ, Scientist, New York.

83. Virgil O. Strickler diary entry, January 3, 1909, Virgil O. Strickler Subject File, Folder 1, MBEL. Mrs. Stetson's quarrelsome nature apparently extended to fisticuffs, as attested by a 1905 altercation revealed in a later lawsuit: "Mrs. Stetson's Eye Is Blackened in a Fight with Business Friend," *Boston American,* November 9, 1909; "Says Man Hit Mrs. Stetson," *Boston Post,* November 9, 1909.

84. Mary Baker Eddy to Laura Lathrop/John Carroll Lathrop, April 8, 1899, L02446, MBEL. A pair of letters written two years earlier helps illustrate both Mrs. Eddy's astute assessment of Mrs. Stetson and her deep desire to keep her on track. "Can you fail to see the snake in the grass!" Mrs. Eddy bluntly asked Laura Lathrop, clearly pointing to Augusta. Mary Baker Eddy to Laura Lathrop, December 10, 1897, L04378, MBEL. On the very same day, she penned a stern letter of rebuke to Augusta: "No person on earth will ever again bear from you what I have borne from your manipulation of my students," ending with the plea, "I beg that you open your eyes and do only to others as you would be done then you will be safe God will bless you and Mother will love you and help you on in the end." Mary Baker Eddy to Augusta E. Stetson, December 10, 1897, V01554, MBEL.

85. Mary Baker Eddy to Ruth B. Ewing, January 8, 1895, L08510, MBEL.

86. Augusta arrived in November, leaving her husband in the care of her parents. To her credit,

she visited as often as she could and eventually purchased a spacious home for them in Somerville, Massachusetts. After her father passed on in 1894, she eventually persuaded her mother and husband to move to New York to live with her. *Lincoln Journal Star,* March 4, 1901. As for the initial move to New York, Mrs. Eddy had a different view of how events transpired. In a reply to Augusta that she drafted but never sent, Mrs. Eddy wrote, "Your letter astounds me with its contortions of history.... I thought if you were removed from Boston you would do better and you did. But you treated my students in New York badly even those that were doing well." Mary Baker Eddy/Calvin A. Frye to Augusta E. Stetson, December 13, 1895, L09587, MBEL.

87. Just a month after Augusta's arrival, for instance, Mrs. Eddy wrote, "I am shocked by what I hear from New York! It does not come from a student of mine but from good authority that you are telling that I sent you to N. York to watch my <u>students</u> there! I cannot credit it that ever you said a thing so far from the facts." Mary Baker Eddy to Augusta E. Stetson, December 27, 1886, V00985, MBEL. And in a later letter she wrote, "You resent having a student meddle with your student but do not hesitate to do this yourself with even mine!" Mary Baker Eddy to Augusta E. Stetson, April 2, 1894, V01300, MBEL.

88. Mary Baker Eddy to Augusta E. Stetson, January 19, 1888, V01037, MBEL.

89. Mrs. Stetson's first pulpit was a makeshift affair fashioned from a fabric-covered crate in a humble hall above a Caswell & Massey drugstore. "Christian Science in New York," *Broadway Magazine,* May 1907.

90. In her letter to the Board notifying them of her decision, Mrs. Eddy wrote, "The Bible and 'Science and Health with Key to the Scriptures' shall henceforth be the Pastor of The Mother Church. This will tend to spiritualize thought. Personal preaching has more or less of human views grafted into it. Whereas the pure Word contains only the living health giving Truth." Mary Baker Eddy to the Christian Science Board of Directors, December 19, 1894, L02748. Mrs. Eddy notified her Church of the broader change in a *Journal* article that began, "Humbly, and as I believe, Divinely directed, I hereby ordain, that the Bible, and Science and Health with Key to the Scriptures, shall hereafter be the only pastor of the Church of Christ, Scientist, throughout our land, and in other lands." Mary Baker Eddy, "Church and School," *The Christian Science Journal* 13 (April 1895): 1.

91. Mary Baker Eddy to Laura Lathrop, July 7, 1897, L04373, MBEL.

92. Relinquishing the readership apparently required some nudging from Mrs. Eddy. "God loveth a cheerful giver," she reminded Augusta. "Without the cross there is no crown." Mrs. Eddy asked her to resign promptly her post "so as not to be behind those who have acted so nobly so unselfishly in obeying God in this direction...." Mary Baker Eddy to Augusta E. Stetson, July 24, 1902, V00311, MBEL. Augusta maintained her position as a trustee of the church and continued drawing a salary of $5,000 a year as "reader emeritus." "Faith in Mrs. Stetson," *New York Sun,* November 25, 1909. $5,000 is worth approximately $142,000 in 2018 dollars.

93. For instance, in a stern letter written in the summer of 1891, Mrs. Eddy noted that Augusta was "still looking up my students and trying to control them," against Mrs. Eddy's explicit orders not to. "I have begged of you to leave my students to me and for you to take care of

your own. To give no direction whatever to the course my students take. You have promised you would not and in a week I would find you breaking this promise...." Mary Baker Eddy to Augusta E. Stetson, August 29, 1891, L02564, MBEL. It also came to light that, in the wake of Flavia Knapp's passing, Augusta was trying to gain control of her students, one of whom was Irving Tomlinson. Mrs. Eddy would write him, "Beware! never come under her influence. She is as far from your former teacher as the sky from dust." Mary Baker Eddy to Irving C. Tomlinson, January 9, 1898, L03641, MBEL, quoted in Tomlinson, *Twelve Years,* 276, and Tomlinson reminiscences, 486, MBEL. Later that year, she would again write, "Now dear I warn you again beware of wolves clad in sheep skins or rather a wolf that is beginning to work outside of the skin and snap her teeth at her benefactor." Mary Baker Eddy to Irving C. Tomlinson, October 1, 1898, L03644, MBEL, quoted in Tomlinson, *Twelve Years,* 277, and Tomlinson reminiscences, 486, MBEL.

94. Mary Baker Eddy to Augusta E. Stetson/Carol Norton, December 28, 1893, V01279, MBEL.

95. This came after an embarrassing public imbroglio with Second Church, headed by Laura Lathrop, whom Augusta saw as her chief rival. Laura heeded Mrs. Eddy's pleas for unity, dutifully remaining at First Church before finally gaining permission to leave and start another branch church. Eventually, Second Church of Christ, Scientist, New York purchased a lot at 68th and Central Park West for their edifice. Mrs. Stetson regarded this as an encroachment on her turf and tried to get the owner of the lot to break his contract and sell instead to her. Failing that, she purchased a lot of her own ridiculously close by. The *New York Times,* with a headline that dubbed the kerfuffle a "Merry War of Churches," noted that "the novel spectacle of two churches of the same denomination within two blocks of each other may yet be witnessed." "Merry War of Churches," *New York Times,* June 24, 1898. Mrs. Eddy had sterner words. "Another fight is calling on me for umpire," she wrote to Judge Septimus Hanna, detailing Augusta's latest maneuverings. "Oh how disgusting this appears in so large a city and especially between Christian Scientists." Mary Baker Eddy to Septimus J. Hanna, June 19, 1898, L05225, MBEL.

96. Approximately $38 million in 2018 dollars. The famous Beaux-Arts architectural firm Carrère and Hastings, who would also be responsible for the New York Public Library, was hired to design the magnificent edifice.

97. "A New Million-Dollar Church," *National Magazine,* March 1904, 707-709.

98. "Unique and Costly," *Christian Science Sentinel* 6 (December 12, 1903): 227; reprinted with edits in *Miscellany,* 194. Four services were required to accommodate the throngs that gathered for the elaborate dedication exercises on November 29, 1903, which kicked off with an anthem written especially for the occasion and concluded with the Hallelujah Chorus. Estimates put the attendees at 4,000, with another 1,000 turned away for lack of room. *Broadway Magazine,* May 1907, reprinted as "History of the New York Organizations" in the *Christian Science Sentinel* 9 (May 4, 1907): 655-657.

99. "Mrs. Stetson Is Expelled By Mrs. Eddy," *Boston Post,* October 2, 1909.

100. "Exiled, They Say, by Mrs. Stetson," *New York Times,* October 18, 1909. *Poems: Written on the Journey from Sense to Soul,* and first published in 1901, contains 29 poems by Augusta

ranging in subject matter from the biblical to voyages she took across the sea in her early twenties.

101. *New York Times,* October 18, 1909.

102. Virgil O. Strickler diary entry, July 2, 1909, Virgil O. Strickler Subject File, Folder 1, MBEL.

103. *Broadway Magazine,* May 1907. For those who weren't so fashionable, a coatroom containing donated furs and other fine garments was available so those of humbler circumstances might dress the part. As for the marble and brick mansion that Mrs. Stetson built next door, one report described it as "one of the most beautiful and wonderful houses in New York." Ibid.

104. "Built from Plans 'Divinely Revealed,'" *New York Times,* November 30, 1903. There were darker things as well, including reports from disaffected members of a "secret service" of tattletales who ferried information about the congregation back to Augusta. These kinds of tactics struck fear in those who dared to disapprove or disagree. "The Mafia strikes with steel," said one, ominously foreshadowing what would later come to light about Mrs. Stetson's methods. "Here you are confronted by a sort of mental Mafia and mental assassination." "Controversy Among Christian Scientists," *New York Times,* November 29, 1903. Another source would later report that the ostracism began as soon as Mrs. Stetson labeled someone disloyal. "It went so far that we soon found ourselves meeting our old friends in First Church on the streets or in the street cars and having them cut us dead." "Stetson Teachers Split on Doctrine," *New York Times,* November 9, 1909.

105. Tomlinson reminiscences, 488, MBEL.

106. Peel, *Authority,* 334.

107. Tomlinson reminiscences, 488-489, MBEL.

108. For instance, a member of the Christian Science Board of Directors told Virgil Strickler in July 1909 that the "outside world" expected "that as soon as Mrs. Eddy passed out some very strong personality would arise and take the leadership," which was contrary to their views (and also Mrs. Eddy's) that the future of the Church rested not on personal leadership but on Principle. He warned that Christian Science was confronted with "the same dangers that confronted the Christian religion in the time of Constantine and unless it could be saved from everything like personal leadership it would be lost to humanity for a long period just as Christianity had been for a long time. . . ." Virgil O. Strickler diary entry, July 4, 1909, Virgil O. Strickler Subject File, Folder 1, MBEL. In *Rolling Away* (371-379), Gottschalk points out that although Augusta Stetson always publicly denied any aspirations to succeed Mrs. Eddy as leader, "she had a large following and thus an unparalleled power base in the largest field in the movement outside Boston, and her appetite for power was well known." See also Peel, *Authority,* 330-345.

109. "Consistency," *Christian Science Sentinel* 11 (December 5, 1908): 270; "One Mother Church in Christian Science," *Christian Science Sentinel* 11 (December 5, 1908): 270. See also *WKMBE* Vol. II, 494; Peel, *Authority,* 334-335; and Gottschalk, *Rolling Away,* 368.

110. Mary Baker Eddy to Augusta E. Stetson, December 7, 1908, H00126, MBEL; Mary Baker Eddy to Augusta E. Stetson, December 9, 1908, H00127, MBEL.

111. Mary Baker Eddy to Adolph H. Stevenson, December 9, 1908, L08971, MBEL. Stetson, *Reminiscences, Sermons, and Correspondence,* 16-18. Elizabeth Kelly recalled that coachman Adolph Stevenson "overheard the entire conversation and, when he returned, he tried to tell me what was said." Mrs. Kelly refused to let him, admonishing, "What do you suppose Mrs. Eddy would think if she knew she had someone here who would do such a thing?" Kelly reminiscences, 11-12, MBEL. Adolph Stevenson was dismissed from Mrs. Eddy's service on December 18, 1908 and replaced by Frank Bowman.

112. Tomlinson reminiscences, 488, MBEL.

113. Mary Baker Eddy, "The Way of Wisdom," *Christian Science Sentinel* 11 (January 16, 1909): 390. The article would be reprinted in *The Christian Science Journal* 26 (February 1909): 696-697, and in *Miscellany,* 356-357. Mrs. Eddy is referencing Matthew 23:5. ("But all their works they do for to be seen of men: they make broad their phylacteries, and enlarge the borders of their garments.")

114. Virgil O. Strickler diary entry, July 14, 1909, Virgil O. Strickler Subject File, Folder 1, MBEL. See also Peel, *Authority,* 332. Mrs. Stetson also continued to castigate those whom she deemed disloyal and rail against her perceived enemies to the extent of raining "curses and maledictions" down upon them under the guise of metaphysics. William Rathvon reminiscences, 242, MBEL. Strickler's diary also goes into great detail on this issue.

115. The value of the gold totaled $260, or nearly $7,500 in 2018 dollars. The gift from her students was presented to Mrs. Stetson on the boardroom table in gold pieces laid out in the shape of a crown. Virgil O. Strickler diary entry, July 10, 1909, Virgil O. Strickler Subject File, Folder 1, MBEL. Contemporaneous sources note that Mrs. Stetson's students were frequently asked to pray for her affluence, to "'treat' for gold," and to give her money. "Always when they contributed to Mrs. Stetson it was in gold coin." *New York Times,* November 9, 1909. Excerpts from the composite letter to Mrs. Eddy that accompanied the gift of gold pieces would be published and condemned in a blunt editorial entitled, "'None Good But One,'" by Archibald McLellan, *Christian Science Sentinel* 11 (July 31, 1909): 950.

116. Mary Baker Eddy, "A Letter by Mrs. Eddy," *Christian Science Sentinel* 11 (July 17, 1909): 910. In her reply, Mrs. Eddy thanked Mrs. Stetson for the money, told her that she intended to donate it to a "charitable purpose," and warned, "Beloved! you need to watch and pray that the enemy of good cannot separate you from your Leader and best earthly friend." History would have been vastly different had Augusta heeded the warning.

117. Mary Baker Eddy to the Christian Science Board of Directors, July 22, 1909, L00613, MBEL. Mrs. Eddy was wise to keep out of the line of fire. On several occasions she would be tempted to write letters to Mrs. Stetson, including in October, when William Rathvon reported: "[Adam Dickey] read the *New York Herald* article about Mrs. Stetson's misbehavior to our Leader and she became quite stirred about it. She dictated several letters and then finally decided to keep out of it entirely. This perhaps is best for it will relieve her of much that might otherwise be aimed at her. She will let the Directors carry it through." William Rathvon reminiscences, 244-245, MBEL. For their part, the Directors endeavored to protect Mrs. Eddy, as one member told Virgil Strickler in July

Chapter 12: The Crowning Years

1909, explaining that it was "the chief business of everyone connected with the Mother Church to . . . shield her as much as it was possible; that in addition to having to meet the world's hatred and opposition to Truth she also had to meet the world's belief of old age and that wherever it was possible to save her from taking any action that would give her additional things to meet or wherever it was possible for the action to be taken in the name of someone besides herself it was done. . . ." Virgil O. Strickler diary entry, July 24, 1909, Virgil O. Strickler Subject File, Folder 1, MBEL.

118. Mary Baker Eddy to Augusta E. Stetson, July 23, 1909, H00131, MBEL.

119. Mary Baker Eddy to the Christian Science Board of Directors, July 24, 1909, L00614, MBEL.

120. The final sentence in Section 13 of Article XI reads: "Each church shall separately and independently discipline its own members,—if this sad necessity occurs." *Church Manual,* 55.

121. "A New By-Law," *Christian Science Sentinel* 11 (July 31, 1909): 950. "Mrs. Eddy Orders Mrs. Stetson Out," *Boston Post,* August 6, 1909; "Not Aimed at Mrs. Stetson," *New York Sun,* August 7, 1909.

122. Exercising the Matthew code (Matthew 18:15-17; see also *Church Manual,* 50-51) in his capacity as First Reader at First Church of Christ, Scientist, New York, Mr. Strickler also admonished Mrs. Stetson for her behavior. His diary offers hair-raising details of Augusta's daily sessions with her inner circle. On February 3, 1909, for instance, he recorded the most "violent and vitriolic tornado of maledictory prayer from Mrs. Stetson that we have ever had," as she stated "I strike to kill" and worse. These pseudo-metaphysical tirades occurred nearly every day that year as Augusta lashed out at her perceived enemies, which included just about everyone else in the New York and Boston fields. She also taught her own peculiar views about human generation (she disapproved of it, and of marriage in general); positioned herself as infallible; as the one through whom salvation was to come to the whole human race; as the only witness; as the teacher of the whole world; and more. It would also come to light that Mrs. Stetson and her inner circle had perjured themselves on at least one occasion by testifying in the "fourth dimension of Spirit," as Augusta styled it—speaking in the absolute under oath. Virgil O. Strickler diary, Virgil O. Strickler Subject File, Folders 1-2, MBEL. See also "Tell of a Stetson Fourth Dimension," *New York Times,* November 7, 1909.

123. The Christian Science Board of Directors to Mary Baker Eddy, September 8, 1909, IC 002dP2.03.026, MBEL. The letter describes a branch church "in turmoil," rife with "verified evidence of malpractice, perjury, and continued efforts toward mental assassination." The Directors painted a picture of a woman so "enraged" by the actions against her by the Board and others that her "malice knows no bounds." She was working day and night, along with a large majority of her inner circle under her direction, "for the destruction of those who she feels are standing in the way of her progress." They detailed instances in which Augusta had alluded to herself as the Christ and terrorized her fellow church members with "threats and curses." The accusations made it to the press as well. "We practitioners were taught by Mrs. Stetson that she was Christ, truth, and we were her disciples," Henry Ward Beecher's granddaughter Margaret Beecher White told one

newspaper. She described a "Paschal feast" at Augusta's home before the June communion service, in which Augusta had them stand in a circle while she passed around fish, bread, and lemonade colored with raspberry juice. "Mrs. Stetson Here to Fight Expulsion," *Boston Post,* November 15, 1909.

124. Mary Baker Eddy to the Christian Science Board of Directors, September 9, 1909, L00622, MBEL.

125. As William Rathvon colorfully described it on September 24: "The Directors are still in the midst of examinations with the New York bunch, having a fresh lot on the grill today." William Rathvon reminiscences, 242-243, MBEL.

126. The evenings of September 25 (the day the Board reached its decision), and September 28 were particularly difficult for Mrs. Eddy, William Rathvon wrote in his diary, noting, "We are holding steadfastly to 'no reversal' and I believe will win out." He also mentioned that rumblings of a renewal of activity by the attorneys for the 1907 Next Friends suit may have added to Mrs. Eddy's distress. Ibid., 232.

127. "The action caused a tremendous surprise here," the *Boston Post* reported from Manhattan, "for Mrs. Stetson has been all powerful in the New York church and her authority nearly absolute." "Mrs. Stetson Is Expelled by Mrs. Eddy," *Boston Post,* October 2, 1909.

128. As Robert Peel put it, "they were powerful moves toward safeguarding the structure of her church against future struggles for personal control, as well as toward protecting her teachings from dismemberment by personal interpretation." Peel, *Authority,* 344.

129. *Church Manual,* Article XXIII, Sect. 12, 74; Article XXVI, Sect. 2, 83; Sect. 6, 84; and Sect. 7, 84-85, respectively. "A New By-Law," *Christian Science Sentinel* 12 (October 9, 1909): 110; "Amended By-laws," *Christian Science Sentinel* 12 (October 16, 1909): 130.

130. Mary Baker Eddy, "Take Notice," *Christian Science Sentinel* 12 (October 16, 1909): 130. This would later be edited slighty and republished in *Miscellany,* 358-359.

131. "First Church Now Defies Mrs. Eddy," *New York Times,* November 5, 1909. Emotions ran so high that a police guard was posted in the lobby and outside.

132. "Mrs. Stetson Gets Full Exoneration," *Boston Post,* November 5, 1909.

133. *New York Times,* November 5, 1909.

134. *Boston Post,* November 5, 1909.

135. "Second Admonition for Mrs. Stetson," *New York Times,* November 6, 1909. Although he declined to speculate on what would happen next, Boston spokesman Alfred Farlow told the *Times,* "One of the important duties of the Directors of the Mother Church is to maintain the purity of Christian Science and prevent the promulgation of an adulteration in the name of Christian Science. I desire to say parenthetically that the peculiar teachings and practices described in the public press in connection with this New York situation are entirely contrary to the teachings of Christian Science."

136. "A Letter from Mrs. Eddy;" "Correspondence Between a Committee of Inquiry and the Directors," *Christian Science Sentinel* 12 (October 16, 1909): 130, 170. The trustees insisted that the Board had overstepped their authority with regard to branch church affairs; the Board defended its jurisdiction, replying "The relation between The Mother Church and

its branches necessarily gives to this Board such supervision over the branches as may be necessary to preserve the purity and integrity of the Christian religion which it represents." "Further Correspondence Between a Committee of Inquiry and the Board of Directors," *Christian Science Sentinel* 12 (November 6, 1909): 190; "To Whom It May Concern," *Christian Science Sentinel* 12 (November 13, 1909): 210. In the latter issue, Mrs. Eddy also reprinted an article from the July 1895 *Journal* that she had written on malpractice, later republished in *Miscellany,* 363-364.

137. Ella Rathvon reminiscences, November 6, 1909, MBEL. The quotation marks around the last phrase seem to indicate that these were Mrs. Eddy's words.

138. Augusta Stetson was accompanied by Hayne Davis, her student and legal counsel and one of the practitioners in her inner circle.

139. At issue for the New York branch church were two points: (1) whether or not to accept Mrs. Stetson's offer that she made in the wake of her first admonishment—to resign her office as a trustee and relinquish her salary as "reader emeritus"—and (2) whether or not to remove Virgil Strickler as First Reader.

140. "Mrs. Stetson Here to Fight Expulsion," *Boston Post,* November 15, 1909. "Mrs. Stetson Faces The Mother Church," *New York Times,* November 15, 1909.

141. "Civil War in the Church," *New York Sun,* November 14, 1909.

142. Willard S. Mattox, "Letters to Our Leader," *Christian Science Sentinel* 12 (December 4, 1909): 272. In a postscript worthy of an espionage novel, two copies of the letter were delivered, one to the trustees at First Church, New York, and the other, unbeknownst to them, to First Reader Virgil Strickler—just in case the trustees refused to read their copy aloud to the membership. Mr. Strickler was instructed to wear a white carnation and meet a large red-haired man with a red mustache and a matching white carnation for the handoff at the train station. Mary Baker Eddy to Virgil O. Strickler, November 13, 1909, L11124, MBEL.

143. Richard P. Verrall, "Letters to Our Leader," *Christian Science Sentinel* 12 (December 4, 1909): 271. The members of First Church, New York, would also pass a resolution noting that Mrs. Eddy's "words of advice [were] so potent that not only was a crisis in the history of this church amicably settled, but dissensions in the church were thereby healed. . . ." "Letters to Our Leader," *Christian Science Sentinel* 12 (November 27, 1909): 252.

144. Peel, *Authority,* 342.

145. "Name Ordered Off the Rolls," *Boston Daily Globe,* November 19, 1909. A New York acquaintance noted, not without a touch of *schadenfreude,* "Writing declarations of unswerving fidelity and undying zeal in the cause of Christian Science when she gets in a tight place is one of the best things Mrs. Stetson does. She has done it before, and then continued her offences against the rules and laws of the church." "Another Day Before Board," *Boston Daily Globe,* November 18, 1909.

146. "Mrs. Eddy's Church Ousts Mrs. Stetson," *New York Times,* November 19, 1909. See also "Stetson Faction Stunned," *Boston Post,* November 19, 1909. During this time, "Mrs. Eddy called her students to her room and said 'Take no side neither for nor against Augusta

E. Stetson leave it all in the hands of God!'" Calvin A. Frye diary entry, November 17, 1909, EF053, 61, MBEL.

147. Tomlinson reminiscences, 490, MBEL. Over the coming weeks, letters flowed in from Christian Scientists in New York and far corners of the field, expressing solidarity with the Board. First Church, New York soon voted to accept Mrs. Stetson's resignation as a trustee and rescind her salary. By June 1910, Virgil Strickler would tell some members of Mrs. Eddy's household, "the regenerated First Church is coming along nicely." William Rathvon reminiscences, June 21, 1910, 246, MBEL. Augusta herself withdrew into seclusion for a time, then emerged and continued teaching and practicing her version of Christian Science, albeit without the approval of The Mother Church, and with a much smaller following.

148. *Boston Daily Globe,* May 13, 1908.

149. "Mrs. Eddy's Statements," *Christian Science Sentinel* 11 (June 12, 1909): 810. This would be reprinted in *Miscellany,* 143.

150. Dickey, *Memoirs,* 116-117. *WKMBE* Vol. II, 444-445.

151. Tomlinson, *Twelve Years,* 268.

152. Mrs. Eddy would approve the final revision of the *Church Manual* (89th edition) in late November 1910, just weeks before her passing.

153. Mary Baker Eddy to Allison V. Stewart, March 31, 1910, L03271, MBEL. Mrs. Eddy would appoint Adam Dickey to oversee the committee of translators.

154. *Boston Daily Globe,* May 13, 1908.

155. Ibid.

156. "Roosevelt and Mrs. Eddy Agree," *Detroit Free Press,* May 7, 1908. Mrs. Knott, a longtime resident of Detroit who helped establish Christian Science in that city, was interviewed while she was there visiting her son Frank.

157. "Letters to Our Leader," *Christian Science Sentinel* 12 (May 14, 1910): 731.

158. *WKMBE* Vol. II, 483.

159. "War," *Christian Science Sentinel* 10 (April 11, 1908): 630. This statement would be reprinted in *The Christian Science Journal* 26 (May 1908): 65, and in *Miscellany,* 286. Interestingly, when, as Associate Editor of the Christian Science periodicals, Annie Knott was asked by the *Detroit Free Press* to share her views on Mrs. Eddy's statement, she told them that she herself belonged to a peace society in Boston, and acknowledged that many in the Christian Science church "were inclined to oppose the Rooseveltian pet projects for peace through the extension of the American navy." But, she added, "since Mrs. Eddy has given us her views, we have gladly conformed with her ideas. She is so far-sighted, and has such clear, penetrating insight, that we are perfectly willing to accept her judgment in the matter." *Detroit Free Press,* May 7, 1908.

160. Theodore Roosevelt to Hayne Davis, April 20, 1908, L09772, MBEL. Mr. Davis had sent a copy of Mrs. Eddy's statement to President Roosevelt. Peel, *Authority,* 496n55.

161. "Letters to Our Leader," *Christian Science Sentinel* 12 (May 7, 1910): 711; "Letters to Our

Leader," *Christian Science Sentinel* 12 (May 14, 1910): 731.

162. Mary Baker Eddy/M. Adelaide Still, September 1910, A10352, MBEL.

163. Mary Baker Eddy/Adam H. Dickey, September 1910, A10267, MBEL.

164. Orcutt, *Mary Baker Eddy and Her Books*, 126.

165. Ibid., 128.

166. These words appear in Adam Dickey's foreword to *Poems*, dated September 10, 1910.

167. Set to music, "Laus Deo!" was played on the Church's chimes and sung by the congregation at the dedication services in January 1895. Ethel Munro Goss, "Laus Deo, it is done," *Christian Science Sentinel* 37 (May 18, 1935): 745. Published September 12, 1866 in the *Lynn Reporter*, "I'm Sitting Alone" was written shortly after Mrs. Eddy's second husband, Daniel Patterson, deserted her.

168. Tomlinson, *Twelve Years* 130.

169. William Rathvon reminiscences, 118-119, MBEL. For an interesting account of how Mrs. Eddy came to write the poem "Signs of the Heart," see *WKMBE* Vol. I, 332-333.

170. *WKMBE* Vol. II, 438.

171. This final change was made in 1909.

172. Orcutt, *Mary Baker Eddy and Her Books,* 127.

173. "Our Leader's Poems," *Christian Science Sentinel* 13 (November 5, 1910): 190.

174. Mary Baker Eddy/M. Adelaide Still, October 1910, A10355, MBEL.

175. "Principle and Practice," *Christian Science Sentinel* 20 (September 1, 1917): 10.

176. Mary Baker Eddy, "Instruction by Mrs. Eddy," *Christian Science Sentinel* 13 (September 3, 1910): 10.

177. Blanche Hersey Hogue, "The Church Manual," *Christian Science Sentinel* 13 (September 10, 1910): 23.

178. Mary Baker Eddy, "Take Notice," *Christian Science Sentinel* 13 (September 17, 1910): 50; reprinted in *The Christian Science Journal* 28 (October 1910): 485, and later in *Miscellany*, 237.

179. Mary Baker Eddy, "Take Notice," *Christian Science Sentinel* 13 (October 1, 1910): 90; reprinted in the October 8 and 15 issues of the *Sentinel* (pages 110 and 130), as well as *The Christian Science Journal* 28 (November 1910): 555, and *Miscellany*, 242.

180. Irving C. Tomlinson to Jerry DeWitt, October 6, 1943, LMC.

181. *Brooklyn Daily Eagle,* February 6, 1934.

182. Scott reminiscences, 14, MBEL.

183. *Proceedings in Equity*, 491. Adam Dickey's testimony paints a vivid, if brief, portrait of Mary Baker Eddy, whom he describes as having "a wonderfully intelligent face," as being "quick and active in her mental perception and recognition of what was going on about her," and possessing "a wonderful capacity for reading character and understanding the thought of those with whom she came in contact...."

184. William R. Rathvon, "Our Leader," 1914, 11-13, LMC.

185. "Annual Meeting of The Mother Church," *Christian Science Sentinel* 23 (June 18, 1921): 784-785.

186. Mrs. Eddy told the Committees on Publication, "Tell them they cannot know me in my personality, but in my books and my writings and in my love for them and all mankind." George Shaw Cook to the Christian Science Board of Directors, November 10, 1927, George Shaw Cook Subject File, MBEL. See pages 340-341 for a full account of this 1909 visit.

187. *Science and Health*, xii. Imparting correct teaching was paramount to Mrs. Eddy, as evidenced by her use of the phrase "Christian Science as taught by me," which appears 1) in the 1898 Deed of Trust establishing The Christian Science Publishing Society, 2) in the 1907 Deed of Trust transferring the management of her estate to a trusted trio: her lawyer cousin Henry Baker; chairman of the Christian Science Board of Directors Archibald McLellan; and banker Josiah Fernald; and 3) in her Last Will and Testament. Deed of Trust Organizing The Christian Science Publishing Society, given by Mary Baker Eddy January 25, 1898, reprinted June 15, 2004, MBEL; Meehan, *Late Suit in Equity*, 36-39; Mary Baker G. Eddy, "Last Will and Testament," MBEL. In 1), Mrs. Eddy included a clause requiring that the trustees be "loyal, faithful, and consistent believers and advocates of the principles of Christian Science as taught by me in my book, 'Science and Health with Key to the Scriptures'"; in 2), one of the provisions for payments from the income of her 1907 trust includes "such sums as I may personally desire to use for the advancement of the cause and doctrines of Christian Science as taught by me"; and in 3), her Will directs that after fulfilling specific bequests and requirements, the "rest, residue, and remainder" of her estate be bequeathed to The Mother Church, The First Church of Christ, Scientist, in Boston, "for the purpose of more effectually promoting and extending the religion of Christian Science as taught by me." In a deposition of June 24, 1919, taken in California and presented before the Massachusetts Supreme Court on July 24-25, 1919, Judge Septimus Hanna, former editor of the Christian Science periodicals, First Reader of The Mother Church, and member of the Board of Lectureship, testified about Mrs. Eddy's reasons for the Deed of Trust establishing The Christian Science Publishing Society. During a conversation he had with her a few days before she signed the deed, she told him "that she wished especially in establishing the new trust to protect and preserve the literature of the movement in its purity and from aggressive attempts by enemies of the movement to adulterate the literature by injecting into it thoughts and teachings which would tend to becloud or destroy her teachings of Christian Science and thereby create chaos and confusion in the Christian Science ranks as well as to misrepresent her teachings to the outside world…." *Proceedings in Equity*, 538.

188. Still reminiscences, 4, MBEL.

Image Credits

© The Mary Baker Eddy Collection.   p. 110, 120, 146, 148, 189, 263, 371
   Original in The Mary Baker Eddy Library.
   Used with permission.

Courtesy of The Mary Baker Eddy Collection.   p. 88, 108, 145, 182, 184, 193, 224, 225
   Original in The Mary Baker Eddy Library.

The Bostonian Society   p. 192

Brookline Historical Society   p. 191

Harvard University Archives   p. 243 (HUD 3123 [1910 Poster],
                                                OLVWORK366836)

inGRACE photography   p. 19, 140-141, 155, 201

Kheel Center, Cornell University   p. 47

Library of Congress, Prints and Photographs Division   p. 10-11, 68, 209, 244-245, 269, 328, 348, 352, 361

Smithsonian National Air and Space Museum   p. 246 (NASM 92-5877)

Special Images

**Recent gifts to Longyear Museum from The First Church of Christ, Scientist, in
Boston, Massachusetts:** p. 52 (Calvin Frye's desk); 63 (Adam Dickey framed
portrait); 68 (Abraham Lincoln engraving); 81 (wicker rocking chair); 111 (sleigh bells);
152 (monogrammed linens); 155 (Bohemian pitcher and cups); 201 (household tableware);
211 (Prescott upright piano); 214-215 (Pianola roll, music box, and music disc); 220-221
(Victrola accessories and gramophone record).

Index

G

H

U, V

University Press, 326, 361

W

Walker, Robert, 8-9, 12, 377n13, 377n15

Watson, Walter, 329, 394n18

Weygandt, Minnie, 36, 51, 86-87, 139, 153-154, 172, 184-190, 193, 202, 239, 316, 323-324, 379n41, 381n35, 383n23, 385n43, 393n6, 394n32, 404n89, 407n10, 409n40, 409n42, 409n45, 410n52, 410n53

White Steam touring car (White Steamer), 106-107, 177, 227, 231-233, 248, 398n87, 416n13

Whittier, John Greenleaf, 197, 411n73

Wilbur, Sibyl, 47, 49, 51, 113, 278, 289, 383n26, 384n40, 385n44, 425n18

Wilcox, Martha, 37, 107, 114-119, 138, 153, 172, 179, 193, 201, 210, 233, 247, 249, 278, 305, 319, 331, 381n33, 383n15, 399n11, 399n13, 399n18, 402n67, 407n10

Woodbury, Josephine, 288, 426n35

Y

Young, Bicknell, 201